THE CAMBRIDGE COMPANION TO
THE AGE OF PERICLES

Mid-fifth-century Athens saw the development of ~~~ empire, the radicalization of Athenian democracy through the empowerment of poorer citizens, the adornment of the city through a massive and expensive building program, the production of classical Athenian tragedy, the assembly of intellectuals offering novel approaches to philosophical and scientific issues, and the end of the Spartan-Athenian alliance against Persia and the beginning of open hostilities between the two greatest powers of ancient Greece. The Athenian statesman Pericles fostered where he did not initiate these events and "Periclean Athens" has represented for many the height of classical Athenian history. Although it is no longer fashionable to view Periclean Athens as a social or cultural paradigm, study of the history, society, art, and literature of mid-fifth-century Athens remains central to any understanding of Greek history. This Companion volume reveals the political, religious, economic, social, artistic, literary, intellectual, and military infrastructure that made the Age of Pericles possible. Previous volumes on subjects directly relevant to mid-fifth-century Athens (including the Cambridge Companions to *Early Greek Philosophy* and *Greek Tragedy*) have permitted an approach here that focuses on the historical factors that undergirded, characterized, and threatened Periclean Athens.

Loren J. Samons II is Professor and Chairman of Classical Studies at Boston University, where he received the Metcalf Award for excellence in teaching in 1998. He is the author of *What's Wrong with Democracy? From Athenian Practice to American Worship* (2004), *Empire of the Owl: Athenian Imperial Finance* (2000), and, with Charles W. Fornara, *Athens from Cleisthenes to Pericles* (1991). He has been a Visiting Senior Associate Member of the American School of Classical Studies in Athens and has contributed to many journals, including *Classical Quarterly, Historia, Arion*, and *Zeitschrift für Papyrologie und Epigraphik*.

THE CAMBRIDGE COMPANION TO
THE AGE OF PERICLES

Edited by

LOREN J. SAMONS II
Boston University

CAMBRIDGE
UNIVERSITY PRESS

CAMBRIDGE UNIVERSITY PRESS
Cambridge, New York, Melbourne, Madrid, Cape Town, Singapore, São Paulo

Cambridge University Press
32 Avenue of the Americas, New York, NY 10013-2473, USA

www.cambridge.org
Information on this title: www.cambridge.org/9780521807937

First published 2007

Printed in the United States of America

A catalog record for this publication is available from the British Library.

Library of Congress Cataloging in Publication Data

The Cambridge companion to the Age of Pericles / edited by Loren J. Samons II.
p.   cm.
Includes bibliographical references and index.
ISBN-13: 978-0-521-80793-7 (hardback)
ISBN-10: 0-521-80793-x (hardback)
ISBN-13: 978-0-521-00389-6 (pbk.)
ISBN-10: 0-521-00389-x (pbk.)
1. Greece – History – Athenian supremacy, 479–431 B.C.   2. Athens
(Greece) – History.   I. Samons, Loren J.   II. Title.
DF227.C35   2006
938′.04 – dc22   2006012922

ISBN   978-0-521-80793-7 hardback

ISBN   978-0-521-00389-6 paperback

To my students

Contents

Illustrations and Maps

(Illustrations follow page 144)

MAPS

CONTRIBUTORS

DEBORAH BOEDEKER is Professor of Classics at Brown University and the author of *Descent from Heaven: Images of Dew in Greek Poetry and Religion* (Chico, CA: Scholars Press, 1984).

JEFFREY HENDERSON is Aurelio Professor of Greek and Dean of the College of Arts and Sciences at Boston University and General Editor of the Loeb Classical Library. His four-volume edition and translation of Aristophanes was published in the Loeb series (Cambridge, MA: Harvard University Press, 1998–2002).

LISA KALLET is Cawkwell Fellow and Tutor in Ancient History, University College, Oxford, and author of *Money and the Corrosion of Power in Thucydides* (Berkeley: University of California Press, 2001).

KENNETH LAPATIN is Assistant Curator of Antiquities at the J. Paul Getty Museum, Los Angeles, California, and author of *Chryselephantine Statuary in the Ancient Mediterranean World* (Oxford: Oxford University Press, 2001).

J. E. LENDON is Professor of History at the University of Virginia and author of *Soldiers and Ghosts: A History of Battle in Classical Antiquity* (New Haven: Yale University Press, 2005).

CYNTHIA PATTERSON is Associate Professor of History at Emory University and the author of *The Family in Greek History* (Cambridge, MA: Harvard University Press, 1998).

KURT A. RAAFLAUB is David Herlihy University Professor, Professor of Classics and History, and Chair of the Program in Ancient Studies at Brown University. He is the author of *The Discovery of Freedom in Ancient Greece* (Chicago: University of Chicago Press, 2004).

P. J. RHODES is Honorary Professor of Ancient History at the University of Durham and author of *A Commentary on the Aristotelian Athenaion Politeia* (Oxford: Oxford University Press, 1981; revised reprint, 1993).

L. J. SAMONS II is Professor and Chairman of Classical Studies at Boston University and author of *Empire of the Owl: Athenian Imperial Finance*, Historia Einzelschriften 142 (Stuttgart: Steiner, 2000).

R. SEALEY is Emeritus Professor of History at the University of California, Berkeley, and author of *The Athenian Republic* (University Park: Pennsylvania State University Press, 1987).

J. P. SICKINGER is Associate Professor of Classics at the Florida State University and the author of *Public Records and Archives in Classical Athens* (Chapel Hill: University of North Carolina Press, 1999).

ROBERT W. WALLACE is Professor of Classics at Northwestern University and author of *The Areopagos Council* (Baltimore: Johns Hopkins University Press, 1989).

ABBREVIATIONS

ABSA	*Annual of the British School at Athens*
AC	*L'Antiquité classique*
AHB	*Ancient History Bulletin*
AJA	*American Journal of Archaeology*
AJAH	*American Journal of Ancient History*
AJP	*American Journal of Philology*
AP	*Athenaion Politeia (Constitution of the Athenians),* attributed to Aristotle
ATL	B. D. Meritt, H. T. Wade-Gery, and M. F. McGregor, *The Athenian Tribute Lists,* 4 vols. (Cambridge, MA, and Princeton: American School of Classical Studies at Athens, 1939–1953).
BICS	*Bulletin of the Institute of Classical Studies*
CA	*Classical Antiquity* (formerly *California Studies in Classical Antiquity*)
CAH III.3²	*The Cambridge Ancient History,* vol. 3, part 3, *The Expansion of the Greek World, Eighth to Sixth Centuries B.C.,* second edition, John Boardman and N. G. L. Hammond, eds. (Cambridge: Cambridge University Press, 1982).
CAH V²	*The Cambridge Ancient History,* vol. 5, *The Fifth Century B.C.,* second edition, D. M. Lewis, J. Boardman, J. K. Davies, and M. Ostwald, eds. (Cambridge: Cambridge University Press, 1992).
CAH VI²	*The Cambridge Ancient History,* vol. 6, *The Fourth Century B.C.,* second edition, D. M. Lewis, J. Boardman, S. Hornblower, and M. Ostwald, eds. (Cambridge: Cambridge University Press, 1994).
CJ	*Classical Journal*
CP	*Classical Philology*

CQ   *Classical Quarterly*

CR   *Classical Review*

CT   Simon Hornblower, *A Commentary on Thucydides*, 2 vols.
            (Oxford: Oxford University Press, 1991–1996).

DK   H. Diels and W. Kranz, *Die Fragmente der Vorsokratiker*,
            3 vols., sixth edition (Berlin: Weidmann, 1952).

FGrHist   F. Jacoby et al., *Die Fragmente der griechischen Historiker*
            (Berlin and Leiden: Brill, 1923–).

Fornara   C. W. Fornara, ed. and trans., *From Archaic Times to the
            End of the Peloponnesian War*, second edition
            (Cambridge: Cambridge University Press, 1983);
            references are to item numbers.

G&R   *Greece & Rome*

GRBS   *Greek, Roman and Byzantine Studies*

GSW   W. K. Pritchett, *The Greek State at War*, 5 vols.
            (Berkeley: University of California Press, 1971–1990).

Harding   P. Harding, ed. and trans., *From the End of the
            Peloponnesian War to the Battle of Ipsus* (Cambridge:
            Cambridge University Press, 1985); references are to
            item numbers.

HCT   A. W. Gomme, A. Andrewes, and K. J. Dover, *A
            Historical Commentary on Thucydides*, 5 vols. (Oxford:
            Oxford University Press, 1945–1981).

HSCP   *Harvard Studies in Classical Philology*

IG   *Inscriptiones Graecae*

JdI   *Jahrbuch des Deutschen Archäologischen Instituts*

JHS   *Journal of Hellenic Studies*

KA   R. Kassel and C. F. L. Austin, *Poetae Comici Graeci*
            (Berlin: de Gruyter, 1983–).

LSJ   H. G. Liddell, R. Scott, and H. S. Jones, *A Greek-English
            Lexicon*, ninth edition (Oxford: Oxford University Press,
            1940; with supplement, 1968).

ML   Russell Meiggs and David Lewis, *A Selection of Greek
            Historical Inscriptions to the End of the Fifth Century B.C.*,
            revised edition (Oxford: Oxford University Press, 1988).

PAPh   *Proceedings of the American Philosophical Association*

PP   *La Parola del passato*

SEG   *Supplementum Epigraphicum Graecum* (1923–).

TAPA   *Transactions and Proceedings of the American Philological
            Association*

Tod	M. N. Tod, ed., *Greek Historical Inscriptions*, 2 vols. in 1 (reprint, Chicago: Ayer, 1985).
TrGF	*Tragicorum Graecorum Fragmenta* (Göttingen, 1971–).
YCS	*Yale Classical Studies*

* Abbreviations of ancient authors and their works generally follow the style of the *Oxford Classical Dictionary*, third edition, S. Hornblower and A. Spawforth, eds. (Oxford: Oxford University Press, 1996), occasionally translated or expanded in the interest of clarity.

PREFACE

Like the best companions, this volume neither asks nor answers all questions. It seeks to provoke as much as to inform, to stimulate the reader to further inquiry rather than to put matters to rest. Mid-fifth-century Athens generates as much interest and contention as any era in history, and scholars of the period operate within a long and fruitful tradition of bitter disputes. The contributors, although they share a belief in the importance of the Age of Pericles, often differ in their general conceptions of the period or on points of detail. A volume without discord would hardly do justice to a period as rife with intellectual and political battles as with those on land and sea.

I thank Beatrice Rehl of Cambridge University Press for the invitation to undertake this volume and for the support she has provided over the many years of its completion. The anonymous readers for the Press offered numerous helpful suggestions on the prospectus. I am deeply in debt to the contributors for their willingness to participate in this project and for their generosity and patience while it came to fruition. The volume was completed during a sabbatical from the Department of Classical Studies at Boston University, and I thank my colleagues and the Dean of the College of Arts and Sciences, Jeffrey Henderson, for the support they have offered. Of the many others to whom I owe thanks, I must single out Amanda Lynch for her three years of invaluable assistance while I served as an administrator and attempted to keep this and other projects afloat. Especially during that time – but also before and since – my students have helped me focus on the rewards of studying antiquity.

My wife Jamie deserves more thanks than I can offer in these pages.

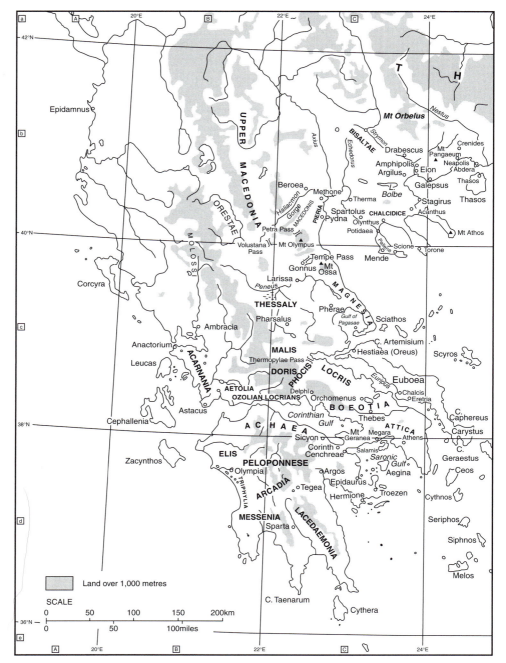

MAP IA. Greece and western Asia Minor

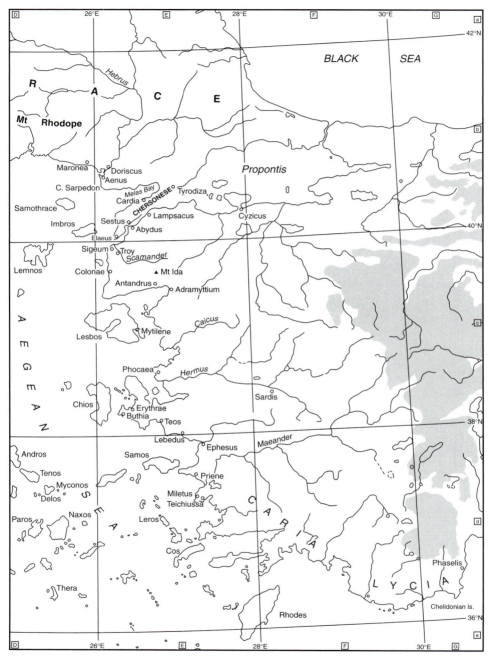

MAP I B.

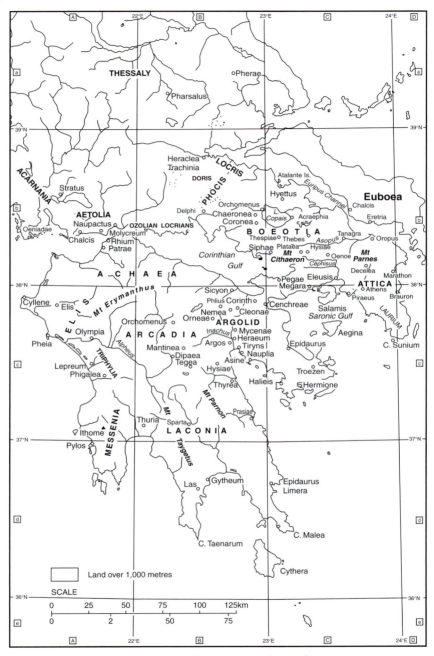

MAP 2. Attica, the Peloponnese, and central Greece

INTRODUCTION: ATHENIAN HISTORY AND SOCIETY IN THE AGE OF PERICLES

L. J. Samons II

SOURCES

Our literary sources for the study of mid-fifth-century Athens consist of contemporary Greek historians (especially Herodotus and Thucydides), Athenian orators and intellectuals (especially Andocides, Antiphon, Plato, and the anonymous author known as Pseudo-Xenophon or "The Old Oligarch"), and Aristotle's works analyzing Athenian and Greek political life (the *Politics* and the *Constitution of the Athenians*, the latter probably but not certainly composed by Aristotle).[1] Besides the references to older (but no longer extant) works found in such late authorities as Plutarch and the Hellenistic and Byzantine commentators, we also possess a significant number of fifth-century decrees (*psephismata*) passed by vote in the Athenian assembly. The Athenians often inscribed these measures on stone pillars (*stelai*), and fragments of many of these decrees (and other inscribed documents) have survived into the present age.

Plutarch composed his biography of Pericles (and those of his contemporaries Themistocles, Aristeides, Cimon, Nicias, and Alcibiades) between ca. A.D. 90 and 120. The biographer was therefore removed from his fifth-century B.C. subjects by more than five centuries. Plutarch's anecdotal style and purpose – to shed light on his subjects' characters rather than their political careers – make his work difficult for the historian to exploit confidently. Nevertheless, Plutarch had access to contemporary fifth-century sources lost to us, and any attempt to flesh out Athenian life or understand Athenian politics in the Age of Pericles must rely heavily (if often uneasily) on his biographical works.

Sometimes historians are able to supplement our picture of mid-fifth-century Athenian life with inferences drawn from contemporary dramatic works, especially those of Aeschylus, Sophocles, and Aristophanes. However, the tragedians usually depicted Greece in its mythic or heroic past, and scholars differ on the degree to which those depictions reflect contemporary Athenian life. Although Aristophanes usually set his comedies in explicitly contemporary circumstances, his works require careful analysis of dramatic context and authorial intent: Aristophanes meant to entertain his audience and win a competition, not to inform posterity about real Athenian life. However, as several contributions to this volume demonstrate, his works provide an invaluable resource for gauging many aspects of Athenian life and politics in the period just after Pericles' career.[2]

As a non-Athenian contemporary of Pericles, and one who traveled widely in (and apparently outside) the Greek world, Herodotus tantalizes the modern historian as a potential source about Periclean Athens. However, Herodotus focused his attention on the period before and during the Persian Wars (490–479), providing little explicit information on mid-fifth-century Greece. If Herodotus, as sometimes alleged, was a member of a "Periclean circle" or even a friend of the statesman, his reticence might seem surprising. In any case, even certainty about Herodotus's extended residence in Athens or his membership in such a circle would do no more than confirm that Athens attracted intellectuals and artists from all over Hellas in this period, and that Pericles regularly befriended such individuals – facts to which other sources already testify.[3] Unfortunately for our purposes, Herodotus was neither a product nor a chronicler of Periclean Athens, and thus his work can do little more than suggest a kind of prose that might have been popular late in Pericles' life or thereafter.

Thucydides' history remains the single best source for the Periclean period and the statesman himself. An Athenian and younger contemporary of Pericles – born perhaps ca. 470–460 – and witness to the entire course of the Peloponnesian War (431–404), Thucydides tells us that he began composing his great work as soon as the war began, because he believed he was witnessing an unprecedented conflict (1.1).[4]

Thucydides' chronicle of the war begins in earnest with events ca. 435 and breaks off in 411/10, yet he also provides us with a crucial (if brief) narrative of events between the Persian and Peloponnesian Wars (479–ca. 439: 1.89–117). Because he served as an Athenian general in the war against Sparta and came from a politically prominent Athenian family, Thucydides was well placed to provide an account of fifth-century Athenian history. Even after his exile in 424/3, Thucydides' wealth and aristocratic connections enabled him to move around the Greek world gathering material from sources that included the Peloponnesians themselves (Thuc. 5.26). Along with invaluable information about the war, Thucydides also presents three long speeches by Pericles. If scholars dispute how much of these speeches derives from the historian rather than the statesman, they nonetheless agree that the orations are crucial sources for attempting to reconstruct Periclean policies and politics.[5]

In a kind of eulogy to Pericles after his last speech in the history, Thucydides praises the Athenian statesman for his political character and his ability "to lead rather than be led by the people" (2.65), contrasting him with more demagogic leaders that followed. This passage and the admiration modern historians often feel for Periclean democracy have led many scholars to conclude that Thucydides' praise of Pericles as a leader – one able to make what was "in name a democracy, in fact the rule of the first citizen" – equates to admiration of Athenian democracy or specific Athenian/Periclean policies (such as imperial expansion or war with Sparta). Such a conclusion is belied, however, by Thucydides' explicit praise for the moderate oligarchical government that ultimately resulted from, and for at least one of the core oligarchs (Antiphon) who was responsible for, the revolution that briefly ended Athens's democratic government in 411 (8.68, 97). Thucydides clearly felt free both to praise a democrat like Pericles for his political integrity and leadership and to praise an oligarch and revolutionary for his intelligence and oratorical skill. In short, Thucydides cannot be treated as a straightforward "admirer" of Pericles or of Pericles' particular policies. (Thucydides' independence of mind should actually increase the modern historian's confidence when approaching his treatment of Pericles.) We may, however, see Thucydides as a product both of the intellectual hotbed Athens became under Pericles' leadership and, perhaps even more, of the embattled – and ultimately defeated and demoralized – city she became after his death.[6] For although Thucydides may have begun work on his history during the last days of the Periclean age when Athens was at the height of her powers, he composed most of that work during and after the debilitating Peloponnesian War.

A late authority deserving of special mention is the first-century B.C. Greek historian Diodorus Siculus. Diodorus composed a kind of world history, which drew heavily on the work of previous authors. For the mid-fifth century, he relied primarily on the now lost fourth-century work of the historian Ephorus, and Diodorus's value consists primarily in preserving for us something of Ephorus's work. However, it seems unlikely that Ephorus himself possessed much better information on the mid–fifth century than what he could read in Thucydides. Moreover, Diodorus's adaptation of Ephorus is confused and chronologically inaccurate. Where he contradicts Thucydides he is usually mistaken, and where he supplements Thucydides he is often untrustworthy. Modern historians therefore must employ his work with great caution.

Finally, the physical remains uncovered by increasingly scientific archaeological methods in the last 150 years have contributed greatly to our understanding of Pericles' Athens. Beyond the ongoing excavations in the Athenian *agora* (marketplace) and study of the Acropolis, work in such areas as the Peiraeus harbor and the silver-mining region of southern Attica has fleshed out the image of Athens appearing in our literary sources. In the last several decades, this work has helped scholars come closer to capturing the bustling, culturally and economically complex imperial city that was Periclean Athens.[7] More than a city of poets, philosophers, and statesmen, it was a place of miners, farmers, artisans, slaves and slavers, foreign traders, shipwrights, shield makers, potters, and prostitutes.

ATHENS AND POLIS GOVERNMENT

Ancient Greece, which the Greeks (Hellenes) called Hellas, was dominated by hundreds of independent, self-governing city-states (*poleis*, singular *polis*).[8] The origins of the polis are controversial, but this form of settlement was firmly established in Greece by the eighth century B.C.[9] A typical polis comprised a town or city center (*astu*) surrounded by land (*chora*) farmed and owned by the polis's citizens. Goods were exchanged and formal and informal public interaction took place in the main square and marketplace (*agora*) in the city center. Some poleis possessed a citadel, often located on defensible and/or fortified high ground. At Athens, this citadel came to be called the *akropolis* ("high city").

Greek poleis ranged in size from tiny villages with perhaps fewer than several hundred citizens to super poleis, of which Sparta and Athens were probably the largest. Athens covered an area (known as Attica) of approximately 1,000 square miles and probably had at least 30,000–40,000 adult male citizens for most of the classical period. Attica's total population is unknown and depends to a large degree on variables like the number of slaves or resident foreigners ("metics") living there at any given time, but it cannot have been less than 100,000 souls and may have been as great as 400,000 or more.[10]

Despite the wide range of sizes among Greek poleis, so far as we are able to tell, most possessed fairly similar governments by the classical period (ca. 500–323 B.C.). Each polis relied on an assembly of adult male citizens that acted as a more or less sovereign authority within the state. In the assembly, citizens of each polis might vote to elect magistrates; approve legislation, treaties, and decisions about war or peace; and, at least in some cases, render judicial decisions.[11] In Athens, this assembly was known as the *ekklesia* and it eventually consisted of all free citizen males, regardless of whether they owned property or not.

Most of the poleis' executive functions were fulfilled by magistrates elected by the citizenry (the *demos*) or chosen by lot, although some offices were restricted to the members of certain families or economic classes.[12] In Athens, the chief magistracy originally consisted of an annual board of nine archons (plus a secretary), at first elected but after 487 chosen by lot from a list of elected candidates (*AP* 8.1, 22.5). Among these magistrates were the eponymous archon, who gave his name to the year and perhaps originally acted as chief magistrate; the *polemarchos*, or "war archon;" and a primarily religious official called simply the *basileus*, or "king" (sometimes translated as "king-archon").

After 487 and the advent of lot-based selection of Athens's archons, the elected office of general (*strategos*, plural *strategoi*) played an increasingly important political role in Athenian government. Pericles, for example, served as one of Athens's ten elected generals for fifteen consecutive years, making the office the formal basis of his power in the state. But in the fifth century, many other *strategoi* – including Themistocles, Aristeides, Cimon, Cleon, and Alcibiades – acted as both military and political leaders, proposing policies and addressing the people in the council or assembly and then commanding the armies that implemented those policies.

A small council (often of elders or former magistrates) usually completed the tripartite arrangement of polis government. In Sparta this council consisted of twenty-eight elected elders plus the two Spartan kings.[13] In Athens the oldest (known) council was the Areopagus. This body consisted of all former archons, who served for life, and it acted as a high court for certain kinds of offenses and served in a general advisory (and perhaps supervisory) role in early Athenian government.[14]

Of course, this composite picture of "typical" polis government, with assembly, council, and magistrates, must be adjusted when we possess enough evidence to describe any particular city-state in detail.

For example, when around 507 B.C. Athens instituted the government that would become known as *demokratia*, the Athenians created a second council (the *boule*), this one of 500 citizens chosen (at least eventually) by lot from the citizen body and serving for one year. This *boule* of 500 became the most important council of the Athenian state.[15] It prepared business for and provided members to preside over meetings of the assembly, heard embassies from foreign powers, supervised financial and military matters, and could act as a kind of court. For one-tenth of each year, the fifty members of the council representing one of the ten Athenian tribes[16] acted as a standing committee for the council as a whole, and these *prytaneis* ("presidents") had to remain in Athens for this entire period (thus known as a "prytany"). Again, the members of the council of 500 (or *bouleutai*) were chosen by lot, apparently from all Athenian citizens that possessed a moderate amount of property, although by the fourth century, even the poorest citizens were apparently able to serve.[17]

Property qualifications for citizenship or office-holding were apparently common in Greek poleis. In many poleis ownership of a small farm and the consequent ability to afford the arms necessary to fight in the infantry phalanx as a hoplite (i.e., one with a *hoplon* – a large shield) probably qualified one for citizenship.[18] However, one of the defining qualities of Athens's *demokratia* – a word combining the basic ideas of power (*kratos*) and the people (*demos*) – was the absence of a property qualification for citizenship. Thus at Athens even the poorest individuals had the opportunity to cast their votes in the assembly and (at least eventually and perhaps unofficially) to serve on the council of 500.[19]

Nevertheless, both before and after the institution of *demokratia*, the Athenians did divide their citizen body into stratified groups based on the ownership of property and restrict certain offices to those reaching a given property qualification. According to Athenian tradition, the lawgiver Solon (ca. 594/3) separated the Athenians into four categories based on the agricultural production of their land: the *pentakosiomedimnoi* (possessing land yielding 500 *medimnoi* of dry or wet produce per year) formed the highest group, followed by the *hippeis* ("horsemen"), *zeugitai* ("yokemen"), and *thetes* ("laborers").[20] Athenian archons initially had to belong at least to the class of *hippeis*, but after the year 457 the *zeugitai* also could hold this office (*AP* 26.2). The treasurers (*tamiai*) of the sacred wealth of Athena, in some ways Athens's highest financial position in the fifth century, had to belong to the highest property class.[21]

Solon's property qualifications actually represented a radical movement in Greek politics, because they formally separated the qualifications for office-holding from one's birth.[22] At an earlier point in Athenian history, perhaps even into the period just before Solon's reforms, it appears likely that only the members of Athenian families known as *eupatridai* (literally, the "well-fathered") were able to hold Athens's highest offices. After Solon, any citizen rich enough to join the *pentakosiomedimnoi* could (theoretically) hold any political position in Athens. Nevertheless, the members of the clans of the *eupatridai*, which claimed descent from the ancient Athenian aristocracy, continued to play a major role in Athenian government and society through their control of particular religious cults and their potential influence in the social groups that made up the demos as a whole.[23]

These smaller religio-social units represent another way in which the Athenian demos divided itself into component elements.[24] Membership in one of the aristocratic families or clans (*gene*) obviously provided advantages for those wishing to wield power in Athens, both in terms of the land and wealth these clans usually controlled and because of the supposed antiquity and religious associations of the families. The aristocratic clans in turn apparently wielded significant influence in the phratries ("brotherhoods"), poorly understood organizations based at least theoretically on common descent and connected through religious cults. It seems likely that the phratries approved citizenship for individual Athenians before the institution of *demokratia*, and thus the aristocratic clans probably played a crucial role in determining who was and who was not considered an Athenian citizen.[25] Larger than the phratries were the original four tribes (*phylai*) into which the members of the demos were divided. These tribes also related (theoretically) to descent, and most Ionian Greeks (the ethnic/linguistic subgroup of Hellenes into which the Athenians fell), whether they lived in mainland Greece, the islands, or Asia Minor, were divided into similar *phylai*.[26] Like the phratries and the clans, these tribes were religious as well as social and military organizations, with their own cults, priests, and rituals.

The Athenian demos of Pericles' day was thus divided in both economic and religio-social ways into subgroups that played particular roles within the polis (and in most cases probably resembled similar divisions in other poleis). Aside from their religious functions, the tribes and phratries, for example, almost certainly served (at least originally) as organizing units for the Athenian military.[27] But the demos as a whole also functioned as a unit, particularly in the worship of the polis's tutelary goddess, Athena.[28] The city came together to propitiate and celebrate the goddess in a festival known as the Panathenaea, held once every year and every four years with special splendor. The celebrations included a procession to the Acropolis, where the temple of Athena was located and her sacred treasure was stored.[29]

Eligibility for Athenian office-holding did not depend only on the actual wealth of the would-be magistrate. Every Athenian chosen by lot or election for office went through a vetting process known as the *dokimasia*, in which his citizenship was checked and anyone who wished could lodge a complaint against him.[30] A prospective member of the council of 500 or a candidate for the office of archon also answered certain questions put to him by the council of 500, including whether he was enrolled in certain cults, whether he treated his parents well, and whether he had served in the military when called upon and paid his taxes.[31] Candidates for other magistracies answered similar questions before a court of Athenian jurors.[32] In this way, the Athenians placed formal checks on the persons that could hold their most important offices, even if the individuals were selected by lot from the citizen body. But one must emphasize that prospective Athenian officials faced questions about their character and behavior and not about their knowledge, intelligence, experience, or technical skills.[33]

ATHENS IN THE SIXTH CENTURY B.C.

Understanding of the Age of Pericles requires some attention to the century that preceded it. Not long after the period of Solon's reforms, Athens fell under the control of the tyrant Peisistratus and his sons (ca. 561–511/10).[34] Like many Greek tyrants, Peisistratus was simply an "unconstitutional" ruler, someone who had seized power in a polis and had done so outside the normal avenues of political action. The position of tyrant in sixth-century Greece did not carry the particularly negative connotations later associated with the term. Peisistratus was said to have left the traditional Athenian constitution in place, only ensuring that his own supporters held the most important offices.[35]

The period of Peisistratid rule is especially crucial for understanding Periclean Athens because so many of the trends that developed under the *demokratia* seem to have their origins under the Athenian tyrants. Coming to power during and in part because of conflict between rival aristocratic factions, Peisistratus perhaps styled himself a kind of champion of the demos – one who claimed to protect the common people of Athens from the aristocrats who controlled so much of Athenian political and social life and drew the members of the demos into their struggles. Besides suppressing these conflicts, Peisistratus seems to have opened up avenues of citizenship to those of questionable birth or connections, thereby increasing the ranks of his supporters while undermining his aristocratic opponents.[36]

Other important trends that began under Peisistratus include the expansion of Athenian power into the Aegean, especially in the area around the Hellespont. Peisistratus (or his sons) apparently also constructed a major temple to Athena on the Acropolis (later partially destroyed by the Persians and then replaced by the Parthenon and Erechtheion), and may have offered loans to poor farmers, as well as instituting the first tax on agricultural produce in Attica.[37] He also used economic power apparently derived at least partly from mines in Thrace and in Attica to fund the military support on which he relied. In all these ways, Peisistratus and his sons set important precedents for fifth-century, democratic Athens.[38]

The overthrow of the Athenian tyrants in 511/10 was accomplished not by the Athenians themselves but by the Spartans. Peisistratus's son Hippias had become a harsh ruler after the murder of his brother Hipparchus in 514 by a pair of insulted aristocratic lovers, one of whom had rebuffed the tyrant's amorous brother. After Hippias's subsequent expulsion of certain aristocrats from Athens, some of the exiles apparently then tried to oust the Peisistratids from power, but failed. Fortunately for these Athenian aristocrats, the sixth-century Spartans made something of a habit of destroying tyrannies, and their overthrow of the Peisistratids allowed the reestablishment of the more typical style of polis government in Athens.[39]

After the Spartans removed the Peisistratids in 511/10, the Athenian aristocrats returned to power and apparently resumed their quarreling. Eventually an Athenian named Cleisthenes (a former brother-in-law of the tyrant Peisistratus and the grandson of another tyrant, Cleisthenes of Sicyon) seemingly determined, in effect, to reconstitute the faction that had supported Peisistratus. By appealing to the demos for support against the other aristocrats, Cleisthenes was able to defeat his rivals and pass the reforms that would create the government eventually known as *demokratia*. The Spartans most probably took Cleisthenes' regime for a new form of tyranny (since the only forms of Greek regime known to them at that time were rule by a tyrant or the typical aristocratic/timocratic polis government) and returned to Athens to force Cleisthenes and his family (the Alcmeonids) from power. The Athenians dutifully expelled Cleisthenes and his relatives. But when the Spartans then attempted to dismantle Cleisthenes' political reforms, the Athenians balked and ejected the Spartans, who ultimately decided to accept Athens's new regime.[40]

Precisely what Cleisthenes accomplished ca. 507 and by what means he managed it are problematic questions. It appears that he partially separated control of citizenship from the potentially aristocratdominated phratries and gave more power in this and other areas to the individual residents of the villages/neighborhoods of Attica (the *demoi*, or "demes"). After Cleisthenes, a man's citizenship would be determined (at least in part) by his neighbors, and not (at least technically) primarily by his connection with aristocratic families or patrons.[41] At the same time, Cleisthenes created a new council of state, made up not of the aristocratic former archons (as was the Areopagus) but rather of 500 citizens (at least eventually) chosen by lot.[42] These 500 would be chosen through the increasingly important demes. The demes themselves were now allocated into ten new tribes, each containing some demes from the coastal region of Attica, some from the interior region around the city of Athens, and some from the city itself (*AP* 21). Each new tribe therefore represented a geographical microcosm of the polis as a whole, perhaps reflecting a desire to use the ten tribes as organizational tools for the Athenian military, as well as for the political and religious arrangement of the polis.[43] After 501/0, each tribe elected one of the polis's ten generals, although at some point in the fifth century the specific allocation of one general per tribe was abandoned.

By around 500 B.C. the structure of Athens's government had taken the basic form it was to have for nearly two centuries (apart from two brief periods of oligarchic rule). The most unusual aspects of Athenian government at this time – what at least arguably made it *demokratia* as opposed to the type of polis government that might be called either *aristokratia* (rule by the *aristoi*, or "best") or *oligarchia* (rule by the rich *oligoi*, or "few"), depending on one's point of view – was the absence of any property qualification for participation in the assembly and the influence on citizenship and the council of 500 (and thus on government policy) of the neighborhood demesmen. The demes now became in some ways the most significant subdivision of the Athenian polis.[44]

We know very little about precise legislative and judicial procedures in this early period of *demokratia*. The Athenian assembly passed decrees (*psephismata*) by majority vote on issues placed before it by the council of 500. The council had the option of putting an actual measure before the assembly (which might then be amended), or simply placing an issue on the agenda, a procedure that permitted specific proposals from the floor of the assembly.[45] Although fourth-century Athenians distinguished between permanent and general "laws" (*nomoi*) – regulations either laid down by a lawgiver like Solon or (later) created by a special process of lawmaking – and particular "decrees" passed in the Athenian assembly, this may not have been true in the early fifth century. At that time, whatever the assembly decreed by vote seems to have had the same force as Solon's (or Drakon's earlier) law code.

ATHENIAN HISTORY IN THE FIFTH CENTURY B.C.

In the period just after the institution of *demokratia* ca. 507, Athens withstood threats from its Greek neighbors. Both the Boeotians and the Chalcidians apparently wished to test the new Athenian regime, and according to Herodotus, the Spartans also planned to overthrow the new government and reinstall a tyrant.[46] The alleged Spartan invasion fell apart, and the Athenians then defeated the Boeotians and Chalcidians, even seizing prime land on Euboea from the latter and settling Athenians there (Hdt. 5.75–77). In a well-known passage describing Athens's victories over these forces ca. 506, Herodotus comments that this success showed how quickly Athens became a military power after achieving *isegoria* ("equality of speech").[47]

Athenian self-confidence appears to have continued to rise, because in 498 Athens sent twenty warships to Asia Minor to help the (largely Ionian) Greek cities there in their rebellion against the Great King of Persia. Although the Athenians withdrew after only one campaign (and the Ionian revolt eventually ended in disaster), Athens's brief participation in the failed action led ultimately to Persian retribution. In 490 a large Persian force (accompanied by the Peisistratid Hippias, Athens's former tyrant) landed at Marathon, located in northeast Attica about twenty-seven miles from the city center of Athens. The Athenians, apparently fearing possible betrayal of the city to Persia if they remained within their city walls, marched out to meet the Persians. First awaiting Spartan assistance (which came only too late), the 10,000 or so Athenians (assisted by a few hundred allies from Plataea) eventually determined to attack the much larger Persian army. Making their assault on the run, the Athenian infantry won a great (and very unexpected) victory. The Athenian hoplites then hurried back to Athens in time to prevent a Persian landing there.

For the moment, Athens had been saved from Persian domination.[48] Nevertheless, in the next decade the Athenians carried out reprisals against leading citizens suspected of supporting the Peisistratid tyranny or "medizing" (taking a stance sympathetic to the Medes and Persians), voting to exile certain individuals from Athens for a period of ten years.[49] This procedure for temporary banishment (called "ostracism," from the broken potsherds, or *ostraka*, on which the Athenians wrote the desired victim's name) allowed the banished individual to reclaim his property (and resume his political activities) after his return to Athens, and it continued to be an important part of the Athenian political landscape through the late fifth century.

In addition to several significant ostracisms, including those of Pericles' father and uncle, the 480s also saw an epochal change in Athenian public finance and national defense. In 483/2 the Athenians struck a particularly rich vein in the public silver mines located in southern Attica. Previously, profits deriving from the mines had apparently been distributed to the citizens at large. But in this year, the Athenian Themistocles proposed that the polis collectively use this money to construct a larger fleet as protection against Athens's island neighbor and enemy Aegina (which had a large fleet) and/or against the expected return of the Persians (Hdt. 7.144; Thuc. 1.14). Voting to follow Themistocles' advice, the Athenians practically overnight became a naval superpower and soon possessed a fleet of two hundred or so warships.

When the Persians under their new Great King, Xerxes, did invade again in 480, the now publicly enriched Athenians provided the bulk of the allied Greek fleet that opposed them. However, only about thirty Greek poleis chose to stand against the tens and probably hundreds of thousands of invading Persians and their subjects (including other Greeks). At the head of the allied Greeks were the Spartans, who as the greatest Hellenic power commanded both the land and sea operations against Xerxes.

In a series of battles and with the aid of some timely storms, which wrecked much of the Persian fleet, the Greek allies repulsed the Persians in 480–479 and expelled them from mainland Greece.[50] Seaborne operations against the Persians continued on the coast of Asia Minor and around the Hellespont in 479, freeing eastern Greek states that had been compelled to join the Persians. However, the Spartans seem to have been unwilling to continue campaigning overseas during the winters of 479/8 or 478/7. Meanwhile their commander Pausanias had made himself obnoxious to the allied Greeks, allegedly in part by adopting Persian habits. Connected with many of the freed Greeks of Asia Minor by their Ionian heritage and providing most of the allied fleet in any case, the Athenians now seemed the logical choice to lead any continuing actions against Persia in the eastern Aegean. By spring 477 the Spartans acquiesced in this situation.[51]

After the Spartans withdrew, the Athenians and other Greeks formed a new alliance, often called the "Delian League" by moderns because it held its meetings and initially stored its common funds on the island of Delos, a center of Ionian Greek cult. The Athenian Aristeides received the task of determining the amount of annual contributions (*phoros*, or "tribute") the Greek allies that did not provide ships would pay to the league, while Athenian treasurers were selected to steward the money. The ostensible purpose of these payments, the historian Thucydides tells us, was the plan "to ravage the Persian Great King's land" as an act of vengeance for all he had perpetrated against the Greeks.[52] But, in the coming years, the Athenians seemingly launched few campaigns against the Great King's territory. Instead, other Greek states were forced into the league and Athenian settlements were established in the Aegean.[53]

By the mid-460s, some members of the alliance were seeking to leave the league. But the Athenians refused to allow this, even after a great Hellenic victory over Persian land and sea forces at the Eurymedon River in southern Asia Minor (ca. 466) effectively ended the immediate threat of Persian activity in the Aegean.[54] Subsequently, the large island of Thasos (a member of the league) and Athens apparently disputed the Thasians' control of certain mines and markets located in the northern Aegean region. When Thasos attempted to leave the alliance and retain its control over these mines, the Athenians blockaded and then reduced the city (ca. 465–463; Thuc. 1.100–101). Perhaps equally discomforting to some members of the Delian League, which had been designed at least in part to punish the Persians, in 462/1 the Athenians abandoned their alliance with Sparta against Persia, made a new alliance with previously medizing Thessaly and Argos (the latter Sparta's bitter enemy), and ostracized the pro-Spartan Athenian general Cimon (Thuc. 1.102; Plut. *Cim.* 17).

The occasion for this reversal in foreign policy was provided by a major domestic political reform. Before 462/1 the Athenian assembly apparently could act as a huge court (the *heliaia*) in certain cases, while the ancient and much smaller Areopagus council heard cases involving homicide (and probably other matters).[55] In 462/1 the Athenian

Ephialtes put forward proposals to restrict the Areopagus's powers, and thereafter most cases were heard before courts (*dikasteria*) made up of very large numbers of Athenian citizen-jurors ("dicasts," numbering from hundreds to even thousands). These jurors were chosen by lot and allocated to particular courts from a roster of 6,000 selected each year.[56] Probably in the late 450s, Pericles proposed that these dicasts should be paid, and eventually they received 3 obols (one-half of one drachma, or about a day's wage for an unskilled laborer in the mid-fifth century) per day for their service.[57] Payment of jurors led to payment for other public services, including membership on the council of 500 and (in the fourth century) even attendance at the assembly.[58]

The reforms of Ephialtes arguably radicalized the Athenian democracy, in part by removing power from the more conservative Areopagus and (ultimately) by distributing some of this power to the courts made up of common Athenians. Cimon's ostracism left the more conservative pro-Spartan Athenians without their former leader, and Ephialtes' murder shortly thereafter apparently allowed Pericles to emerge as a leader of the progressive faction. By the 450s Athens's foreign and domestic policies usually take on what we can identify as a "Periclean" character. Hostilities with Athens's former allies Corinth and Sparta were opened ca. 460, while the Athenians concurrently sent a major expedition to Egypt (which was in revolt from Persia).

Athens's expedition to Egypt ended in disaster in 454 (Thuc. 1.104, 109), around the same time that the Athenians decided to move the common treasury of the Delian League to Athens. Subsequently Athens's public expenditures seem to have ballooned, with payments to jurors on Athenian courts and funding for an expensive building program, centered on the Acropolis, but affecting other parts of Attica.[59] In 451/0 Pericles proposed that Athenian citizenship be restricted to those with Athenian mothers as well as fathers, a law that effectively limited the aristocratic practice of marrying sons to the daughters of wealthy non-Athenians, and that probably also reflected the financial benefits (through public payments) now attaching to Athenian citizenship.[60]

Despite Athens's failure in Egypt, the so-called First Peloponnesian War against Sparta and Corinth resulted in Athenian gains in central Greece (Boeotia) and even in the Peloponnese. After Cimon returned from ostracism, he effected a brief policy reversal in Athens, negotiating a five-year truce (451) with the Spartans that confirmed Athens's gains (Thuc. 1.103, 105–108, 112). Cimon then led a major campaign against Persian forces in Cyprus but died before the Athenians won a great victory. This success apparently led to negotiations between the Persian Great King Artaxerxes and the Athenians and to the end of actual hostilities between Athens and Persia.[61]

Whether a formal "Peace of Callias" (as the alleged Atheno-Persian treaty that followed the Cyprus campaign is commonly called, after the Athenian credited with the negotiations) existed or not, the de facto state of peace that followed Cimon's victory and death allowed Pericles to focus the Athenian demos's attention on consolidating what had become a Greek empire.[62] The Athenians embraced this mission with great enthusiasm, as several decrees of the assembly from the early to mid-440s demonstrate.[63] And although Athens lost most of its holdings in central Greece and the Peloponnese after a major defeat in 447/6 forced it to accept a thirty years' truce with Sparta in 446/5, the Athenian grip on the allied states continued to produce rich rewards in the form of yearly tribute payments. With this source of wealth added to their native supply of silver, the Athenians of Pericles' day were able to maintain a great stockpile of ready cash in the city, pay their jurors and other officials, and continue to erect new buildings, statues, and walls.[64] Meanwhile, in 441/0 Athens intervened in a conflict between Samos and Miletus – two of the larger and more powerful members of the Athenian alliance – taking the side of the Milesians and imposing a democracy on formerly autonomous Samos. When the Samians resisted, the Athenians besieged the city for nine months, and having taken it, they compelled the Samians to pay the costs of the war (Thuc. 1.115–17).

In 433 the Athenians received a request for alliance from the Corinthian colony of Corcyra, a powerful island in the Adriatic off the northwestern coast of Greece. The Corcyreans and Corinthians had come to blows over another city, Corcyra's own colony Epidamnus. The Corinthians, for their part, suggested that an Athenian alliance with Corcyra would break the spirit of the treaty of 446/5 between Athens and Sparta. This treaty had included Sparta's allies, of which Corinth was by far the most important and powerful. Apparently already eyeing possible expansion into the central Mediterranean, the Athenians nonetheless concluded a defensive pact with Corcyra.[65] This ultimately resulted in their participation in a naval battle between Corcyra and Corinth on the Corcyrean side. Shortly after this, in 432 the Athenians took aggressive steps against another Corinthian colony, Potidaea, which happened to be a tribute-paying member of the Athenian empire. Fearing Corinthian reprisals over Corcyra, the Athenians demanded that the Potidaeans destroy part of their city wall, give hostages, and dismiss their Corinthian magistrates. In response, the Potidaeans revolted from

Athens and accepted Corinthian assistance. The Athenians besieged the city, located in the northwest Aegean on the westernmost prong of the Chalcidice (Thuc. 1.56–67).

Corinth, along with other Peloponnesian allies, now complained to Sparta that Athens had grown too powerful and must be checked. The Spartans were ultimately compelled to agree, and in 431 they invaded Attica, beginning the well-known Peloponnesian War. In the first years of this war, Pericles encouraged the Athenians to refuse any concessions to the Spartans and Athens endured a devastating plague and expended most of its ready cash. By 428, Pericles was dead and the Athenian demos determined to levy a tax on wealthier Athenians' property in order to continue the war and pay the democracy's expenses.

To their descendents Pericles and his contemporaries had bequeathed not only the war with Sparta but also a powerful empire and a political society that relied heavily on the wealth and economic opportunities the empire generated. Perhaps, therefore, it should not surprise us that, despite Pericles' death, the Athenians voted to continue the war he had supported. The first phase of this war continued until the year 421, when Athens and Sparta agreed to a treaty.[66] Despite this treaty and a brief period of alliance, in 418 an Argive–Athenian army fought (and lost) a major land battle against Sparta at Mantinea in the Peloponnese. In 416 the Athenians besieged and reduced the Spartan colony on the island of Melos, killing all the men and enslaving the women and children.[67] The next year, the Athenians launched their major invasion of Sicily, aimed ultimately at the Corinthian colony Syracuse, a Peloponnesian ally and the dominant power on the great island.

Blunders in command and the failure of the city to support the expedition adequately led to the disastrous defeat of the Athenians in Sicily in 413. Meanwhile, the Athenians had provoked renewed hostilities with Sparta in mainland Greece (Thuc. 6.105, 7.18). The Spartans responded by occupying the Attic village of Decelea, using it as a base to raid Athenian territory.[68] Enriched by Persian subsidies, the Spartans then built a fleet and began campaigning in the eastern Aegean, leading to revolts among Athens's most important allies.

By 411 the Athenians had completely exhausted their once vast monetary reserves and had begun relying entirely on the yearly income from their subjects' tribute payments and local taxation to fund the war effort. In this environment, the exiled Athenian general Alcibiades, who had at first cooperated with the Spartans and then assisted the Persians, now suggested that he could bring Persia (and the Great King's money) over to Athens's side if the Athenians would agree to alter their form of government. In response to Alcibiades' offer, a group of Athenians proposed and carried measures to suspend public pay for jury service and the like, to select a new council of 400 to replace the council of 500 previously chosen by lot, and to restrict the citizen body to the 5,000 or so Athenians who could afford to serve as hoplites in the Athenian army.[69] Essentially, they hoped to end Periclean democracy and to make Athens's regime more like the older form of polis government that still provided democracy's greatest competitor in the Greek world.

The Athenians passed these reforms in a special meeting of the assembly, with many members of the demos present undoubtedly believing that such measures offered the hope of defeating Sparta and maintaining the empire. But the actual citizen body of 5,000 never materialized, and the Four Hundred in fact dominated Athens (even assassinating some of their enemies) for about four months in mid-411. Eventually a few of the Four Hundred and some agitated hoplites began to suspect pro-Spartan sympathies among the core oligarchs. The Athenians soon voted to remove the Four Hundred from power and install a "moderate" government based on a limited (but real) citizen body of about 5,000. Those of the Four Hundred who remained in Athens were tried and executed; most fled the city, including Plato's cousin Critias.[70] The moderate regime lasted only a little longer than the Four Hundred, and by 410/9 Athens's *demokratia* in its Periclean form – including citizenship for all free Athenian males and payments for public services – had been reinstituted.[71]

In the last years of the war, the Athenians received offers of peace based on the status quo from the Spartans. However, Alcibiades was once more acting as an Athenian general, and he and other commanders won important victories in the northeastern Aegean that restored Athenian confidence. The Athenians consequently refused Sparta's proffered peace treaties, choosing even to melt down the gold statues of their goddess Athena Nike (Athena "Victory") to coin the money necessary to continue the war. Only in 405, when the Athenian fleet was caught off guard and almost completely annihilated at Aegospotami in the Hellespont and Athens's grain supply was subsequently cut off, did the Athenians seriously consider treating for peace. After enduring a blockade of several months, they agreed in 404 to terms dictated by the Spartans: Athens's empire and the walls connecting the city to its harbor were to be dismantled and its fleet reduced to a paltry twelve ships. Athens's foreign policy was to be under Spartan control. But this treatment was lenient; Sparta's allies Corinth and Thebes had apparently wanted Athens to suffer the same fate it had imposed on the Melians and others – namely, execution of the men and enslavement of the women and children.[72]

Many Athenians who witnessed Athens's humiliation at the end of the Peloponnesian War had witnessed the height of the city's power and prosperity under Pericles. And although the period of Pericles' leadership lasted for only about three decades (ca. 460–429), the Athenian statesman continued, augmented, or set in motion many trends that dominated Athenian history for much of the fifth century. Expansion and consolidation of the Greek empire (even at Sparta's expense) combined with liberalization of the Athenian political regime remained hallmarks of Athenian policy after Pericles' death, and such policies arguably contributed both to Athens's greatness and to her downfall. The interplay between such forces, the social, economic, religious, and political contexts that spawned or perpetuated them, and the fulcrum for Athenian history provided by the Age of Pericles serve as the focus for the remaining chapters of this volume.[73]

NOTES

1   In most cases I have provided references only to the most important ancient sources. I have indicated certain secondary works (and usually only those in English) that may be profitably consulted by those wishing to pursue individual issues. Years in the Athenian calendar (which ran from summer to summer) are conventionally expressed in the form 462/1. Expressions such as 462–461 denote the period covered by (in this case two) modern calendar years.

2   For drama in the Age of Pericles, see the chapter by Henderson in this volume. For the use of Aristophanes as a historical source, see especially the chapters by Boedeker, Kallet, and Patterson.

3   On Pericles' friends and acquaintances, see Plutarch *Pericles*, esp. 4–6, 24, 31–2; V. Ehrenberg, *Sophocles and Pericles* (Oxford: Blackwell, 1954); D. Kagan, *Pericles of Athens and the Birth of Democracy* (New York: Simon & Schuster, 1991); and A. Podlecki, *Perikles and His Circle* (London: Routledge, 1998). On Athens's attraction of intellectuals, see the chapter by Wallace below.

4   Thucydides' birth date is unknown, but the traditional view that places his birth ca. 455 relies in large part on the questionable inferences that he was not much older than thirty when he served as a general in 424/3 and was a young admirer of Pericles when the war began: see C. W. Fornara, "Thucydides' Birth Date," in R. M. Rosen and J. Farrell, eds., *Nomodeiktes: Greek Studies in Honor of Martin Ostwald* (Ann Arbor: University of Michigan Press, 1993), pp. 71–80.

5   For these speeches see the conclusion to this volume.

6   Good introductions to Thucydides are provided by F. E. Adcock, *Thucydides and His History* (Cambridge: Cambridge University Press, 1963); K. J. Dover, *Thucydides*, Greece & Rome New Surveys in the Classics, no. 7 (Oxford: Oxford University

Press, 1973); and S. Hornblower, *Thucydides*, second edition (London: Duckworth, 1994). For the philosophical/sophistic currents running through Athens in this period, see the chapter by Wallace.

7   See especially the chapters of Lapatin, Patterson, and Kallet. For the agora, see John Camp, *The Athenian Agora: Excavations in the Heart of Classical Athens* (London: Thames and Hudson, 1986); for the Acropolis, see J. Hurwit, *The Athenian Acropolis* (Cambridge: Cambridge University Press, 1999).

8   A few areas of Greece had a more rudimentary form of regime or settlement, sometimes based on tribes or federations and (often) extended territory. On these *ethne* ("nations"), see, e.g., A. M. Snodgrass, *Archaic Greece* (Berkeley: University of California Press 1980), pp. 42–7. This view of the *ethnos*, however, has more recently been criticized; see Jeremy McInerney, *The Folds of Parnassos: Land and Ethnicity in Ancient Phokis* (Austin: University of Texas Press, 1999), esp. pp. 18–35, and cf. Edward E. Cohen, *The Athenian Nation* (Princeton: Princeton University Press, 2000), pp. 22–9.

9   On the rise of the polis, see Sealey in this volume, pp. 238–40; V. D. Hanson, *The Other Greeks* (New York: Free Press, 1995), esp. pp. 108–26; A. M. Snodgrass, "The Rise of the Polis: The Archaeological Evidence," and K. A. Raaflaub, "Homer to Solon: The Rise of the Polis. The Written Sources," in M. H. Hansen, ed., *The Ancient Greek City-State* (Copenhagen: Royal Danish Academy of Sciences and Letters, 1993), pp. 30–40, 41–105; and Lynette G. Mitchell and P. J. Rhodes, eds., *The Development of the Polis in Archaic Greece* (London: Routledge, 1997).

10   The numbers are impossible to fix: cf. P. J. Rhodes, *CAH* VI².566–67; M. H. Hansen, *The Athenian Democracy in the Age of Demosthenes* (Oxford: Blackwell, 1991), pp. 55, 90–94; and Cohen (n. 8), pp. 12–15. For metics and slaves, see the chapter by Patterson.

11   See P. J. Rhodes, with D. M. Lewis, *The Decrees of the Greek States* (Oxford: Oxford University Press, 1997), esp. pp. 1, 502, and R. Sealey, *The Athenian Republic* (University Park: Pennsylvania State University Press, 1987), pp. 91–8. Cf. Rhodes, *CAH* V².78, 91–5, and Nicholas F. Jones, *Public Organization in Ancient Greece: A Documentary Study* (Philadelphia: American Philosophical Society, 1987).

12   Sparta retained two hereditary kings, with primarily religious and military duties, throughout the classical period (see Hdt. 6.52–9; Xen. *Constitution of the Spartans*, esp. 13, 15). However, the Spartans' ephors and the members of their council of elders (the *gerousia*) were elected (see also Arist. *Pol.* 1270b, II.9.19–1271a, II.9.28). At Athens, some important priesthoods were restricted to particular families, and it seems likely that most other poleis possessed some offices filled only by members of certain families.

13   See n. 12 above. For the council's role in Greek government and the concept of *probouleusis* (roughly speaking, preparing or approving business for the assembly), see Rhodes (n. 11), pp. 475–501 and see below at nn. 15–16 and 45.

14   On the Areopagus and its controversial origins and early history, see R. W. Wallace, *The Areopagos Council* (Baltimore: Johns Hopkins University Press, 1989).

15   On the council of 500, see P. J. Rhodes, *The Athenian Boule* (Oxford: Oxford University Press, 1972; revised reprint, 1984).

16   These ten tribes were primarily geographical, electoral, and military units created during the Cleisthenic reform ca. 507, and had nothing to do with descent.

17   On the qualifications for *bouleutai*, see Rhodes (n. 15), esp. pp. 1–30.

18 See Hanson (n. 9), pp. 201–19.

19 For the Athenians' willingness to overlook property qualifications in the fourth century, see *AP* 7.4, 47.1.

20 See *AP* 7.

21 *AP* 8.1; on the office and Athena's treasury in general, see L. J. Samons, *Empire of the Owl: Athenian Imperial Finance* (Stuttgart: Steiner, 2000), pp. 30–50.

22 Some moderns therefore treat Solon as the real founder of Athenian democracy; see, e.g., R. W. Wallace, "Solonian Democracy," in I. Morris and K. A. Raaflaub, eds., *Democracy 2500? Questions and Challenges* (Dubuque, IA: Kendall/Hunt, 1998), pp. 11–29. Aristotle (*AP* 9.1; *Pol.* 1274a, II.12.3) believed that it was Solon's supposed admission of all citizens to the juries that made his constitution "democratic," but such participation in juries probably did not actually begin until the mid-fifth century.

23 On the *eupatridai*, cf. P. J. Rhodes, *A Commentary on the Aristotelian Athenaion Politeia* (Oxford: Oxford University Press, 1981; revised reprint, 1993), pp. 74–6, 183–7; A. Andrewes, *CAH* III².3.367–8, 393; Hansen (n. 9), pp. 27–8. For their control of cults, cf. Robert Parker, *Athenian Religion: A History* (Oxford: Oxford University Press, 1996), pp. 63–6.

24 For these subgroups, see J. D. Mikalson, *Athenian Popular Religion* (Chapel Hill: University of North Carolina Press, 1983), pp. 83–90.

25 On the phratries, see esp. S. D. Lambert, *The Phratries of Attica* (Ann Arbor: University of Michigan Press, 1993); Rhodes (n. 23), pp. 68–71; Andrewes, *CAH* III.3².366–68; Parker (n. 23), pp. 64, 108–9. For the *gene* see Rhodes, ibid., Andrewes, *CAH* III.3².367–68, and Hansen (n. 10), p. 46. The precise nature of the clans and their possible role in the phratries have become very controversial subjects: see esp. Rhodes (n. 23), p. 768; Félix Bourriot, *Recherches sur la nature du génos* (Lille: Université de Lille, 1976); Denis Roussel, *Tribu et cité* (Paris: Les Belles Lettres, 1976); and Nicholas F. Jones, *The Associations of Classical Athens: The Response to Democracy* (Oxford: Oxford University Press, 1999), esp. pp. 195–220, 242–9.

26 On the Ionian tribes, cf. Rhodes (n. 23), pp. 67–8, 71; Snodgrass (n. 8), pp. 25–8; Andrewes, *CAH* III.3².361, 366; and Parker (n. 23), pp. 16–17. On Greek ethnic divisions in general, see Jonathan Hall, *Ethnic Identity in Greek Antiquity* (Cambridge: Cambridge University Press, 1997).

27 For the (later ten) tribes, see, e.g., Hdt. 6.111. For the possible military role of the phratries, see Hansen (n. 10), p. 46; Roussel (n. 25), pp. 109–21; and A. Andrewes, "Phratries in Homer," *Hermes* 89 (1961): 129–40. For Athenian soldiers divided by tribe, see, e.g., *IG* i³ 1147, = ML 33 = Fornara 78; cf. Thuc. 2.34, *SEG* XXXIV. 45, with Lewis, *CAH* V².113.

28 The demos as a whole also participated in the worship of Dionysos – especially during Athenian festivals such as the City Dionysia (at which comedies and tragedies were performed) – and other gods (such as those worshipped by initiates to the mysteries at Eleusis): see, e.g., Parker (n. 23), pp. 89–101.

29 For the Panathenaea, see Parker (n. 23), pp. 75–6, 89–92, and J. Neils, ed., *Worshipping Athena: Panathenaia and Parthenon* (Madison: University of Wisconsin Press, 1996).

30 On the *dokimasia*, see *AP* 45.3, 55, 59.4, with Rhodes (n. 23), pp. 614–17; and Hansen (n. 10), pp. 218–20.

31 *AP* 55.3; Rhodes (n. 15), pp. 176–8.

32 Hansen (n. 10), p. 219.

33 See ibid., pp. 218–20.

34 Peisistratus first came to power in 561/0, but did not secure permanent control of Athens until probably the 540s: see *AP* 13.3–15.3, with Rhodes (n. 23), pp. 191–9.

35 Hdt. 1.59; Thuc. 6.54; *AP* 16.1–3, 7–8.

36 See esp. Hdt. 1.59–64; Arist. *Pol.* 1305a, V.5.9; and *AP* 13–17, with Rhodes (n. 23), esp. pp. 185–227, 255–6; and cf. C. W. Fornara and L. J. Samons, *Athens from Cleisthenes to Pericles* (Berkeley: University of California Press, 1991), pp. 14–17, 151–7; R. Sealey, *A History of the Greek City States* (Berkeley: University of California Press, 1975), pp. 134–44; and A. Andrewes, *The Greek Tyrants* (London: Hutchinson, 1956), pp. 100–115.

37 The dating of the so-called "Peisistratid" temple of Athena is controversial; see, e.g., Hurwit (n. 7), esp. pp. 116–22, who argues that the temple of Athena constructed in the late sixth century belongs to the early democratic rather than to the tyrannical regime.

38 See L. J. Samons, *What's Wrong with Democracy? From Athenian Practice to American Worship* (Berkeley: University of California Press, 2004), pp. 101–4. Cf. Andrewes (n. 36), pp. 100–115, and *CAH* III.3².398–416; and Michael Stahl, *Aristokraten und Tyrannen im archaischen Athen: Untersuchungen zur Überlieferung, zur Sozialstruktur und zur Entstehung des Staates* (Stuttgart: Steiner, 1987).

39 On the Peisistratid tyranny's overthrow, which according to tradition was actually instigated by exiled Athenians, see Hdt. 5.55–7, 62–5; Thuc. 1.20, 6.53–9; *AP* 17–19; and p. 286 below.

40 Hdt. 5.66, 69–73; *AP* 20–21. See L. J. Samons, "Mass, Elite and Hoplite-Farmer in Greek History," *Arion* 5.3 (1998): 110–15, and Fornara and Samons (n. 36), pp. 37–58.

41 For deme membership and citizenship, see Hansen (n. 10), p. 46, citing Isoc. 8.88 and Dem. 57.46, and M. Ostwald, *CAH* IV².312.

42 For Cleisthenes' reforms see also Sealey in this volume, pp. 240–42. I leave aside the issue of an older council of 400, perhaps created by Solon: *AP* 8.4, with Rhodes (n. 23), pp. 153–4.

43 For the tribes and the *trittyes* ("thirds") into which they were divided, see esp. John S. Traill, *The Political Organization of Attica: A Study of the Demes, Trittyes, and Phylai, and Their Representation in the Athenian Council* (Princeton: American School of Classical Studies at Athens, 1975); N. F. Jones (n. 25); Ostwald, *CAH* IV².312–15; and Rhodes (n. 23), pp. 251–4. Cleisthenes associated each tribe with a semimythical or heroic "founder," and each tribe had its own religious officials and rites. See *AP* 21.6, with Parker (n. 23), pp. 103–4, 117–21. For the tribes' potential relationship to the navy, see Dem. 14.22–3.

44 The deme was also the most important religious organization within the community: see Parker (n. 23), p. 102.

45 See *AP* 45.4, with Rhodes (n. 15), pp. 52–81.

46 Hdt. 5.74. For the unlikelihood of any real friendship between the Spartans and the Athenian tyrants, see at n. 39 above, Samons (n. 38), p. 213 n. 41, and P. J. Rhodes (n. 23), p. 237.

47 Hdt. 5.78 (cf. 5.66). The historian here ignores the Athenians' earlier expansion under the Peisistratids and before.

48 See Hdt. 6.102–17. On the campaign of Marathon, see Hammond, *CAH* IV².506–16; C. Hignett, *Xerxes' Invasion of Greece* (Oxford: Oxford University Press, 1963), pp. 55–74; and W. K. Pritchett, "Marathon," *University of California Publications in Classical Archaeology* 4, no. 2 (1960): 137–89.

49 *AP* 22, with Hdt. 6.115, 121–5.

50 For the campaigns of 480–479, see Hdt. bks. 7–9, and Hignett (n. 48). For a contemporary reaction, see Aeschylus's *Persians*.

51 Thuc. 1.94–5; Hdt. 8.3. On Athenian-Spartan relations in this period, see Fornara and Samons (n. 36), pp. 117–26, and, in general, the chapter of Lendon in this volume.

52 Thuc. 1.96; on the foundation of the league and the institution of tribute payments, see Samons (n. 21), pp. 84–91. For the league's history, see the chapter by Rhodes in this volume.

53 Thuc. 1.98–99. See also Rhodes in this volume, pp. 25–6.

54 For the Eurymedon, see esp. Thuc. 1.100; Plut. *Cim.* 12–13.

55 M. H. Hansen has argued that the *heliaia* was not the assembly acting as a court but a separate court of sworn jurors instituted by Solon: Hansen (n. 10), pp. 30, 191, with references there; cf. Rhodes (n. 23), pp. 160–62, 771. In any case, the *heliaia* pre-dated the reforms of Ephialtes.

56 For Ephialtes' reforms, see *AP* 25; for analysis, see the chapters by Rhodes and Sealey in this volume; Rhodes (n. 23), pp. 314–17, and *CAH* V².67–75; Wallace (n. 15), pp. 83–7; and Fornara and Samons (n. 36), pp. 59–72. For the system of dicasteries, see Hansen (n. 10), pp. 178–224, and Sealey, in this volume; for the numbers of dicasts, see Rhodes (n. 23), pp. 728–9, and Hansen (n. 10), p. 187.

57 Arist. *AP* 27.3, *Pol.* 1274a8–9; see Hansen (n. 10), pp. 188–9, and for the date of the institution of jury pay, cf. Rhodes (n. 23), pp. 338–40, and Fornara and Samons (n. 36), pp. 67–75.

58 For payment of the councilmen, see Thuc. 8.69.4 with Rhodes (n. 15), pp. 13–14; for the assembly, see *AP* 41.3.

59 On the transfer of the treasury from Delos, its date, and its effects, see Samons (n. 21), pp. 92–163. On the building program, see esp. Wycherley, *CAH* V².215–22, and J. S. Boersma, *Athenian Building Policy from 561/0 to 405/4 B.C.* (Groningen: Wolters-Noordhoff, 1970).

60 Payment for public service such as jury duty was apparently very unusual. There is little evidence of state pay in classical Greece outside of Athens: see Rhodes (n. 23), p. 338. On the citizenship law, see Cynthia Patterson, *Pericles' Citizenship Law of 451/0 B.C.* (New York: Arno, 1981) and her chapter in this volume.

61 On Cimon's campaign in Cyprus, see Thuc. 1.112; Diod. 12.3–4; Plut. *Cim.* 18–19.

62 For the debate about the Peace of Callias, see L. J. Samons, "Kimon, Kallias and Peace with Persia," *Historia* 47 (1998): 129–40; E. Badian, *From Plataea to Potidaea: Studies in the History and Historiography of the Pentecontaetia* (Baltimore: Johns Hopkins University Press, 1993), pp. 1–72; A. J. Holladay, "The Détente of Kallias?" *Historia* 35 (1986), 503–7; Russell Meiggs, *The Athenian Empire* (Oxford: Oxford University Press, 1972), pp. 129–51; David Stockton, "The Peace of Callias," *Historia* 8 (1959): 61–79; and Rhodes in this volume, n. 20.

63 See, e.g., the Athenians' regulations for Chalcis (*IG* i³ 40 = ML 52 = Fornara 103; cf. Fornara 99–100, 102). The dates of many imperialistic decrees conventionally placed in the early 440s based on their letter forms (especially the sigma) are

controversial. H. B. Mattingly has argued that most of them belong in the 420s and thus reflect Cleon's policies rather than Pericles': see Mattingly, *The Athenian Empire Restored* (Ann Arbor: University of Michigan Press, 1996). Recent investigations support Mattingly's basic contention that the letter forms alone cannot provide a sound criterion for dating inscriptions. However, at least some of the inscriptions he discusses (e.g., the regulations for Erythrae and Chalcis) probably still belong in the 440s or earlier. See also Rhodes in this volume, pp. 24, 33 with n. 55. For the once conventional view of this period, see Lewis, *CAH* V².121–46; for arguments supporting this view, see esp. R. Meiggs and D. Lewis, *A Selection of Greek Historical Inscriptions to the End of the Fifth Century* B.C., revised edition (Oxford: Oxford University Press, 1988), esp. pp. 119–21.

64 On the use of this money, see Lisa Kallet, "Accounting for Culture in Fifth-Century Athens," in Deborah Boedeker and Kurt A. Raaflaub, eds., *Democracy, Empire, and the Arts in Fifth-Century Athens* (Cambridge, MA: Harvard University Press, 1998), pp. 43–58, and Samons (n. 21).

65 See Thuc. 1.31–45. Athens's interests in the West may perhaps be inferred from her treaties with Rhegium and Leontini, Greek city-states located in southern Italy and eastern Sicily, respectively. These treaties existed by 433/2 at the latest: see ML 63–4 (= Fornara 124–5), with commentary.

66 On Spartan-Athenian relations before the Peloponnesian War, see the chapter by Lendon below. On the first ten years of the war (431–421), see Thuc. 2–5.17, with Meiggs (n. 62), pp. 306–23; Donald Kagan, *The Archidamian War* (Ithaca, NY: Cornell University Press, 1974); and Lewis, *CAH* V².370–432.

67 See Thuc. 5.18–116, with Meiggs (n. 62), pp. 338–45, and Donald Kagan, *The Peace of Nicias and the Sicilian Expedition* (Ithaca, NY: Cornell University Press, 1981).

68 On the Sicilian expedition and the Decelean War, see Thuc. bks. 6–7, with Meiggs (n. 62), pp. 345–74; Kagan (n. 67); and Andrewes, *CAH* V².446–63.

69 See Thuc. bk. 8, esp. 47–54, 64–70; *AP* 29–33.

70 On the overthrow of the Four Hundred and the brief regime of the Five Thousand, see esp. Thuc. 8.80–98; *AP* 33–34; D. Kagan, *The Fall of the Athenian Empire* (Ithaca, NY: Cornell University Press, 1987), pp. 187–246; and Andrewes, *CAH* V².474–85.

71 *AP* 34.1 and Andoc. 1.96–98, with Rhodes (n. 23), pp. 414–15.

72 See Xen. *Hell.* 2.2.3, 10, 16–23, 3.5.8, 6.5.36, 46; Andoc. 1.142, 3.21; Isoc. 14.31; Justin 5.8.4–5; Plut. *Lys.* 14.

73 I wish to thank the University of California Press for permission to reprint and adapt portions of Loren J. Samons II, *What's Wrong with Democracy? From Athenian Practice to American Worship* (Berkeley: University of California Press, 2004).

I: DEMOCRACY AND EMPIRE

P. J. Rhodes

In the past half-century it has often seemed paradoxical, and to the politically correct embarrassing, that Athens in the second half of the fifth century was democratic, and indeed a champion of democracy in the Greek world, and therefore admirable, but was also the head of the greatest empire in which Greeks controlled other Greeks, and therefore deplorable.[1] One advantage available to those who challenged the orthodox dating criteria for fifth-century Athenian inscriptions, and moved to the 420s texts which orthodoxy placed ca. 450, was that the more extreme manifestations of imperialism could be associated not with Pericles, of whom (following Thucydides) we ought to approve, but with Cleon, of whom (again following Thucydides) it was respectable to disapprove: "None of the inscriptional evidence for fully organized Athenian imperialism can be dated before 431 B.C. Even the very language of imperialism does not seem to have been current until the last years of Perikles' ascendancy."[2] G. E. M. de Ste. Croix, in an avowedly if idiosyncratically Marxist interpretation of ancient history, developed the idea first expressed by G. Grote (who in the nineteenth century did more than anybody else to make Athenian democracy an object of praise) that, despite the judgment of Thucydides that the Athenians exercised their power as far as they could, as was natural, and their subjects hated it, as also was natural,[3] in fact the Athenian empire was unpopular only with upper-class oligarchs in the member cities and was popular with lower-class democrats: "It is unique among past empires known to us in that the ruling city relied very much on the support of the lower classes in the subject states."[4] Elsewhere he claimed, "Although Athens certainly exploited her allies to some extent, I see no evidence that she did so in any extensive way."[5] On the other hand, M. I. Finley, who took an interest both in Athenian democracy and in

Athenian imperialism, wrote, "Athenian imperialism employed all the forms of material exploitation that were available and possible in that society;"[6] but he also wrote, "We must acknowledge that other societies can act, and have acted, *in good faith* in moral terms other than ours, even abhorrent to us. Historical explanation is not identical with moral judgment."[7] Let us in that spirit investigate the connections between the Athenians' democracy and their empire.

Thucydides' digression (1.89–117) on the Pentecontaetia, the period of (nearly) fifty years between the Persian War and the Peloponnesian War, is not just a chronicle but was placed in book 1 with a purpose, to show how Athens set out from innocent beginnings to become so powerful as to be perceived by Sparta as a threat.[8] There is no need to doubt that the beginnings were innocent.[9] In 483/2 the Athenians had spent surplus revenue from their silver mines on shipbuilding, as a result of which they had been able to contribute 200 ships to the Greek navy which fought against the Persians in 480, more than half of the total.[10] At the end of 479 nobody could be sure that the Persian War was at an end even in the short term, and in 478 fighting against the Persians continued under Spartan leadership. But in 478/7, after the Spartan regent Pausanias had made himself unpopular with the allies, Athens took over as the leader of the Greeks who still wanted to continue the fighting, appropriately because of its large navy and because it was regarded as the mother city of the Ionian Greeks, who occupied many of the islands of the Aegean and the central part of the Aegean coast of Asia Minor. This new organisation, with its headquarters originally on the island of Delos, is known to modern scholars as the Delian League (Thuc. 1.94–97.1).

Thucydides' purpose is to outline the growth of Athenian power, and it is likely enough that before ca. 449 there was a good deal of campaigning against the Persians, which he does not report, with which the League members were entirely happy. The League appears in fact to have been a full and permanent offensive and defensive alliance (*AP* 23.5), but that is not incompatible with a declared anti-Persian aim. However, from the beginning, in the period when the Athenian commander was Cimon, Athens found ways of advancing its own interests through the activities of the League. Eïon, on the north coast of the Aegean, was indeed a surviving Persian outpost in Europe, but after its capture Athenian settlers were sent there.[11] The island of Scyros had nothing to do with the Persians, but it lay on the route from the Hellespont to Athens, and this time Thucydides does mention the Athenian settlers.[12] Carystus, at the southern end of Euboea, after being sacked by the Persians in 490, had supported them in 480 and had afterwards been punished by the Greeks:[13] it too lay near to the route from the Hellespont to Athens, and it was attacked and forced to join the League (Thuc. 1.98.3). Naxos, for whatever reason, wanted to leave the League, but it was forced back and (metaphorically) enslaved (Thuc. 1.98.4). Thucydides then comments on Athens's strict insistence on the allies' obligations: an unending alliance was to mean unending service in campaigns under Athenian leadership (Thuc. 1.99). For the revolt of Thasos he does give a reason, a dispute over Thasos's trading-posts and mines in its *peraia*, the territory which it possessed on the mainland opposite: after a long siege Thasos was made to demolish its walls, surrender its ships, pay tribute in cash, and give up its possessions on the mainland.[14] The seizure of opportunities to advance Athens's interests and the use of force to crush opposition thus quickly became established.

In the late 460s Cimon disagreed with his opponents both on foreign and on domestic policy: he stood for good relations with Sparta, and took a force to help Sparta against the rebelling Messenians. His chief opponent, Ephialtes, had not wanted to help Sparta; and after the Spartans had sent Cimon and his soldiers away Athens broke off the alliance with Sparta which had been in force since 481 and instead made alliances with Argos and other enemies of Sparta in Greece.[15] At first the supporters of Ephialtes extended the area within which Athens could be ambitious rather than the nature of Athens's ambitions. Fighting against Persia led the Athenians to Cyprus, where Pausanias and Cimon had gone before, and an invitation received there led them on to fight against the Persians in Egypt and Phoenicia.[16] They also became involved in the First Peloponnesian War, and started building up their power in mainland Greece (Thuc. 1.102.4, 103.3–4, 105–8, 111).

A further stage, about which we learn more from inscriptions and from later literary sources than from Thucydides, was reached in the years around 450. About 454 the Egyptian campaign ended in disaster, and the campaigning in Greece ran out of steam; in 451 Athens made a five-year truce with the Peloponnesians and Argos made a thirty-year peace with Sparta.[17] Persia seems to have been willing to exploit this apparent weakness: it had tried unsuccessfully to incite Sparta against Athens during the Egyptian war (Thuc. 1.109.2–3); the League treasury may have been moved from Delos to Athens in 454 because a small island in the middle of the Aegean seemed unsafe;[18] the first of the tribute lists (strictly, the lists of offerings to Athena of $\frac{1}{60}$ of the tribute, calculated separately on each member state's payment) which began in 453 show considerable variations from one year to the next, and point to unrest in the League; and it appears from Athens's decree for Erythrae, probably of the late 450s, that rebels there had Persian support.[19] Cimon, back in Athens after his period of ostracism, campaigned again to Cyprus and Egypt, but he died, and the Athenians, though victorious, withdrew (Thuc. 1.112.1–2). Whether the Athenians made a treaty with the Persians, the so-called Peace of Callias, continues to be disputed, but it is not disputed that after Cimon's death regular campaigning against Persia came to an end.[20]

What was to become of the League? The likelihood that no tribute was collected in 448, and Plutarch's report of an invitation from Athens to all the Greeks to discuss what looks like the foundation of a new league, may be seen as signs that Athens considered the question seriously. The resumption of collection in 447, with the numbering of the lists resumed probably in 446 as if there had never been an interruption, and the abandonment of the congress proposal when Sparta declined the invitation,[21] show that Athens's final answer to the question was to keep the Delian League in being although it was not going to continue regular warfare against Persia. In 447–446 most of Athens's mainland acquisitions succeeded in asserting their independence, but the Thirty Years' Peace of 446/5 effectively recognised the division of the Greek world into a Spartan bloc based on the Greek mainland and an Athenian bloc based on the Aegean (Thuc. 1.113–115.1).

It is in the middle of the century that we start finding evidence for Athens's setting up democracies in allied states;[22] requiring offerings at the festival of the Panathenaea, perhaps at first only from allies which were Ionian in the strict sense of the term, but eventually from all the allies;[23] transferring lawsuits from local courts to Athenian courts;[24] sending garrisons and governors and other officials to allied states;[25] and simply changing the language used in oaths and in Athenian decrees, so that "the allies" became "the cities," or even "the cities which Athens controls," and they were required to promise obedience to Athens.[26] Above all, allies which had been disloyal were liable to have some of their land confiscated and given to colonies or "cleruchies" of Athenian settlers: this device will both have installed unofficial garrisons to keep an eye on allies of doubtful loyalty and have provided land for Athenians – particularly poorer Athenians – at the allies' expense.[27] There were opportunities for richer Athenians as well: normally only citizens of a city could own land in the city's territory, but we happen to know that a man called Oeonias, one of those involved in the religious scandals of 415, owned land in Euboea which was sold in Athens along with the rest of his confiscated property and which realised the enormous sum of 81⅓ talents.[28] From the middle of the century we can justifiably say with Finley that "Athenian imperialism employed all the forms of material exploitation that were available and possible in that society."[29]

After the reforms of Ephialtes in 462/1, Athens was self-consciously democratic, with a regime in which the poorer citizens were encouraged to play an active part. I have argued that, although particular provocations help to explain why the reforms were made when they were, the reformers did consciously want to transfer power from the council of the Areopagus (of which men who had served as archons became members for life) to bodies more representative of the Athenian people (the council of five hundred, the assembly, and the jury-courts); we perhaps see in Aeschylus's *Suppliant Women*, probably of 464/3, the concept of *demokratia* at the time when it was coined;[30] by the middle of the fifth century Athens was encouraging or requiring democratic regimes in allied states;[31] and by the time of the Peloponnesian War Athens was perceived as a champion of democracy and Sparta of oligarchy.[32]

Democracy was literally "people-power;" but the *demos*, the "people" among whom power was shared, was limited to free adult males of Athenian descent. Indeed, Pericles' citizenship law of 451/0 defined the *demos* more strictly than before by requiring an Athenian mother as well as an Athenian father − probably not, as a fourth-century writer thought, to restrict the size of the citizen body, but to guarantee its quality and ensure that what were perceived as the growing benefits of belonging to the Athenian *demos* were enjoyed only by those who were genuinely Athenian.[33] Large numbers of citizens were actively involved in running the democracy, through machinery which required a very high level of participation: decision-making, by an assembly of citizens guided but not dominated by the council of five hundred, whose membership changed each year; administration, by large numbers of officials and boards, again changing each year, supervised by the council; law-courts with amateur chairmen and juries of hundreds or thousands. The empire added to the business which the citizens had to transact: more decisions had to be taken by the assembly; there was more administration to be done and more officials and committees were needed;[34] there were more lawsuits to be decided, especially when Athens took to having cases transferred from local courts to Athenian courts. Not every citizen was an activist − there were "quiet Athenians," uninvolved in public affairs[35] − but the system could not have worked unless a substantial proportion of the citizens were willing to play an active part at least in some years of their life. Pericles in his funeral oration is represented as saying that Athens alone regards the uninvolved not as leisured but as useless (Thuc. 2.40.2).

This high degree of involvement for the citizens was possible only because of the many non-citizens who were not and could not be involved. While a citizen was attending the assembly or sitting on a jury or doing the work of some office or simply talking to other citizens in the Agora, ordinary economic life had to continue, in the house and in the field, in making and transporting and selling and buying goods. Much of a citizen family's economic work would be done by the citizen's wife and children, and if he could afford any by his slave or slaves; much of the making and transporting and selling of goods was in the hands of metics, free men and women who were not of Athenian descent, and who unless granted it as a special privilege were not allowed to own land and houses in Attica and therefore needed non-agricultural forms of livelihood. It was still easier to devote much of one's time to public life if one was rich rather than poor. As the modern world has found, unless one adopts a communist regime (in which case there is a danger that open financial advantage will disappear only to be replaced by other kinds of advantage), the advantages of wealth cannot be abolished, but they can be moderated: Athens, in order to moderate them and make it easier for poorer citizens to play an active part, introduced modest payments for performing the various civilian duties of a citizen, beginning with service on juries, probably in the 450s, and culminating with attendance at the assembly, in the 390s.[36]

The empire generated more business and more officials for the democracy, but it also helped to pay for the democracy. By the 440s, nearly all the members of the Delian League were paying tribute in cash rather than contributing ships to the League's forces. As we have seen, the League's treasury, originally kept on the island of Delos, was apparently in 454 moved to Athens. This treasury was kept separate from Athens's other treasuries until ca. 411, when it and the main treasury of the state were amalgamated,[37] but at any rate between ca. 449, when regular campaigning against Persia came to an end, and 431, when the Peloponnesian War began, the income from tribute must greatly have exceeded the sums spent for League purposes. In any case, from 453 onwards, $\frac{1}{60}$ of the tribute was given as an offering to the (Athenian) treasury of the goddess Athena; and, whatever may have been done with the surplus tribute,[38] the fact that Athenian military and naval expenditure was a legitimate charge on the tribute meant that Athens could afford out of its own funds expenditure for other purposes (including payment to Athenian juries and officials) which it might otherwise not have been able to afford.

Rowing the Athenian navy's ships was primarily the responsibility of the poorer citizens, the *thetes*, those too poor to be able to equip themselves to fight in the army as hoplites. Athens's leadership of the Delian League meant that it would continue to have a use for a large navy and a large number of oarsmen, as a result of which the poorer citizens would be more important to the city's military success in Athens than in most cities. Cimon opposed the democratic reforms in 462/1 and was ostracised (Plut. *Cim.* 15; *Per.* 9.5): the hoplites stood to gain as much as the *thetes* from the transfer of powers from the Areopagus to more representative bodies, and the reforms should not be seen in any crude sense as a triumph for the *thetes*. Nor is there any occasion when the assembly is known to have divided on class lines, with the hoplites voting one way and the *thetes* the other, though the absence from Athens in 411 of many of the *thetes* (who were serving in the fleet, based at Samos) made it easier for the oligarchs to get acceptance by the Athenian assembly for their revolution, by which ostensibly the hoplites would remain full citizens but the *thetes* would not.[39]

It would be wrong to claim too simple a link between social class, the dominant mode of fighting, and the distribution of political power; and H. van Wees has argued recently that Athens's naval power encouraged the development of democracy only by increasing the confidence of lower-class citizens who were in any case ambitious for more power.[40] However, it is still true that the League enabled the navy and the *thetes* to enjoy more importance in Athens than they did in other cities, and that this will have had some effect on the ethos of the city and the way in which the city confronted its enemies and fought its wars: "It is right that there [i.e., at Athens] the poor and the *demos* have more than the noble and the rich, for this reason, that it is the *demos* that rows the ships and surrounds the city with strength . . . far more than the hoplites and the noble and the good."[41]

But how far did the democracy in turn affect the way in which Athens treated the League? There is no sign that anybody in Athens disapproved of the empire or of the way in which Athens treated the allies. In the 440s and 430s Athens was spending large sums on buildings on the Acropolis and elsewhere,[42] which were paid for certainly indirectly and probably to a considerable extent directly out of surplus tribute from the League. The criticism attributed to the democracy's aristocratic opponent Thucydides son of Melesias is only that it was wrong to spend on beautifying Athens tribute collected for war against the Persians (Plut. *Per.* 12–14). The criticism made by Bdelycleon in Aristophanes' *Wasps* is that the money collected from the allies enriches politicians like Cleon rather than ordinary citizens (Ar. *Wasps* 655–712). The oligarchs in 411 wanted not to abandon the empire but to substitute oligarchic regimes for democratic in the allied states as well as in Athens, though Thucydides both states himself and attributes to Phrynichus the view that what the allies wanted was freedom rather than any particular kind of constitution imposed on them by Athens.[43] Until the beginning of the Peloponnesian War, the level of tribute was kept generally constant; there were then sharp increases, in 428 (probably) and in 425, imposed specifically in order to help pay for the war rather than in order to enrich Athens at the allies' expense.[44] The speech *Against Alcibiades* which purports to have been written in connection with Athens's last ostracism, in 415, makes it a point of complaint against Alcibiades that he and his fellow tribute-assessors had presumed to double the original amount levied; but this passage would be unique in fifth-century Athenian texts in suggesting that there was anything wrong in the extraction of tribute from the allies, and its inclusion is one reason among several for thinking that this is not an authentic speech of 415 but a later composition.[45]

Speculation about how things might have differed in other respects if they had differed in one respect is artificial and not very profitable, but I will indulge in it for one paragraph. We have seen the first signs of imperialism visible already under the leadership of Cimon and before the reforms of Ephialtes; it is possible to imagine a scenario in which Cimon was still dominant in the 450s, democratic reforms were delayed, and while Cimon remained dominant campaigning in and beyond the Aegean continued but conflict with the Peloponnesians was avoided. Increasing interference with and control of the allied states might yet have taken place. It is hard to believe that an empire which depended on Athens's navy, and which increased the volume of business to be transacted and the number of officials to be appointed by a state in which, after the reforms of Cleisthenes in 508/7, citizen involvement was already becoming important, would not have moved in the direction of democracy eventually even if it had not done so in 462/1. And, when we see how the Thirty Years' Peace of 446/5 proved unsustainable, even though after it Athens was not powerful in mainland Greece, it is also hard to believe that, even if the pro-Spartan policies of Cimon had continued for a time, the power of Athens would not in the end have led to conflict between Athens and Sparta. While the course which history actually took was not inevitable, it is the course which history actually took, and maritime empire and democracy were natural partners.

Since this book is a *Companion to the Age of Pericles*, it is appropriate to ask how far the Athenian combination of democracy and empire is to be attributed to Pericles himself. Despite the claim made by Thucydides, what we find in Periclean Athens cannot have been "in theory democracy but in fact rule by the first man" (Thuc. 2.65.9) – because that is not how Athens worked.[46] Pericles was frequently elected general, according to Plutarch for each of the last fifteen years of his life (Plut. *Per.* 16.3), and in the heyday of the Delian League the generals were the political as well as the military leaders of Athens. Nevertheless, as general Pericles was one of a board of ten men, who were constitutionally equal, and he and his colleagues had little formal power inside Athens. To be general he had to be elected, year after year (and in 430 he was deposed, but subsequently re-elected[47]). To direct Athenian policy he had to ensure that the assembly voted as he wanted, again and again, on proposal after proposal; and in a society without disciplined political parties nobody, however influential, could be certain of achieving that on every occasion. It does, however, seem likely that from the 450s to the 430s Pericles was sufficiently influential to ensure that the assembly did vote as he wanted, not on every occasion but more often than not. The assembly could easily take a decision which impeded or conflicted with another decision taken earlier, at a previous meeting or even at the same meeting; but in so far as Athens pursued a consistent policy during this period we can reasonably assume that Pericles approved of that policy and was working for it.[48]

We have seen above that the development of the empire began under Cimon's leadership, while after Cimon's ostracism his opponents pursued more ambitious policies; and that Cimon's opponents were responsible for the development of a self-conscious democracy. If we look for items explicitly attributed to Pericles, we find, in internal affairs, that he was a prosecutor of Cimon (allegedly not as zealous as he might have been),[49] and was associated with Ephialtes in the reform of the Areopagus;[50] he was responsible, perhaps in the 450s, for the introduction of jury pay,[51] and in 451/0 for requiring two Athenian parents as a qualification for citizenship (*AP* 26.4, Plut. *Per.* 37.3). He is said to have fought in the Athenian forces at Tanagra ca. 457 (Plut. *Per.* 10.2); he was in command of an expedition to Sicyon and Acarnania ca. 454 (Thuc. 1.111.2–3), in the Sacred War for Delphi in the early 440s,[52] in Euboea and the Megarid in 446 (Thuc. 1.114, Plut. *Per.* 22–3), and in the Samian war of 440–439 (Thuc. 1.115.2–117, Plut. *Per.* 25–28). He is credited also with colonising expeditions, to the Chersonese, perhaps in the 440s, and to the Black Sea, perhaps in the 430s (Plut. *Per.* 19.1, 20.1–2). He was the author of the invitation to the Greeks to a congress to discuss what may have been a plan of the early 440s to convert the Delian League into a league of all the Greeks (Plut. *Per.* 17). He is associated also with public works: in particular, with the works on the Acropolis in the 440s–430s, and with defending the expenditure of surplus tribute from the Delian League on these works;[53] also with the Odeum, said to be an imitation of a Persian building (Plut. *Per.* 13.9–11), and the Middle Wall, running close to the more northerly of the Long Walls between Athens and the Piraeus which had been built in the 450s.[54] Although it now seems to be established that Athens's inscription concerning an alliance with Egesta, despite its older form of sigma, is to be dated 418/7, this does not automatically invalidate the earlier dates proposed for all disputed inscriptions, and some signs of imperial behaviour are still probably to be found in the middle of the century.[55] In the 430s Pericles is credited with the decision to make a defensive alliance with Corcyra (when the Athenians could, if they were anxious to avoid trouble, have refused to involve themselves in the dispute between Corcyra and Corinth);[56] and with the first, "reasonable and humane," decree against the Megarians, and with the insistence that the decree imposing sanctions on them should not be repealed.[57] Although by no means everything that Athens did in this period was done on Pericles' formal proposal or under his leadership, he is associated with enough, over a sufficient range, to justify the view that the policies which Athens was pursuing were Pericles' policies.

In 427 Cleon tried to prevent the revision of the decision taken by Athens on his proposal to execute all the men of Mytilene and enslave all the women and children. He is represented by Thucydides as stating that democracy is incapable of ruling an empire, because the citizens' trust of one another is carried over into trust of the allies, and they are not willing to take and to keep to the firm decisions that are needed (Thuc. 3.37). In fact, by Greek criteria there was nothing paradoxical about a democracy's ruling an empire. The foundation of democracy was not human rights but citizens' rights, and, just as a democracy felt no obligation to grant equal rights within the state to metics and slaves, it felt no obligation to treat as equals the allies which it gained in the wider Greek world. It would favour democratic regimes among the allies, both because it believed in the principles of democracy (interpreted as above) and because it found other democracies easier to deal with,[58] but its primary commitment was to its own *demos* and the interests of its own *demos*.

Independence for one's local community was a persistent desire in Greece: for the strong and ambitious, independence for themselves could be combined with the absorption or subjection of lesser, neighbouring communities; for the weak and unambitious the best that could be hoped for was often a measure of local freedom and independence combined with a measure of subordination to a more powerful neighbour. The Greek word *autonomia* (from which the English "autonomy" is derived) may have been coined in connection with that lesser hope, and in particular with the hopes of the members of the Delian League.[59] Thucydides states that the members of the League were "autonomous at first" (Thuc. 1.97.1), probably not because there was any foundation document which stipulated that they should be, but because it never occurred to anybody at the time that states which voluntarily joined an alliance might not be autonomous. Every state which enters into an alliance loses something of the total freedom to make all decisions without reference to anybody else, but no previous alliance in Greece had gone beyond committing its participants to joint action in the area with which the alliance was concerned.[60] But Thucydides can use the term "enslaved" of Athens's suppression of a revolt from the League;[61] and when he is dealing with the League in its later state the concept of "subjects" (*hypekooi*) appears both in his own narrative and in the speeches of Athenians and others.[62]

According to Thucydides, Sparta's last demand to Athens before the Peloponnesian War was that Sparta wanted peace, and there could be peace if Athens would leave the Greeks autonomous.[63] He tells us later that at the beginning of the war people's sympathies were in general with the Spartans, particularly because they proclaimed that they were going to liberate Greece (Thuc. 2.8.4). Pericles' response to the Spartan demand was, "We shall leave the cities autonomous if they were autonomous when we made the treaty [sc. the Thirty Years' Peace]" (Thuc. 1.144.2). Athens may have regarded none of the League members as autonomous, though there were a few with which it had interfered comparatively little: in 428 the Mytilenaeans apply the word only to themselves and the Chians (Thuc. 3.10.5–11.3). In the Peace of Nicias, in 421, it was stated that six north-eastern cities returned to Athens were to be autonomous, free from attack by Athens and remaining neutral if they wished, as long as they paid tribute at the original rate (attributed to Aristides in 478/7): their status is contrasted with that of other cities, about which the Athenians could decide as they saw fit (Thuc. 5.18.5, 8).

At the end of the war, after Athens had capitulated and accepted Sparta's terms, "Lysander sailed into the Piraeus and the exiles returned and they began to demolish the walls to the music of pipe-girls, with great enthusiasm, thinking that that day was the beginning of freedom for Greece."[64] Thus by the late fifth century the League was perceived as an organisation through which Athens infringed the freedom of the other Greek states.

Athens was a major state for which freedom meant not only freedom from receiving orders from superiors but also freedom to give orders to inferiors;[65] and through the Delian League Athens succeeded in obtaining that kind of freedom for itself, on a scale and to an extent unparalleled in Greece. At the beginning of the Peloponnesian War Pericles is represented as telling the Athenians that what was at issue for them was not just slavery or freedom but loss of the empire and danger from those whose hatred they had incurred through the empire: it was not possible to give the empire up; it was like a tyranny, and, although it may have been wrong to acquire it, it would be dangerous to let it go (Thuc. 2.63.1–2). The image of Athens the tyrant city is found also in speeches of the Corinthians and of Cleon and Euphemus – and in Aristophanes' *Knights*.[66] Councils of the allies probably ceased meeting when the treasury was moved to Athens.[67] The formal independence of the member states as separate *poleis* with their own separate political institutions was preserved: they were not treated as demes of a greater Athens as, later, cities around the Mediterranean were to be treated as *municipia* (municipalities with their own local government but with no pretence of greater power or independence) of a greater Rome, and to that extent their pride was safeguarded. However, by prescribing a form of constitution, transferring major lawsuits from local courts to Athenian courts, and forbidding cities to issue their own silver coins and to use their own weights and measures,[68] Athens had imposed forms of submission to which states which aspired to be independent had not previously been subjected.

Economically, there were probably advantages for all in belonging to the Athenian power bloc which dominated the Aegean, rather than standing outside it and in opposition to it, but the advantages depended on the retention of Athens's favour. Athens had learned that control of the sea meant not only that it could import whatever it wanted to import from wherever it wanted (Thuc. 2.38.2, [Xen.] *AP* 2.6–7), but also that it could help its friends to import what they wanted and hinder its enemies.[69] The cost of paying the tribute would fall mostly on the richer citizens of the allied states, and the rich would suffer more than the poor, quantitatively though perhaps not proportionally, when part of a city's land was acquired individually or through a cleruchy[70] by Athenians. On the other hand, while having a few ships of its own would bring a city a sense of security as well as pride, it might cost less in terms both of cash and of demands on manpower to pay tribute than to maintain those ships and send them to serve in the League's navy.[71] Moreover, not all the opportunities for employment provided by the League benefited Athenian citizens only: to an unquantifiable extent the allies provided oarsmen for the Athenians' ships, and metics and slaves worked alongside citizens on the various building projects.[72]

We need to ask, as de Ste. Croix did, whether Thucydides was right to suggest that the citizens of the states which Athens treated in this way all hated it.[73] His attempt to distinguish between an "editorial" Thucydides, revealing his own opinions in the speeches and a few direct comments, and a narrative of events which proves the editorial opinions to be mistaken,[74] was too simple. Whatever degree of authenticity we think Thucydides aimed for, and achieved, in his speeches, the extent to which he allowed speakers to contradict one another makes it clear that we can never interpret a speech simply as a vehicle for his own opinions. Notoriously, in the debate on Mytilene, Cleon says, "Do not pin the blame on the oligarchs and acquit the people, for all alike attacked us," while Diodotus replies, "At present the people in all the cities are well disposed to you, and either refuse to join the oligarchs in rebellion or, if compelled to join them, promptly become enemies of the rebels" (Thuc. 3.39.6, 47.2). And Thucydides' narrative of events is not straightforward. Mytilene when it rebelled against Athens was oligarchically governed; after it had been besieged during the winter, and there was no sign of the promised further help from Sparta, the Spartan commander Salaethus armed the ordinary citizens for a final attack on the Athenians, but they refused to obey orders, accused the leading men of hoarding food, and demanded a fair distribution (Thuc. 3.27). De Ste. Croix focused on their refusal to obey orders and argued that they were pro-Athenian; D. W. Bradeen focused on their demand for food and argued that they had reached the limit of their endurance.[75]

From Naxos in the League's early years to various states in the last phase of the Peloponnesian War, including states on the Asiatic mainland, which seem not to have been greatly deterred by Sparta's intention of returning them to Persian control,[76] we can construct a substantial list of revolts, but there were also of course many occasions when a state did not revolt even though it might have done so with a reasonable chance of success. It must be remembered that both Athens and Sparta were much larger and more powerful than most Greek cities, so that if a force from one arrived outside a city, threatening to take hostile action if it did not receive cooperation, it might seem prudent to that city to cooperate with the attacker for the time being, and to express penitence and plead that they had succumbed to irresistible force if the other great power sent a retaliatory expedition later, whatever its true sympathies.[77]

One distinction needs to be emphasised. We may assume that most poorer men are likely to have preferred democratic regimes, under which they had political rights, to oligarchic, under which they did not, while some though not all of the richer men will have preferred oligarchic regimes, under which they did not have to share political rights with the poor. Desire for a congenial regime will have had to be balanced against the desire for a city to be free to make its own choice, which Thucydides and Phrynichus believed to be a stronger motivating factor.[78] But we have evidence from many places at many times in Greek history that, whatever the attitude of ordinary citizens may have been, leading politicians frequently preferred being on the winning side in their city thanks to outside intervention, despite the loss of autonomy which that involved, to being on the losing side in a city which was free from outside intervention and retained its autonomy. In the second half of the fifth century this tended to result in leading democrats' looking to Athens for support and leading oligarchs' looking to Sparta.[79] Men who did have strong reason to be pro-Athenian were those democratic leaders who were in a powerful position in their cities because Athens had imposed or encouraged a democratic constitution, and who might lose their powerful position if Athenian support was withdrawn. Even in oligarchic Mytilene in 428 the men who acted as Athenian *proxenoi* (local representatives of Athens) warned Athens of the city's impending revolt (Thuc. 3.2.3). One consequence of Athens's transferring major lawsuits from local courts to Athenian courts was that it helped Athens to support these pro-Athenian politicians: Athenian courts were likely to give a favourable hearing to pro-Athenian democrats.[80]

The Athenian democracy was first overthrown in 411, after the great Sicilian expedition of 415–413 had ended in disaster and the Persians had begun to support Sparta, and it could no longer be claimed that the democracy was making a success of the war. It was overthrown again in 404, when the democracy had lost the war, the empire had been taken away from Athens, and indeed Athens had been limited to a navy of twelve ships.[81] The democracy was restored again in 403 and then survived unchallenged until it was overthrown by the Macedonians in 321, though it appears that there was now a change of atmosphere if not a fundamental change in the principles of the democracy.[82] There was still payment for civilian service in the fourth century,[83] though without the empire it must have been harder to pay for the democracy. Moreover, the prediction which Thucydides puts into the mouths of Athenian envoys to Sparta in 432, that if Sparta were to take over the empire it would quickly become more unpopular than Athens (Thuc. 1.76.1, 77.6), was to be fulfilled: after the Peloponnesian War Sparta took to interfering in the internal affairs of the Greek cities to such an extent that in 378 Athens founded a new league (cf. below) whose declared purpose was "So that the Spartans shall allow the Greeks to be free and autonomous, and to live at peace occupying their own territory in security."[84]

Athens soon recovered its ambitions. In 395 it joined with some of Sparta's allies in the Corinthian War against Sparta; ca. 390 the Athenian Thrasybulus embarked on what looks like an attempt to recreate the fifth-century Empire, but the impetus was lost when he was killed. In 386 Sparta imposed on the Greek world the (Persian) King's Peace (Peace of Antalcidas), by which the Greeks of Asia Minor were handed over to Persia, and in return Persia gave its backing to the provision that otherwise, with very few exceptions, "all cities and islands" were to be autonomous[85] – which Sparta proceeded to interpret to suit its own interests. In 378 Athens founded a new alliance to resist Spartan imperialism, the Second Athenian League. A prospectus for the League promises that the League will be a defensive alliance based on freedom and autonomy, and that Athens will not do various things which it had done in the Delian League: prescribe constitutions, install garrisons and governors, collect tribute, allow Athenian citizens to acquire land in allies' territory.[86] Athens's promises, and dissatisfaction with Sparta's conduct, made the League popular at first; but the League's original purpose was made irrelevant by Thebes' defeat of Sparta at Leuctra in 371 and liberation of Messenia from Sparta in 370/69. Athens then turned to Sparta in alliance against an increasingly powerful Thebes, and the League found no purpose other than the furtherance of Athenian interests. Sooner or later the original promises were broken: even in the 370s, after promising that there would be no collection of "tribute" (*phoros*), Athens found it necessary to start collecting "contributions" (*syntaxeis*);[87] from the 360s land was made available to individual Athenians through the establishment of cleruchies, particularly in Samos;[88] we know some instances, though admittedly not many, of the sending of governors and garrisons to allied states and of interference in their internal affairs. However, the little evidence that we have suggests that there was no parading of power in this League as in the Delian League, and in particular that the "contributions" were not large and were not under the sole control of Athens; Athens was perpetually short of money until Eubulus, in the late 350s, argued for a change to a less ambitious foreign policy.

The Second League was never a source of power and profit for Athens as the Delian League had been. In the time of Philip of Macedon the Athenian Demosthenes tended to identify democracy with freedom from control by Philip;[89] but in 338 Philip defeated a combination of Athens and Thebes at Chaeronea, and after that the Second League came to an end when he united all the mainland Greeks except Sparta in a new league, the League of Corinth, under his own leadership. Athens was now not the leader of an alliance but a subordinate member.[90]

SUGGESTIONS FOR FURTHER READING

R. Meiggs, *The Athenian Empire* (Oxford: Oxford University Press, 1972) gives a general account of the empire and of problems in its history. P. J. Rhodes, *The Athenian Empire*, Greece & Rome New Surveys in the Classics 17 (Oxford: Oxford University Press, 1985; reissued with addenda 1993), is a survey of the main problems and of relevant bibliography. P. J. Rhodes, "Who Ran Democratic Athens?" in P. Flensted-Jensen et al., eds., *Polis and Politics: Studies in Ancient Greek History Presented to Mogens Herman Hansen on His Sixtieth Birthday* (Copenhagen: Museum Tusculanum Press, 2000), pp. 465–77, discusses the extent to which Pericles and other leaders could control Athenian policy. R. K. Sinclair, *Democracy and Participation in Athens* (Cambridge: Cambridge University Press, 1988) discusses the democracy and the involvement of the citizens in it. D. Stockton, *The Classical Athenian Democracy* (Oxford: Oxford University Press, 1990) discusses the development and working of the democracy to the end of the fifth century.

NOTES

1 Cf. C. W. Fornara and L. J. Samons II, *Athens from Cleisthenes to Pericles* (Berkeley: University of California Press, 1991), pp. 76–7.

2 H. B. Mattingly, "Periclean Imperialism," in *Ancient Society and Institutions: Studies Presented to Victor Ehrenberg on his Seventy-Fifth Birthday* (Oxford: Blackwell, 1966), pp. 193–223 at 212–13, revised in G. Wirth (ed.), *Perikles und seine Zeit*, Wege der Forschung 412 (Darmstadt: Wissenschaftliche Buchgesellschaft, 1979): 312–49

at 335; republished as H. B. Mattingly, *The Athenian Empire Restored* (Ann Arbor: University of Michigan Press, 1996), pp. 147–79 at 178. (I am not aware that any of those who favour downdating has openly formulated the conclusion which I give in the text.) On the dating of fifth-century Athenian inscriptions cf. p. 33 with n. 55 below.

3 Succinctly expressed by the Athenians in the Melian Dialogue: "The strong do what they can and the weak put up with it" (Thuc. 5.89).

4 G. E. M. de Ste. Croix, *The Class Struggle in the Ancient Greek World* (London: Duckworth, 1981), p. 290; earlier G. Grote, *A History of Greece*, 12 vols. (London: Murray, 1869–84), VI. 9–10, 182–4, = V. 149–51, 319–21 (10-vol. edition, 1888); de Ste. Croix, "The Character of the Athenian Empire," *Historia* 3 (1954–1955): 1–41, an article which elicited many responses, expressing varying degrees of agreement or disagreement.

5 G. E. M. de Ste. Croix, *The Origins of the Peloponnesian War* (London: Duckworth, 1972), p. 43.

6 M. I. Finley, "The Fifth-Century Athenian Empire: A Balance Sheet," in P. D. A. Garnsey and C. R. Whittaker, eds., *Imperialism in the Ancient World* (Cambridge: Cambridge University Press, 1978), pp. 125–6.

7 M. I. Finley, *Democracy, Ancient and Modern*, second edition (London: Hogarth/ New Brunswick: Rutgers University Press, 1985; orig. edition, 1973), pp. 95–6.

8 It is enclosed by reiterations, in 1.88 and 118.2, of the "truest reason" given in 23.6 for the war, Athenian power and Spartan fear of it.

9 Contr. N. D. Robertson, "The True Nature of the 'Delian League,' 478–461 B.C.," *AJAH* 5 (1980): 64–96, 110–33; cf. H. D. Meyer, "Vorgeschichte und Gründung des delisch-attischen Seebundes," *Historia* 12 (1963): 405–46.

10 483/2: Hdt. 7.144, Thuc. 1.14.3, *AP* 22.7. 480: Hdt. 8.1–2, 14, 43–8 (nearly two thirds of 400, Thuc. 1.74.1).

11 Thuc. 1.98.1 (476/5?); Athenian settlers: Plut. *Cim.* 7–8.2 (not mentioned by Thucydides).

12 Thuc. 1.98.2 (476/5?).

13 490: Hdt. 6.99.2; 480: 8.66.2; Greek retaliation: 8.112.2, 121.1.

14 Thuc. 1.100–101 (465/4–463/2).

15 Thuc. 1.101–2, Plut. *Cim.* 16.9–10; cf. Ar. *Lys.* 1138–44.

16 Thuc. 1.104, 109–10; ML 33 = *IG* i^3 1147, trans. Fornara 78 (the only source for Phoenicia). Pausanias: Thuc. 1.94.2; Cimon at the River Eurymedon, in Asia Minor opposite Cyprus, 1.100.1.

17 Athens and Peloponnesians: Thuc. 1.112.1; Argos and Sparta: Thuc. 5.14.4, 22.2.

18 Treasury on Delos: Thuc. 1.96.2. Treasury in Athens: first tribute list, 454/3, *IG* i^3 259; Delos unsafe, cf. Plut. *Per.* 12.1.

19 ML 40 = *IG* i^3 14, trans. Fornara 71. 26–9.

20 See, for instance, P. J. Rhodes, *The Athenian Empire*, Greece & Rome New Surveys in the Classics 17 (1985), pp. 25–6; D. M. Lewis, *CAH* V².121–7.

21 Tribute: *IG* i^3 264, 264, with Lewis, *CAH* V².123–5; congress invitation: Plut. *Per.* 17.

22 E.g., Erythrae, probably late 450s (ML 40 = *IG* i^3 14, trans. Fornara 71); Samos, 440 (Thuc. 1.115.3); Miletus, not later than 434/3 (inscription published by P. Herrmann, "Zu den Beziehungen zwischen Athen und Milet im 5. Jahrhundert,"

Klio 52 [1970]: 163–73: date corrected from his 437/6 in the light of E. Cavaignac, "Les dékarchies de Lysandre," *REH* 90 [1924]: 285–316 at 311–14). For the dating of inscriptions with the older style of Athenian lettering see p. 33 with n. 55, below.

23 Ionian Erythrae: ML 40 = *IG* i³ 14, trans. Fornara 71.24; generally ML 46 = *IG* i³ 34, trans. Fornara 98. 41–3.

24 [Xen.] *AP* 1.16–18, Antiph. 5. *Murder of Herodes* 47, Chamaeleon fr. 44 Wehrli *ap.* Ath. 9.407 B; cf. ML 40 = *IG* i³ 14, trans. Fornara 71.31; ML 46 = *IG* i³ 34, trans. Fornara 98.31–43; also Thuc. 1.77.1–4, where the Athenians make a virtue of resorting to lawsuits rather than simply exercising their power.

25 E.g., Erythrae: ML 40 = *IG* i³ 14, trans. Fornara 71.13–15.

26 "The allies": ML 40 = *IG* i³ 14, trans. Fornara 71.24 etc.; "the cities": ML 46 = *IG* i³ 34, trans. Fornara 98.67 etc.; "the cities which Athens controls": *IG* i³ 19.8–9 and 27.14–15 (verb restored in both cases); obedience: ML 52 = *IG* i³ 40, trans. Fornara 103.21–32, cf. similar language in ML 47 = *IG* i³ 37, trans. Fornara 99.43–51.

27 Plut. *Per.* 11.5–6, cf. Diod. Sic. 11.88.3, Paus. 1.27.5. Poorer Athenians: ML 49 = *IG* i³ 46, trans. Fornara 100.43–6.

28 *IG* i³ 422.375–8, cf. Andoc. 1. *Myst.* 13: that was not the whole of his property, and other offenders had property overseas which was sold at the same time. For these scandals see especially Thuc. 6.27–9, 53, 60–1; Andoc. 1. *Myst.* 11–70.

29 Cf. pp. 24–5 with n. 6.

30 Rhodes, *CAH* V². 67–77; Aesch. *Supp.* 600–607, with *demou kratousa cheir*, "the powerful hand of the people," in 604.

31 Cf. p. 27 with n. 22.

32 E.g., Thuc. 3.82.1, [Xen.] *AP* 1.14, 16, 3.10–11.

33 *AP* 26.4 with P. J. Rhodes, *A Commentary on the Aristotelian Athenaion Politeia* (Oxford: Oxford University Press, 1981; revised reprint, 1993), ad loc.

34 *AP* 24.3 has 700 domestic and 700 overseas officials, but the second 700 is probably the result of a textual corruption (for a defence of the first 700 see M. H. Hansen, "Seven Hundred *Archai* in Classical Athens," *GRBS* 21 [1980]: 151–73).

35 Cf. L. B. Carter, *The Quiet Athenian* (Oxford: Oxford University Press, 1986).

36 *AP* 27.3–5 (juries), 41.3 (assembly); 62.2 (third quarter of fourth century). Many of the fifth-century payments to officials are not attested in the fourth, and it is disputed whether they continued to be made: see M. H. Hansen, "Misthos for Magistrates in Classical Athens," *SO* 54 (1979): 5–22; V. Gabrielsen, *Remuneration of State Officials in Fourth Century B.C. Athens*, Odense University Classical Studies xi (Odense: Odense University Press, 1981).

37 *AP* 30.2 with Rhodes (n. 33), ad loc.

38 Cf. pp. 30–31 and 33.

39 The crucial assembly was held not inside the city walls but a short distance outside, at Colonus (Thuc. 8.67.2): with the countryside exposed to the Spartan forces based at Decelea, in the north of Attica, the poorer of the citizens still in Athens, who could not afford armour, will probably have been disproportionately deterred from attending.

40 H. van Wees, "Politics and the Battlefield: Ideology in Greek Warfare," in A. Powell, ed., *The Greek World* (London: Routledge, 1995), pp. 153–78, esp. 153–62.

41 [Xen.] *AP* 1.2. Pericles' strategy for Athens in the Peloponnesian War was to abandon the countryside of Attica and move the population into the single forti-fied area of Athens and the harbour town of Piraeus, relying on Athens's control of the sea to import all that was needed (Thuc. 1.143.4–5, 2.13.2, 14–17, 62.3, cf. 65.7): on this defiance of the normal hoplite-based conventions of Greek warfare see especially J. Ober, "The Rules of War in Classical Greece," in M. Howard et al., *The Laws of War* (New Haven: Yale University Press, 1994), pp. 12–26 with 227–30, and "Thucydides, Pericles, and the Strategy of Defense," in *The Craft of the Ancient Historian: Essays in Honor of Chester G. Starr* (Lanham, MD: University Press of America, 1985), pp. 171–88, republished as *The Athe-nian Revolution* (Princeton: Princeton University Press, 1996), pp. (53–)55–71 and (72–)73–85.

42 For once the buildings can be dated, from the accounts published by the boards of overseers of the different projects: the Parthenon, beginning 447/6, *IG* i³ 436–51; the gold and ivory statue of Athena, which the Parthenon housed, *IG* i³ 453–60; the Propylaea, *IG* i³ 462–6. Probably in 434/3, the winding-up of the Acropolis building programme was ordered in the decrees of Callias, ML 58 = *IG* i³ 52, trans. Fornara 119.

43 Thuc. 8.64, cf. (Phrynichus) 48.5–7.

44 Tribute record conveniently summarised by R. Meiggs, *The Athenian Empire* (Oxford: Oxford University Press, 1972), pp. 538–61, app. xiv. An increase in 428 depends on the dating of *IG* i³ 281–4; the increase in 425 is attested by ML 69 = *IG* i³ 71, trans. Fornara 136.

45 [Andoc.] 4. *Alc.* 11–12: see Rhodes, "The Ostracism of Hyperbolus," in *Rit-ual, Finance, Politics: Athenian Democratic Accounts Presented to David Lewis* (Oxford: Oxford University Press, 1994), pp. 85–98 at 88–91 (415 is certainly the date for the ostracism implied by the speech, and although I do not think the speech was written then I am prepared to believe that the ostracism was held then).

46 See P. J. Rhodes, "Who Ran Democratic Athens?" in P. Flensted-Jensen et al., eds. *Polis and Politics: Studies Presented to Mogens Herman Hansen on His Sixtieth Birthday* (Copenhagen: Museum Tusculanum Press, 2000), pp. 465–77.

47 Diod. Sic. 12.45.4, Plut. *Per.* 35.4–5; cf. Thuc. 2.59. 2,65.2–4.

48 However, for caution against assuming that policies can be attributed to Pericles without supporting evidence see A. W. Gomme, *HCT* I.306–7; de Ste. Croix (n. 5), pp. 78–9.

49 *AP* 27.1, Plut. *Cim.* 14.5, *Per.* 10.6.

50 Arist. *Pol.* 2.1274 A 7–8, Plut. *Cim.* 15.2, *Per.* 9.3–5.

51 Arist. *Pol.* 2.1274 A 8–9, *AP* 27.3–4, Plut. *Per.* 9.2.

52 Plut. *Per.* 21 (commander not named by Thuc. 1.112.5).

53 Plut. *Per.* 12–14; cf. possibly the Anonymus Argentinensis (P. Strasbourg 84, verso), of which Fornara 94 translates no fewer than three reconstructions.

54 Plat. *Gorg.* 455 E, Plut. *Per.* 13.7. The original Long Walls are mentioned by Thuc. 1.107.1, without attribution to any individual.

55 The old view of the change in letter forms goes back to nineteenth-century German scholars. A major challenge to that view has been advanced over many years by H. B. Mattingly, many of whose articles on this subject are collected in his *The Athenian Empire Restored* (Ann Arbor: University of Michigan Press, 1996).

Among defences of the old orthodoxy the strongest was that of M. B. Walbank, "Criteria for the Dating of Fifth-Century Attic Inscriptions," in D. W. Bradeen and M. F. McGregor, eds., *ΦΟΡΟΣ: Tribute to Benjamin Dean Meritt* (Locust Valley, NY: Augustin, 1974), pp. 161–9, revised as "Criteria for Dating" in Walbank's *Athenian Proxenies of the Fifth Century B.C.* (Toronto and Sarasota: Stevens, 1978), pp. 31–51, ch. 2. However, it seems finally to have been established that Antiphon, the archon of 418/7, is to be read in one disputed text, ML 37 = IG i³ 11, trans. Fornara 81: A. P. Matthaiou, "περὶ τῆς IG I³ 11," in Matthaiou, ed., *ΑΤΤΙΚΑΙ ΕΠΙΓΡΑΦΑΙ. ΠΡΑΚΤΙΚΑ ΣΥΜΠΟΣΙΟΥ ΕΙΣ ΜΝΗΜΗΝ Adolf Wilhelm (1864–1950)* (Athens: ΕΛΛΗΝΙΚΗ ΕΠΙΓΡΑΦΙΚΗ ΕΤΑΙΡΕΙΑ, 2004), pp. 99–122. Earlier dates for inscriptions can no longer be ruled out on grounds of letter forms alone, but they are not necessarily wrong in every disputed case.

56 Plut. *Per.* 29.1–3 (neither Pericles nor anybody else is named by Thuc. 1.44).

57 Plut. *Per.* 29.4–31.1; cf. on the sanctions decree Thuc. 1.140.3–5. On the chronology of the items mentioned by Plutarch I agree with de Ste. Croix (n. 5), pp. 246–51.

58 For this kind of affinity cf. Thuc. 5.29.1, 31.6.

59 M. Ostwald, *Autonomia* (Atlanta: Scholars Press, 1982); P. Karavites, "ἐλευθερία and αὐτονομία in Fifth Century Interstate Relations," *RIDA* 29 (1982): 145–62; cf. E. J. Bickerman, "Autonomia: Sur un passage de Thucydide (I. 144. 2)," *RIDA* 5 (1958): 313–44 (suggesting that the word was first coined in connection with the Greeks of Asia Minor under Persian rule). For a perhaps too rigid discussion of the meaning of the word see M. H. Hansen, "The 'Autonomous City-State': Ancient Fact or Modern Fiction?" in M. H. Hansen and K. Raaflaub, eds., *Studies in the Ancient Greek Polis*, Historia Einzelschriften 95 (Stuttgart: Steiner, 1995), pp. 21–43.

60 Thuc. 1.19 states that "the Spartans led their allies without making them liable for tribute, but merely took care by means of oligarchy that they should conduct their politics in a manner advantageous to themselves;" but there is no evidence that before the fourth century Sparta intervened in its allies' internal affairs as Athens did.

61 Cf. p. 26.

62 E.g., Thuc. 1.35.3, 77.2, 5, 117.3.

63 Thuc. 1.139. 3, cf. 140.3.

64 Xen. *Hell.* 2.2.23, cf. Plut. *Lys.* 15.5.

65 Cf. Pericles in Thuc. 2.63.1 (summarised below), Diodotus in 3.45.6, Alcibiades in 6.18.3.

66 Thuc. 1.122.3, 124.3; 3.37.2; 6.85.1; Ar. *Knights* 1111–20, cf. 1330, 1333.

67 Thuc. 1.97.1, 3.10.5, 11.4, is not enough to prove that, but there is no positive evidence for meetings later, and the Athenians certainly took decisions which ought to have been taken by the council of the allies if the council did still exist.

68 If that is how we should still interpret ML 45 = IG i³ 1453, trans. Fornara 97, despite the reinterpretation of T. J. Figueira, *The Power of Money: Coinage and Politics in the Athenian Empire* (Philadelphia: University of Pennsylvania Press, 1998).

69 [Xen.] *AP* 2.3, 11–12; cf. (helping friends) ML 65 = IG i³ 61, trans. Fornara 128.34–41; IG i³ 62.1–5; (hindering enemies) Thuc. 1.120.2, cf. 3.86.4, Ar. *Ach.* 719–958. Despite de Ste. Croix (n. 5), pp. 251–89, Athens's notorious decree

against the Megarians (Thuc. 1.67.4, 139.1–2, 144.2, cf. Ar. *Ach.* 515–39, 719–835) should be seen as the imposition of economic sanctions.

70 Cf. p. 27.

71 Cf. Thuc. 1.99.3.

72 Oarsmen, e.g., Thuc. 1.121.3, 143.1, 7.63.3; contrast special fleets manned by citizens and metics, 3.16.1, or by citizen hoplites, 3.18.3–4. For building projects see in particular the Erechtheum records, *IG* i³ 474–9, with R. H. Randall, Jr., "The Erechtheum Workmen," *AJA* 57 (1953): 199–210.

73 Cf. p. 24 with nn. 3–4.

74 De Ste. Croix (n. 4, 1954–1955): 2–3.

75 De Ste. Croix (n. 4, 1954–1955): 4; his view is more nuanced but not changed in essence in (n. 5), pp. 40–41. D. W. Bradeen, "The Popularity of the Athenian Empire," *Historia* 9 (1960): 257–69 at 263–4.

76 However, in 411 Persian garrisons were expelled by Miletus (the Milesians had been told that they must put up with servitude for the time being by Lichas, who not much earlier had himself objected to the prospect of Sparta's imposing Persian rule rather than freedom on the Greeks), and by Antandrus and Cnidus: Thuc. 8.84.4–5, 108.4–109.1; Lichas earlier, 43.3, 52.

77 See especially J. de Romilly, "Thucydides and the Cities of the Athenian Empire," *BICS* 13 (1966): 1–12; also H. D. Westlake, "Ionians in the Ionian War," *CQ* n.s. 29 (1979): 9–44, republished in his *Studies in Thucydides and Greek History* (Bristol: Bristol Classical Press, 1989), pp. 113–53. The Spartan Brasidas in his speeches at Acanthus and elsewhere, described by Thucydides as "attractive but untrue," is represented as offering genuine freedom rather than a change of regime accompanied by a change of master, but also as threatening to take hostile action if his offer is not accepted: Thuc. 4.85–87.1 + 87.2–6; threat acted on, 109.5; Thucydides' comments, 108.5, cf. 88.1.

78 Cf. p. 31 with n. 43.

79 In general: Thuc. 3.82.1, cf. Plat. *Rep.* 8.556 E; a particular instance, Megara in 424: Thuc. 4.66.1–3, 71, 74.2–4.

80 Cf. [Xen.] *AP* 1.16, 3.10–11.

81 Andoc. 3. *Peace* 11–12, Xen. *Hell.* 2.2.20, Diod. Sic. 13.107.4 (ten ships), Plut. *Lys.* 14.8 (number of ships to be decided).

82 Change in atmosphere, Rhodes, "Athenian Democracy after 403 B.C.," *CJ* 75 (1979/80): 305–23. More fundamental change, M. Ostwald, *From Popular Sovereignty to the Sovereignty of Law* (Berkeley: University of California Press, 1986); R. Sealey, *The Athenian Republic* (University Park: Pennsylvania State University Press, 1987); M. H. Hansen, *The Athenian Democracy in the Age of Demosthenes* (Oxford: Blackwell, 1991), pp. 296–304.

83 Cf. p. 29 with n. 36.

84 *IG* ii² 43 = Tod 123, trans. Harding 35.9–12.

85 Xen. *Hell.* 5.1.31, cf. Diod. Sic. 14.110.3.

86 *IG* ii² 43 = Tod 123, trans. Harding 35.9–51.

87 Thp. *FGrHist* 115 F 98, trans. Harding 36; cf. for instance *IG* ii² 123 = Tod 156, trans. Harding 69.11, and *IG* ii² 233 = Tod 175, trans. Harding 97.20.

88 No cleruchies were established in the territory of states which joined the League in time to be included in the list of members on *IG* ii² 43 = Tod 123, trans. Harding 35, a list to which no additions were made, for whatever reason, after (probably) 375.

The more benign view of the League presented by J. L. Cargill, *The Second Athenian League: Empire or Free Alliance?* (Berkeley: University of California Press, 1981), depends on the assumption that only states included in that list were members of the League.

89   Cf. P. J. Rhodes, "On Labelling Fourth-Century <Athenian> Politicians," *LCM* 3 (1978): 207–11.

90   My thanks to the editor both for his invitation to contribute to this volume and for his helpful comments on my first draft.

2: ATHENIAN RELIGION IN THE AGE OF PERICLES

Deborah Boedeker

ristophanes' hero Strepsiades brings the *Clouds* to a boisterous finale by burning down the Thinkery, whose leader Socrates has been subverting the minds and morals of young Athenians. Strepsiades himself was a short-term convert to the comic philosopher's slick sophistry and outlandish new gods – which include Cosmic Spin (*Dinos*), Aether, and especially the Clouds – but events in the play cause him to recognize his error and repent. With his parting words, he berates the Socratic crew for their otherworldly speculations:

> What were you thinking when you outraged the gods
> and peered at the seat of the Moon?
> Chase them, hit them, stone them – for lots of reasons,
> but most of all because they wronged the gods.
>
> *Clouds* 1506–9[1]

This chapter will focus on the *right* ways to treat the gods, by outlining the major beliefs and practices of Athenian religion(s) in the time of Pericles.

First, a disclaimer: no ancient Greek word corresponds to our term "religion." Acts performed in recognition of unseen powers intermingled constantly with other aspects of daily life, rather than defining a discrete area of human activity. There were no widely accepted dogmatic texts, no priestly class, no creed. Nevertheless, activities and objects set apart for the gods had a particular status (*hieron*).[2] The unseen entities that Strepsiades knows as *theoi* or *daimones* had a special claim on one's attention, as *Clouds* makes clear, and *nomizein tous theous*, "doing the customary things for the gods," was considered essential to the city's well-being.

GODS OF ATHENS

Let us visit the shining land of Pallas,
to see Kekrops' lovely country, rich in men,
where there is reverence for the ineffable rites . . .
and offerings to the heavenly gods. . . .
Chorus of Clouds: Clouds 300–302, 305

Like most ancient societies, classical Athenians recognized a plurality of divine powers. Among the most prominent were the twelve Olympian gods, a family more or less united under their father/consort/brother Zeus. Characters in *Clouds* mention many Olympians (Zeus, Athena, Poseidon, Demeter, Apollo, Artemis, Hermes, and Dionysos), along with their relatives the Muses and Charites ("Graces"). These deities were widely honored, individually or in groups, throughout the Greek world.

Greek gods and heroes are known to modern audiences largely from myths. In the ancient world, too, traditional stories yielded communal knowledge about the *daimones*, their past interactions with humans, and their influence in the world. Such narratives were pervasive: painted on vases, painted or sculpted in sanctuaries, retold informally, publicly performed by trained singers or actors. In Athens, bards performed the Homeric *Iliad* and *Odyssey* at the Panathenaia festival (discussed below), and heroic myths were the basis of almost all Athenian tragedies and satyr plays.[3]

A number of local myths shaped and reflected classical Athens's view of itself. The politically important claim that Athenian citizens were autochthonous, born from Attic soil rather than descended from invaders, is supported by the tale of Erichthonius, the first king of Athens. He was born of Earth when Athena, avoiding Hephaistos's attempt to rape her, cleaned off his ejaculate and dropped the semen-soaked tuft onto the ground. The heroism of good king Theseus, a figure to rival Heracles himself, prefigures Athens's role in protecting its fifth-century allies.[4] Attica also figures as a locus of divine favor and civilizing arts in the story of Demeter's gift of agriculture to Triptolemos, who spread the cultivation of grain to other lands.

In their cults, the gods were known by particular titles, specific to each sanctuary. Such names could be geographical (Aphrodite *en Kepois*, "in the Gardens"), functional (Zeus *Polieus*, "of the City"), or connected to another attribute (Athena *Parthenos*, "Maiden"). In prayers or ordinary speech, a god's most appropriate title might be cited: Strepsiades tells his son to honor *Paternal* Zeus by helping his father attack the Thinkery (*Clouds* 1468).

Besides the twelve Olympians, Pericles' contemporaries worshipped Demeter's daughter Kore/Persephone, various nymphs, Kourotrophos ("Child-nurturer"), Earth, Mother (i.e., of the gods), the river Kephisos, Boreas the north wind, and many others. Athenians also honored a host of divinities named for psychological, ethical, or political qualities, such as Peitho, "Persuasion," Dike, "Justice" (whose very existence is debated in *Clouds* 902–8), and Eukleia, "Glory."[5]

Dozens of deities were honored in Athens, but the city's namesake clearly stood above the rest, from the dominant position of her temple on the Acropolis to the administration of her wealth: treasurers kept track of Athena's financial assets in one account and (at least by the late 430s[6]) those of the "other gods" in another.[7] Athena also held a special place in her people's hearts and lore; the miraculous regrowth of her sacred olive tree heartened Athenians after the Persians sacked their city in 480 (Hdt. 8.55). Athena's festivals outweighed those of other gods in number and splendor, and from a young age citizens honored her with song and dance: Aristophanes' character Better Argument fondly recalls how the youths used to hymn "Pallas [Athena], dire City-Sacker" (*Clouds* 966–7).

Athenians did not claim that only the deities recognized by their city existed. Everyone knew that foreign peoples had their own gods. Sometimes these were equated with Greek counterparts, as if they were the same gods under different names; Pericles' contemporary Herodotus, for example, could write, "In Egyptian, Apollo is Horos, Demeter is Isis, and Artemis is Bubastis" (2.156.5). Likewise, as Aristophanes and his audience recognized, non-Athenian Greeks honored the familiar Olympians somewhat differently: in *Lysistrata*, Spartans with stage-Doric accents sing the praises of "Asana (Athena) Bronze-House" (*Lys.* 1299), a title not used in Athens. Moreover, non-Greek gods such as Thracian Bendis could be worshipped by their devotees in Attica (see below), as long as the demos did not prohibit it.

New gods were occasionally accepted into public worship. We hear of several deities admitted to state cult in the fifth century. Soon after 490, Pan was introduced from the Peloponnese, after he appeared to the

Athenian runner Pheidippides as he raced to seek Sparta's help against the Persians at Marathon. The goat-god asked why Athens did not worship him, despite his goodwill. The Athenians believed Pheidippides' report, and soon after their victory established a shrine of Pan under the Acropolis (Hdt. 6.105–6). Archaeological evidence shows that Pan was also introduced into other Attic nymph-sanctuaries around this time.[8] Similarly, after Xerxes' invasion in 480–79, Athens established a cult of Boreas in thanksgiving for his destruction of Persian ships with a storm before the battle of Artemisium (Hdt. 7.189).

Pan and Boreas, both Greek figures, were introduced into Athenian state worship in Pericles' youth; about the time of his death, it appears, the Thracian Bendis became an official god of Athens as well.[9] We have no story explaining why Bendis rose from a tolerated foreign deity to one whose cult was overseen and financed by the city; possibly her upgrade was meant to gratify Thracians working in the Piraeus (who had worshipped her privately) and the Thracian king Sitalces, with whom Athens was negotiating an important alliance as the Peloponnesian War began (Thuc. 2.29).[10]

The first-century B.C.E. geographer Strabo thought that classical Athens more readily accepted new gods than did other Greek cities: "Just as in other respects the Athenians welcome foreign things, so too with the gods" (10.3.18). In any case, the introduction of a new god probably occasioned considerable public debate in Periclean Athens, thanks to the demos's involvement with all such matters. The Athenian pantheon was stable, but flexible enough to adjust to changing circumstances.

IMMORTAL MORTALS

> – And tell me, which manly man among Zeus's sons do you think had the best spirit and toiled through the most labors? Speak up!
> – In my opinion, no man was better than Heracles.
> Worse Argument and Better Argument: *Clouds* 1048–50

Not only gods but heroes too were revered in the Greek world, mainly at sites believed to be their tombs. Heroes sometimes received chthonic offerings or holocausts (animal sacrifices wholly consumed by fire); in Athens, however, they were evidently honored much like gods.[11] Their nature, nonetheless, was considered distinct: heroes were thought of as mortals of an earlier time who possessed great, though localized, powers after their death – especially the power to heal or defend.

Several Attic heroes were known from Panhellenic poetry. Menelaus's helmsman Phrontis, for example, perished near Cape Sounion on the way home from Troy (*Od.* 3.276–85); he was worshipped at his alleged tomb there.[12] Some heroes enjoyed cults in more than one place. Heracles had many shrines, including several in Attica.[13] As they faced the Persians at Marathon, the Athenian hoplites camped successively in two Heraclean sanctuaries (Hdt. 6.116); after the battle, an inscription indicates, Heracles' annual festival at Marathon was expanded, thanks no doubt to his help in defending the homeland.[14]

Of all Attica's heroes, however, Theseus took pride of place. He was already a popular figure in the sixth century, but if he had a fixed place of worship before the classical period, it has not yet been found. In myths, Theseus was a civilizing hero: he eliminated outlaws on the road to Athens, killed the lethal bull of Marathon, and slew the Cretan Minotaur. The classical period remembered him as the king who unified the separate settlements of Attica. Nor were his exploits restricted to the distant past: he was seen at Marathon in 490, helping defeat the Persians. Sometime around 475, the Athenian leader Cimon claimed that an eagle had led him to Theseus's bones where they lay buried on the island of Skyros. Cimon brought the remains home with processions and sacrifices; Plutarch assures us that they were welcomed enthusiastically, "as if [Theseus] himself were returning to the city" (Plut. *Thes.* 36.1–2; cf. *Cim.* 8.5–6).

Theseus's popularity is evident in vase paintings, public murals (including the "Painted Stoa" in the Agora, dated to the 460s, which showed him fighting at Marathon), and architectural sculpture (especially on the Hephaistos temple overlooking the Agora), as well as in the construction of his own sanctuary, the still undiscovered Theseion. Two choral songs by the lyric poet Bacchylides celebrate his exploits.[15] He also figures in a number of fifth-century tragedies, where he can embody the political and military virtues claimed by Athens: courage against aggressors, defense of suppliants, even "democratic" consultation with his subjects (see esp. Eur. *Suppl.* 399–455).[16] Theseus could thus serve as figurehead for the Delian League and its successor, the Athenian Empire, as well as the democracy that claimed him as its founder.[17] Such a figure demonstrates well the interface between religion and other cultural forms.

One group of Attic heroes had played a prominent civic role ever since ca. 508–7, when Cleisthenes established ten new *phylai*, "tribes," each named for a local hero, as the official divisions of the citizen body for most religious, administrative, and military purposes.[18] In Pericles' time, images of the Eponymous Heroes stood together in the Agora; the fence around them became a message board (as reflected in Ar. *Eq.* 977–80), where notices were posted of lawsuits, honors, military assignments, and the like. Statues of the ten heroes were also erected at Delphi, thereby legitimizing Athens's tribal structure in Apollo's Panhellenic sanctuary.[19]

> – By Zeus, Socrates, I beg you, tell me who are those females who intoned that noble song? Not some sort of Hero-*ettes*, are they?
>
> Strepsiades: *Clouds* 314–15

As Strepsiades' question acknowledges, immortalized mortals came in both genders.[20] Some heroines were well known in myths as well as cults. Iphigenia, for example – whose father Agamemnon sacrificed her to Artemis so that the Greeks could sail to Troy – was worshipped together with Artemis at Brauron on the Attic coast, a sanctuary important for rites of prepubescent girls.[21] Dionysos's mother Semele received annual offerings in the Attic deme Erchia, as well as in her home town of Thebes, at Delphi, and elsewhere.[22] The Athenian princess Aglauros leapt off the Acropolis, either to save the city by self-sacrifice or because she was terrified when she peeked into a basket concealing the snake-formed baby Erichthonios. Athenian ephebes included her in their famous oath of allegiance to their city.[23] Inscriptional evidence suggests that heroines usually received less costly offerings than their male counterparts; a common gift was the vegetal *trapeza* (table offering) rather than an animal sacrifice.[24]

Not all immortalized mortals came from the heroic past. By the time of Pericles, even some contemporary Athenians were honored posthumously as heroes.[25] Harmodios and Aristogeiton, who in 514 assassinated Peisistratus's son Hipparchos, enjoyed heroic honors as Tyrannicides in the fifth century and long after: their images were set up in the Agora, and each year the war archon made offerings at their tombs. Though not called "heroes" in our sources, the Tyrannicides were publicly celebrated and remembered with songs and annual sacrifices, like gods or cult heroes.[26]

Other historical figures also enjoyed annual worship after their death. Founders (*oikistai*) of Greek colonies, many of which were established in the archaic and classical periods, were typically buried inside their new city rather than in a cemetery outside its walls; their tombs were treated as shrines, and they received sacrifices and games.[27] In a unique case, an Athenian oikist of Pericles' time may have received comparable honors while still alive. When Athens finally succeeded in making a permanent settlement at Amphipolis in the northern Aegean in 437, the expedition's leader Hagnon was for a time recognized as oikist, even though he did not remain in the colony.[28]

Classical Athens also paid heroic-style honors collectively to contemporary war dead. Most notably, the hoplites who died defeating the Persians at Marathon (mentioned as paradigmatic figures at *Clouds* 985–6) came to receive regular offerings at their Bronze Age-style tomb near the battlefield.[29] Their leader Miltiades was commemorated with a statue at Delphi, near those of the Eponymous Heroes.[30]

Others who died patriotically may also have been treated as heroes. After the expulsion of Persians from mainland Greece in 479, Athens was engaged almost every year in military activity. At an appointed time, the annual war dead, their ashes repatriated for the purpose, were solemnly buried in the Kerameikos cemetery outside the city and honored with sacrifices, athletic contests, and a funeral oration (Thuc. 2.34).[31] If these offerings recurred as an annual festival (as seems likely from Thucydides' report), the festival resembles a continuing cult of the dead rather than just a grand public funeral.

For Greeks of the classical period to worship contemporaries even after death[32] would have been extraordinary, though tomb cult (repeated offerings at the grave site) had been practiced sporadically in various parts of archaic Greece. Herodotus, it is true, reports a few instances in which maltreated Greek warriors (none of them Athenian) received cultic honors in the generation or two before Pericles.[33] This privilege, however, came as Delphi's response to marvelous post mortem signs suggesting the power of the deceased, something that did not happen for the ordinary war dead. Plutarch cites a funeral oration from 439 B.C.E., in which Pericles suggests that those who fell in battle became deathless (*athanatoi*) like the gods, who are considered to be immortal "because of the honors they receive and the good things they provide" (Plut. *Per.* 8.9). Although Athens honored its military casualties with festivals and offerings much as it honored traditional heroes, the city of Pericles apparently stopped short of declaring a new metaphysical status for its war dead: as with the Tyrannicides, the term *heros* was not applied to one who died in battle.[34]

SANCTUARIES, SACRIFICES, FESTIVALS

> There are offerings for the heavenly gods,
> high-roofed temples and sacred images,
> holiest processions for the Blessed Ones,
> the gods' sacrificial victims with their garlands, and festivals
> in every kind of season . . .
>
> Chorus of Clouds: *Clouds* 305–10

In Attica as throughout Greece, temples were built as homes for gods. The interiors of these buildings were not used for religious services; rather, the entire sanctuary (*temenos*), even without a temple, was a focus for religious practices. An outdoor altar provided a place for offerings; architectural reliefs might include narrative scenes featuring the god whose image was housed in the temple; votive objects, sometimes of great value, could be displayed or stored within the sanctuary.

Besides bringing honor to the gods to whom they were dedicated, these public structures also made social and political statements. A new temple enhanced a community's prestige as well as displaying its piety. In Periclean Athens, the *absence* of temple construction also conveyed a message. When Xerxes' army attacked Athens in 480 and 479, the Acropolis was burned and its temples destroyed. The Greek victors soon reclaimed the city, but did not rebuild the damaged structures. A well-known tradition (and one disputed since antiquity) maintains that before the battle of Plataea in 479, the Greek allies swore an oath to leave burned and pillaged temples unrestored – a lasting sign of Persian hubris.[35] Authentic or not, the Oath of Plataea points to the situation in Athens, where ruined temples were left in disrepair for decades. Then in mid-century, perhaps after a peace treaty was concluded with the Persians,[36] the city of Pericles undertook a monumental building program. New temples were designed and built on the Acropolis; work on the magnificent Parthenon would continue for fifteen years (447– 32). Sanctuaries were enhanced elsewhere in Attica, too, for example at Sounion, where a fine temple of Poseidon was built overlooking the sea.[37] Pericles himself, reportedly a friend of the architect Iktinos and master sculptor Pheidias, was a strong proponent of the building program (Plut. *Per.* 12–14).[38] Many scholars believe (though this view has been challenged[39]) that tribute from Athens's subject cities largely financed the work. If so, the religious monuments of Athens profited greatly from the city's political and military preeminence.

Doubtless, the Periclean building program had many motives, including gratitude to the gods and desire to secure their favor. Yet however many pious goals there were, the monuments this program produced unquestionably had great propaganda value.[40] The rebuilt Acropolis, in particular, recalled Athens's heroic role in the Persian Wars.[41] The north bastion of the Acropolis used structural elements of older temples that were destroyed by the Persians in 480, turning the devastation of the city into a visible statement of barbaric outrage versus Athenian resistance and renewal.[42] At the same time, the new temples and statues on the Acropolis put the powerful city and its patron deity Athena magnificently on display for both domestic and foreign audiences.

In the same period, probably also under the influence of Pericles, the sanctuary at Eleusis was likewise liberally expanded – the site to which devotees from many parts of the Greek world came each year to celebrate the Mysteries of Demeter and her daughter. Athens thus enhanced the splendor and prestige of its most successful Panhellenic cult,[43] where, as Aristophanes' Cloud-chorus describes it, "the house that receives initiates is opened up during the pure mystic rites" (*Clouds* 302–4).

If temples were the most visible structures of Greek religion, its most salient practices were public rituals honoring the gods, most of them performed at prescribed times by the city or a deme, tribe, phratry, or other group. Prominent among these were animal sacrifices, in which domesticated food animals (usually cattle, sheep, pigs, or goats) were ceremoniously led to the altar of a sanctuary and ritually killed. In most sacrifices, certain parts of the victim (especially bones and fat) were burned for the god(s); the rest was cooked and shared among the human participants.

Roles at a sacrifice were typically divided by gender. In elaborate sacrifices, young women carried the basket in which the sacrificial knife was hidden, and women trilled the *ololugmos* cry as the animal was struck. The sacrificer (*mageiros*) was male, even at women's rites; and in visual representations, only men are present as the meat is cooked and distributed.[44] The presiding official, however, could be either male or female, depending on the cult. This priest or priestess might receive the valuable hide or a special portion of meat.

Some rites, such as major oaths, called for holocausts, in which the entire victim was burned. In others, the offerings were bloodless: first fruits or other vegetal or animal products such as cakes, milk, honey, and wine were brought to the altar. Besides prescribed offerings in public sanctuaries, small-scale sacrifices were held within a household, with the head of the family serving as priest.

A very common kind of offering (often a private, informal one) was the libation. At occasions where wine was consumed, including the male drinking parties known as *symposia*, a little wine was first poured out while calling on a god (especially Zeus in one of his manifestations) or hero. Libations were also used to effect formal acts, especially peace treaties, which were even called *spondai*, "libations" (e.g., Thuc. 1.35). In another variation, the entire contents, not just the first drops, were poured onto the ground for heroes or for the dead.[45]

Sacrifices were clearly meant to please and appease the powers to which they were directed; the rituals also served important functions for their participants. Shared cultic activities defined groups of all sorts.[46] Virtually all kinship, vocational, and social groups gathered for sacrifices. The ten tribes sacrificed to their eponymous heroes; old families (*gene*) might be linked with particular gods and private sanctuaries;[47] guilds of workers offered sacrifices to their patron gods or heroes; the supposed kinship groups called phratries each worshipped their own Zeus Phratrios and Apollo Patroos. Other organizations, known as *orgeones*, "enactors of rituals" of a hero or deity, had as their foundation a shared cult apart from the official state religion.[48] And as we have seen, the Attic demes had their own sacrificial calendars, as did the polis itself.

Yearly festivals (*heortai*) are another salient characteristic of Greek religion, perhaps more frequent and elaborate in classical Athens than elsewhere.[49] Thucydides' Pericles praises them as a mark of the quality of life enjoyed in his city: "We have provided for the spirit the greatest number of respites from labor, establishing annual contests and festivals . . . " (Thuc. 2.38.1). The fifth-century pamphleteer known as the Old Oligarch maintained that Athens had twice as many festivals as any other city (Ps.-Xen. *AP* 3.2, 8), but took a more cynical view of their motivation, as a way devised by ordinary citizens to enjoy sacrifices, rites, festivals, and sanctuaries that no poor man could afford: "They sacrifice many victims publicly as a city, but it is the demos that has a good time and gets the victims allotted to it" (2.9).

In addition to the sacrifices, feasts, prayers, and processions common to many festivals, a bewildering array of unique activities took place. A small sample can only suggest the variety: drinking the new wine in somber silence at the Anthesteria; driving two human scapegoats out of the city at the Thargelia; cleaning a hallowed image of Athena in the sea at the Plynteria; verbally abusing initiates of Demeter on their way to her great mysteries at Eleusis; collecting the remains of sacrificed piglets from the pits where they had decayed, to mix with the seed corn at the Thesmophoria; registering the year's newly fledged adult citizens in the phratries at the Apatouria. Some festivals were occasions for retelling stories of gods and heroes: Homeric epics were performed at the Panathenaia, and the City Dionysia featured elaborate choral and dramatic performances (dithyrambs, tragedies, and satyr plays) based on mythical narratives.

The Athenian festival calendar can be seen as a cycle of propitiating and collaborating with higher powers to carry out the community's important tasks. The seasons of the agricultural year, for example, are perceptible in the nature of some rites and their position in the calendar.[50] While the cycles of fertility and food production were fundamental elements in the festival calendar, as they were in the lives of many citizens, the agrarian cycle does not tell the whole story: Attic festivals had civic significance as well. Periclean Athens's largest and most spectacular religious events clearly were organized with an eye to public impact, showcasing the splendor and might of the imperial city.

The Panathenaia, an annual festival for the city's namesake (celebrated more elaborately every fourth year), included competitions with extravagant prizes, topped by a 1,000-drachma gold crown and 500 drachmas cash for the winning kitharode (performer of Homeric epic).[51] The city was evidently attempting to put its festival on a par with the prestigious Panhellenic "Crown Games" (Olympian, Pythian, Isthmian, Nemean), although its costly prizes contrast sharply with their traditional victors' garlands of sacred leaves. The Panathenaia, moreover, required participation by the members of Athens's empire. By mid-century, indeed, the tribute-paying cities were made to send contributions to several major Athenian festivals: a sacrificial cow and set of hoplite armor for the Panathenaia, a phallos for the procession at the City Dionysia, and first fruits to the Eleusinian Mysteries (a practice that other Greek cities were invited to follow).[52]

Other evidence from the religious sphere also reflects Athenian hegemony. Beyond Attica – on the islands of Samos, Euboea (at Chalkis), and Kos – fifth-century boundary stones were inscribed to "Athena who rules Athens." This goddess has no known temples, and scholars disagree as to whether the inscriptions refer to a local cult of Athena (presumably established or encouraged by Athens) or simply identify her as owner of the designated territory, which would suggest Athenian expropriation of the land in question.[53] One way or another, the boundary stones mark the sway of the goddess and her imperial city outside of Attica.

Just as Athens did not restrict all cult participation to its own residents, so too Athenians did not necessarily restrict their religious activities to Athenian cults. Delphi, Dodona, and other oracles were consulted by individuals and by the state. Athenian men competed in Olympic festivals and other great games; winners enhanced their city's reputation as well as their own – as Alcibiades claimed for his Olympic chariot racing (Thuc. 6.16). Like other poleis, Athens sent official observers to the Panhellenic games and other important festivals, to attend and sacrifice on behalf of the city. Groups of women were also sent every second year to join maenadic rites for Dionysos in the mountains around Delphi.

RELIGION AND THE DEMOCRACY

The Athenian state took its relationship to the gods very seriously. Not only were thousands of Athenians, male and female, involved in public festivals each year, but also the city's political and judicial business constantly utilized religious rituals.[54] Meetings of the Assembly, for example, began with piglet sacrifices, purifying fumigations, and prayers; jurors swore by Zeus, Poseidon, and Demeter to vote in accordance with the laws and cursed anyone who did not abide by the oath; the new archons were inducted each year with an impressive ritual that included oaths sworn first in the Agora, and then again on the Acropolis;[55] inscriptions recording public decisions frequently began (a bit opaquely) with the single word *theoi*, "gods."

Religious duties, moreover, were an important part of the responsibilities of administrative and military officials. The war archon sacrificed to the Tyrannicides and administered games in honor of the war dead; the archon basileus was responsible for conducting many rituals during his year in office, and his wife served as the bride of Dionysos at the Anthesteria. Generals conducted pre-battle sacrifices at which seers inspected the victims' organs for omens; soldiers sang a paean before battle; a share of the booty was dedicated in sanctuaries of helpful gods.[56]

During the course of the fifth century, the demos became increasingly involved with oversight of religious practices. The Assembly admitted new public cults and determined salaries and perquisites for cultic officials. According to a decree dated to 448,[57] for example, the new priestess of Athena Nike would receive fifty drachmas a year, plus the legs and hides of sacrificed animals (*IG* i³ 35). Priests, like other magistrates, had to give an account of their year in office. Religious officials who failed to conduct their duties properly were liable to fines and worse: the Eleusinian hierophant Archias was reportedly executed for performing an unauthorized sacrifice (Ps.-Dem. 59.116).[58]

The demos also demanded a strict account of temple treasuries and income – and considered that wealth available for its own use in an emergency. [59] In 441–439 the city borrowed funds from Athena (*IG* i³ 363), and at the start of the Peloponnesian War, Pericles counted among the city's resources the gold on Athena's statue in the Parthenon (Thuc. 2.13.3–5). Public religion was publicly financed as well, by taxes and other revenues. Merchants and ship owners apparently were assessed landing taxes that supported the cults of several gods.[60] Gods also owned property, not only the objects dedicated to them but also land that could be leased for agricultural purposes; accounts were kept of their assets and debits.[61] Wealthy citizens – as many as 100 each year – were tapped by the city to finance certain festival expenses; such "liturgies" supported, for example, the choruses that performed tragedies, comedies, and dithyrambs at the City Dionysia.

Religious practices obviously intersected with political activities in Athens, but it is difficult to determine exactly what public religion had to do with that most notorious aspect of Periclean politics, democracy. Some scholars have found democratizing aspects in certain Athenian festivals, especially the City Dionysia. Robert Connor thinks this celebration contributed to Athens's democratic ideology, with its sense of inclusiveness, freedom, and equality.[62] Simon Goldhill also considers the Dionysia a democratic festival, pointing to actions that generated civic pride and unity in the theater, as when the allies' tribute was displayed, the city's benefactors were honored, and an age-class of war orphans were presented as new citizen-soldiers.[63] These features might better be characterized as patriotic, rather than specifically democratic.[64] Yet democratic in some sense is the sheer number of citizens who participated in the festival (1,000 men and boys performed in the dithyrambic choruses alone), as well as the procedures for selecting judges for the competitions.[65]

Democratizing tendencies might be expected in the appointments of priests and priestesses. The prestigious priesthoods of Athens were traditionally "gentilician," passed along within the old aristocratic clans (*gene*). Did these give way to religious magistrates selected "democratically" in the Athenian sense, that is, annual offices chosen by lot from among eligible male citizens? Were female priesthoods suppressed in Athens, to accord with the democracy's apparent suppression of females' prominence in other areas of society?

On the one hand, it appears that no gentilician priesthood was discontinued in the democracy, nor was any female official replaced by a male. The Eteoboutadai continued to provide the priest of Poseidon Erechtheus on the Acropolis, as well as the venerable priestess of Athena Polias, who held office for life. The Eumolpids and Kerykes continued to supply hierophants, heralds, and torchbearers for the Mysteries at Eleusis. On the other hand, the *gene* did not supply officials for all *new* cults introduced under the democracy.[66] Some duties were assigned to an archon (for example, the war archon for the Tyrannicides cult). Occasionally, a new priesthood was established along more democratic lines, though perhaps not before Pericles' death. When Bendis was introduced into Athenian state cult, her priest(ess?) seems to have been chosen by lot from all Athenian men (or perhaps women: the relevant inscription is mutilated[67]). A new priestess of Athena Nike was selected from all Athenian *women*, although she was apparently chosen for life and thus "undemocratically."[68] The existence of lifelong female office-holders points to a gap between Athenian religious and political cultures.[69] Still, the Nike office was open to all citizen women, rather than just a particular family or economic class. With important differences in terms of gender and length of term, priesthoods for cults introduced by the demos do seem to have been influenced by the principles for selecting citizens for civic magistracies.

PRIVATE RELIGIOUS ACTIVITIES AND BELIEFS

> – Then will you not believe in any god now except the ones
>   we do:
> this Void here, and Clouds and Tongue, these three?
> – Yes, I wouldn't talk to the other gods even if I bumped
>   into them,
> and I wouldn't sacrifice or pour libations or offer them
>   incense either.
>
> Socrates and Strepsiades: Clouds 423–6

The very public nature of much Athenian cult by no means tells the whole story of religious practices and attitudes in the city. As Strepsiades' reply to Socrates assumes, individuals also had private ways of interacting with gods and heroes, and could articulate their belief or criticism. If dramatic (especially comic) dialogue is any reflection of ordinary speech, we can conclude that it was common to call upon gods, especially in informal oaths (*Clouds* 245–6, 455, 483, etc.). Prayers are also frequent (e.g. *Clouds* 793, 1478–82), as are references to myths (Zeus's imprisonment of Kronos: *Clouds* 902–6).

Not every festival, moreover, was fully funded and organized by the demos. Strepsiades, for example, recalls family gatherings, which featured barbecues and new toys, at the Diasia (*Clouds* 408, 864), a spring festival of Zeus Meilichios (Thuc. 1.126.6) celebrated outside of Athens.[70] Other festivals, including a famous one celebrated by women for Aphrodite's mortal lover Adonis, seem to have existed apart from the civic calendar.

Private citizens frequently offered votive objects in sanctuaries, as thank-offerings or in hope of divine favors, and of course as a display of the donor's generosity and piety. In the archaic period, individuals even dedicated large marble or bronze statues of young women or men (some of them, at least, representing deities) on the Acropolis. This practice was curtailed, however, during the ascendancy of Pericles, probably reflecting the fledgling demos's desire to restrict conspicuous expenditures by families. Surviving inscriptions on statues or other votive objects give insight into the dedicators' motives, or at least the sentiments they published. One mid-fifth-century inscription from the Acropolis reads, "Lady [Athena], Menandros of Aigilia, son of Demetrios, set up this [. . .] as a first-fruit offering, fulfilling his vow and rendering thanks to you; do you, daughter of Zeus, returning the favor, preserve his prosperity."[71] Even women could speak publicly through such inscriptions: "O Lady Deo, Lysistrate daughter of Stephanos (?), an attendant of your and your daughter's secret rites, set up this beautiful image (*agalma*) as a decoration for your portal; she does not spare her possessions but, within her power, she is generous to the gods."[72]

Very different sentiments characterize a class of inscriptions first attested late in the fifth century, when some Athenians began to scratch curses or binding spells onto lead tablets, which were then buried or cast into bodies of water. These curse tablets, as well as "voodoo dolls" and other magical charms, attempted to constrain the attentions of a would-be lover, or to incapacitate (usually temporarily) an enemy or rival.[73] The earliest examples of this genre tend to give only the name of the person to be bound, or the simple declaration "I bind N;" in later periods, binding inscriptions would call on many deities by name. Literature from the Periclean period, especially the Furies' "binding song" directed against Orestes in Aeschylus's *Eumenides*, shows that cursing or binding was familiar in Athens before the appearance of written spells. Binding magic is an important example of individuals making use of unseen powers. What makes it "magic" instead of "religion" (the distinction is not entirely a modern invention[74]) is largely a matter of context, not function; after all, many civic festivals aimed to effect a change in the material world. Magic tends to be secretive, individualistic, and (however widespread its practices actually were) subject to social or even legal disapproval.[75]

CRITICISM OF TRADITIONAL RELIGION

Aristophanes' *Clouds* has as its real villain the sophistry that allegedly taught Athenians to doubt their traditional gods. Strepsiades, having learned from Socrates to scorn the state religion, laughs when one of his rebuffed creditors calls on the gods:

> – No way, by great Zeus and all the gods,
> will you get away with this!
> – It's amazing to hear you say "gods,"
> and swearing by Zeus is hilarious to those in the know.
> Creditor and Strepsiades: *Clouds* 1239–41

Such disbelief is readily associated with the sophists of Pericles' time, yet criticism of the traditional gods, or doubt about their existence, is as old as our earliest Greek literature. In the *Odyssey*, when Odysseus finally comes home and punishes the suitors, his aged father can exclaim, "Then you *do* still exist, you gods on Olympus, if the suitors have been punished for their outrageous behavior!" (*Od.* 24.351): obviously Laertes had doubted that the gods were there at all. In sixth-century Ionia, thinkers such as Xenophanes and Heraclitus more trenchantly criticized traditional religious ideas and practices.[76]

The Periclean era (as *Clouds* attests) was a time of heightened intellectual ferment, including religious skepticism. Some critics were reportedly associates of Pericles: the cosmologist and philosopher Anaxagoras of Clazomenae, who taught that the sun was a rock, not a god, and the sophist Protagoras of Abdera, notorious for claiming, "Man is the measure of all things," and for explicit agnosticism. Another sophist was Prodikos of Keos, who maintained that Demeter and Dionysos were human inventors of agriculture and viticulture, later deified by grateful beneficiaries. Dramatists too presented characters with dissonant ideas about the gods; a fragment of the lost *Sisyphus* (attributed usually to Critias) voices the radical idea that gods were invented by a clever mortal, to frighten people into thinking that evil-doers would be punished even if their misdeeds went undetected by men.[77]

It is surely not coincidental that critics of traditional religion were drawn to Athens, wherever they came from originally. The city of Pericles had a reputation for tolerance (according to a Spartan saying, "In Athens, *panta kala* – *anything* is fine!" Plut. *Lac. Apophth.* 236b–c). In his Thucydidean funeral oration, Pericles himself declares, "We conduct public business with freedom and – concerning that mutual suspicion about habits of everyday life – we do not get angry with a neighbor if he does something to please himself" (Thuc. 2.37.2). That tolerance was limited, however; it is equally clear that maintaining good relations with the gods was important to the city. Arguments used in forensic speeches, all dating from a slightly later period, prove that an Athenian jury would be expected to accept traditional ideas about the gods. Thus when the exiled Andocides defends himself against charges of impiety, he argues that he must be innocent: though he sailed many times in dangerous conditions, the gods never destroyed him (*On the Mysteries* 137–9).

Especially in troubled times, actions and teachings deemed impious were liable to receive harsh punishment. In 415, just before Athens sent a huge armada against Sicily, a large number of herms (schematic stone representations of Hermes, commonly found on Athenian streets and doorways) were defaced by persons unknown. This sacrilege was taken very seriously (Thuc. 6.27), as a bad omen and even a plot against the democracy. Informers then reported another act of impiety: a private parody of the Eleusinian mysteries. The controversial general Alcibiades was accused by his political enemies of participating in these outrages (Thuc. 6.28), resulting in his removal from office and defection to Sparta.[78]

Most notoriously, a generation after Pericles, the Athenian Socrates was put to death on a charge of impiety: not only did he "corrupt the young," but also he did not worship the state's gods, introducing instead new gods of his own. According to Socrates' defense in Plato's *Apology* (19b–c), this indictment was influenced by his portrayal in the *Clouds*. The "real" reasons for Socrates' execution are debated, but doubtless partly political: the philosopher had close connections with some of the harsh oligarchs who came to power in 411 and 404, a fact which must have caused resentment in the restored democracy. Nevertheless, Socrates was formally charged and convicted largely because of his alleged teachings about the gods.[79]

At least one figure of the Periclean era was also charged with impiety at Athens. Diagoras of Melos, a fervent atheist, was condemned for impiety (especially for ridiculing the Eleusinian Mysteries); he fled Athens to avoid execution. Later sources maintain that some of his contemporaries were also judged guilty of impiety in Athens. Prodikos was reportedly executed by hemlock for corrupting the young – just like Socrates. Anaxagoras and Protagoras were supposedly prosecuted for impiety, as was Euripides. Apart from Diagoras and Socrates, however, whose fates are well attested, evidence for these prosecutions is late and thin or inconsistent, leading K. J. Dover to suggest that most of the impiety trials may never have happened.[80] If so, Periclean Athens may perhaps deserve something of its reputation for tolerance.

For most Athenians in Pericles' time, however, gods and heroes were part of the fabric of life. Sanctuaries and temples peppered the landscape, public sacrifices and festivals took place at frequent intervals in demes as well as city, minor rituals such as libations and prayers punctuated private life and public business, oaths regularly called gods to witness commercial and civic transactions, many forms of entertainment relied on myths and took place at religious festivals. Though we cannot hope to quantify "belief" in the gods, it would be wrong to think that the state religion reduced their powers to a formality.[81] Indeed, they could be visibly present, for good or ill. Daimonic powers, especially heroes or "hemitheoi," were known to take part in battle. Not only did Theseus appear at Marathon, but in 446, a hemitheos opposed the Athenian troops as they lost at Koroneia against the Boeotians – and this is not just a casual anecdote, but a matter noted on the official, demos-commissioned war memorial.[82] In times of crisis, moreover, as when the great plague struck Athens at the beginning of the Peloponnesian War, prayers and supplications were increased (Thuc. 2.47.4). Though clearly some in Periclean Athens ridiculed or argued against traditional practices and beliefs, many more would have agreed with Aristophanes' Strepsiades when (as we saw at the beginning of this chapter) he reaffirmed the "ancestral" religion – however much that tradition changed with each generation.

SUGGESTIONS FOR FURTHER READING

Robert Parker, *Athenian Religion: A History* (Oxford: Oxford University Press, 1996) is an indispensable resource. General works on Greek religion include Walter Burkert's dense and authoritative *Greek Religion*, trans. J. Raffan (Cambridge, MA: Harvard University Press, 1985), the more discursive *Ancient Greek Religion* by Jon D. Mikalson (Oxford: Blackwell, 2005), the same author's *Athenian Popular Religion* (Chapel Hill: University of North Carolina Press, 1983), and Jan N. Bremmer's concise *Greek Religion*, second edition (Oxford: Oxford University Press, 1999). Though not restricted to the classical period, John M. Camp's richly illustrated *The Archaeology of Athens* (New Haven: Yale University Press, 2001) is a fine source of information on religious monuments in Attica.

Highly recommended are several collections of essays. *Oxford Readings in Greek Religion*, ed. Richard Buxton (Oxford: Oxford University Press, 2000), offers a lively selection, including Christiane Sourvinou-Inwood's "What Is Polis Religion?" Similarly useful is the anthology *Faith, Hope and Worship: Aspects of Religious Mentality in the Ancient World*, ed. Henk S. Versnel (Leiden: Brill, 1981), in which the chapters by F. T. van Straten, "Gifts for the Gods," and P. A. Meijer, "Philosophers, Intellectuals and Religion in Hellas," are especially relevant to topics discussed in this chapter. *Goddess and Polis: The Panathenaic Festival in Classical Athens* (Princeton: Princeton University Press, 1992), ed. Jenifer Neils et al., contains accessible discussions of Athens's greatest festival.

E. R. Dodds, *The Greeks and the Irrational* (Berkeley: University of California Press, 1951), revolutionary in its time, still provides stimulating discussions of the nature of Greek beliefs. H. W. Parke, *Festivals of the Athenians* (Ithaca, NY: Cornell University Press, 1977) offers standard coverage of its subject matter. On religion and democracy, a good starting place is Michael H. Jameson, "Religion in the Athenian Democracy," in Ian Morris and Kurt Raaflaub, eds., *Democracy 2500? Questions and Challenges* (Dubuque, IA: Kendall/Hunt for the Amer. Inst. of Archaeology, 1997): 171–95. W. Robert Connor, "'Sacred' and 'Secular.' ἱερὰ καὶ ὅσια and the Classical Athenian Concept of the State," *Ancient Society* 19 (1988): 161–88, surveys the interpenetration of divine and human spheres in the fifth century. Robert Garland, *Introducing New Gods: The Politics of Athenian Religion* (Ithaca, NY: Cornell University Press, 1992), engagingly analyzes an important facet of fifth-century religious change. Serious and helpful is the same author's study "Religious Authority in Archaic and Classical Athens," *Annual of the British School at Athens* 79 (1984): 75–123. Bernhard Smarczyk's comprehensive *Untersuchungen zur Religionspolitik und politischen Propaganda Athens im Delisch-Attischen Seebund* (Munich: tuduv, 1990) covers religion and politics in the Athenian Empire. On the subject of criticism of religion, in addition to P. A. Meijer's essay mentioned above, see K. J. Dover's "The Freedom of the Intellectual in Greek Society," *Talanta* 7 (1976): 24–54.

Finally, a great deal can be learned from fifth-century literature, tragedy and comedy above all, about the range of attitudes toward the gods in classical Athens.

NOTES

1 My translations from *Clouds* owe much to Jeffrey Henderson's Loeb edition: *Aristophanes*, vol. 2 (Cambridge, MA: Harvard University Press, 1998). *Clouds*, first produced in 423 and later modified, slightly postdates the Age of Pericles, but its "old-fashioned" religious attitude provides an appropriate background. I thank Kristen Gentile for exemplary assistance with this chapter.

2 W. Robert Connor, "'Sacred' and 'Secular.' ἱερὰ καὶ ὅσια and the Classical Athenian Concept of the State," *Ancient Society* 19 (1988): 161–88; L. J. Samons, *Empire of the Owl: Athenian Imperial Finance* (Stuttgart: Steiner, 2000), pp. 325–9.

3 See Henderson's chapter in this volume.

4 William Blake Tyrrell and Frieda S. Brown, *Athenian Myths and Institutions* (New York: Oxford University Press, 1991), pp. 167–70; David Castriota, *Myth, Ethos, and Actuality. Official Art in Fifth-Century B.C. Athens* (Madison: University of Wisconsin Press, 1992), pp. 58–63, 89–95.

5 Emma Stafford, *Worshipping Virtues* (London: Duckworth, 2000).

6 *IG* i³ 52A.13–31 = ML 58.

7 E.g., in the important measures decreed shortly before the Peloponnesian War: *IG* i³ 52.21–5, discussed by Russell Meiggs and David Lewis, ML 58: pp. 154–61. Cf. also Tullia Linders, *The Treasurers of the Other Gods in Athens and Their Functions* (Meisenheim am Glan: Hain, 1975). On Athenian treasuries and related decrees, see Samons (n. 2), esp. pp. 29–83.

8 Robert Garland, *Introducing New Gods: The Politics of Athenian Religion* (Ithaca, NY: Cornell University Press, 1992), pp. 47–51; Robert Parker, *Athenian Religion: A History* (Oxford: Oxford University Press, 1996), pp. 163–5.

9 Parker (n. 8), pp. 170–5; Garland (n. 8), pp. 111–14.

10 Sitalces: Garland (n. 8), pp. 112–13; Parker (n. 8), p. 173; Hornblower, *CT* 1. 282–9.

11 Cf. Arthur Darby Nock, *Essays on Religion and the Ancient World*, Zeph Stewart, ed. (Cambridge, MA: Harvard University Press, 1972), pp. 578f.

12 H. Abramson, "A Hero Shrine for Phrontis at Sounion?" *CSCA* 12 (1979): 1–19; Parker (n. 8), p. 35.

13 According to a widespread tradition, Heracles was posthumously received into the immortal Olympian family; correspondingly, he was not worshipped at a tomb.

14 Cf. Eugene Vanderpool, "An Inscribed Stele from Marathon," *Hesperia* 11 (1942): 329–37.

15 H. Alan Shapiro, *Myth into Art. Poet and Painter in Classical Greece* (London: Routledge, 1994), pp. 109–23.

16 See Carolin Hahnemann, *Incarnating Democracy* (Ph.D. dissertation: Brown University, 1997).

17 Cf. Castriota (n. 4), pp. 58–63, 90–94.

18 Parker (n. 8), pp. 116–21. On Cleisthenes' reforms see most recently Greg Anderson, *The Athenian Experiment: Building an Imagined Political Community in Ancient Attica, 508–490 B.C.* (Ann Arbor: University of Michigan Press, 2003).

19 Carol Mattusch, "The Eponymous Heroes: The Idea of Sculptural Groups," in W. D. E. Coulson et al., eds., *The Archaeology of Athens and Attica under the Democracy* (Oxford: Oxbow Books, 1994): 73–82, esp. pp. 74–6.

20 See Jennifer Larson, *Greek Heroine Cults* (Madison: University of Wisconsin Press, 1995), esp. pp. 26–42; Deborah Lyons, *Gender and Immortality: Heroines in Ancient Greek Myth and Cult* (Princeton: Princeton University Press, 1997).

21 Cf. Christiane Sourvinou-Inwood, *Studies in Girls' Transitions: Aspects of the Arkteia and Age Representation in Attic Iconography* (Athens: Kardamitsa, 1988).

22 Larson (n. 20), pp. 27, 30.

23 Larson (n. 20), pp. 39–41; Deborah Boedeker, *Descent from Heaven. Images of Dew in Greek Poetry and Religion* (Chico, CA: Scholars Press, 1984), pp. 108f.

24 Larson (n. 20), pp. 27, 29, and *passim*.

25 Joseph Fontenrose discusses a variant heroization pattern of historical figures in "The Hero as Athlete," *CSCA* 1 (1968): 73–104.

26 M. W. Taylor, *The Tyrant Slayers*, second edition (Salem, NH: Ayer, 1991).

27 E.g. Hdt. 6.38.1: the sixth-century Athenian Miltiades as oikist in the Thracian Chersonese.

28 On Hagnon and his replacement-oikist Brasidas, see Irad Malkin, *Religion and Colonization in Ancient Greece* (Leiden: Brill, 1987), pp. 228–32; Hornblower, *CT* II.452–5.

29 The rites are not attested, however, until the second century C.E. (*IG* ii² 1006.69).

30 See Martin Flashar, "Die Sieger von Marathon: Zwischen Mythos und Vorbildlichkeit," in Martin Flashar, Hans-Joachim Gehrke, and Ernst Heinrich, eds., *Retrospektive: Konzepte von Vergangenheit in der griechisch-römischen Antike* (Munich: Biering & Brinkmann, 1996): 63–85.

31 Felix Jacoby, "*Patrios Nomos*. State Burial in Athens and the Public Cemetery in the Kerameikos," *JHS* 64 (1944): 37–66.

32 As argued by Nicole Loraux, *The Invention of Athens. The Funeral Oration in the Classical City*, trans. A. Sheridan (Cambridge, MA: Harvard University Press, 1986 [French original 1981]), pp. 39–41. Similarly, Parker (n. 8), pp. 135–7.

33 The Phocaeans at Agylla (Hdt. 1.167.2) and the Cypriote leader Onesilos (Hdt. 5.114.2). Artachaees, a Persian, also received heroic honors, according to Herodotus (7.117.2).

34 Similarly, Parker (n. 8), pp. 135–7. On avoiding the term *heros*, see also Deborah Boedeker, "Paths to Heroization," in Deborah Boedeker and David Sider, eds., *The New Simonides* (Oxford: Oxford University Press, 2001), pp. 148–63.

35 See the succinct discussion by R. Meiggs, "The Political Implications of the Parthenon," in G. T. W. Hooker, ed., *Parthenon and Parthenos*, Greece & Rome suppl. vol. 10 (Oxford: Oxford University Press, 1963), pp. 36–45.

36 The "Peace of Kallias," weakly attested, is dated by many scholars to 449. Cf. D. Lewis in *CAH* V².121–7; P. J. Rhodes, p. 27 in this volume.

37 John M. Camp, *The Archaeology of Athens* (New Haven: Yale University Press, 2001), pp. 108–9 and 307–8.

38   Camp, *ibid.*, pp. 72–4; Jeffrey M. Hurwit, *The Athenian Acropolis* (Cambridge: Cambridge University Press, 1999), pp. 157–9.

39   Lisa Kallet-Marx, "Did Tribute Fund the Parthenon?" *CA* 8 (1989): 252–66. For a defense of the dominant view, see Samons (n. 2), pp. 41–2, 154–6.

40   Bernhard Smarczyk, *Untersuchungen zur Religionspolitik und politischen Propaganda Athens im Delisch-Attischen Seebund* (Munich: tuduv, 1990), pp. 298–317.

41   Mary Beard, *The Parthenon* (Cambridge, MA: Harvard University Press, 2003), pp. 141–4.

42   Robin Francis Rhodes, *Architecture and Meaning on the Athenian Acropolis* (Cambridge: Cambridge University Press, 1995), pp. 32–4.

43   Camp (n. 37), pp. 106–8; Garland (n. 8), pp. 107–9.

44   For differing interpretations of the gender distinctions, see Marcel Detienne, "The Violence of Wellborn Ladies," in Marcel Detienne and Jean-Pierre Vernant, eds., *The Cuisine of Sacrifice among the Greeks* (Chicago: University of Chicago Press, 1989), pp. 129–47; Robin Osborne, "Women and Sacrifice in Classical Greece," *CQ* 43 (1993): 392–405.

45   On libations see Walter Burkert, *Greek Religion*, trans. J. Raffan (Cambridge, MA: Harvard University Press, 1985), pp. 70–73.

46   Cf. Christiane Sourvinou-Inwood, "What Is Polis Religion?" in Richard Buxton, ed., *Oxford Readings in Greek Religion* (Oxford: Oxford University Press, 2000), pp. 13–37, esp. p. 18; Jon D. Mikalson, *Athenian Popular Religion* (Chapel Hill: University of North Carolina Press, 1983), pp. 83–90.

47   E.g., the Gephyraioi *genos* reportedly owned several temples to which others were not admitted (Hdt. 5.61.2); the *genos* of Isagoras worshipped Carian Zeus (Hdt. 5.66.1).

48   See Stephen J. Lambert, *The Phratries of Attica* (Ann Arbor: University of Michigan Press, 1993); Nicholas F. Jones, *The Associations of Classical Athens: The Response to Democracy* (New York: Oxford University Press, 1999), pp. 249–67.

49   See Jon D. Mikalson, *The Sacred and Civil Calendar of the Athenian Year* (Princeton: Princeton University Press, 1975); H. W. Parke, *Festivals of the Athenians* (Ithaca, NY: Cornell University Press, 1977).

50   See Allaire C. Brumfield, *The Attic Festivals of Demeter and Their Relation to the Agricultural Year* (Salem, NH: Arno, 1981). Lin Foxhall, "Women's Ritual and Men's Work in Ancient Athens," in R. Hawley and B. Levick, eds., *Women in Antiquity: New Assessments* (London: Routledge, 1995), pp. 96–110, proposes that in certain festivals the heavy farm work carried out by men was assisted by ritual work done by women.

51   The figures are based on *IG* ii² 2311 (ca. 370 B.C.E.), translated in Jennifer Neils, et al., *Goddess and Polis: The Panathenaic Festival in Classical Athens*, exhib. cat. (Princeton: Princeton University Press for Hood Museum of Art, Dartmouth College, Hanover, NH, 1992), p. 16.

52   *IG* i³ 34.41–3, 71.55–8 (Panathenaia), *IG* i³ 46.15–17 = ML 49.11–13 (Dionysia), *IG* i³ 78 = ML 73 (Mysteries). See Smarczyk (n. 40), pp. 158–61; Parker (n. 8), pp. 142–4.

53   Smarczyk (n. 40), pp. 58–153; Garland (n. 8), p. 107; Parker (n. 8), pp. 144–5.

54   Mikalson (n. 46) provides many examples.

55   *AP* 55.5, cf. 7.1. Cf. Connor (n. 2), pp. 171–2.

56 See Pritchett, *GSW*, vols. 1, 3, and 4 *passim* (Berkeley: University of California Press, 1971–1985) for data on religion and warfare in the Greek world.

57 Or perhaps ca. 427: see ML 44.

58 Robert Garland, "Religious Authority in Archaic and Classical Athens," *ABSA* 79 (1984): 75–123, at 79.

59 On loans from the gods, see Samons (n. 2), pp. 230–48 and *passim*.

60 Summarized in Parker (n. 8), pp. 125.

61 For a recent overview of accounting in Athens see Diane Harris, "Freedom of Information and Accountability," in Robin Osborne and Simon Hornblower, eds., *Ritual, Finance, Politics: Athenian Democratic Accounts Presented to David Lewis* (Oxford: Oxford University Press, 1994), pp. 213–25.

62 W. Robert Connor, "City Dionysia and Athenian Democracy," *Classica et Mediaevalia* 40 (1989): 7–32.

63 Simon Goldhill, "The Great Dionysia and Civic Ideology," *JHS* 107 (1987): 58–76, also published as "The Great Dionysia and Civic Ideology," in J. J. Winkler and F. I. Zeitlin, eds., *Nothing to Do with Dionysos?* (Princeton: Princeton University Press, 1990), pp. 97–129.

64 P. J. Rhodes, "Nothing to Do with Democracy: Athenian Drama and the *Polis*," *JHS* 123 (2003): 104–119 offers a detailed rebuttal of Goldhill. See also Henk S. Versnel, "Religion and Democracy," in Walter Eder, ed., *Die athenische Demokratie im 4. Jahrhundert v. Chr.* (Stuttgart: Steiner, 1995), pp. 367–87, at pp. 376–7; Michael H. Jameson, "Religion in the Athenian Democracy," in Ian Morris and Kurt Raaflaub, eds., *Democracy 2500? Questions and Challenges* (Dubuque, IA: Kendall/Hunt for the Amer. Inst. of Archaeology, 1998), pp. 171–95.

65 Bernard M. W. Knox, "Athenian Religion and Literature," in *CAH* V². 268–86, at p. 272.

66 See Sara B. Aleshire, "The Demos and the Priests: The Selection of Sacred Officials at Athens from Cleisthenes to Augustus," in Osborne and Hornblower (n. 61), pp. 325–37.

67 *IG* ii² 1283; see Garland (n. 58): 95.

68 Judging from the epitaph for the first Nike priestess, Myrrhine: *SEG* 12.80, ca. 411 B.C.E.

69 Osborne (n. 44).

70 Parker (n. 8), pp. 77–8.

71 Raubitschek 218, cited in F. T. van Straten, "Gifts for the Gods," in H. S. Versnel, ed., *Faith, Hope and Worship: Aspects of Religious Mentality in the Ancient World* (Leiden: Brill, 1981), pp. 65–151 and Plates 1–64, at pp. 72–3.

72 *SEG* 10.321, cited in Straten (n. 71), p. 75. This mid-fifth-century inscription, from the Demeter temple under the Acropolis, is the last extant dedication from a woman in classical Athens; see Elaine Fantham et al., *Women in the Classical World* (New York: Oxford University Press, 1994), pp. 38–9.

73 See Christopher A. Faraone, "The Agonistic Context of Early Greek Binding Spells," in Faraone and Dirk Obbink, *Magika Hiera: Ancient Greek Magic and Religion* (New York: Oxford University Press, 1991), pp. 2–32; John G. Gager, *Curse Tablets and Binding Spells from the Ancient World* (New York: Oxford University Press, 1992); Fritz Graf, *Magic in the Ancient World* (Cambridge, MA: Harvard University Press, 1997), pp. 118–74.

74 Jan Bremmer, "The Birth of the Term 'Magic,'" *ZPE* 126 (1999): 1–12.

75   For a succinct discussion of "magic" vs. "religion," see Robert L. Fowler, "Greek
     Magic, Greek Religion," in R. Buxton, ed., *Oxford Readings in Greek Religion*
     (Oxford: Oxford University Press, 2000), pp. 317–43.

76   Summarized in P. A. Meijer, "Philosophers, Intellectuals and Religion in Hellas,"
     in Versnel (n. 71), pp. 216–63, at pp. 220–24.

77   Meijer (n. 76), pp. 218, 229–32.

78   Profaning the rites at Eleusis seems to have been a particularly serious charge; see
     K. J. Dover, "The Freedom of the Intellectual in Greek Society," *Talanta* 7 (1976):
     24–54, at 26–7.

79   Parker (n. 8), pp. 199–207.

80   Testimonia collected and discussed in Dover (n. 78). For a less skeptical view of
     the prosecutions, see Meijer (n. 76).

81   Connor (n. 2).

82   See Pritchett, *GSW* 3.26.

3: THE ATHENIAN ECONOMY

Lisa Kallet

AN ECONOMIC MENTALITY

Then, listen, pop, and relax your frown a bit.
First of all, calculate roughly, not with counters but on your
    fingers,
how much tribute we receive altogether from the allied cities.
Then make a separate count of the taxes and the many
    one-percents,
court dues, mines, markets, harbors, rents, proceeds from
    confiscations.
Our total income from all this is nearly 2000 talents.

This passage, from Aristophanes' *Wasps* (655–60, trans. Henderson), performed in 422 before thousands of citizens, encapsulates a fascinating feature of fifth-century Athens: the place of money, economic activity, and numeracy in the life of citizens from rich to poor, urban to rural. It suggests an audience with a fondness for calculating and counting, one attuned to economic advantages – in short, an Athenian economic mentality. Aristophanes' verses also encompass many central facets of the fifth-century economy that will be surveyed in this chapter and illuminate the relationship among individual, polis, and empire in the pursuit of financial and economic benefit. Bdelycleon, the speaker, aims to deflate his father Philocleon's conviction that he has great wealth and power as a result of his position as a juror, for which he receives state pay (the ultimate justification, in Philocleon's view, for performing that service). Bdelycleon produces as argument the city's staggering national wealth in order to show how little Philocleon gets out of it. "So the pay we've been getting," Philocleon exclaims, "doesn't even amount to a tenth of the revenue!" (664). The underlying assumption is that individual citizens have a right to benefit materially from the city's power.

Indeed, money, trade, and market infuse the texts of diverse genres such as comedy, tragedy, and history, appearing as topical allusion, as metaphor, and as moral concern. In Aristophanes' *Acharnians*, for example, references to money – in the form of pay, cost, and bribes – permeate the plot, which itself involves the market as metaphor for the democracy. *Wasps* arguably illustrates a perversion of the "right" values, for Philocleon sees his aim in life not as the ability to participate in the democracy because he receives jury pay, but as participation in order to receive pay. The ordinary citizen, as presented, is a calculating citizen, out for individual gain. The language of money and profit removed from a social nexus of reciprocity pervades Greek tragedy, in which the poets explore the value of life, personal relationships, and power through money as metaphor or instrument emblematizing the perversion of social values or the destruction of the *oikos* (e.g., Sophocles' *Oedipus Tyrannus*, in which Oedipus accuses Teiresias of having been bribed for a prophecy, and thinks that money can buy power and information). Elsewhere, traders bring news, or characters act in a commercial role (like Odysseus in Euripides' *Cyclops*). In Thucydides' *History*, money both fuels the polis and becomes the engine of its destruction; and the more that the Athenians seek to extract profit from their empire, the more they aim at overextension – in ancient Greek as well as modern formulations, part of the recipe for disaster. Moral issues aside, the combined evidence of these texts and inscriptions concerned with money, and with domestic and imperial administration, reveals the extent of regular exposure of thousands of citizens to the nuts and bolts of Athens's public and private economy (a conclusion that also vitiates the notion that ancient authors were not interested in economic matters).

Much about the economy of Attica was traditional and timeless: it was an agricultural community in which the vast majority of citizens lived on and worked the land. Like other classical poleis, Athens taxed for revenue. Attica had natural advantages that in combination gave the polis a prosperity surpassing that of other Greek communities: its silver mines at Laurium in the southeastern Attic countryside, and its large port, or *emporion*, the Piraeus. But what makes Athens's fifth-century economic history unique is the combination of those natural advantages and the unprecedented means and opportunity to exploit the Aegean's resources to the imperial city's benefit – not to mention a tendency to treat the Aegean region as an extension of Athens in terms of economic practice.[1]

A momentous decision early in the fifth century neatly illustrates the intersections among the economic, political, and military: the Athenians determined to use the yield from the silver mines to build a fleet. Rather than distribute the profits among the citizenry according (apparently) to normal practice, the Athenians, on Themistocles' proposal, Herodotus tells us (7.144), agreed to forego private gain for the public good (defined as security and power). This decision facilitated the development of Athenian power internationally and gave the city the muscle to enforce decisions that benefited it economically at an early stage of its post–Persian War ascendancy in the Greek world. If this was indeed unusual, then it can justly be said to have ushered in or at least greatly reinforced the idea of public wealth to be spent on the public good.[2] The use of public moneys in military and domestic areas in fact became a hallmark of fifth-century Athens. Of course, for this outlook to be realized, the Athenian collective required steady and substantial sources of revenue.

WITHIN THE POLIS: DOMESTIC ECONOMIC ACTIVITY

Agriculture

Attica, like the rest of Greece, was a collection of households, *oikoi*, consisting of land, animals, and slaves as well as the physical house and family. In elite male ideology, the proper management of the household – *oikonomia*, meaning its economic growth – was explicitly viewed as mirroring in microcosm the proper management of the state, and by extension, the ability to increase the prosperity of the polis. The tension between *oikos* and polis over rights and importance intimately binds together the economic and the political. A conspicuous feature of Periclean Athens, judging by the rhetoric Thucydides ascribes to the leader, was the devaluation of the *oikos* relative to the polis, an attitude reflected concretely in Pericles' war strategy of evacuating the countryside and leaving it vulnerable to annual Spartan invasions in the Peloponnesian War. That this was a hard sell when it mattered most – in times of crisis – is clear from a remark Thucydides gives him: "A man may be personally ever so well off, and yet if his country is ruined he must be ruined with it; whereas a flourishing commonwealth always affords chances of salvation to unfortunate individuals." Pericles continues, attempting to convince the Athenians that their power is so extraordinary that it is capable of unlimited extension on sea, and concludes, "and so, although you think it a great privation to lose the use of your land and houses, still you must see that this power is something widely different; and instead of fretting on their account, you should really regard them in the light of the gardens and other accessories that embellish a great fortune, and as, in comparison, of little moment" (2.60.3, 62.3). (Despite the implication of conspicuous consumption, elites were faced with a democratic ideology of private simplicity that frowned on conspicuous consumption by the rich: houses remained simple and plain by later standards in antiquity.)

While the unique aspects of Periclean Athens (principally economic, naval, and cultural) are in one respect independent of the agricultural land, nevertheless in another respect the land is the very foundation. From a practical, economic standpoint, and for elites, an ideological one as well, the land served to demarcate "rich" and "poor" (the typical Greek fondness for antithesis resisted in-betweens, though in this case both terms were exceptionally fluid) and underlay the ideal of *autarkeia*, "self-sufficiency." For as wealthy as the polis was from its *arche* and its silver mines, permitting sizable public expenditures, affluent citizens, although few in number, played an essential economic role in the life of the city on a regular basis, through performing expensive public services called liturgies (e.g., equipping a warship, financing a dramatic chorus).[3] The liquid wealth of most of these citizens came from the land.[4]

Moreover, the land was tied to the city. Surpluses were brought there to be sold to middlemen (*kapeloi*) in the agora – by the fifth century certainly a permanent market[5] – for cash or to procure other goods or items, another link between land and urban center. To the extent that the *oikos* is a microcosm of the polis, and the polis an aggregate of *oikoi*, the same principle and definition of *autarkeia* applies to both: self-sufficiency – somewhat paradoxically – means having the surplus wealth to purchase what is desired or even needed from outside the *oikos*. Consider this remarkable anecdote in Plutarch about Pericles: Pericles, he says, was not averse to "financial gain," for to prevent his inherited property from dissipation or loss, he "sold all his annual produce all together at once, and then he used it to buy in the agora each item as it was needed, and so provide for the daily livelihood of his household" (*Per.* 16.4) – to the great annoyance of his sons and their wives, Plutarch continues, for there was no surplus in the house: they lived according only to what they needed for maintenance. The fascination of this anecdote lies in showing not only Pericles as a kind of economic rationalist out for profit, but also the transference of the *oikos*, in a sense, to the polis, and their interrelationship. While this practice may be on the extreme end, whether it was unusual is difficult to say. Plutarch may imply that it was, but we should also allow for exaggeration. In any case, elites would have needed money to discharge public obligations such as liturgies or for (other) prestige expenditures. At the same time, those below the elite would have exchanged surplus produce for cash. As mentioned above, money was indispensable, as comedy especially highlights, to the "Athenian lifestyle."

Although scholars disagree on the organization of landholding in Attica, the nature and basis of the rural economy is clear.[6] Most holdings consisted of small lots – the result partly of Attica's large population, partly of the division of plots within an *oikos*. Landowners tended toward a diversity of crops rather than specialization, focusing on the triad of olives, grapes, and barley. Beans and other pods, fruits and nuts, and even a little wheat were grown as well; the last was preferred to barley (and nutritionally superior), but wheat required more water than the climate of Attica produced, hence the city's need to import it (see below). Olive trees were scattered throughout Attica, many of them sacred to Athena, with severe penalties (initially death) imposed on anyone who cut down or planted too close to one. Olives were "protected species" generally, because, alongside silver, they were the most prized product of Attica and a highly profitable export commodity (in fact, a law ascribed to Solon prohibited the export of any produce but olive oil). Landholders also kept animals, chiefly pigs and goats, some for sacrifices; the rich might keep horses. Because of its expense, horse-raising (*hippotrophia*) was the ultimate measure of aristocratic value.

At the same time, the geographically diverse region fostered distinct microclimates; someone owning land in different parts of Attica might reduce risk in a bad year in one crop or region. Indeed, a valuable piece of evidence from the late fifth century, the Attic Stelae recording the sale of confiscated property of those convicted of mutilating the Herms in 415 (ML 79 = Fornara 147), shows that elites might have more than one landholding. Equally interesting, these holdings could be scattered throughout Attica: one Euphiletos owned houses and/or property in several different parts of Attica. Unique to the period of Athens's empire, wealthy citizens also bought land abroad in subject states, a practice so repugnant to the local inhabitants of those areas, and evidently widespread enough, that, when the Athenians attempted to organize a naval league in the fourth century, a clause put into the formal charter explicitly forbade the practice.[7]

The Mines at Laurium

The mines were the catalyst of Athenian naval power; and because that power helped make Periclean Athens unique in wealth, culture, and arguably the form that the democracy itself took, the mines deserve pride of place in any discussion of the Athenian domestic economy. The relationship between public and private economic interests in the mines is typical of economic activity in general in Athens. The polis leased rights to open a new mine or operate an existing one. The individual who bought the lease "owned" the right to work the plot of land and the mining equipment and workers, chiefly slaves; the polis owned the ore under the ground. The mines were extremely productive for both state and private citizens in the fifth century. The purchase price of the leases and, apparently, a percentage of the yield went to the state. Although the great silver strike in the 480s that yielded 100 talents for the state may not have been a single year's yield but rather only a percentage of its total, it nevertheless shows the lucrative nature of mining for the polis (recall Bdelycleon's inclusion of revenue from the mines in his list to Philocleon).[8]

Mine owners stood to reap a considerable profit, both from the renting of slaves and from their portion of a strike. Nicias, the ill-fated Athenian general who died in the Sicilian expedition, owned mining contracts, and, reportedly, 1,000 slaves, rented out through an agent to work in the mines. He was one of Athens's wealthiest men, singled out by Xenophon in his lengthy discussion of the mines and the profitability of renting slaves (*Poroi* 4.14). Owning mining leases could be represented as the ultimate in profit-earning on the comic stage. In Aristophanes' *Knights*, Sausage Seller has been brought in, in accordance with an oracle, to defeat Paphlagon (a thinly disguised Cleon) and become the favorite of the character Demos. They both recognize that a key to victory lies in promising the greatest profits to the public treasury, that is, Demos's money. But first they assert their respective power in an attempt to outdo each other. Says Paphlagon, "But you won't eat up the Milesians' big fish and then run roughshod over them." Sausage Seller responds, "But I will eat sides of beef and buy mining leases" (360–61). Sausage Seller continually "out-demagogues" Paphlagon, chiefly by making the most lavish promises of wealth, and in the end wins.

Wages, Employment, and Other Production

To Praxias, resident of Melite, for [sculpting] the horse and the man visible behind turning it: 120 drachmas (Erechtheium accounts, *IG* i³ 476, for 407)

Resolved by the Council and Assembly . . . to pay fifty drachmas annually to the priestess of Athena Nike (*IG* i³ 35, ca. 448)

Ambassador: You sent us to the Great King, on a salary of two drachmas per diem [eleven years ago].

Dicaeopolis: Oh dear, the drachmas! (Aristophanes *Acharnians* 65–7)

The majority of Athenians, like Greeks generally, worked for themselves on the farm; to work for another compromised the freedom of the individual. This ideology, however, would have been considered a luxury by the many citizens who were wage earners, engaged in the building trades, manufacturing, commerce, retail vending, mining, or the arts. Literary sources from this period tend to emphasize consumption and imports (see below). Production outside the *oikos*, however, whether for local use or export, underlies this preoccupation. Indeed, given the city's size and needs, it would not be surprising to find a high degree of specialization and an abundance of goods produced for exchange. As usual, most evidence of domestic production comes from the fourth century; but fifth-century comedy especially and inscriptions reveal a large number of occupations and specializations, numbering near seventy, with most of them outside the agricultural sector – for example, metalsmiths, fullers, statue-makers, knife-makers, carpenters, and armor and weapons manufacturers – an impressive figure considering how woefully incomplete the evidence is for the Periclean period.[9]

With the exception of public service (see below), an important phenomenon stands out: citizen, metic, and slave often worked side by side at the same task, with the same skills (there were no specifically citizen, metic, or slave occupations in the private sphere); metics and slaves thus served a crucial economic function in the urban economy (conspicuously in the mines as well). For example, in the construction of the Erechtheium, slave, metic, and citizen worked together on the project as masons, all for the same pay. Wages are not as well attested for the fifth century as for later periods;[10] but a living wage for a skilled worker was in the realm of four obols to one drachma a day.

In a different category, thousands of Athenians would have received pay, *misthos*, for public duties in the course of their life: as a juror, council member, priest or priestess of a civic cult, construction worker, rower, or hoplite. Three areas stand out as central to the public economy of Athens in its "redistributive" aspect: political participation and other public duties, military service, and employment on building projects. First, political participation. "The sweetest part of all is when I come home with my pay!" exclaims Philocleon, the gullible juror of *Wasps*. Public pay, a hallmark of Periclean Athens, was attacked by fourth-century critics as illustrative of the excesses of radical democracy; a telling indication that this was a fifth-century viewpoint is that, at the inception of the oligarchical coup of 411, the ringleaders immediately called a halt to all pay for offices. Pericles, usually blamed for creating the "city under pay," receives censure from Plato (*Gorgias* 515e) for having made Athenians "money-lovers" (*philarguroi*). Pericles is usually credited the introduction, probably ca. 460, of jury pay, at the rate of, probably, two obols a day, increased to three by Cleon early in the Peloponnesian War. Likely other political magistracies and offices were paid in the fifth century, like members of the Boule. Most individuals performing a public service of any kind could expect to be paid, from the priestess of Athena to ambassadors, such as the comic envoys living it up for eleven years in Persia at a drachma a day.

Why pay for political participation? Two obols for jury pay, for example, is not a large sum, hardly even a subsistence wage; but neither was it purely token, the way that, say, receiving five dollars a day for jury duty in a U.S. city might be regarded. Philocleon's view of the economic power of his pay is of course punctured by Bdelycleon in his comparison with the annual revenue. But pay in other spheres, e.g., the military, implies that one could subsist on three obols a day, and such recompense therefore can be seen as affording an opportunity for the poor to participate in the political life of the city, mass participation being essential for the democracy, as it evolved in the age of Pericles, to work.

Military pay for citizens (and mercenaries) varied depending on whether one was a mere rower in the fleet or a hoplite, and the figure fluctuates between three obols and one drachma. During the famous Sicilian campaign (415–413), all were paid one drachma a day, though this rate probably was reduced after the debacle. Pay for citizen military service was in fact as radical as pay for political office, since in Greek poleis warfare was normally land-based hoplite warfare, with hoplites providing their own armor and sustenance and receiving no pay. But the rowers in the fleet, the real source of Athens's power, came from the lowest socioeconomic stratum; pay was essential for their service. Pay for light-armed troops, hoplites, and cavalry, well attested for the Peloponnesian War years, would have followed the practice of naval pay, but when is unclear.[11]

The most visible feature of Periclean Athens was the building program. Plutarch, in his biography of Pericles, presents it as a massive public works project designed to bring employment to the masses. Certainly a by-product of the decision to embark on such extensive public building, stimulated partly by the transfer of the Delian League treasury from Delos to Athens in 454, was a huge boost to employment. All together, both domestic and imperial revenues had created a reserve, by mid-century, of some 10,000 talents, mostly stored in temples, *the* "reserve banks" of ancient Greece.[12] While the Athenians likely could have rebuilt their sacred monuments with domestic revenues, some tribute, as the building accounts of the Parthenon show, was indeed used – enough so that Pericles' political enemy, Thucydides (not the historian), tried to incite public moral condemnation of the practice of using imperial moneys for domestic purposes. The people were not persuaded, and Thucydides was ostracized.[13]

The existence of the empire, crucial for understanding any aspect of fifth-century Athens, is vital for the area of employment, both at home and abroad. A tradition reflected in Aristotle (*AP* 24.3) credits Aristeides with creating massive employment opportunities, associated with the creation of the Delian League, and the advice to use the fruits of their imperial control to maintain the population:

> In accordance with Aristeides' proposal, they provided ample maintenance for the common people, so that more than 20,000 men were supported from the tribute, the taxes, and the allies. There were 6,000 jurors; 1,600 archers, and also 1,200 cavalry; the council of 500; 500 guards of the dockyards, and also 50 guards on the Acropolis; about 700 internal officials and about 700 overseas. In addition to these ... they had 2,500 hoplites; 20 guard ships; other ships sent out for the tribute, carrying 2,000 men appointed by lot; also the town hall; orphans; and guardians of prisoners. All these were financed from public funds.

Many of the figures supplied (for internal officials and military personnel) are accurate, though it is impossible to judge the plausibility of the grand total.[14]

Domestic Taxation

The polis did not tax citizens directly as a regular procedure; but in wartime the citizens could order the wealthy among them to pay a property tax, the *eisphora*, which could yield substantial amounts. The first, shortly into the Peloponnesian War, yielded 200 talents (Thuc. 3.19.1).[15] Such irregular taxation was naturally abhorrent, not only because it was unpredictable and remitted immediately, but also because it compromised, through its compulsory nature, one's free status. Tellingly, such direct taxation was regarded as something typically imposed by tyrants – like the Peisistratids in sixth-century Athens[16] – on their subjects. If one thinks of the fact that a common Greek term for one's property was *ousia*, one's "being," it is easier to appreciate more fully the reaction to this kind of taxation. Indeed, wealthy citizens viewed it as a kind of tyranny of the demos – in this context the mass of the poor citizenry – over them, for it was that majority who profited from the expense of a relative few.[17]

The number of wealthy Athenians who could be subject to property taxes (and liturgies) grew over the fifth century. A phenomenon of the period is the emergence of the *nouveaux riches*, either men whose wealth did not derive from generations of inherited property – as did that of a Callias or a Cimon – or those who moved up the economic ladder by virtue of nonagricultural investment and profit, as in the case of Nicias's mines and slaves. Aristophanes could put to good comic use Cleon's (evident) ownership of a tanning factory as part of his scathing attacks on the notorious politician, calling him a mere tanner. (Nicias, however, seems to have escaped the snobbery and ridicule bestowed on men of new wealth.) Snobbery notwithstanding, such newly rich individuals, along with the traditional landed elites, played a vital economic role in the fiscal health, military power, and religious life of the city.

The Athenians welcomed foreigners to the city to take up residence and contribute to, among other areas, the economic life of the polis. Such foreigners were, unlike citizens, subjected to a regular tax, the *metoikion*, as well as a market tax; prostitutes (mostly slaves or metics) had to pay a tax as well. Privileged foreign residents might be exempted from taxation – but they might then, like citizens, be subject to *eisphorai*. It is unknown exactly when the *metoikion* was instituted, but it seems likely that it dates to the Periclean period, for the simple reason that it was at this time, during the heyday of Athens's empire, that foreigners flocked to the city. In the fourth century the tax rate was twelve drachmas a year for men, six for women without male relatives. Unlike the *eisphora*, it was a poll, not a property tax.

The Piraeus

The place of the Piraeus in the city's public and private economy is perhaps best illustrated by the building of the Long Walls in the 450s, linking the urban center of Athens with the Piraeus harbor complex. Symbolically as well as practically the walls marked the reliance on the sea and naval power for imports and signaled the priority of the sea over (native) land; their significance was only enhanced during the Peloponnesian War, when the Attic countryside was often inaccessible.

In the course of the fifth century, the Piraeus became *the* Aegean *emporion*, in large part because Athens's position as the imperial center allowed the city to dictate to a great extent the flow and distribution of goods and commodities, especially grain. The reliance of Aegean communities on imports for their food supply, increasingly controlled by Athens, reinforced the latter's position as imperial center. Thus, consideration of the Piraeus and maritime trade and taxation moves us into an area in which the distinction between the Athenian polis and empire often blurs.

The population of the Piraeus increased during the fifth century (likely in tandem with the prominence of the port in Aegean commerce), a fact that would have also increased the city's need for grain. Much of the population would have been metics; their presence attests to the economic opportunities of the *emporion*, for, with their being debarred from political life, prevented from owning land, and compelled to pay the residency tax, economic opportunity would have been their incentive.

Those involved in facilitating or actively engaging in trade were merchants (*emporoi*), ship-owners (*naukleroi*), retail tradesmen (*kapeloi*), and moneylenders and changers. *Emporoi* and *naukleroi* might be citizens or metics. Scholars have come to recognize that Hasebroek's model of traders as poor, marginalized non-Athenians underestimates the evidence of citizen participation and the potentially lucrative and honored (in time of need) nature of that participation, whether conducted by citizen or foreigner (as evidenced, for example, by honorary decrees to those who imported necessities to the state).[18] Moreover, trade spawned small-scale industries and manufacturing, especially in the areas of ship-building and shield, sword, and furniture production, to name a few.

A ready example of the polis's interest in the Piraeus is the presence of a variety of officials whose functions were to ensure proper procedures and collection of taxes and the importation of sufficient quantities of grain. Such officials include the *pentekostologoi*, "collectors of the two-percent tax," the *agoronomoi*, "market inspectors," the *metronomoi*, "weight and measure inspectors," and the *sitophylakes*, "grain inspectors." Trade was otherwise handled by the private sector, not the polis directly. One notable feature that separates the polis from the economic/commercial sphere is the total absence of interference in lending, in particular, in setting caps on interest rates. Maritime – and landed – loans were a private matter between lender and borrower; the rates could fluctuate widely depending on assessments of the degree of risk and expectation of profit (landed loans, however, were more consistent; interest was based on time alone, and, in the fourth century, interest above one percent a month evoked moral condemnation). All the evidence for maritime lending is from the fourth century, but there is no reason to assume that the fifth century was different.

Imports and Exports

"The greatness of our city draws the products of the world into our harbor, so that to the Athenian the fruits of other countries are as familiar a luxury as those of his own" (Thuc. 2.38.2). So asserts Pericles in the Funeral Oration, numbering the Piraeus and the city's imports among the signs of power emphasized in the speech. The city's imports evidently captivated the Athenian imagination, to judge from their mention in diverse genres. In his rant against Athenian democracy couched in the form of a paean of sorts to its success, the Old Oligarch also links imports with power. The Athenians, he claims, are fond of foreign gastronomic luxuries, importing specialties of Sicily, Italy, Cyprus, Egypt, Lydia, Pontus, the Peloponnese, and other places, and able to do so because of their thalassocracy (II.7). He also alludes to the essentially command economy of the Athenians, in the course of which he specifies imports needed for shipbuilding:

> [The Athenians] alone of Greeks and foreigners can be wealthy: where will a city rich in timber for ship-building dispose of its goods without the agreement of the rulers of

the sea? If a city is wealthy in iron, copper, or flax, where will it dispose of its goods without the agreement of the rulers of the sea? But these are just what I need for ships – wood from one, iron from another, and copper, flax, and wax from others. In addition, exports to any city hostile to us will be forbidden on pain of being barred from the sea. Although I do nothing, I have all these products of the land because of the sea, while no other city has two of them; no city has both timber and flax, but where there is an abundance of flax the ground is level and treeless, nor do copper and iron come from the same city, nor any two or three of the other products from one place but one from one city, another from another.

(II.11)

Still greater detail is provided by this famous fragment of the fifth-century comic poet Hermippus (fr. 63 *apud* Athen. 1.27e–28a) on the products brought in by the shipowner (*naukleros*) Dionysius:

From Cyrene, silphion and ox-hides;
from the Hellespont, mackerel and all kinds of salt fish;
from Sitalces, itching powder for the Lacedaemonians,
and from Perdiccas, many shiploads of lies.
Syracuse sends pork and cheese,
and may Poseidon sink the curved ships of the Corcyreans
since they collaborate with both sides.
That is what comes from that direction.
From Egypt, sails, rigging, and papyrus;
from Syria, incense. Crete the Beautiful
delivers cypress to the gods;
and Libya, ivory for sale; Rhodes, raisins
and dried figs that bring pleasant dreams.
From Euboea, pears and fat sheep;
slaves from Phrygia and mercenary troops from Arcadia.
Pagasae provides slaves and branded serfs;
the Paphlagonians furnish Zeus's acorns and glistening almonds,
the high point of the meal Phoenicia,
palm-fruit and wheat flour of the finest sort;
Carthage, carpets and motley pillows.

The comic potential of this kind of information surely in part derives from the insertion of jabs at the "commodities" provided by targeted traitor states and unreliable allies such as the Corcyreans, with whom the Athenians had formed a defensive alliance before the Peloponnesian War, and Perdiccas, the Macedonian king who shifted allegiances as easily as the wind. But the passage is revealing for its inclusion of both raw and manufactured commodities, for the variety of foodstuffs, and for the intermingling of luxury items such as ivory and carpets with essential commodities such as slaves, wheat, timber, and linen for sails and rigging. The list could be vastly expanded to include both necessities and staples such as salt and luxury items such as gemstones and perfumes.

These passages mislead in implying that all these products are brought in by "the polis:" trade, as mentioned above, was largely a matter of the private sector, watched over, to be sure, by public officials and especially tax officials. But it is important to distinguish between imports driven by public need and nonessential ones driven by private demand and including many luxury must-haves for the elite – such as Persian garments, the fashion statement of the Peloponnesian War years.[19]

The grain trade was paramount to the lifeblood of the city.[20] A critical source was the Black Sea, not only for Athens: Herodotus (7.147), for example, notes grain ships passing through the Hellespont under Xerxes' eyes in 480, bound for Aegina and the Peloponnese. Egypt likely was another provider. One such instance, in the form of a gift from the Egyptian king Psamettichos, occurred in 445/4 during a shortage.

Illuminating evidence of Athens's self-interest in the grain trade comes from a decree (ML 65 = Fornara 128) concerning the north Aegean city of Methone in the 430s that allows it to import grain up to a certain (fragmentary) quantity of *medimnoi* (a *medimnos* is roughly equivalent to a bushel) and alludes to *Hellespontophylakes*, "guards of the Hellespont," Athenian customs officials who levied a tax (possibly a tithe) on cargo and on ships en route from the Black Sea to the Aegean. When the board was instituted is unknown, but it certainly precedes the 430s; indeed the Athenians' desire to control the trade may be detectable early in the history of the Delian League, from their activities in the Hellespontine region. In any case, it is important to appreciate that the Athenians would not have placed a tollhouse at the Hellespont were grain (as well as other commodities) not a regular – and profitable – item of trade from the Black Sea. Finally, Pericles' wartime strategy of the abandonment of the countryside in 431 presupposes a foreign grain pipeline already securely in place.

Athens's security demanded a reliable source of wood and pitch for shipbuilding (recall the Old Oligarch's emphasis on this, among other commodities essential to that purpose such as flax and iron). Moreover, the scale of Athens's mining operation at Laurium would have generated an enormous, continual need for charcoal for the smelting process. It has been estimated that Athens's need for timber probably increased fourfold from the sixth to fifth century due to the navy, public building, industry, and a rise in population.[21] By the last third of the fifth century, the primary supplier was Macedon; earlier sources are unknown, though the wood for the fleet in the 480s may have come from western sources such as southern Italy, since Thrace and Macedon were either under the control of or in alliance with Persia.

Finally, the traffic in slaves was substantial for both public and private use – public, such as the police force of 300 Scythians, and an unquantifiable number of private slaves working in domestic, agricultural, and industrial capacities. Thucydides reports a round figure of 20,000 slaves, many skilled (and probably mine) workers, that deserted Attica late in the Peloponnesian War (7.27.5). Traditionally war captives, especially women and children, were sold as slaves if not ransomed by their families. But the city needed regular sources and these came chiefly from the north, especially the Black Sea, and the east, from Phrygia, Phoenicia, and elsewhere. Although the extent of agricultural slavery in the domestic economy is disputed,[22] diverse literary evidence such as comedy and forensic oratory suggests that slaves were integral to agricultural production, and not just in elite landholdings.

Athens's reliance on imported necessities is thus a crucial factor in the city's public and private economies. This was especially true during the Peloponnesian War because of the partial and then complete incapacitation of the land during the near-annual Spartan invasions between 431 and 425 and the Spartan occupation of Attica in the war's final stage (413–404). The importance of these sources often emerges only when we learn of their loss to the city. In 424, for example, Thucydides notes that the surrender to Brasidas of Amphipolis, an Athenian colony in the north, engendered "great fear" among the Athenians because of the loss of shipbuilding timber (and money). Later in the war, when Euboea revolted (411), the historian signals its importance again through conveying the Athenians' reaction: they were "gripped by panic" because the island "brought them the greatest benefit" (8.96.2); the implication is that it was material and economic in nature (whether foodstuffs or timber).

The Piraeus could be both a transshipment point for goods and the final destination of imports. In turn, Athens chiefly exported silver, ceramics, olives and olive oil (the last, however, leaves no trace in the material record). Silver was an intrinsically fluid metal in terms of its functions: it could be a medium of exchange (money), a commodity in and of itself, or both. Compared with other Aegean sources, Attic silver occupied a unique position: its renowned purity helped make Athenian silver coinage – the "owls" – dominant in the Greek world and helped it achieve the status of *the* international coinage, and therefore guaranteed that Laurium silver would always be an especially profitable and desired export item. Especially in minted form, it enjoyed an enhanced value beyond its weight; demand drove up the price.

Athenian ceramics are found throughout the Mediterranean, both coarseware and fine, painted pottery. As in the case of silver, during the fifth century Attic pottery dominated trade. Although the value of fineware as a commodity is debated between those who downplay its worth and those who elevate it to near-metal value, its presence in the Mediterranean suggests its desirability as an export commodity, and in fact ceramics could be tailored for the preferences of specific markets, as seems to have been the case, for example, in the Levant.[23]

Silver and trade generally provided the greatest potential for individual profit. As part of founding a new city, the Chorus Leader of Aristophanes' *Birds* asks, "How will we give men wealth? For that's something they lust after the most." To which the reply is, "When they consult a diviner, the birds will show them the best mines, and will reveal the most profitable trading voyages" (592–4). Citizens in their public capacity, too, had every reason to ensure imports of both necessities and luxuries, to lure cargoes to the Piraeus and foreigners to the city, and to see to it that sizable revenue accrued to the state from trade. I mentioned above some of the officials involved in the oversight of the *emporion*, many concerned with the collection of taxes. This brings us to maritime taxation.

Maritime Taxation

While the Athenians probably levied overland transit taxes, most goods arrived by sea, and maritime taxation was often the chief and most regular source of public revenue for a Greek polis. Athens's imperial position and control of the Aegean (in varying degrees) allowed the polis to enhance such taxation's potential. Yet much is uncertain when it comes to rates, varieties, and mechanisms of collection, since our sources are, as usual, spotty, or unspecific. Our evidence consists of the *Wasps* passage about the taxes and the one-percents, dated to 422, and references to an empire-wide five-percent maritime tax, the *eikoste*, around 413 (Thuc. 7.28.4); to a two-percent tax that was farmed out in 402/1 (And. 1.133); and to a ten-percent tax (*dekate*),[24] which may or may not have been a local tax.

Athens likely had a plurality of taxes in order to extract as much money from as many sources as possible (as *Wasps* would have us conclude). Thus in the Piraeus, one might expect a harbor tax, a tax on cargo (import and export), another on the ship, and another on passengers. Obviously we would like to know how sizable a chunk of the city's annual income such taxes composed. Recall Bdelycleon's total revenue from all sources, both domestic and foreign, of 2,000 talents. Xenophon, recollecting in the early fourth century, puts the total revenue, both imperial and domestic, collected by Athens at the beginning of the Peloponnesian War at 1,000 talents (*Anab.* 7.1.27). Given comic exaggeration, Xenophon's figure is probably near the mark. Thucydides has Pericles speak of an annual 600 talents coming in from the empire "apart from the other revenue" on the eve of war (2.13.2); this "other revenue" was likely domestic, and less than 600 talents. A figure of ca. 400 talents of domestic revenue would have derived from a combination of tax revenue (the two-percent tax mentioned above may have yielded around fifty talents) and a percentage of the proceeds from the silver mines.

Individuals would expect to profit from tax collection. Each year, contracts to collect taxes were farmed out at a public auction to successful bidders; they might be required to make a down payment, thus ensuring the polis a minimum revenue immediately. One man, Agyrrhius, is said to have made a profit of six talents on the collection of the two-percent tax at the end of the fifth century. So claimed Andocides (1.133) in a speech accusing Agyrrhius of conspiring to eliminate competition at the auction by essentially buying off his competitors with shares in his lease (for which he had underbid, thereby to increase his own profits at the expense of the state). Andocides presents himself as the model citizen who stopped this practice, by outbidding Agyrrhius and his gang and securing the lease for thirty-six talents, still "making a small profit."

Public interest in taxation and money and in schemes to increase the public revenues ran deep. There are hints, however, that many proposals that looked good on paper were decided failures. Indeed, measures concerning taxation and foreign trade as part of fiscal policy were held up to ridicule by Aristophanes in his *Ecclesiazousae*, performed in 393. As an analogy to the absurdity of handing over their property to the state (on order of the women of Athens), one character, the Citizen, recalls other disastrous decrees. He notes the "salt decree," the decree about the copper coinage, and the two and a half-percent tax proposed just recently by Euripides: "weren't we all swearing that it would bring in three million drachmas? And then we looked into it and found out, as usual, that it would not work" (823ff., trans. Sommerstein). That his examples are all economic in nature is especially interesting. To be sure, the special need to raise public revenues was acute following Athens's defeat in the Peloponnesian War, but it suggests a pattern of behavior in crisis that rings true as well for the Peloponnesian War years.

ATHENS ABROAD: THE EMPIRE

The Athenian empire presents an especially instructive case study of the often inseparable interrelationship of the political and the economic. While the ancients emphasized power as a chief goal of conquest, they also recognized that wars were fought for profit (often morally couched in terms of the pursuit of *time*, "honor," which required material expression). More important for our purposes, the Athenians' experiment with *arche*, "rule," was or became a revenue-generating organism whose function and purpose were recognized as such.[25]

Tribute

Best known of imperial revenue is tribute (*phoros*, literally, a "bringing in"). Initially advertised to the allies as essential for the League's naval operations, the Athenians, in their capacity as League treasurers (*Helleno-tamiai*), controlled the moneys. Interestingly, the intake appears to have exceeded military needs – when the League treasury was moved from Delos to Athens in 454, there was evidently an accumulated reserve. Thucydides gives a figure of 460 talents as the total monetary assessment of members at the League's inception in 478;[26] yet the orthodox estimate of the total collected in 454 (when League membership is assumed to have been greater than that in 478) puts it at ca. 400 talents. There are too many unknown variables for a historical reconstruction to explain these developments and figures – e.g., League membership at the outset, changes in the projected League "program," whether there were commonly discrepancies between amounts assessed and what was actually collected, and, insufficiently recognized, whether the orthodox estimate should remain unchallenged.[27] Athens may have enticed prospective members with the expectation of profit (in the form of war spoils) in return for their contributions (including ships); subsequently the League developed into an instrument of Athenian power, paid for by the very peoples whom Athens was subjecting, in a brilliant (from the Athenian standpoint) kind of economic imperialism.

Assessments were calculated on land (area or estimated crop yield), though maritime revenues may have served as a basis in the case of coastal and island communities.[28] Assessments may have been optimistic compared to what was actually collected (a point that applies to the relationship between assessment and collection generally). Indeed members sometimes made partial, late, or no payments, a phenomenon illuminated by the tribute quota lists and other inscriptions concerned with the method of collection that suggests a reactive, forceful (though not necessarily successful) approach to an existing problem.

A twofold trend can be discerned at least by the later fifth century, first that tribute was less effective in producing the revenues required (perhaps only because Athens faced sustained war) and second that the Athenians' focus became even more economic. The most blatant illustration is the decision around 413 to eliminate tribute and substitute a maritime tax, made during a time of acute financial need (during the Sicilian expedition and the Spartan occupation of Attica). This tells us that the Athenians were not receiving the assessed amounts of tribute, or that they needed more in spite of receiving the full complement. Alternatively, perhaps they believed that they could simply reap far more by this means than they could by any other, if only because collection, relying on tax-farming and individual incentive, might be easier than in the case of tribute, and it was a form of revenue less symbolically charged than was tribute by this time.

Other Revenues

As mentioned above, according to Thucydides/Pericles (2.13.3), in 431 Athens regularly received 600 talents of annual imperial revenue, "for the most part consisting of tribute."[29] If the Athenians were collecting ca. 400 talents of tribute, then that leaves ca. 200 talents to account for. Athenian actions early in the Delian League's history show a clear focus on extracting revenues from the Aegean over and above tribute to enhance their own profits. In 476, after capturing the Persian stronghold at Eion at the mouth of the Strymon River in Macedonia, they established an Athenian *emporion* on the site (Thuc. 4.102). Around the same time, the elimination of pirates from the northern Aegean island of Scyros made maritime activity safer for all. Athens's colonization of the island, however, completed a process begun earlier with the capture of Lemnos and Imbros of securing transit points for grain ships. A later observer of the *arche*, Thucydides, in a rationalizing tour de force, saw in the colonization program of the legendary Cretan king Minos a means to eradicate piracy from the Aegean in order to increase his own revenue. The historian provides further evidence of Athens's early interest in maritime trade and profits. Writing of the revolt of the large and important island of Thasos in the mid-460s, he notes that the dispute between the island and Athens arose over *emporia* on the mainland opposite Thasos, as well as over a mine on the island (1.100). The revenue at stake was considerable: according to Herodotus (6.46), Thasian controlled gold and silver mines yielded 200–300 talents annually.

The north Aegean region was especially important to Athens for timber and metals. It sought to strengthen its control of the area by founding Amphipolis in Macedonia at a strategic junction up the Strymon from Eion, finally succeeding (after several attempts) in 437. Our knowledge about the revenues from the colony, mentioned above in connection with its surrender to Brasidas in 424, is especially valuable because the colony was not tributary. It is thus is a precious piece of evidence of evidently sizable revenue besides tribute that came into Athens's coffers.

The religious and economic were intertwined in the empire (as at home). One-sixtieth of the annual tribute (an amount called the *aparche*) was dedicated to Athena, and in her name Athens appropriated allied land, providing sacred rents that went into her treasury. Allies were also required to dedicate a cow and panoply at the Great Panathenaea, and then, sometime during the Peloponnesian War, they were instructed to offer an annual gift of grain to Eleusinian Demeter (nonallies were invited to as well); whatever was not used in the preparation of sacred cakes was sold off. The Athenian (sacred) treasuries benefited.

Likewise, as noted above, the political and the economic were closely aligned throughout the history of the *arche*; punitive measures often took an economic form. The Megarian decree passed sometime in the 430s, in response to Megara's withdrawal from alliance with Athens, provides an explicit example. Athens barred the Megarians from harbors throughout the empire and from the Athenian agora, citing the Megarians' cultivation of sacred land as the ostensible reason (Thuc. 1.67.4, 139.2; Plut. *Per.* 29ff.).[30] That the Athenians had the muscle to enforce the decree and that it had a damaging economic impact is implied by Aristophanes' *Acharnians* (529ff., 729ff.). The play presents the Megarians as slowly starving, subject to inflated grain prices, and unable to purchase salt, the trade that the Athenians controlled. Of course all this could be part of a joke about the decree's ineffectiveness, but the fact that Thucydides has the Megarians complaining to Sparta about the decree, and its role as a chief point of contention between Sparta and Athens in 432, suggests the contrary.

The economic authority exerted by Athens in the empire can appear at times enormous and impressive. The Methone inscription mentioned above implies a closed-sea policy, with restrictions on who can import grain, and with a tax on ships and cargo entering the Aegean from the Black Sea. To the south, by contrast, Athens seems to have successfully marginalized Crete from considerable Aegean trade: imports of Athenian pottery, which appear all over the Aegean and eastern Mediterranean, virtually stop during the Periclean period through the end of the Peloponnesian War; they resume, suggestively, around 400.[31]

Consider also one of the most famous and radical economic/fiscal decisions, that requiring allies to use Athenian silver coinage, weights, and measures (ML 45 = Fornara 97). Its date is uncertain – possibilities proposed range from ca. 450 to ca. 414[32] – but it may be tied to the elimination of tribute and substitution of the *eikoste* in ca. 413, mentioned above, for a concern with uniform metrological standards throughout the empire can best be explained by reference to taxes on trade. If a tax on seaborne traffic were being collected throughout the empire, with the goal of getting as much money to Athens as possible – and, implicitly, as quickly – then uniform standards would facilitate the process. Whenever this intriguing decision is to be placed, it is remarkable and unprecedented for its attempt to create a closed economic system in the Aegean, along with Athens's evident closed-sea policy noted above. Relevant also is the Athenians' interest in the west at the latest by the mid-440s (when a colony at Thurii in southern Italy was founded). They increasingly focused on Sicily, with the twofold goal of preventing the flow of grain to the Peloponnese (according to Thucydides) and enhancing their own economic and financial growth in the Sicilian expedition.

CONCLUSION

The Athenian economy is a slippery entity that resists a single definition or model. Since the late nineteenth century, debate has raged between those who deny the existence of an economic sphere detached from political and social relations in ancient Athens (this is called the primitivist or the substantivist position) and those who regard Athens as having a proto-modern free market economy (the modernist or formalist position). But attempts to force economic activity and behavior in Athens into any "either/or" category always ultimately run aground; evidence for both embedded and detached behavior can be amply adduced, depending on what activities one focuses on (and neither model allows for change).[33] Nor can one quantify and measure important variables, another impediment to definition.

To appreciate the complexity and unique (because of its *arche*) nature of the Athenian economy in the age of Pericles, we must think in terms of economies, keep in mind the coexistence of multiple kinds of economic behavior and practice, and recognize the sometimes blurred lines between a public and private economy (e.g., in the realm of maritime interests).[34] With respect to the public economy that is so striking a feature of fifth-century Athens, the polis exacted direct and indirect revenues from its citizenry, from metics, and from the empire to an unparalleled extent in Greek history. It leased contracts for economic activity such as mining and exacted payments such as court fees and rents. Revenues could be redistributed through pay for public duties, and through expenditure on building projects. Indeed the Athenians, to their allies, doubtless cast the payment of tribute in terms of exchange – money for protection – whereas, to themselves, in terms of security and the extension of power. We can discern the intimate intertwining of the political and the economic (and the military) simultaneous with autonomous economic behavior guided purely by the desire for profit. Moreover, polis and individual were often linked in interests (not surprising given the conception of the polis *as* a collection of individuals). By the fourth century, Xenophon could tie imports, exports, and taxation to the prosperity of both polis and individual, as a kind of investment promoting overall political health through economic growth. But even by the age of Pericles, the city's economic power from its control of the Aegean region (and beyond) was regarded as a source of profit and consumer pleasure for individuals. In fact, the fifth century appears to have been pivotal in the development of economic behavior, both public and private.

SUGGESTIONS FOR FURTHER READING

In addition to the works cited in the notes, J. K. Davies, "Society and Economy," in D. M. Lewis, J. Boardman, J. K. Davies, and M. Ostwald, eds., *The Cambridge Ancient History*, vol. 5, *The Fifth Century B.C.* (Cambridge: Cambridge University Press, 1992), pp. 287–305, is an excellent discussion. A. French, *The Growth of the Athenian Economy*, esp. pp. 107–34 (New York: Barnes & Noble, 1964), although dated, nevertheless is useful for its direct concern (in the pages cited) with the impact of the Athenian empire on the economy. The papers in P. Cartledge, E. E. Cohen, and L. Foxhall, *Money, Labour and Land: Approaches to the Economies of Ancient Greece* (London: Routledge, 2002), while most are not concerned with fifth-century Athens in particular, offer useful perspectives on economic aspects of and in Greek poleis relevant to classical Athens. Among these, the brief preface by G. E. R. Lloyd (pp. xv–xviii) and the Introduction by E. E. Cohen (pp. 1–7) provide valuable methodological discussions.

NOTES

1   At the same time, scholarship on the classical Athenian economy almost invariably focuses on the fourth century B.C., because that is when the evidence, chiefly in the form of forensic oratory, provides the fullest information about economic practices and behaviors. I regret that I am unable to take account of works published since 2002.

2   L. J. Samons, *Empire of the Owl: Athenian Imperial Finance*, Historia Einzelschriften 142 (Stuttgart: Steiner, 2000); see also M. Ostwald, "Public Expense: Whose Obligation? Athens 600–454 B.C.E.," *PAPhS* 139 (1995): 368–79, on the financing of public expenditures chiefly through private means in the period preceding the mid-fifth century.

3   On irregular property taxes imposed on the rich, see below.

4   Wealthy metics spent on liturgies as well. They could not, however, own land; see Patterson, this volume.

5   As E. Harris emphasizes in "Workshop, Marketplace and Household: The Nature of Technical Specialization in Classical Athens and Its Influence on Economy and Society," in P. Cartledge, E. E. Cohen, and L. Foxhall, eds., *Money, Labour and Land: Approaches to the Economies of Ancient Greece* (London: Routledge, 2002), pp. 67–99.

6   Controversy surrounds the issues of nucleated settlements vs. rural farmsteads, the extent of fragmented holdings, the prevalence of wealthy absentee landlords vs. country dwellers, and leasing vs. slave labor. See, e.g., M. Jameson, "Agriculture and Slavery in Classical Athens," *CJ* 73 (1977/78): 122–45; E. M. Wood, *Peasant-Citizen and Slave* (London and New York: Verso, 1988); M. Jameson, "Agricultural Labor in Ancient Greece," in B. Wells, ed., *Agriculture in Ancient Greece* (Stockholm: Swedish Institute of Athens, 1992), pp. 135–46; R. Osborne, *Demos: The Discovery*

of Classical Attika (Cambridge: Cambridge University Press, 1985), and *Classical Landscape with Figures* (Dobbs Ferry, NY: Sheridan House, 1987); S. Isager and J. E. Skydsgaard, *Ancient Greek Agriculture* (London and New York: Routledge, 1992).

7   Tod II.123.35–41 = Harding 35.

8   On the tenuous evidence for mines and their operation in the fifth century, see Samons (n. 2), pp. 202–4.

9   See Harris (n. 5), who counts ca. 170 occupations for the fourth century. The fifth-century figure would doubtless rise significantly if we had the abundance of Old Comedy and inscriptions that existed at the time.

10 For the evidence, see W. T. Loomis, *Wages, Welfare Costs and Inflation in Classical Athens* (Ann Arbor: University of Michigan Press, 1998).

11 For discussions of military pay and the problem of a standard rate, see W. K. Pritchett, *The Greek State at War*, vol. 1 (Berkeley: University of California Press, 1971); Loomis (n. 10).

12 But cf. Samons (n. 2), esp. pp. 73–80, against the view that the reserves brought to Athens were housed in temples. One should note that moneys could be stored in temples while not necessarily dedicated to their particular gods.

13 Most scholars accept the testimony of Plutarch, e.g., L. J. Samons, "Athenian Finance and the Treasury of Athena," *Historia* 42 (1993): 129–38, and (n. 2), p. 156; but cf. L. Kallet-Marx, "Did Tribute Fund the Parthenon?" *CA* 8 (1989): 252–66; A. Giovannini, "Le Parthénon, le tresor d' Athéna et le tribut des alliés," *Historia* 39 (1990): 129–48, and "La participation des alliés au financement du Parthénon: *aparchè* ou tribut?" *Historia* 46 (1997): 145–57.

14 See M. H. Hansen, "Seven Hundred *archai* in Classical Athens," *GRBS* 21 (1980): 151–73.

15 Thus the introduction of the *eisphora* follows the lifetime of Pericles (perhaps not coincidentally), appearing first in 428 (Thuc. 3.19.1), though some scholars have argued that the tax was levied earlier, e.g., R. Thomsen, *Eisphora* (Copenhagen: Gyldendalske Boghandel, 1964), pp. 119–46; J. G. Griffith, "A Note on the First *Eisphora* at Athens," *AJAH* 2 (1977): 3–7; S. Hornblower, *CT* I.404; for 428, see R. Sealey, "The Tetralogies Ascribed to Antiphon," *TAPA* 114 (1984): 71–85; L. Kallet-Marx, *Money, Expense and Naval Power in Thucydides' History 1–5.24* (Berkeley: University of California Press, 1993), pp. 134–5, also with fuller bibliography.

16 Thucydides (6.54.5) refers to a tax of a twentieth, though he calls it "moderate;" cf. Arist. *AP* 16.4 (a tithe on produce). For the general association of tyrants with taxation, see, e.g., Arist. *Pol.* 1313b26–28.

17 E.g., Xen. *Symp.* 4.32. See also L. Kallet, "*Demos Tyrannos*: Wealth, Power and Economic Patronage," in K. Morgan, ed., *Popular Tyranny: Sovereignty and Its Discontents in Classical Athens* (Austin: University of Texas Press, 2003), pp. 117–53.

18 J. Hasebroek, *Trade and Politics in Ancient Greece* (London: G. Bell, 1933); see S. Isager and M. H. Hansen, *Aspects of Athenian Society in the Fourth Century B.C.* (Odense: Odense University Press, 1975); D. Engen, *Athenian Trade Policy, 415–307 B.C.: Honors and Privileges for Trade-Related Services* (Ph.D. dissertation: University of California, Los Angeles, 1996); J. K. Davies, "Ancient Economies: Models and Muddles," in H. Parkinson and C. Smith, eds., *Trade, Traders and the Ancient City* (London: Routledge, 1998), pp. 235–6.

19   See M. Miller, *Athens and Persia in the Fifth Century B.C.* (Cambridge: Cambridge University Press, 1997).

20   There has been a lively controversy over the issue of whether Athens (and other Aegean communities) had a need for imported grain in the fifth century or whether it became essential only in the fourth century. The issue chiefly hinges on population statistics, which are notoriously hard to quantify even for male citizens: fifth-century estimates for this group range from 30,000 to 50,000. See L. Foxhall and H. A. Forbes, "Sitometreia: The Role of Grain as a Staple in the Ancient Greek World," *Chiron* 12 (1982): 41–90; P. D. Garnsey, "Grain for Athens," in P. Cartledge and F. D. Harvey, eds., *Crux: Essays in Greek History Presented to G. E. M. de Ste. Croix* (London: Duckworth, 1985), pp. 62–75, and *Famine and Food Supply in the Graeco-Roman World* (Cambridge: Cambridge University Press, 1988); A. Keen, "'Grain for Athens': Notes on the Importance of the Hellespontine Route in Athenian Foreign Policy before the Peloponnesian War," *Electronic Antiquity* 1 (1993); M. Whitby, "The Athenian Grain Trade in the Fourth Century B.C.," in Parkinson and Smith (n. 18), pp. 102–28.

21   R. Meiggs, *Trees and Timber in the Ancient Mediterranean World* (Oxford: Oxford University Press, 1982), p. 193.

22   See n. 6 above.

23   See D. Gill and M. Vickers, "Reflected Glory: Pottery and Precious Metal in Classical Greece," *JdI* 105 (1990): 1–30; M. Vickers and D. Gill, *Artful Crafts: Ancient Greek Silverware and Pottery* (Oxford: Oxford University Press, 1994); J. Boardman, "Trade in Greek Pottery," *OJA* 7 (1988): 27–33; for the Levant: B. Shefton, "Reflections on the Presence of Attic Pottery at the Eastern End of the Mediterranean during the Persian Period," *Transeuphratène* 19 (2000): 75–81.

24   The date of this reference, from Callias decree A (ML 58 = Fornara 118), is controversial. Candidate years proposed range from 434 to 418; for 434, see B. D. Meritt, H. T. Wade-Gery, M. F. McGregor, eds., *The Athenian Tribute Lists*, vol. 3 (Princeton: The American School of Classical Studies at Athens, 1950), pp. 320, 326–34; 433/2: Samons (n. 2), pp. 114–33; 432/1: L. Kallet-Marx, "The Kallias Decree, Thucydides, and the Outbreak of the Peloponnesian War," *CQ* 39 (1989): 94–113; 422/1: H. B. Mattingly, *The Athenian Empire Restored* (Ann Arbor: University of Michigan Press, 1997), pp. 215–46; 418/7: C. W. Fornara, "The Date of the Callias Decrees," *GRBS* 11 (1970): 185–96.

25   On the economic goal of the *arche*, see L. Kallet, *Money and the Corrosion of Power in Thucydides: The Sicilian Expedition and Its Aftermath* (Berkeley: University of California Press, 2001), pp. 195–217. On imperial revenues and the Athenian treasuries, see Samons (n. 2).

26   Meritt, Wade-Gery, and McGregor, *ATL* III.236–43, argue that the figure of 460 talents included ship contributions as well as money; but this distorts what Thucydides, our source for this information, says. See M. Chambers, "Four Hundred Sixty Talents," *CP* 53 (1958): 26–32; Kallet-Marx (n. 15), pp. 49–52. See also the succinct discussion in R. Meiggs, *The Athenian Empire* (Oxford: Oxford University Press, 1972), pp. 50–67.

27   The editors of *ATL*, the exhaustive publication of the fragments of the tribute quota lists, have to a great extent controlled the kinds of questions asked in connection with tribute, and too often treated many as settled that are fundamentally uncertain, including the arrangement and chronology of many of the fragments of quota lists.

28 For recent discussion of the controversial problem of assessment bases, see, e.g., L. Nixon and S. Price, "The Size and Resources of Greek Cities," in O. Murray, ed., *The Greek City: From Homer to Alexander* (Oxford: Oxford University Press, 1990), pp. 137–70; T. Figueira, *The Power of Money: Coinage and Politics in the Athenian Empire* (Philadelphia: University of Pennsylvania Press, 1998), pp. 298–9, 312–13; Samons (n. 2), pp. 91 n. 37, 182.

29 The phrase is controversial; see Hornblower, *CT* vol. 1, *ad loc.*, for discussion and references.

30 Cf. Lendon, pp. 270–71, 273–4, in this volume.

31 See B. L. Erickson, *Late Archaic and Classical Crete. Island Pottery Styles in an Age of Historical Transition, ca. 600–400 B.C.* (Ph.D. dissertation: University of Texas, Austin, 2000).

32 R. Meiggs and D. Lewis (in ML 45) provide a useful discussion of the early date, for which see also *ATL* III.281; Figueira (n. 28), *passim*. Mattingly (n. 24), pp. 5–52, 403–6, 521, places the decree in the 420s; for ca. 414, Kallet (n. 25), pp. 205–26.

33 On the nature and development of the debate beginning with K. Bücher, E. Meyer, and K. J. Beloch through K. Polanyi and M. I. Finley, see, e.g., E. M. Burke, "The Economy of Athens in the Classical Era: Some Adjustments to the Primitivist Model," *TAPA* 122 (1992): 199–226; Davies (n. 18), pp. 225–56.

34 For a fine statement of the complex economic realities with respect to late classical Olynthus, see N. Cahill, *Household and City Organization at Olynthus* (New Haven: Yale University Press, 2002), pp. 281–2.

4: WARFARE AND ATHENIAN SOCIETY

Kurt A. Raaflaub

I n 432, Sparta and its allies, fearing the growth of Athens's power
and its aggressive policies, decided to go to war. In subsequent
negotiations, the Spartans raised specific demands that, if accepted,
might have avoided war. Urged by Pericles, the Athenians decided not
to negotiate about ultimatums; any disagreements were to be resolved by
arbitration, as envisaged by the Thirty Years' Peace of 446. A few months
later, fighting began. After almost three decades of war, interrupted by
a short period of ineffective peace, Sparta prevailed. In 404, starved and
exhausted, the Athenians capitulated.[1]

Pericles died in 429. Only the outbreak and first two years of this
war were his responsibility. Thucydides explains its catastrophic outcome by the mistakes and rivalries of Pericles' successors. In his view,
Pericles' plan, strategy, and calculations were sound; had the Athenians
followed his advice, they could have won (2.65.8–10).[2] He supports this
judgment by a comprehensive assessment that he lets Pericles formulate
in a speech before the war (1.140–44): Financial reserves and a centralized, unified process of deliberation and decision-making are crucial for
success in war. Both are typical of Athens but not of the enemy. In a
single land battle, the Peloponnesians can take on the rest of Greece, but
they do not have the resources to fight the type of war that is required
to defeat the Athenians. They are farmers, not sailors, used to engaging
in short infantry wars with neighbors but unable to spend much time
away from home and lacking experience in fighting long wars overseas. Using their traditional strategy of invading the enemy's territory,
they will do limited damage to the Attic countryside, but Athens will
retaliate in kind. More importantly, they have no competitive navy and,

lacking the money and manpower needed, cannot hope to build one quickly. Nor is seamanship easily learned: the Athenians themselves, despite decades of experience, have still not entirely mastered it.

Athens's control of seapower and its "insular" position will be decisive in this war.

> Suppose we were an island, would we not be absolutely secure from attack? As it is we must try to think of ourselves as islanders; we must abandon our land and our houses, and safeguard the sea and the city. We must not, through anger at losing land and homes, join battle with the greatly superior forces of the Peloponnesians. . . . What we should lament is not the loss of houses or of land, but the loss of men's lives.
>
> (1.143.5; cf. 2.62.2–3)

Overall, Pericles concludes, if the Athenians stick to their war plan, maintain discipline, and do not overextend themselves, they will win (see below).

Some of these thoughts are arguably based on Thucydides' own hindsight, anticipating later developments. Still, and despite ongoing debate about the authenticity of Thucydides' speeches, it is reasonable to attribute the gist of the argument to Pericles himself. This raises a number of questions. What was Pericles' strategy? Why was he certain that Athens could and would win this war? What were the resources and the "military culture" he could rely upon? Asked more broadly: what had brought Athens to such a height of power and self-confidence that its leader could predict victory in a war with Sparta – the polis that had enjoyed military pre-eminence and leadership in Greece for more than a century? Why was Pericles able to convince his fellow citizens to accept his "hawkish" policies? How did they think about war and experience war? Even if women and children, resident aliens (metics), and slaves had no say in politics, how were they affected by the momentous decision they were witnessing? How, finally, was Athens as a community prepared to cope with the war and the losses or gains to be expected?

With such questions I am throwing my net widely. As far as possible, I will look at the relevant issues from the perspective of the people of Athens: mostly the citizens and their families, but also the noncitizens. This perspective has too often been neglected.[3] Then as today, war was utterly brutal and wasteful, destroying the defeated and dehumanizing the victors. Throughout history, admiration for great and memorable deeds has tended to obscure the suffering caused by them. Like Homer, we should be respectful of both.

The sources we rely upon to answer our questions are both informative and limited. Thucydides, though rich on political and military developments, does not usually describe matters familiar to his readers, including the social, economic, or religious background or impact of war.[4] Inscriptions add incidental evidence, for example, on casualty figures or the financial management of the war. So do later authors, though often using distorted sources of dubious reliability. Both comedy and tragedy are surprisingly helpful, throwing light on aspects not covered elsewhere (such as the leaders' corruption, the demos's pride in their power, or the suffering of the victims of war). Especially on generic issues, that is, aspects not tied specifically to conditions prevailing in the Age of Pericles, we will need to use evidence not directly related to events of this period. Even so, the picture will inevitably remain spotty.

ATHENS'S RESOURCES

By any criterion, Athens was an exceptionally large polis. Sparta's territory was even larger, but in citizen numbers Athens had a great advantage: at its height, it counted 40–50,000, Sparta perhaps 7,000 or fewer. Sparta, however, counted as full citizens (Spartiates) only those who qualified for the heavily armed infantry army (the hoplites); in war, these were supplemented by noncitizen contingents, consisting of *perioikoi* (inhabitants of semiautonomous settlements controlled by Sparta) and even slaves (helots, sometimes freed in advance, sometimes not).[5] Athens did not make full citizenship dependent on property or military qualifications. Thousands of lower class citizens (thetes) who did not qualify for hoplite service helped row the fleet. Hence an anonymous critic of democracy observes, "It is right that [in Athens] the poor and the ordinary people should have more power than the noble and the rich, because it is the ordinary people who man the fleet and bring the city her power" (Ps.-Xen. *AP* 1.2). Metics served as both hoplites and rowers. Additional crews for the ships were hired among mercenaries and slaves. Most likely, the proportion of citizens was initially high and declined somewhat over time. Presumably many rowers worked in the shipyards in the Piraeus in the off season.[6]

We are reasonably well informed about only two figures. First, the full complement for one trireme was 200 men, including officers and *epibatai* (hoplites who fought on deck); hence a fleet of 100 triremes required up to 20,000 men. For comparison, 9,000 Athenian and a few hundred Plataean hoplites defeated the Persians at Marathon. In 431 Athens had 300 battle-ready ships (Thuc. 2.13.8). The manpower needs of the fleet were thus horrendous.[7] Second, when discussing Athenian resources, Thucydides lists the total of hoplites: They "had 13,000 hoplites in addition to the 16,000 others who were in various garrisons and those engaged in the actual defense of the city. This ... force was drawn from the eldest and the youngest of the citizens in the army together with the resident aliens who were qualified as hoplites" (2.13.6–7). These categories are unclear, the figures much debated. Mogens Hansen concludes reasonably that ca. "15,000 hoplites aged 20–49 in the field army correspond to ca. 18,000 hoplites of military age (19–59) and accordingly there will have been some 32,000 thetes to man the fleet, to serve as light armed troops in the field and to assist in defending the walls."[8] In addition, Thucydides (2.13.8) lists 1,200 cavalry, including mounted archers (citizens, except for the latter) and 1,600 regular archers (mercenaries).

All these soldiers were paid for their service (this was obvious for mercenaries but an innovation for citizens and metics, made imperative by the length of naval campaigns). The community's financial needs, particularly in extended warfare, were astronomical. It cost roughly one talent to build a trireme and between one half and one talent to pay the crew for a month (1 talent = 6,000 drachmas or 6,000 mandays at 1 dr. per day).[9] A three-month campaign with 150 ships would thus have cost 225–450 talents. According to Thucydides (1.96.2), the total assessed tribute of the Delian League in the first year amounted to 460 talents; 1,400 talents were spent on the campaign to crush the rebellion of Samos in 441–439, that is, more than the 1,200 or 1,300 for the Parthenon, including Athena's gold-ivory statue.[10] As Thucydides lets Pericles point out, "victory in war depended on a combination of intelligent resolution and financial resources" (2.13.2).

Financial planning and management thus assumed unprecedented importance. On financial resources, Pericles gives the following details: "apart from all other sources of revenue," 600 talents of average yearly tribute from the empire; a reserve on the Acropolis of 6,000 talents of coined silver (reduced from a maximum of 9,700 talents by expenses for buildings on the Acropolis and the siege of Potidaea); uncoined gold and silver in offerings by individuals or the state, the sacred vessels and furniture used in processions and games, the spoils taken from the

Persians, and other resources of various kinds, totaling no less than 500 talents; money in other temples, and, as a last resort, the gold on Athena's statue, weighing forty talents (2.13.3–5). Total revenue from "other sources" amounted to at least several hundred talents. In addition, wealthy citizens contributed by assuming the special obligation ("liturgy") of outfitting a trireme ("trierarchy"). A special tax (*eisphora*) was levied only in emergencies. Such figures appear impressively big, but a few years of intensive campaigning sufficed to empty the barrel and cause financial problems – especially since a substantial part of the revenues was expended for other (not least political and cultural) purposes. Shortages and the need to resort to an *eisphora* occurred already in 428 and grew more severe later in the Archidamian War. All this suggests that Pericles was not anticipating an extended war.[11]

Clearly by far the largest source of income, through tribute and other revenues, was the empire. It was indispensable in other ways too. Apart from the personal profits that many Athenians drew from it, it supplied most of the mercenaries. A few poleis, especially Lesbos and Chios, still maintained substantial navies, and allies outside the empire (for example, Corcyra) contributed naval contingents as well. Moreover, the cities of the empire, largely located along the coasts of the Aegean, provided shelter and supply bases for the Athenian fleet and thus allowed it to move freely and rapidly throughout the entire area it controlled. This was especially important because the triremes, highly specialized warships, were unable to store more than a minimum of food and other supplies.[12] Hence, once they moved out of their power sphere, the Athenians needed either to take along transporters or to find supplies in unfriendly territory. But this was not Pericles' concern in 432.

We may not feel as optimistic about Athens's resources as Thucydides makes Pericles sound. Yet we must avoid thinking from hindsight. At the time, and with a specific strategy and type of war in mind, Athens must have seemed extraordinarily well prepared and resourceful. No Greek polis had ever amassed such huge reserves, was so firmly in control of a large area with immense resources, had so much experience in war, and could rely on such a large, committed, dynamic, and politically active citizen body. This is echoed, for example, in the superlatives Thucydides uses repeatedly to describe Athens as the "greatest, most self-sufficient, and freest of all cities," probably reflecting an "ideology of power and freedom" that was developed at that very time. It is confirmed by Pericles' unusual belief that it was possible to calculate with almost unfailing certainty the risks and outcome of a complex war and by the extraordinary collective character portrait Thucydides lets the Corinthians draw of the Athenians (1.70).[13]

What Pericles could not foresee, of course, was the plague that soon began to ravage Athens, overcrowded as it was by tens of thousands of evacuees from rural Attica (Thuc. 2.48–54). Even so, Thucydides insists, and despite all the mistakes of later politicians, the Sicilian disaster, mass revolts of allies, and Persian as well as Sicilian support for the enemy, the Athenians could have won the war if they had not "destroyed themselves by their own internal strife. . . . So overwhelmingly great were the resources which Pericles had in mind at the time when he prophesied an easy victory for Athens over the Peloponnesians alone" (2.65.12–13).

PERICLES' STRATEGY

Resources alone were not sufficient. What, then, was Pericles' strategy to secure that victory? Thucydides offers several clues. In his first speech, Pericles warns the Athenians "not to add to the empire while the war is in progress," and to avoid involving themselves in new perils. "What I fear is not the enemy's strategy, but our own mistakes" (1.144.1; cf. 2.65.7). Elsewhere, Pericles announces his plan to retaliate with naval expeditions for Peloponnesian devastation of Attica (1.142.2–5), to avoid engaging the Spartans in land battles even for the defense of Attica, to evacuate the country population into the city, and to keep the allies under firm control (2.13.2). Pericles' intention thus was to fight a defensive war without taking risks. Sparta's superior land army was to be deprived of any chance to achieve a decisive victory. The population of Attica, protected by the fortifications of the city and the Piraeus, was to be supplied from the sea, which was controlled by Athens's navy. Unable to defeat Athens and to fight an extended war, Sparta would thus be forced to come to an agreement. Athens did not need to defeat Sparta in the field. Since Sparta had been the aggressor, a draw formally acknowledging the status quo was equivalent to an Athenian victory. This is essentially what was accomplished by the Peace of Nicias. Pericles or any prudent leader, Thucydides implies, would have accepted Sparta's peace offers after Athens's successes at Pylos and Sphacteria in 425.[14]

This may seem to us unsatisfactory, but it was a sound strategy that might have worked, especially if the Athenians had succeeded in doing some serious damage to the Peloponnesian countryside. It was also a highly remarkable strategy because it turned the conventional ideology of war among Greek poleis on its head. Typically, when an army invaded a polis's territory and threatened to destroy farms and crops, the defenders were supposed (and forced) to face the aggressors in open battle or to seek an agreement.[15] The keys to the success of Pericles' strategy were fortifications, control of the sea, and discipline. The last was the crux. For the first two the Athenians had prepared themselves over many decades. It is time, therefore, to examine the evolution of the Athenian military.

MILITARY DEVELOPMENTS TO THE MID-FIFTH CENTURY

In the great wars against the Persians, the Athenians had played a crucial role. At Marathon their hoplites defeated an army invading by the sea. In 480 and 479, their ships formed by far the largest contingent of the allied Greek navy that held off the Persian fleet at Artemision, overwhelmed it at Salamis, and with its marines crushed it at Mycale, while 8,000 Athenian hoplites contributed decisively to destroying the last Persian army at Plataea. In the winter of 478/7 disagreements prompted the withdrawal of the Peloponnesians from allied campaigns and the formation of a new alliance (called the "Delian League") under Athenian leadership. From then on, the Athenians were involved almost incessantly (on average in two out of three years) in military actions, involving substantial naval and/or hoplite forces, that were directed against Persians, rival Greeks, and rebellious allies, and took place on the Greek mainland, in the Aegean, around Cyprus, and even in Egypt.[16]

Such constant and intense military activity was unprecedented among Greeks, a result of the introduction of naval warfare on a large scale in the confrontation between Greeks and Persians, and of Athens's imperial policies. In the archaic period, when hoplite warfare predominated, wars had been intermittent, short, and usually decided in one battle. Naval campaigns were different. In fact, naval warfare changed the entire face of war.

Although the trireme supposedly was invented in the seventh century, few poleis could afford this expensive and highly specialized weapon. The battle at Lade at the end of the Ionian revolt against Persia (500–494) was the first securely attested naval battle in which large numbers of triremes were involved.[17] A few years later, the Athenians made a particularly rich strike in the silver mines at Laurium. Involved in an ongoing rivalry with neighboring Aegina and aware of the impending threat of a large-scale Persian invasion, they decided to invest this wealth in a large fleet – thus changing the course of history. In a second, equally momentous decision, they opted in 478/7 for continuing the war against Persia with their own allies. Without this turn of events, naval warfare based on large fleets of triremes might have remained an exception. Now it became permanent. The navy, as Athens's main weapon, served not only to realize the purposes of the Delian League, but also to increase and solidify Athens's control over the allies who soon found themselves subjects in a tightly controlled empire. The league provided most of the resources required to operate this fleet. The availability of such resources was an indispensable condition for the formation of an empire. Only a handful of other ancient city-states (Carthage and Rome among them) were in a position to achieve the same goal.[18]

Naval warfare often lasted weeks, sometimes months, or even years. It was carried out over long distances. In principle, it could reach any corner in Athens's sphere of influence and far beyond, as the Egyptian campaign of the 450s demonstrates. Ships could be used to transport troops and equipment. Hence naval operations often supported sieges, and the Athenians soon became the foremost experts of siege warfare – although, compared with later centuries, siege technology was primitive and the best way of reducing a city was to blockade and starve it into submission. Given the enormous financial and manpower needs involved, only a power with similar resources could even hope to compete with Athens. Moreover, crews needed to be trained: the intricate and coordinated movements to outmaneuver the opponents, circle around them, sheer off their oars, or ram them in order to enable the *epibatai* to storm them required intensive exercise. This was a task the Athenians never considered complete, although they constantly had a small fleet at sea for precisely this purpose.[19] The lack of experience among other Greeks is illustrated by the first battle between Corcyra and Corinth in 432, which, according to Thucydides (1.49.1–3), was "of a somewhat old-fashioned kind," fought more like a land than a sea battle.

Great quantities of lumber, leather, metal, and other raw materials, large shipyards, and thousands of workers were needed to build and maintain the ships, and extensive harbor facilities with suitable ship sheds to keep them safe and dry during the winter. Most of the materials were not available in Attica. They needed to be procured by trade agreements or force – for which the navy again was indispensable.[20]

Except for emergencies, citizens qualifying as hoplites or horsemen served on ships only as *epibatai* or officers. Hoplites provided their own equipment and were mostly independent farmers. They fought in a specific formation, the "hoplite phalanx" (below), that had evolved in the Archaic Age to suit wars typical among poleis: neighborhood conflicts about booty and the control of land, farmers fighting on their land for their land. When and how exactly the phalanx emerged and how long it predominated is much debated.[21]

The Athenian hoplites had their glory days in the Persian Wars. The "fighters of Marathon" (*marathonomachai*) were still celebrated fifty years later in Aristophanes' comedies, representing the traditional values of upright citizens. Their role in war, though reduced by increasing reliance on the navy, remained significant.[22] In the double battle at the Eurymedon in the early 460s and during the 450s, when Athens gained control over much of central Greece, they won crucial victories – but soon lost their gains in bitter setbacks. Even during the Peloponnesian War they were involved in several important land battles – with a rather poor record. Many naval operations too were decided by combined fighting rather than pure sea battles.

Even in hoplite battles light-armed troops perhaps played a more important role than has often been assumed, though in a rather unorganized way. As highly mobile slingers, archers, and javelin throwers, they tried to disturb the enemy ranks before the battle even began, and they were useful in the pursuit of the defeated. Well into the Peloponnesian War, however, Athens did not have an organized light-armed corps. At the battle of Delium in 424/3, Thucydides notes, "there were no properly armed light troops present on this occasion, nor did Athens possess any" (4.94). Their significance increased rapidly in the course of the war, in which several campaigns were marked by unconventional modes of fighting (such as surprise and night attacks).[23]

Owning a horse and enough land to maintain it, and being able to use a horse in war, had been a distinguishing trait of early Greek aristocracies. In Athens members of the property class above the hoplites were called *hippeis* (horsemen). Even so, most of them apparently used their horses to ride into battle rather than fighting on them. Athens established an organized cavalry corps consisting of elite Athenians only in the mid-fifth century; it is proudly represented in the Parthenon Frieze. Opportunities to prove their value came in the early years of the Peloponnesian War, when they harassed the Peloponnesians who ravaged the Attic countryside, and crucially in the war's last decade, when Sparta permanently occupied a fort in Attica.[24]

Finally, the fortifications. Athens lay inland, several miles from the sea. In 493 its main harbor had been moved from the open bay of Phaleron to the Piraeus with three well-protected harbors. After the Persian Wars both the city and the Piraeus were fortified. In the 450s the city, Piraeus, and Phaleron were connected by the Long Walls; a few years later, a third (middle) leg from the city to Piraeus was added.[25] These fortifications, defended by the home guard mentioned in Thuc. 2.13.7, protected the fleet and the vital shipyards, as well as the tens of thousands of citizens and metics who lived in the Piraeus and Athens. They offered shelter to the population of Attica in times of enemy invasions and guaranteed that food supplies would reach Athens safely from its harbor. They were completed when Athens was involved in the "First Peloponnesian War" (ca. 460–446/5). It is possible, therefore, that Pericles' strategy, to sacrifice the Attic countryside and fight a war entirely by means of the fleet from the fortress "island" Athens/Piraeus, was developed much earlier.

All this explains Pericles' optimism in 432. Athens was as well prepared for the impending war as it could be. His policies were accepted by a majority of citizens. They must have shared his assessment of resources and risks. Was this enough to make them support Pericles? How did the Athenians experience war and think of it?

THE SOLDIERS' EXPERIENCE OF WAR

Although information on this topic is deplorably scarce, some insight can be gained from scattered references. In the late fourth century, the education of young men (*epheboi*) for their functions as citizens and soldiers was fully regulated: they spent one year in "basic training" and guard duties in the harbor, the second year patrolling the borders of Attica (Arist. *AP* 42). Some elements of this system originated much earlier, and some form of *ephebeia* probably existed already in the fifth century, but we know virtually nothing about it. Nor do we know much about how the hoplites prepared for war once they reached adulthood. The Spartans, freed by their labor force of slaves (helots) from daily work, were professional warriors, spending much time in training. The Athenians were proud of avoiding such a strict regimen. They too must have practiced, but how exactly and how often they did this is unclear and debated.[26] Only hoplites and horsemen were liable to serve; except for emergencies, service in the fleet apparently was voluntary. Registers of those meeting the hoplite census were perhaps kept in the local districts (demes). Lists were compiled of those who were called up for an impending campaign and posted in the Agora, at the monument of the "eponymous heroes."[27]

On the day indicated, the soldiers, streaming into Athens from all areas of Attica, assembled in the Agora by tribal regiments. The northwest corner of the Agora was crowded with monuments celebrating Athenian victories. For example, the "Painted Stoa," erected by Cimon probably in the 460s, was decorated with four great paintings of mythical and historical Athenian victories, including that of Marathon. It also eventually displayed as trophies some shields taken from the Spartans at Pylos in 425/4. During the festival of Athena (the Panathenaea), competitions that included military events were held in the Agora. At other occasions, the war dance (*purrhiche*) was performed here. The Agora thus was the center of civic activity both in the political and in the military sense.[28]

Before leaving town for war, the army offered sacrifices to heroized maidens called Hyakinthides. According to myth, the daughters of Erechtheus, Athens's first king, had sacrificed themselves to secure their community's victory. Hence offerings at their shrine were supposed to guarantee victory in battle. All campaigning of the year ultimately ended with the solemn rituals of the state burial of the war dead (below). Great victories (especially those over the Persians) were celebrated annually. The battle too was framed by sacrifices, the taking of omens, and libations; the site of victory was marked by an improvised monument (*tropaion*), a thank offering to the gods composed of collected arms and armor, and usually a tenth of the spoils was dedicated to the gods.[29]

On the battlefield the army arranged itself in the tight phalanx formation, hundreds of men wide and eight or more rows deep. Its purpose was to maintain its order, to wear out the enemy through furious fighting among the front lines, and then to close the ranks even more tightly and break the opposing line in a shoving match. Once one side caved in, the battle was over. The losers ran for their lives; the victors pursued them and then erected the *tropaion*. Losses were often heavy among the defeated, relatively light among the winners.[30]

By the Peloponnesian War, changes in equipment had increased the hoplites' mobility, and light-armed troops as well as cavalry played in increasingly important role.[31] Thucydides' description of the first encounter between Syracusans and the invading Athenian army in 415 offers an impression of such a battle.

First the stone-throwers, slingers, and archers on both sides engaged each other in front of the main lines of battle.... The soothsayers brought forward the usual victims for sacrifice and trumpeters sounded the charge to the hoplites.... The armies now came to close quarters, and for some time no ground was yielded on either side.... It was the Argives who first forced the Syracusan left wing back, and then the Athenians broke through the troops in front of them. The Syracusan army was now cut in two and took to flight. The Athenians did not pursue them far, prevented by the numbers of still undefeated Syracusan cavalry.... They collected their dead, put them on a pyre, and camped there for the night. Next day they gave the Syracusans back their dead under an armistice ..., collected the bones of their own dead ..., and, taking with them the arms which they had stripped from the enemy, sailed back.

(6.69–71)

Whenever possible, the bones of the fallen would be brought back to Athens to be buried in the public cemetery.

As in all premodern wars, these battles were decided in hand-to-hand combat between men who tried to kill their opponent lest they be killed themselves. The fierceness and ugliness of such fighting and the sheer courage required to hold one's place in the battle line defy imagination. Homer's *Iliad* offers vivid illustrations.[32] In describing how Achilles reacts to the death of his best friend, Patroclus, avenges it by mutilating the body of Hector, and goes berserk when returning to battle, this epic also grasps the psychological impact of war on the fighters – a phenomenon well known from recent wars but hardly noticed otherwise by ancient sources.[33] The wounded would be cared for as well as possible and brought back home: war invalids must have been a frequent sight in Athens's streets. Captives were killed on the spot or taken back to be ransomed or sold into slavery. If the victory offered an opportunity for looting, the gods, the community, and the leaders received privileged shares; the rest was distributed among the soldiers.[34]

It is easy to imagine the joyous reception at home of a victorious army. The news of a defeat was a different matter. "It was at night that the Paralus [the messenger ship] arrived at Athens. As the news of the disaster was told, one man passed it on to another and a sound of wailing arose and extended first from Piraeus, then along the Long Walls until it reached the city. That night no one slept" (Xen. *Hell.* 2.2.3).

No campaign could begin, of course, before it had been talked over and approved by the assembly. Hence we should take a brief look at some political aspects of war.

POLITICS OF WAR

Proposals on military matters, like all other issues in Athens, were discussed first by the democratic council of 500.[35] Often its motions were amended or new ones proposed in the course of debate in the assembly. A famous example is the decision, taking up his boastful claims, to put Cleon himself in charge of the campaign at Pylos in 425 (Thuc. 4.27–8). Indeed, many of those who voted upon a specific proposal for military action were going to be among the soldiers fighting to realize it in the field. Most of them had served in several campaigns on land or sea and thus were thoroughly familiar not only with the technical, logistic, and tactical issues, but also with the empire and thus with much of the "territory" in which such actions were going to take place. Despite frequent criticism of the assembly's incompetence, the Athenians must have brought to most decisions on military matters a level of personal experience matched by few modern societies.

Given the long history of collaboration, rivalry, and warfare between Athens and the Peloponnesians, there were probably few unknown factors even in the assembly's debate in 432 about the impending war. Both sides were thoroughly familiar with the other's policies, habits, modes of fighting, resources, strengths, and weaknesses.[36] This too must have contributed to Pericles' confidence in choosing a winning strategy and predicting the outcome. Things were different when a campaign was to be led into less familiar territory, such as, in Pericles' early years as a statesman, the large naval expedition to Egypt or, long after his death, that to Sicily. In the latter case, Thucydides emphasizes, perhaps more than the facts warranted it, how woefully uninformed the Athenians were about the land and the peoples they were hoping to conquer, and how this made them vulnerable to deception, false predictions, and exaggerated expectations.[37]

Yet public discussion about war (or peace) had serious disadvantages too. For example, it jeopardized secrecy, the lack of which could hurt both military plans and diplomatic negotiations. In 428/7, news of the impending departure of an Athenian expedition reached the rebel

Mytilenians "through a man who crossed over from Athens to Euboea, went on foot to Geraestus, found a merchant ship on the point of sailing, and got by sea to Mytilene on the third day after he had left Athens" (Thuc. 3.3). This enabled the Mytilenians to reinforce their fortifications and harbor and prepare for the attack. In 425 a promising peace offer of Sparta was withdrawn because Cleon insisted on public discussion of the terms (Thuc. 4.22).[38]

In the Greek polis issues of foreign policy and war provided the bulk of political contention. Especially in Athens, the assembly decided on all matters, large and small, and the competition among ambitious leaders caused a close watch to be maintained on every issue and every campaign. It was here that distinction could be gained, and here fierce political battles were fought. A great reputation for leadership depended on success in action and victory, not on caution and peace. Hence in the Age of Pericles proposals for activist and aggressive policies usually had a better chance; experience and expertise easily lost out to emotional frenzy, and the hawks tended to prevail – often enough to the detriment of the community.

This problem, as critics pointed out, was aggravated because the demos made the decisions but did not accept responsibility for them. In a debate in 427 about the fate of the defeated Mytilenians, Thucydides lets one speaker elaborate upon this point. In order to win support for their proposals, he says, politicians are forced to speak against their better knowledge and to flatter the people. Even a politician with good intentions has "to tell lies if he expects to be believed." Yet

> we who give you our advice ought to be resolved to look rather further into things than you whose attention is occupied only with the surface – especially as we can be held to account for the advice we give, while you are not accountable for the way in which you receive it. For indeed you would take rather more care over your decisions, if the proposer of a motion and those who voted for it were all subject to the same penalties.
>
> (3.43)

Indeed, when the news of the Sicilian disaster reached Athens in 413, "for a long time people would not believe it.... And when they did recognize the facts, they turned against the public speakers who had been in favor of the expedition, as though they themselves had not voted for it" (8.1.1).

The assembly was entitled to honor meritorious citizens. Herodotus mentions debates among the allies after Persian War battles about who had been "the best" soldier or general. Themistocles supposedly won such a competition because all other leaders placed him second after themselves (Hdt. 8.123). In democratic Athens such honors were not bestowed upon individual fighters. Monuments erected in the Agora for victories in the Persian Wars or at Eion in Thrace (in 476/5), celebrated the Athenians' collective achievements without even mentioning the generals.[39] Except for the Tyrannicides, Harmodius and Aristogeiton, no individuals were honored with statues in the Agora before the early fourth century.

TOTAL WAR

Greek conventions of war were simple. The victors had the right to dispose of the defeated in any way they wanted. For most of the archaic period, wars were fought among neighboring communities for booty, control of fertile land, and honor. Until the mid-fifth century, wars rarely affected the survival of the defeated community. It is a black mark on the Athenian honor sheet that, under the pressure of their long and bitter war with Sparta, they reintroduced into warfare among Greeks the "Homeric" custom of destroying conquered cities and enslaving their populations. Thucydides set a monument for all these victims in his "Melian Dialogue" (5.84–113), highlighting the fate of the tiny island of Melos, which refused in 416/5 to "give up in a short moment the liberty which our city has enjoyed from its foundation for 700 years" (5.112). The Melians resisted bravely but eventually "surrendered unconditionally to the Athenians, who put to death all the men of military age whom they took, and sold the women and children as slaves. Melos itself they took over for themselves, sending out later a colony of 500 men" (5.116). Mytilene, one of Athens's oldest allies, barely escaped the same fate in 427 (Thuc. 3.36, 49–50). Others did not.[40] When the Athenians were about to lose the war, Xenophon writes, "they could see no future for themselves except to suffer what they had made others suffer, people of small states whom they had injured not in retaliation for anything they had done but out of the arrogance of power" (*Hell.* 2.2.10).

All this happened after Pericles' time. Yet under his leadership, Aegina fared no better. Forced into the Athenian alliance in 457, this neighbor and long-standing rival in 432 complained to Sparta that

Athens was not respecting its autonomy as guaranteed in the Thirty Years' Peace. In the war's first summer, "the Athenians expelled the Aeginetans with their wives and children . . . , accusing them of having been largely responsible for the war," and occupied the island themselves. The exiles were partly settled on Spartan territory (and almost wiped out a few years later), partly "scattered about throughout the rest of Hellas" (Thuc. 2.27). A few survivors eventually returned after the war.

For decades, Athens also enslaved rebellious allies, not literally but politically. After their defeat, every citizen had to swear an elaborate oath of allegiance to Athens that ended with the words "I shall obey the People of the Athenians" – an unmistakable indication of their servitude.[41] The measures the Athenians enacted to control these poleis clearly violated their constitutional and legal autonomy. Many of these measures were eventually extended even to those allies who had not revolted. As a result, most members of the Delian League, despite initial autonomy and equality, became subjects to Athenian rule in a far-flung and well-organized empire.[42] Thucydides (3.1–14, 36–50) used the occasion of Mytilene's revolt to illustrate in detail both the allies' complaints and Athenian discussions about the principles that were to guide their reaction to such revolts.

As these examples show, the Peloponnesian War was an ancient equivalent of a "total war," fought with every means available, affecting virtually the entire Greek world, depriving most communities even of the possibility of remaining neutral, displacing tens of thousands of persons, and causing untold miseries. Its after-effects, visible not least in armies of refugees and hordes of unemployed mercenaries, plagued the Greek world for decades to come.[43]

How did the Athenians themselves react to all this? The tragedies of Aeschylus and the early plays of Sophocles offer insight into how independently and critically Athenian intellectuals dealt with the issues of Athenian imperialism.[44] Strong reactions to problems connected with war are visible only much later, during the Peloponnesian War, for example, in Aristophanes' peace plays (*Acharnians*, *Peace*, and especially *Lysistrata*). In *Suppliant Women*, *Andromache*, *Hecuba*, and *Trojan Women*, Euripides raises doubts about the justification of wars and the motives of the political leaders promoting wars. He questions the glory and benefits accruing to the victors and demonstrates that they too lose out by paying a price that is far too high. He dramatizes the plight of the victims of war and focuses on the dehumanizing impact of war on those fighting it.[45]

ATHENS'S CIVIC IDEOLOGY

Other sources tell us much about how the Athenians as a community dealt with war in Pericles' time. From the late sixth century, the Acropolis housed monuments and dedications celebrating Athenian successes and commemorating outstanding citizens. After the Persian Wars, honorary monuments sprang up in the Agora as well. Beginning in the 440s, under Pericles' leadership a massive building program was realized on the Acropolis, culminating in the Parthenon with its statue of Athena, the virgin warrior goddess – an expression of gratitude to the goddess and a monument to Athens's imperial might.[46] Wherever the Athenians went in their harbor and in the public spaces of their city, buildings and monuments reminded them of the glorious past and the power of their community. The same message was impressed upon them in political events and festivals and often also in the theater. Through constant involvement in war, through a unique series of victories and successes, and through unique dedication and sacrifice on the part of the citizens, their city had achieved unique power and greatness. They were now called to live up to the example set by their ancestors. All this conditioned the Athenians from early on to accept war as inevitable and even desirable. The epigrams on the Eion memorial near the Painted Stoa made this explicit:

> Those who come after may read and from this memorial take courage, and in their country's cause march no less bravely to war.
>
> (Plut. *Cim.* 7)

Similarly, at the state funeral of the first year's war dead (below), Thucydides' Pericles reminds his audience of their ancestors' virtue that preserved their country's freedom (against the Persians), of their fathers' efforts that acquired the empire, and of the present generation's achievement that increased the empire and made Athens self-sufficient both in war and in peace (2.36).[47]

Every four years, at the Great Panathenaea, Athena received a panoply (the hoplite's equipment) from each of the cities of the empire. A hoplite race and several equestrian events underscored the martial nature of her festival. At the opening ceremony of the Great Dionysia, the ten generals offered libations; the war orphans who had reached adulthood were announced with their own and their fathers' names, equipped with shield and spear, and dismissed from state care; and the tribute of the empire was displayed in the orchestra.[48] Most importantly, the community appropriated the commemoration and burial of the war dead. An impressive ceremony took place every year after the end of the campaigning season. The bones of the fallen were displayed; families made their offerings and mourned their relatives; in a solemn procession coffins, each containing the bones of one tribe, were brought to the public burial-place and buried there; one empty bier was "decorated and carried in the procession: for the missing, whose bodies could not be recovered" (Thuc. 2.34).

This public cemetery lined the street in front of the Dipylon Gate. Inscribed with an epigram that honored the dead and with their names, arranged by tribes, the tombs formed a panorama of civic virtue. Since competitions were part of the state funeral, it is likely that the Athenian war dead were honored as heroes. In their praise, a distinguished citizen gave a speech. The funeral oration soon became a particular genre of patriotic oratory, recounting in great detail the ancestors' martial glory and the achievement of those to be buried who had sacrificed themselves for their community. Shared pride in communal glory helped overcome grief and loss and prepared the citizens for further ordeals.[49] Examples survive from the fourth century.

Thucydides uses the opportunity of Pericles' Funeral Oration in 431 to convey his understanding of the civic ideology promoted by Pericles' democracy. He focuses on the spirit, way of life, and institutions that make martial accomplishment and imperial greatness possible (2.36.1–4). The collective character portrait he draws of the Athenians complements that sketched earlier by the Corinthians, who focused on their restless "activism" (*polupragmosune*, 1.70–71). Here, Pericles emphasizes the citizens' total dedication to the common good. In dying, they have proved their civic excellence (*arete*) and acted like lovers (*erastai*) of their polis, subordinating their self-interest to its needs and demands and thereby overcoming whatever limitations they may have had individually. The common goal, worthy of receiving the highest priority in each citizen's life, is to contribute to the community's greatness, glory, and power (2.43; cf. 60).

All this helps us understand why the Athenians of Pericles' age committed themselves over such a long time to a policy of aggressive imperialism. A reaction is visible only much later in the war, when the Sicilian disaster, the defection of many allies, a string of Spartan successes, and Persian support for the enemy had greatly reduced the prospects of victory in this war. On the intellectual level, such reactions are echoed in Aristophanes' *Lysistrata*. On the political level they resulted in the oligarchic coup of 411. Neither is our concern here. But we need to consider the question of losses and hardships, for it must have influenced the Athenians' thoughts about war.

LOSSES AND GAINS

The destruction of the Attic countryside by invading Peloponnesian armies clearly upset the Athenians; it had the desired psychological effect, although its long-term economic impact is debated.[50] As Pericles had emphasized, material assets could be replaced but human life was most precious. Despite their naval skills, the Athenians were not immune to the heavy losses inevitably caused even among the victors by naval warfare. Some information survives about Athenian casualty figures. A stele from the *demosion sema* preserves the record of one of the ten tribes in 460 or 459: "Of Erechtheis these died in the war, in Cyprus, in Egypt, in Phoenicia, at Halieis, on Aegina, at Megara, in the same year." The list comprises around 180 names, corresponding roughly to 3.5–4.5 percent of the tribe's men in fighting age. This was perhaps exceptional but hardly unique. In Pericles' early years, 8,000 citizens or more (perhaps one out of five or six adult men!) are estimated to have perished in Egypt. Total losses in the Peloponnesian War may have amounted to 20,000.[51] The majority of the victims were lower class citizens who could probably not rely on an extended support network such as was typical of farming populations. Their deaths must have caused great hardship to their families. What did the community do about it?

In the Funeral Oration, Pericles says that the children of those buried "will be supported at the public expense by the city, until they come of age. This is the crown and prize which she offers, both to the dead and to their children, for the ordeals which they have faced. Where the rewards of valour are the greatest, there you will find also the best and bravest spirits among the people" (Thuc. 2.46.1). The message is clear: knowing that their families will be cared for, the citizens will commit themselves more to the common cause. Support for war orphans supposedly dated back to the early sixth century. More likely, it was introduced or at least enhanced when naval warfare became the norm and perhaps a great disaster (such as that in Egypt in 454) had raised public awareness of such needs. No clear information survives about support measures for daughters (who elsewhere received a dowry), wives, and parents of the war dead. The words Pericles addresses to them (which seem quite problematic to modern Western sensitivities) do not allude to such support (2.44–46). Nor, it seems, were the families of the thousands of metics who fought and died along with the citizens cared for. The conclusion seems unavoidable that these measures, limited to young male citizens, were intended to boost the morale of the citizen fighters and to bring up future soldiers.[52] A law establishing state support for war invalids (though on a very low level) was attributed to Solon or Peisistratus; more likely, this law too originated in the fifth century, when their numbers increased greatly.[53]

Because Sparta decided in 404 not to follow its allies' demand to destroy and enslave Athens, the Athenian women were spared the fate their men had imposed on many others (above). Their suffering, caused by loss of husbands and sons, widowhood, and lonely old age, mostly remains unmentioned, though Pericles tersely alludes to it (above) and the poets occasionally draw it on center stage. Euripides does so indirectly, for example, at the end of *Suppliant Women*, through the suicide of a mythical war-widow who throws herself on her husband's pyre, and the laments of her desolate father. Aristophanes in *Lysistrata* lets us feel directly the pain of Athenian wives whose husbands have been away for months, depriving their families of fathers and strength, whose men or sons have died, and whose daughters will not find a husband.[54]

Slaves, of course, were not the state's responsibility. Their Athenian masters' extraordinary involvement in politics and war affected their position in society. The "Old Oligarch" acknowledges, with exaggeration and sarcasm, that they were better off and enjoyed more equality of speech (*isegoria*), that is, were more equal and freer in Athens than elsewhere. "There is good sense behind the apparently surprising fact that they allow slaves to live in luxury. . . . In a state relying on naval power it is inevitable that slaves must work for hire so that we may take profits from what they earn" (Ps.-Xen. *AP* 1.10–12). One of Aristophanes' characters exclaims: "To hell with this war: I can't even punish my slaves anymore" (*Clouds* 6–7). Some slaves served in the navy along with their masters. Toward the end of the war, when manpower became critical, great numbers were enlisted and rewarded with freedom or, exceptionally, even with citizenship. When the Peloponnesians held the fort at Decelea and controlled the Attic countryside, supposedly over 20,000 slaves ran away (Thuc. 7.27.5). On a less pronounced scale, slave desertion was a problem from the beginning of the war. In wartime, the chances of slaves to escape and find a haven among the enemy increased greatly; no wonder their masters treated them well.[55]

Economically, at the end of the war, the Athenians suffered badly. They increasingly lost control of their empire and of the seas; hence their manpower, money, and food supplies were disrupted. Hoplites and elite citizens manned the ships and perished in naval defeats. Refugees who were expelled and repatriated from cleruchies and other settlements abroad aggravated the problems. Finally, Athens was starved into submission. In Pericles' time, however, such possibilities must have seemed remote, almost unthinkable – even if intellectuals such as Herodotus and Sophocles worried about the inevitable fall of the mighty and Thucydides lets Pericles mention this possibility (2.64.3).[56] True, Pericles reminds his fellow citizens that the policy they have chosen entails suffering (inconveniences and material losses), but these were expected to be temporary, more than balanced by future gains (2.60–64). Overall, despite suffering and hardships, in the minds of many Athenians the "balance sheet" of war and empire contained a number of positive entries – not only on the level of pride and honor (which Pericles stresses in the same speech) but also on that of individual and collective prosperity.

To mention only the main points, public building, shipyards, and service in the fleet and in official functions throughout the empire provided thousands of Athenians with jobs and income. In a rare comment on such matters, Thucydides illustrates the extent to which the Athenians had become used to such income: popular enthusiasm for the Sicilian expedition in 415 was great not least because the "mass of the people, including those in the army, [were seduced by] the prospect of getting pay for the time being and of adding to the empire so as to secure permanent paid employment in the future" (6.24.3). An estimated 10,000 lower class citizens reached hoplite status because of land they acquired on allied territory. Fleet and empire protected massive imports of grain on which the population depended, swollen as it was by economic opportunity. The Piraeus had become the major port of trade in the Aegean, providing more jobs and making goods from all over the world accessible to the Athenians. Citizens of communities throughout the empire, coming to Athens for political, legal, or business reasons, offered more income. The elite, as is to be expected, profited even more, by acquisition of land in allied territory, booty, interest from loans, fees for representing foreigners, and bribes. The records of auctions disposing of the property of citizens convicted in the aftermath of religious scandals in 415, some of Aristophanes' plays, and other sources offer illuminating insights. Moreover, the large flow of public revenue relieved tax pressure on the wealthy and made them more willing to go along with democracy and its policies.[57]

How much such economic considerations really mattered in motivating the citizens to fight and toil for the greatness of their city is much debated; in my view they should not be underestimated even if they were perhaps not decisive.[58]

There were other collective benefits, not least in the political sphere. Naval policies, the empire, and democracy interacted with each other, at least initially depended on each other, and developed together. Although this too is debated, I suggest that without the empire and the predominant role the fleet and through it the lower citizen classes played in maintaining and enhancing it, Athenian democracy in its fully developed, "radical, Periclean" form would never have materialized.[59]

CONCLUSION

Overall, then, there were many and good reasons for Pericles' optimistic assessment of Athens's chances in its confrontation with the Peloponnesians and for his trust that the citizens would support his policies. Pericles was the last Athenian politician who was able to maintain his political predominance over a long period of time. He provided the strong and consistent leadership that democracy needed to keep its balance and pursue a clear political line – even though its excessive stress on equality did not easily tolerate such authority. It is quite possible, therefore, that Thucydides is correct when he insists that the war would have had a different outcome if Pericles had lived longer. Conversely, as much as he was able to maintain discipline and respect limits in his policies, Pericles was also an aggressive imperialist and almost compulsive "hawk." Without him, quite possibly, Athens would not have gone to war – at least not then and not for the reasons it did. Yet again, one of his successors, Cleon, whom Thucydides blames for some of the war's mistakes and who proved an even more rabid hawk, was active already before Pericles died. Ultimately, it is impossible to second-guess history. Its balance sheet records things more broadly. Some of Athens's greatest intellectual and artistic achievements were intimately connected with, or even inspired by, war and the empire. Without "the (or a) Peloponnesian War, there would have been no Thucydides (nor perhaps Euripides, Aristophanes, and Plato, at any rate in their existing forms)."[60]

Suggestions for Further Reading

Generally on warfare in antiquity: H. Delbrück, *Warfare in Antiquity* (Lincoln: University of Nebraska Press, 1975); A.Ferrill, *The Origins of War* (Boulder: Westview, 1997); P. Sabin et al., eds., *The Cambridge History of Greek and Roman Warfare* (Cambridge: Cambridge University Press, forthcoming).

On Greek warfare: J.-P. Vernant. ed., *Problèmes de la guerre en Grèce ancienne* (Paris: Mouton, 1968); Pritchett, *GSW*; J. K. Anderson, "Wars and Military Science: Greece," in M. Grant and R. Kitzinger, eds., *Civilizations of the Ancient Mediterranean* (New York: Scribner, 1988), 1. 679–702; P. Ducrey, *Warfare in Ancient Greece* (New York: Schocken, 1985); M. M. Sage, *Warfare in Ancient Greece: A Sourcebook* (London: Routledge, 1998); V. D. Hanson, *The Wars of the Ancient Greeks* (London: Cassell, 1999); H. van Wees, ed., *War and Violence in Ancient Greece* (London: Duckworth, 2000), and *Greek Warfare: Myths and Realities* (London: Duckworth, 2004).

On Greek and Athenian infantry warfare: J. K. Anderson, *Military Theory and Practice in the Age of Xenophon* (Berkeley: University of California Press, 1970); J. G. P. Best, *Thracian Peltasts and Their Influence on Greek Warfare* (Groningen: Wolters-Noordhoff, 1969); V. D. Hanson, *The Other Greeks: The Family Farm and the Agrarian Roots of Western Civilization* (New York: Free Press, 1995); V. D. Hanson, ed., *Hoplites: The Classical Greek Battle Experience* (London: Routledge, 1991); V. D. Hanson, *The Western Way of War: Infantry Battle in Classical Greece* (New York: Knopf, 1989); F. Lissarrague, *L'autre guerrier: Archers, peltastes, cavaliers dans l'imagerie attique* (Paris: La découverte, 1990); D. Pritchard, "'The Fractured Imaginary': Popular Thinking on Military Matters in Fifth-Century Athens," *AH* 28 (1998), 38–61. On cavalry, see G. R. Bugh, *The Horsemen of Athens* (Princeton: Princeton University Press, 1988); I. Spence, *The Cavalry of Classical Greece* (Oxford: Oxford University Press, 1993); R. A. Gaebel, *Cavalry Operations in the Ancient Greek World* (Norman: University of Oklahoma Press, 2002). On naval warfare: L. Casson, *Ships and Seamanship in the Ancient World* (Princeton: Princeton University Press, 1971); L. Casson, *The Ancient Mariners*, second edition (Princeton: Princeton University Press, 1991); B. Jordan, *The Athenian Navy in the Classical Period* (Berkeley: University of California Press, 1975); B. S. Strauss, "The Athenian Trireme: School of Democracy," in J. Ober and C. Hedrick, eds., *Dêmokratia* (Princeton: Princeton University Press, 1996), pp. 313–25, and "Perspectives on the Death of Fifth-Century Athenian Seamen," in van Wees, *War and Violence* (above), pp. 261–83; V. Gabrielsen, *Financing the Athenian Fleet* (Baltimore: Johns Hopkins University Press, 1994), H. T. Wallinga, *Ships and Sea-Power before the Great Persian War* (Leiden: Brill, 1993); and J. S. Morrison et al., *The Athenian Trireme*, second edition (Cambridge: Cambridge University Press, 2000).

On social aspects of war: Y. Garlan, *War in the Ancient World: A Social History* (London: Chatto and Windus, 1975); J. Rich and G. Shipley, eds., *War and Society in the Greek World* (London: Routledge, 1993); K. Raaflaub and N. Rosenstein, eds., *War and Society in the Ancient and Medieval Worlds* (Washington, DC: Center for Hellenic Studies, 1999); on economic aspects: Y. Garlan, *Guerre et économie en Grèce ancienne* (Paris: La découverte, 1989); P. Millett, "Warfare, Economy, and Democracy in Classical Athens," in Rich and Shipley (above), pp. 177–96; V. D. Hanson, *Warfare and Agriculture in Classical Greece*, revised edition (Berkeley: University of California Press, 1998); L. Foxhall, "Farming and Fighting in Ancient Greece," in Rich and Shipley (above), pp. 134–45; and J. A. Thorne, "Warfare and Agriculture," *GRBS* 42 (2001): 225–53; on religious aspects: *GSW*, vol. 3; R. Lonis, *Guerre et religion en Grèce à l'époque classique* (Paris: Belles Lettres, 1979); the chapters by M. H. Jameson and A. H. Jackson in V. D. Hanson, ed., *Hoplites* (above); and the chapters by S. Deacy and R. Parker in van Wees, *War and Violence* (above).

NOTES

1 See relevant chapters in *CAH* V²; D. Kagan, *The Peloponnesian War* (New York: Viking, 2003). Translations (often modified): for Thucydides and Xenophon, R. Warner (London: Penguin, 1972; 1966); for Pseudo-Xenophon, *AP*, and Aristotle, *AP*, J. M. Moore, *Aristotle and Xenophon on Democracy and Oligarchy* (Berkeley: University of California Press, 1975).

2 See D. M. Lewis in *CAH* V².370–80; on Thucydides: see A. Rengakos and A. Tsakmakis, eds., *Brill's Companion to Thucydides* (Leiden: Brill, forthcoming) and Samons, pp. 2–3 with n. 6 in this volume.

3 See Y. Garlan, *War in the Ancient World: A Social History* (London: Chatto and Windus, 1975); K. Raaflaub and N. Rosenstein, eds., *War and Society in the Ancient and Medieval Worlds* (Washington, DC: Center for Hellenic Studies, 1999).

4 See *HCT* 1.1–25; S. Hornblower, "The Religious Dimension to the Peloponnesian War," *HSCP* 94 (1992): 169–97. Lisa Kallet (nn. 10, 37 below) demonstrates, however, how much can be extracted from his text on financial matters. Impact: P. Cartledge, "The Effects of the Peloponnesian (Athenian) War on Athenian and Spartan Societies," in D. R. McCann and B. S. Strauss, eds., *War and Democracy* (Armonk, NY: M. E. Sharpe, 2001), pp. 104–23.

5 Sparta: Lendon, this volume. Athens: A. W. Gomme, *The Population of Athens in the Fifth and Fourth Centuries B.C.* (Oxford: Blackwell, 1933); M. H. Hansen, *Three*

Studies in Athenian Demography (Copenhagen: The Royal Danish Academy, 1988), pp. 14–28.

6   Metics and slaves: Patterson, this volume. See P. Hunt, *Slaves, Warfare, and Ideology in the Greek Historians* (Cambridge: Cambridge University Press, 1998); V. Rosivach, "Manning the Athenian Fleet," *AJAH* 10 (1985 [1993]): 41–66; V. Gabrielsen, *Financing the Athenian Fleet* (Baltimore: Johns Hopkins University Press, 1994), chapter 5.

7   Gabrielsen (n. 6), p. 106.

8   Hansen (n. 5), p. 24.

9   Pay: Pritchett, *GSW* I.3–29; W. T. Loomis, *Wages, Welfare Costs and Inflation in Classical Athens* (Ann Arbor: University of Michigan Press, 1998), chapter 2 and pp. 266–9.

10 Gabrielsen (n. 6), chapters 5 and 6; Samos: R. Meiggs, *The Athenian Empire* (Oxford: Oxford University Press, 1972), p. 192; C. W. Fornara, "On the Chronology of the Samian War," *JHS* 99 (1979): 7–18. Parthenon: R. S. Stanier, "The Cost of the Parthenon," *JHS* 73 (1953): 68–76; first tribute: L. Kallet-Marx, *Money, Expense, and Naval Power in Thucydides'* History *1–5.24* (Berkeley: University of California Press, 1993), pp. 49–52; L. J. Samons, *Empire of the Owl: Athenian Imperial Finance* (Stuttgart: Steiner, 2000), pp. 84–91.

11 Kallet-Marx (n. 10): chapters 3–6; Samons (n. 10). Trierarchy: Gabrielsen (n. 6), pt. 1; *eisphora*: R. Thomsen, *Eisphora* (Copenhagen: Gyldendal Boghandel, 1964); other purposes: L. Kallet, "Accounting for Culture in Fifth-Century Athens," in D. Boedeker and K. A. Raaflaub, eds., *Democracy, Empire, and the Arts in Fifth-Century Athens* (Cambridge, MA: Harvard University Press, 1998), pp. 43–58, 357–64.

12 Gabrielsen (n. 6): 118–19. Personal profits: Meiggs (n. 10), chapter 14; M. I. Finley, *Economy and Society in Ancient Greece*, B. Shaw and R. Saller, eds. (New York: Viking, 1982), chapter 3.

13 C. Meier, *The Greek Discovery of Politics*, trans. D. McLintock (Cambridge, MA: Harvard University Press, 1990), chapter 8; K. A. Raaflaub, "Democracy, Power, and Imperialism in Fifth-Century Athens," in J. P. Euben et al., eds., *Athenian Political Thought and the Reconstruction of American Democracy* (Ithaca, NY: Cornell University Press, 1994), pp. 103–46, and *The Discovery of Freedom in Ancient Greece* (Chicago: University of Chicago Press, 2004), chapter 5.2.

14 Thuc. 4.15–22, 41. Athenian strategy: Kagan (n. 1), pp. 50–54; Lewis (n. 2), pp. 380–88; I. Spence, "Perikles and the Defense of Attika during the Peloponnesian War," *JHS* 110 (1990): 91–109; J. Ober, *The Athenian Revolution* (Princeton: Princeton University Press, 1996), chapter 6.

15 See, e.g., Thuc. 4.84–8.

16 For details, see Thuc. 1.89–117; Meiggs (n. 10); C. W. Fornara and L. J. Samons, *Athens from Cleisthenes to Pericles* (Berkeley: University of California Press, 1991), chapters 3 and 4; *CAH* V², chapters 3, 5–6. Frequency: Garlan (n. 3), p. 15.

17 Hdt. 6.7–15. Triremes: H. T. Wallinga, *Ships and Sea-Power before the Great Persian War* (Leiden: Brill, 1993).

18 K. A. Raaflaub, "City-State, Territory, and Empire in Classical Antiquity," in A. Molho et al., eds., *City-States in Classical Antiquity and Medieval Italy* (Stuttgart: Steiner, 1991), pp. 565–88.

19 Plut. *Per.* 11.4; Arist. *AP* 24.3. Training: *GSW* I.225–7; J. S. Morrison et al., *The Athenian Trireme*, second edition (Cambridge: Cambridge University Press,

2000), pp. 115–17. Naval warfare: V. D. Hanson, "Democratic Warfare, Ancient and Modern," in McCann and Strauss (n. 4), pp. 3–33.

20 Morrison (n. 19), chapter 10; Finley (n. 12), pp. 53–7; R. Meiggs, *Trees and Timber in the Ancient Mediterranean World* (Oxford: Oxford University Press, 1982), chapter 5; Gabrielsen (n. 6), chapters 6 and 7; R. Garland, *The Piraeus from the Fifth to the First Century B.C.* (Ithaca, NY: Cornell University Press, 1987), pp. 95–100.

21 W. R. Connor, "Early Greek Land Warfare as Symbolic Expression," *PP* 119 (1988): 3–29; V. D. Hanson, *The Other Greeks: The Family Farm and the Agrarian Roots of Western Civilization* (New York: Free Press, 1995); Raaflaub and Rosenstein (n. 3), pp. 129–41; H. van Wees, "The Development of the Hoplite Phalanx," in V. D. Hanson, ed., *War and Violence in Ancient Greece* (London: Duckworth, 2000), pp. 125–66; P. Krentz, "Fighting by the Rules: The Invention of the Hoplite Agôn," *Hesperia* 71 (2002): 23–39; H. van Wees, *Greek Warfare: Myths and Realities* (London: Duckworth, 2004).

22 R. T. Ridley, "The Hoplite as Citizen," *AC* 48 (1979): 508–48; V. D. Hanson, "Hoplites into Democrats," in J. Ober and C. Hedrick, eds., *Dêmokratia* (Princeton: Princeton University Press, 1996), pp. 289–312.

23 H. van Wees, "Politics and the Battlefield: Ideology in Greek Warfare," in A. Powell, ed., *The Greek World* (London: Routledge, 1995), pp. 153–78, and *Greek Warfare* (n. 21), chapter 6; K. A. Raaflaub et al., *Origins of Democracy in Ancient Greece* (Berkeley: University of California Press, forthcoming), chapter 5; J. G. P. Best, *Thracian Peltasts and Their Influence on Greek Warfare* (Groningen: Wolters-Noordhoff, 1969); J. Roisman, *The General Demosthenes and His Use of Military Surprise* (Stuttgart: Steiner, 1993).

24 G. R. Bugh, *The Horsemen of Athens* (Princeton: Princeton University Press, 1988); I. Spence, *The Cavalry of Classical Greece* (Oxford: Oxford University Press, 1993); R. A. Gaebel, *Cavalry Operations in the Ancient Greek World* (Norman: University of Oklahoma Press, 2002); I. Jenkins, *The Parthenon Frieze* (Austin: University of Texas Press, 1994).

25 Garland (n. 20), pp. 22–2, 167–9; R. E. Wycherley, *The Stones of Athens* (Princeton: Princeton University Press, 1978), chapter 1.

26 Ephebes: P. J. Rhodes, *A Commentary on the Aristotelian Athenaion Politeia* (Oxford: Oxford University Press, 1981; revised reprint, 1993), pp. 493–5. Training: Thuc. 2.39; Plato, *Laches*; Pritchett, *GSW* I.208–21. Sparta: J. F. Lazenby, *The Spartan Army* (Warminster: Aris & Phillips, 1985).

27 Lists: *CT* I.256. Fleet: above n. 6.

28 Army: P. Siewert, *Die Trittyen Attikas und die Heeresreform des Kleisthenes* (Munich: Beck, 1982), pp. 150–53. Stoa: John M. Camp, *The Athenian Agora: Excavations in the Heart of Classical Athens* (London: Thames and Hudson, 1986), pp. 66–72; monuments: ibid., pp. 74–7. Panathenaea: D. G. Kyle, "The Panathenaic Games: Sacred and Civic Athletics," in J. Neils, ed., *Goddess and Polis: The Panathenaic Festival in Ancient Athens* (Princeton: Princeton University Press, 1992), pp. 77–101; P. Ceccarelli, *La pirrica nell'antichità greco romana* (Pisa: Istituti editoriali e poligrafici internazionali, 1998), chapter 2.

29 W. Burkert, *Greek Religion*, trans. J. Raffan (Cambridge MA: Harvard University Press, 1985), p. 267; V. D. Hanson, ed., *Hoplites: The Classical Greek Battle Experience* (London: Routledge, 1991), chapters 8 and 9. Pritchett, *GSW* vol. 3, is dedicated entirely to religion and war.

30 V. D. Hanson, *The Western Way of War: Infantry Battle in Classical Greece* (New York: Knopf, 1989), and *Hoplites* (n. 29), chapters 1–6; P. Krentz, "Casualties in Hoplite Battles," *GRBS* 26 (1985): 13–20.

31 J. K. Anderson, *Military Theory and Practice in the Age of Xenophon* (Berkeley: University of California Press, 1970); S. Mitchell, "Hoplite Warfare in Ancient Greece," in A. B. Lloyd, ed., *Battle in Antiquity* (London: Duckworth, 1996), pp. 87–105.

32 J. Lazenby, "The Killing Zone," in Hanson (n. 29), pp. 87–109; S. Mitchell (n. 31); J. E. Lendon, *Soldiers and Ghosts: A History of Battle in Classical Antiquity* (New Haven: Yale University Press, 2005). Aeschylus *Persians* 353–432 describes a sea battle (Salamis).

33 J. Shay, *Achilles in Vietnam* (New York: Simon & Schuster, 1994), and *Odysseus in America: Combat Trauma and the Trials of Homecoming* (New York: Scribner, 2002); L. Tritle, "Hector's Body: Mutilation of the Dead in Ancient Greece and Vietnam," *AHB* 11 (1997): 123–36, and *From Melos to My Lai* (London: Routledge, 2000).

34 Wounded: van Wees, *Greek Warfare* (n. 21), pp. 146–48; invalids: Lys. *Or.* 24; captives: P. Ducrey, *Le traitement des prisonniers de guerre dans la Grèce antique* (Paris: De Boccard, 1968), Pritchett, *GSW* V.203–312; booty: ibid., pp. 68–541.

35 For political aspects, see Rhodes, Sealey, this volume.

36 As is well illustrated, e.g., by Thuc. 1.70–71 (despite the Corinthians' contrary claims), 1.140–44.

37 Thuc. 6.1.1; cf. *HCT* IV.197 and the entire passage 6.1–26 with J. Ober, "Civic Ideology and Counterhegemonic Discourse: Thucydides on the Sicilian Debate," in A. L. Boegehold and A. C. Scafuro, eds., *Athenian Identity and Civic Ideology* (Baltimore: Johns Hopkins University Press, 1994), pp. 102–26; deception: L. Kallet, *Money and the Corrosion of Power in Thucydides: The Sicilian Expedition and Its Aftermath* (Berkeley: University of California Press, 2001), pp. 69–79.

38 Cf. Hdt. 3.82.2 and *Pap. Mich.* 5982: A. Andrewes, "The Theramenes Papyrus," *ZPE* 6 (1970): 35–8. S. Lewis, *News and Society in the Greek Polis* (Chapel Hill: University of North Carolina Press, 1996).

39 E.g., Fornara 51; Plut. *Cim.* 7, cf. 8.1; Aeschin. 3.186.

40 Ducrey (n. 34); P. Karavites, *Capitulations and Greek Interstate Relations* (Göttingen: Vandenhoeck and Ruprecht, 1982); P. Rahe, "Justice and Necessity: The Conduct of the Spartans and the Athenians in the Peloponnesian War," in M. Grimsley and C. J. Rogers, eds., *Civilians in the Path of War* (Lincoln: University of Nebraska Press, 2002), pp. 1–32. On the fate of Plataea, Sparta's responsibility, see Thuc. 3.52–68, 6.18.

41 *IG* i³ 40 = ML 52.20–33 = Fornara 103, one among several extant examples; J. M. Balcer, *The Athenian Regulations for Chalkis* (Wiesbaden: Steiner, 1978).

42 See n. 16 above; W. Schuller, *Die Herrschaft der Athener im ersten attischen Seebund* (Berlin: de Gruyter, 1974).

43 E.g., Cartledge (n. 4); J. Seibert, *Die politischen Flüchtlinge und Verbannten in der griechischen Geschichte* (Darmstadt: Wissenschaftliche Buchgesellschaft, 1979); H. W. Parke, *Greek Mercenary Soldiers* (Chicago: Ares, 1981). Thucydides' treatment of the civil war in Corcyra illustrates the impact of war on domestic relations: 3.70–85: J. Price, *Thucydides and Internal War* (Cambridge: Cambridge University Press, 2001).

44 C. Meier, *The Political Art of Greek Tragedy* (Baltimore: Johns Hopkins University Press, 1993); D. Rosenbloom, "Myth, History, and Hegemony in Aeschylus," in

B. Goff, ed., *History, Tragedy, Theory* (Austin: University of Texas Press, 1996), pp. 91–130.

45   J. Henderson, "*Lysistrate*: The Play and Its Themes," *YCS* 26 (1980): 153–218; H.-J. Newiger, "War and Peace in the Comedy of Aristophanes," *YCS* 26 (1980): 219–37; J. Gregory, *Euripides and the Instruction of the Athenians* (Ann Arbor: University of Michigan Press, 1991); N. T. Croally, *Euripidean Polemic: The Trojan Women and the Function of Tragedy* (Cambridge: Cambridge University Press, 1994).

46   T. Hölscher, "Images and Political Identity: The Case of Athens," in Boedeker and Raaflaub (n. 11), pp. 153–83; B. Smarczyk, *Untersuchungen zur Religionspolitik und politischen Propaganda Athens im Delisch-Attischen Seebund* (Munich: tuduv, 1990), pp. 31–57, 298–317; J. M. Hurwit, *The Athenian Acropolis* (Cambridge: Cambridge University Press, 1999).

47   Raaflaub (n. 13), pp. 181–93, and "Father of All, Destroyer of All: War in Late Fifth-Century Athenian Discourse and Ideology," in McCann and Strauss (n. 4), pp. 307–56.

48   Neils (n. 28); Smarczyk (n. 46), esp. pp. 501–618; S. Goldhill, "The Great Dionysia and Civic Ideology," *JHS* 107 (1987): 58–76, also published in J. J. Winkler and F. I. Zeitlin, eds., *Nothing to Do with Dionysos?* (Princeton: Princeton University Press, 1990), pp. 97–129.

49   C. W. Clairmont, *Patrios Nomos: Public Burial in Athens during the Fifth and Fourth Centuries B.C.*, 2 vols. (Oxford: B.A.R., 1983); N. Loraux, *The Invention of Athens: The Funeral Oration in the Classical City*, trans. A. Sheridan (Cambridge, MA: Harvard University Press, 1986); R. Parker, *Athenian Religion: A History* (Oxford: Oxford University Press, 1996), pp. 131–3.

50   Thuc. 2.21, 59. V. D. Hanson, *Warfare and Agriculture in Classical Greece* (Pisa: Giardini 1983; second edition, Berkeley: University of California Press, 1998); L. Foxhall, "Farming and Fighting in Ancient Greece," in J. Rich and G. Shipley, eds., *War and Society in the Greek World* (London: Routledge, 1993), pp. 134–45; J. A. Thorne, "Warfare and Agriculture," *GRBS* 42 (2001): 225–53.

51   *IG* i³ 1147 = ML 33 = Fornara 78. Another example: ML 48. See B. S. Strauss, *Athens after the Peloponnesian War* (Ithaca, NY: Cornell University Press, 1986), pp. 179–82; Hansen (n. 5), pp. 14–28.

52   Raaflaub, in Boedeker and Raaflaub (n. 11), pp. 30–32. On Thuc. 2.46 (women), see chapters by P. Cartledge and L. Kallet-Marx in R. M. Rosen and J. Farrell, eds., *Nomodeiktes: Greek Studies in Honor of Martin Ostwald* (Ann Arbor: University of Michigan Press, 1993), pp. 125–32, 133–43.

53   Plut. *Sol.* 31.3–4; cf. Lys. *Or.* 24; M. Manfredini and L. Piccirilli, *Plutarco, La vita di Solone* (Milan: Mondadori, 1977), p. 278.

54   D. Schaps, "The Women of Greece in Wartime," *CP* 77 (1982): 193–213.

55   Hunt (n. 6), chapters 6–8, and "The Slaves and the Generals of Arginusae," *AJP* 122 (2001): 359–80; R. Osborne, "The Economics and Politics of Slavery at Athens," in Powell (n. 23), pp. 27–43.

56   J. Moles, "Herodotus Warns the Athenians," *Papers of the Leeds International Latin Seminar* 9 (1996): 259–84; Raaflaub, "Philosophy, Science, Politics: Herodotus and the Intellectual Trends of His Time," in E. J. Bakker et al., eds., *Brill's Companion to Herodotus* (Leiden: Brill, 2002), pp. 164–83; B. Knox, *Word and Action* (Baltimore: Johns Hopkins University Press, 1979), chapter 8.

57   Meiggs, Finley (n. 12); Raaflaub (1994, n. 13), pp. 132–4; W. Schmitz, *Wirtschaftliche Prosperität, soziale Integration und die Seebundpolitik Athens* (Munich: tuduv, 1988).

58   M. I. Finley, *The Ancient Economy*, new edition (Berkeley: University of California Press, 1999), chapter 6; P. Rahe, "The Primacy of Politics in Classical Greece," *AHR* 89 (1984): 265–93.

59   Raaflaub, in Raaflaub and Rosenstein (n. 3), pp. 141–6; Raaflaub et al., *Origins of Democracy in Ancient Greece* (Berkeley: University of California Press, 2006), chapter 5.

60   Cartledge (n. 4), p. 117. See, more generally, Boedeker and Raaflaub (n. 11).

5: ART AND ARCHITECTURE

Kenneth Lapatin

Suppose that Sparta were to become deserted and only the temples
and foundations of buildings remained, I think that future generations would, as time passed, find it very difficult to believe that
the place had really been as powerful as it was reputed to be. . . . If,
on the other hand, the same thing were to happen to Athens, one
would conjecture from what met the eye that the city had been
twice as powerful as it actually is.

Thucydides (1.10.2)

The monuments of fifth-century Athens, and its Acropolis (Figure 1) in particular, have come to embody the "Glory of
Ancient Greece" to such a degree that Thucydides might be
faulted for underestimation. While the knee-high remains of Sparta are
today unimpressive, the Acropolis, a UNESCO World Heritage Site,
averages over a million visitors annually. It appears constantly on travel
brochures, postage stamps, restaurant menus, and olive oil containers,
and even in less relevant contexts, such as Las Vegas casino chips and
Japanese telephone cards. What accounts for the pervasiveness and continuing power of this imagery? Why are the art and architecture of
fifth-century Athens so renowned?

There is no single answer, of course, but any explanation must
take into account the extraordinary aesthetic quality of the monuments.
Over half a millennium after their construction Plutarch wrote

The works of Pericles are even more admired – though built
in a short time they have lasted for a very long time. For,
in its beauty, each work was, even at that time, ancient, and
yet, in its perfection, each looks even at the present time
as if it were fresh and newly built. Thus there is a certain

bloom of newness in each building and an appearance of being untouched by the wear of time. It is as if some ever-flowering life and unaging spirit had been infused into the creation of these works.

(Life of Pericles 13)

Although no longer untouched by the ravages of time, the beauty and refinement of the Acropolis monuments – and more modest objects such as marble reliefs and painted pots – remain apparent to even the most casual viewers. The pleasing symmetry and grace of Classical Athenian artifacts in diverse media mark the acme of long-standing craft traditions. Quality aside, the visual arts have a unique capacity to affect us directly and immediately.

Received opinion is another factor that plays heavily upon perceptions. In the fourth century B.C., long before Plutarch called buildings on the Acropolis "delightful adornments" that brought "the greatest amazement to the rest of mankind" (Life of Pericles 12), Attic orators cited them as evidence of a past golden age. Subsequently, Athenian classicism was adopted and adapted by other Greeks, Romans, and those still farther afield in both time and space, living under very different social and political circumstances. Visual quotations, imitations, and variations (not to mention the appropriation and possession of the artifacts themselves) obviously draw on the authority of the past, but they also simultaneously confer on the originals still greater prestige. Thus Classical Athenian creations, from the battered Acropolis temples to red-figured ceramics, have long served as emblems of high culture, as yardsticks against which the art of other cultures and periods has been measured. Today we often take their consequence, both aesthetic and political, for granted.[1]

The significance of ancient objects to those who made, commissioned, and saw them, however, is not always easy to pin down. Plutarch, for example, described the construction of the Parthenon and other Acropolis monuments as a great democratic public works program intended by Pericles to put money into the hands of Athenian tradesmen. But he lived nearly 600 years after the fact, at a time when Roman emperors and well-to-do citizens competed to display their own generosity through costly construction projects. Composing the Life of Pericles, moreover, Plutarch evidently drew on the untrustworthy partisan political invective of fifth-century and later debates. His aims in writing the Life cannot all be recovered, of course, and his motives should not be reduced to a single objective. Nor, for that matter, should Pericles' and the Athenians'. The Acropolis buildings were certainly expensive, but contemporary building accounts preserved on stone indicate that they were fashioned by foreigners and slaves, as well as citizens, and that all were paid the same wages. Thucydides, a contemporary witness, had no doubt that the buildings were meant to project power. But the Parthenon, Propylaia, Erechtheion, and Nike Temple also served important religious functions, replacing cult buildings that had been destroyed by the Persians in 480/79 B.C. A democratic reading of the Acropolis monuments may be defensible, but it alone is far from satisfactory.

The same can be said of interpretations of the early fifth-century B.C. marble statue of a young man from the Acropolis (Figure 2), conventionally known as the *Kritios Boy*, that celebrate the figure as an embodiment of democratic ideals. Earlier male statues, the *kouroi* (sing. *kouros*), such as those excavated at the sanctuary of Poseidon at Sounion and at cemeteries in Attica (Figure 3), also stood nude with one leg advanced and both arms at the sides, a pose derived in the seventh century from Egyptian prototypes and popular throughout Greece in the sixth. The Acropolis youth breaks free from the stiff Archaic formulae. Rather than standing balanced between two straight legs, he rests his weight on the left, while the right is advanced, flexed, and relaxed. No longer a mere agglomeration of parts, this young body responds to the weight shift in the tilt of hips and shoulders. The anatomy is integrated; bones and muscles react to movement and operate together as a rational system. The head, moreover, is turned slightly to the side, and this additional departure from the rigid symmetry and frontality of the *kouroi* gives the youth an impression of inner life, as if he might be contemplating some potential course of action. The physical and (perhaps) intellectual gravity of this figure and other contemporary works, which also lack the artificial smile of their predecessors, have been thought to reflect a greater sense of liberty, individualism, responsibility, and humanism – attitudes considered appropriate to a new, democratic era.

But are such imputations of deep meaning to stylistic advances sustainable – especially when we do not know whom this statue represents, who commissioned it, or even precisely when it was carved (a date around 480 B.C. is widely accepted)? Such dedications on the Acropolis were expensive and were often the offerings of aristocrats, just like the earlier *kouroi* and their female counterparts, the *korai*. The *Kritios Boy* might depict Theseus, as some have proposed, but even though this hero became increasingly popular in democratic Athens, the statue still seems to represent a paradigm of elite virtue. The aristocratic leader and sometime opponent of Pericles, Cimon, in fact, presented himself as a "new Theseus." Although the *Kritios Boy* certainly represents a kind of progress from the *kouroi*, such formal developments do not necessarily correspond to those that occurred contemporaneously in Athenian politics. In fact, there is nothing demonstrably democratic about him.[2]

The *Kritios Boy* and other fifth-century Athenian monuments are, nonetheless, regularly employed as illustrations of the values embodied in such encomiastic texts as Pericles' Funeral Oration and the choral odes of Sophocles. To be sure, those who created them may have shared something of the outlook of politicians and poets, and we see in Athenian art, too, the quest for and expression of timeless ideals. But in a society where people looked more often than they read, the visual arts did not function as passive reflections so much as active participants in the construction of the world they purportedly depict. Despite the apparent naturalism of their style – the result of their makers' increasingly accurate representation of optical experience – Classical Greek statues and paintings are not transparent windows onto "daily life" or straightforward delineations of fixed mythological narratives. Rather, in keeping with the public contexts in which they were exhibited and their high degree of idealization, they functioned as normative images that served ideological ends. Like their Archaic counterparts, Classical images provided examples, both positive and negative, of qualities and behaviors to be emulated and avoided. From the colossal gold and ivory statue of Athena that stood inside the Parthenon to the red-figure pots sold in the lower city, the images created, commissioned, and viewed by the inhabitants of Athens were cultural constructs that played crucial roles in the formation of social identities. That they were attractive made them more palatable, and their mastery of form made (and continues to make) them more convincing. In a way, they functioned not unlike the carefully composed billboards and magazine and television advertisements that surround us today, but they were intended to convey cultural and political messages, rather than merely to sell merchandise. By reading the monuments in their own contexts, so far as those can be recovered, we can hope to glean some of the many meanings they might have held for their ancient viewers. Yet we must always beware of projecting onto them our own biases and desires, attitudes that have developed over the intervening two and a half millennia.

When the Athenians returned home after the defeat of the Persians at Plataia in 479 B.C., they found their city in ruins. Before the battle, according to some ancient sources, the Greek allies had vowed not to rebuild the temples and shrines destroyed by the invaders, but to leave them as a lasting memorial of barbarian impiety. Whether or not this "Oath of Plataia" was formally sworn, the Athenians' first concern must have been to reconstruct their houses, defenses, water supply, and other infrastructure. Fortifications were quickly rebuilt, and some new civic and religious buildings in the lower city were commissioned by aristocrats in keeping with age-old traditions of public benefaction: Themistocles, for example, financed a small Temple of Artemis Aristoboule ("of the Best Counsel") west of the Agora (Figure 4). Cimon's brother-in-law Peisianax erected the *Peisianakteion*, a colonnaded *stoa* that provided sheltered space to the public while advertising his generosity. Cimon himself, among other projects, beautified the city with shade trees and underwrote construction of the Long Walls to Piraeus (which Pericles completed), as well as the walls of the Acropolis, where elements of two temples damaged by the Persians were prominently displayed. The rebuilding of the Acropolis temples themselves, however, did not begin until after the middle of the fifth century, perhaps after peace with Persia nullified the terms of the oath.[3]

In contrast to such projects undertaken by wealthy individuals, the Athenian *demos*, as early as 477/6 B.C., commissioned two local sculptors, Kritios and Nesiotes, to replace the bronze statues of the "Tyrannicides," Harmodios and Aristogeiton, that Antenor had fashioned for the fledgling democracy some thirty years earlier. The Persian king Xerxes had carried off Antenor's bronzes, no doubt understanding their importance as emblems of Athens's freedom. We have no record of their appearance, but Kritios's and Nesiotes' replacements were reproduced on Athenian ceramics, coins, and reliefs; and full-scale marble copies and fragmentary plaster casts survive from the Roman period (Figures 5, 6). These statues functioned as emblems of Athens's liberation from tyranny, for although Harmodios's and Aristogeiton's attempt to kill the tyrant Hippias was unsuccessful (they managed only to kill his brother Hipparchos, and did so on account of a love quarrel), the Athenians heroized them as if they had actually freed the city from despotic rule. Harmodios and Aristogeiton were aristocrats, but they were widely credited with bringing *isonomia* ("equality before the law") to Athens. Thus, celebrating them as champions of democracy served Athenian ideology. Popular songs honored the pair, and their descendants were granted tax exemptions and other special privileges. In fact, ancient authors emphasize that Antenor's statues were the first *state-sponsored* commemorative images in Greece, and the speed with which the Athenians replaced them after the Persian Wars indicates their continuing significance.

Kritios's and Nesiotes' wedge-shaped action group was erected in the Agora not far from the site of the assassination attempt. It contrasted the prudence of the older man with the rash enthusiasm of his lover. The bearded Aristogeiton employs his scabbard and the cloak draped over his extended left arm defensively, as he prepares to thrust with the sword held in his withdrawn right hand. The smooth-cheeked Harmodios, in contrast, boldly raises his weapon above his head, exposing his entire body to counterattack. A fragment of the epigram carved on the base of the statues survives: "A great light shone for the Athenians when Harmodios and Aristogeiton slew Hipparchos." Publicly displayed in the Agora, Kritios's and Nesiotes' bronzes embodied and dramatically projected the idea, which recurs in Thucydides, that Athenians will zealously sacrifice their strength, prowess, and lives on behalf of the *demos*. Thus the statues served as both models for citizens and a warning to any future tyrant: indeed, their dynamic composition cunningly placed the viewer in the position of the victim.[4]

The *Tyrannicides* are one of the few major sculptural monuments of fifth-century Athens that seem to have an explicitly democratic message. Although the statues do not survive, their form and meaning have been interpreted with considerable confidence on account of the wealth of preserved evidence, both physical and literary. The roughly contemporary *Kritios Boy* (Figure 2, so-called by moderns on account of the superficial resemblance of his head to later copies of Kritios's statue of Harmodios) allows far less certainty. Nonetheless, his eyes, hollowed for inlays of stone or glass, his fine, wispy hair, and his integrated anatomy all link him to contemporary works in bronze, the premier sculptural medium of the early fifth century.

Most ancient bronzes have fallen victim to the melting pot. Exceptions, ironically, have been preserved by ancient earthquakes, landslides, and shipwrecks. Surviving statue bases and literary sources attest to the existence of numerous bronze statues in fifth-century Athens. Among these the group of *Eponymous Heroes* erected in the Agora also satisfied the needs of the Athenian state. Standing in the city center, they served as emblems of the ten tribes created by Kleisthenes, the backbone of his reorganization of the city's political structure ca. 507. The creator(s) of this group is unfortunately unknown, as is the appearance of the heroes themselves, although some of them were likely depicted nude, just as were the *Tyrannicides* and other Greek heroes in their prime. Nor can the Athenian monument to the *Eponymous Heroes* be accurately dated. Nonetheless, the traveler Pausanias, writing in the second century A.D., reports that bronze statues of the Athenian *Eponymoi* also appeared in another group that was erected at the sanctuary of Apollo at Delphi and financed from a tithe of the spoils taken at Marathon. Pausanias reports that the Delphi group was fashioned by the Athenian sculptor Pheidias and also featured bronze statues of Athena, Apollo, and, perhaps alone among mortals, Miltiades, Cimon's father. Thus scholars reasonably date its dedication prior to Cimon's ostracism in 461 B.C. But whatever its date, the Delphi group is unlikely to have projected precisely the same messages as its Athenian counterpart, for not only did it bear the stamp of Cimon's agenda, but it also must have been aimed at celebrating Athens's victories against a foreign enemy, and it did so in a Panhellenic setting.[5]

There is no secure evidence for the appearance of the Athena Pheidias fashioned at Delphi, but a roughly contemporary marble relief found on the Acropolis (Figure 7) features the goddess standing with her weight on one leg, the other flexed. As in other Early Classical images of women, the drapery here is relatively subdued (hence, and because of the absence of the "Archaic" smile, works of this period are sometimes called "Severe"). However, the intense pigments originally applied to ancient statuary would have enlivened it substantially. The goddess's crested helmet is tilted back so that she might look down at a short stone slab, and this mysterious *stele* is the key to the image. Some have thought it an inscribed list of Athenian war casualties and have called the relief the "Mourning Athena." Others have noted that the goddess is barefoot: taking her to be standing on sacred ground, they have identified the *stele*, and the relief itself, as a boundary-stone marking the perimeter of a holy precinct. Others still have suggested that the *stele* represents the inscribed accounts of the goddess's treasures stored on the Acropolis, or a turning post in a stadium. Thus the relief has also been considered the dedication of magistrates or the offering of an athletic victor. The solution is elusive, but whatever this image represents, its solemn, reflective mood, like that of the *Kritios Boy*, seems to point forward to calm, introspective monuments of the high Classical style of the second half of the fifth century.[6]

Surviving statues from early fifth-century Athens provide important evidence of changes in style, but owing to the absence of contextual information they are, paradoxically, often more difficult to interpret than better documented lost works known from ancient literary sources. Among the most impressive of the latter was the colossal *Bronze Athena* that Pheidias erected on the Acropolis. It too was a state dedication financed from Persian War booty, literally transforming enemy spoils into a gleaming image of the goddess who guided the Athenians to victory. The statue is known from ancient descriptions, representations in other media, and fragments of both its stone base and inscribed accounts recording payments made for materials and labor. Popularly called the *Promachos*, it depicted Athena standing at ease, guarding the western approach to the Acropolis (see Figure 26). Precise details of its imagery are uncertain, but standing approximately forty feet tall, it was one of the most conspicuous monuments in Athens: the crest of the goddess's helmet and tip of her spear could be seen from the sea. Visible to anyone approaching the city, this colossal bronze epitomized the Athenians' wealth, power, and technology, as well as their piety. It took nine years to fashion, and the inscribed accounts record the purchase of copper, tin, lead, and silver, as well as coal, firewood, and even goats' hair (to prevent shrinkage of the clay molds). Modern scholars estimate that its total cost may have been as high as eighty-three talents, about twelve times the total amount thought to have been spent annually by twenty-eight *choregoi* on performances at the City Dionysia, or enough to build more than forty triremes.[7]

The Athenians celebrated their victories with paintings as well as statuary. Cimon's brother-in-law, Peisianax, commissioned Polygnotos of Thasos, as well as the Athenians Mikon and Panainos (a relative of Pheidias), to decorate the interior of the *Peisianakteion*, the *stoa* he built at the northern edge of the Agora. These monumental paintings became so famous that the building came to be called the "Painted Stoa;" they constituted programmatic political statements aimed at a broad public, for the building was employed for a variety of purposes, including the meetings of philosophers (hence the "Stoics"). The paintings depicted Athenian military victories in the Persian Wars, especially at Marathon (with emphasis on the roles of Theseus and Miltiades), along with images of mythological battles presented as antecedents and analogues: Theseus leading the Athenians against Amazons and the aftermath of the fall of Troy. Cimon also honored Theseus, whose bones he recovered from the island of Skyros, by commissioning Polygnotos to decorate the *Theseion* with paintings of the Amazonomachy, the Centauromachy, and the recovery of Minos's ring from the sea. These compositions implicitly glorified their patron as well as the state, for their age-old themes could now be also read as allegories of Cimon's on-going exploits against the Persians, who were androgynous like the Amazons, oriental like the Trojans, and hubristic like the centaurs. Theseus's recovery of Minos's ring, meanwhile, exemplified Athens's maritime supremacy. Painted on large wooden panels, these works are lost, but we have descriptions of them, and echoes of their compositional innovations – such as irregular ground lines, transparent drapery, and livelier, more expressive faces, conveying the mood of figures – have been recognized on contemporary red-figured pottery (Figure 8). Slightly later, Agatharchos of Samos, another immigrant to Athens, apparently made the first systematic experiments in perspective. According to the Roman architect Vitruvius (7 praef. 11), Agatharchos painted a temporary stage setting for one of the dramas of Aischylos and wrote a commentary on his method that influenced the philosophers Demokritos and Anaxagoras, who were also concerned with vision, perspective, and representation.[8]

As the paragraphs above demonstrate, historians of ancient art today rely not only on preserved (and often damaged) artifacts, but also on writings of later Greek and Roman authors that often focus on the contributions of specific individuals to the development of style. Such concerns conveniently parallel those of many modern scholars, who trace "advances" – in multiple media – from the stiff, highly patterned images of the Archaic period to the fluid, seemingly more naturalistic representations of the Classical. Contemporary Athenian notions of art, however, were different from ours today. As difficult as it is for us to define, "art" is derived from the Latin *ars*, a term denoting skill or craft. Its Greek equivalent, *techne*, likewise has the practical sense of applied knowledge, which remains at the root of such words as *technique* and *technology*. Although *techne* could be considered in the abstract, the ancients thought of it in real terms and thus spoke of the *techne* of physicians, ship captains, charioteers, fishermen, generals, and cowherds, as well as sculptors, painters, architects, metalworkers, and gem carvers.[9]

The creations of ancient artisans and craftsmen (*technitai* and *banausoi* in Greek), which we have come to call "artworks" made by "artists," were not intended to be displayed in museums. There was a "museum" in fifth-century Athens: the *Museion*, a shrine of the Muses, on a hill of the same name, west of the Acropolis, south of the hill of the Nymphs and the Pnyx (see Figure 4). The Muses were lovely maidens, the daughters of Zeus and Mnemosyne (Memory). They nurtured literature, poetry, dance, and music. There was no muse of the visual arts. These were patronized by the lame smith-god Hephaistos, the only Olympian to fall short of physical perfection. Aristocratic authors scorned the physical labor required by craft production, for, as Xenophon, writing in the early fourth century B.C., had Socrates say,

> the manual crafts (*banausikaí*), as they are called, are spoken against, and are, naturally enough, held in utter disdain in our states. For they spoil the bodies of the workmen and the foremen, forcing them to sit still and live indoors, and in

some cases to spend the day at the fire. The softening of the
body involves a serious weakening of the mind. . . . In fact,
in some cities, and especially in those reputed to be good at
war, it is not lawful for citizens to practice such crafts.

This outlook (with its positive reference to Sparta) is extreme, and
plentiful evidence indicates that Athenian citizens (as well as foreigners)
practiced crafts. Nonetheless, Aristotle considered the craftsman to be a
kind of slave because he worked for others. And, as both Plutarch and the
satirist Lucian observed in the Roman imperial period, however much
people might admire the creations of accomplished sculptors such as
Pheidias, no one would want to be like them.[10]

The gleaming white marbles and painted pots that we associate
most readily with Athenian visual culture of the fifth century B.C.
are workshop products, the creations of (mostly anonymous) craftsmen and, in a few cases, women. As admirable as they are, the artifacts that fill modern galleries were made to serve other functions: as
votive or funerary offerings, decorations of temples and other public
buildings, or drinking and storage vessels. The high quality of Classical
Athenian ceramics and stonework testifies to the skill of their creators
and to the aesthetic refinement of ancient patrons, but these durable
artifacts hardly represent the top of the pyramid. The objects praised
most highly by Greek and Latin authors and recorded in ancient temple
inventories were fashioned from precious metals and other intrinsically
valuable materials: statues, cups, furniture, and implements of gold and
silver, ivory, and fine woods, as well as elaborate textiles.[11] Most such
items are lost: metals were melted down for reuse, and organic materials
have disintegrated. Surviving examples, however, are exquisite, and their
styles and motifs parallel those in better-preserved media (Figures 9–10).
Engraved gemstones (Figure 11) are more durable and survive in larger
numbers, but are highly portable and their post-antique history often
cannot be traced. Nonetheless, literary evidence and physical remains
indicate that fifth-century Athens welcomed numerous foreign craftsmen, and sumptuous creations as well as pottery were widely exported.

The expense of the substances from which sumptuous artifacts
were fashioned ensured that important commissions were entrusted to
the most skilled craftsmen, and the physical properties of their materials
allowed a greater degree of elaboration. The symbolic and magical associations of these often exotic materials, moreover, frequently enhanced
their value and carried spiritual connotations. Gold, for example, is
incorruptible; the poet Pindar called it "the child of Zeus" (frag. 209).

Items fashioned from it and other precious materials were thus appropriate for the most significant contexts.

The single most important object in fifth-century Athens was, without doubt, the colossal gold and ivory statue of Athena that Pheidias fashioned for the interior of the Parthenon. Completed in 438 B.C., it is now lost, but its appearance can be recovered from ancient descriptions as well as representations and adaptations in other media: statuettes, coins (Figure 12), tokens, plaques, vase paintings, et cetera. The so-called *Parthenos* stood over 40 feet high, dominating the interior of the temple built to house it (Figure 13). Its drapery and weapons were formed from over a ton of gold: forty-four talents according to the Athenian historian Philochoros, the equivalent of 616 talents of silver, or 3,696,000 silver drachmas (about 7 1/2 times the cost of the bronze *Promachos*; more than imperial Athens's foreign income at the beginning of the Peloponnesian War; enough to construct a fleet of more than 300 triremes). And this was just the cost of the gold. The underlying armature was crafted from expensive hard woods, and the goddess's eyes were probably precious stones. Her exposed flesh and other details, meanwhile, were rendered in ivory imported from Africa and/or the Near East.

Greeks had employed ivory for statues and other sumptuous items since the second millennium B.C., but before Pheidias made the *Parthenos* the size of ivory images was limited by the dimensions of the tusks from which sculptors carved either whole figures or individual components (heads, hands, arms, feet) that could be assembled around a wooden core. Pheidias's achievement was to overcome the problem of scale by adapting ancient furniture-making and bronze-casting techniques. He evidently unscrolled tusks into long, thin sheets of ivory that could be chemically softened, molded to shape, and mounted on an armature.[12]

The colossal *Athena*, like the temple it inhabited, was remarkable not only for its materials, scale, and construction, but also for its imagery. Both Parthenon and *Parthenos* were adorned with numerous subsidiary scenes, the significance of which was highly charged, and together they formed a coherent program. Like the bronze *Promachos*, the *Parthenos* stood fully armed, but at rest. The *Parthenos*, however, was being crowned by a gold and ivory Nike that alighted on her extended right hand, the physical manifestation of Athenian victories past, present, and future. The goddess's shield was decorated inside and out with depictions of mythological combat: the Olympian gods defeating the giants and the Athenians battling Amazons – scenes that also appeared on the external sculptures of the Parthenon, as on other contemporary monuments, where they functioned as allegories of the defeat of foreign enemies. Set on the slopes of the Acropolis, moreover, the Amazonomachy on the goddess's shield effectively rewrote history, for although the Persians had managed to sack Athena's sacred rock, Pheidias, like Polygnotos before him, depicted the Amazons being repulsed. Lapiths fighting centaurs, another allegory for the forces of civilization overcoming barbarism, decorated the goddess's thick-soled sandals. Meanwhile, Athena's triple-crested helmet was adorned with more ancient power symbols: the sphinx, two pegasoi, and, on each of the raised cheekpieces, griffins – half lion, half eagle – famed as guardians of gold. A snake, representing the Athenian hero Erichthonios, was coiled at her side. The statue's base bore reliefs depicting the birth of Pandora, probably not the baneful story known to us from Hesiod, but more likely a positive local variant, symbolizing Athena's gifts to mankind.

Literally and symbolically, the *Parthenos* embodied the benefits of the goddess's favor. The statue manifested the wealth and power of the state and the resources Athens could bring to bear against any enemy. Illuminated by the temple's wide doorway and two flanking windows in its eastern wall and framed by a two-tiered, $\prod$-shaped colonnade, the massive figure filled the interior of the temple (Figure 14). Reflected in a shallow pool of water (a later addition that helped maintain humidity beneficial to its ivory), the huge, gleaming image functioned as an epiphany, making the goddess present to mortal viewers. The enormous statue, moreover, was surrounded by treasure because the Parthenon, like other Greek temples, served as a repository of wealth. (Unlike synagogues, churches, and mosques, ancient temples did not shelter congregations of worshippers, for the indispensable ritual of sacrifice customarily took place at an altar in the open air (see Figure 39). On such occasions, temple doors would be opened so the deity, in the form of its statue, could witness the event.) The contents of the Parthenon, now lost, were inventoried on stone by the Treasurers of Athena. Surviving inscriptions record the presence of gold wreaths, coined money and bullion, statuettes, jewelry and gemstones, Persian daggers overlaid with gold and other weapons, gold horse trappings, gilt baskets and boxes containing precious items, gold and ivory flutes and lyres, incense-burners and ritual implements, richly inlaid tables, thrones, and couches, and numerous gold and silver vessels, some of which were employed during the great religious festivals that honored the goddess.

Thus the Parthenon itself served as a richly appointed jewel box. Like other Greek temples, it was essentially a rectangular block surrounded by a ring of columns on a stepped platform (Figures 14, 15). This traditional form allowed the architect (literally "master builder") considerable leeway for adjustments in plan, proportion, and decoration. The Parthenon was deliberately built to be the most elaborate temple of its day. Although Thucydides had Pericles in the Funeral Oration (2.40) say of the Athenians, "We combine love of beauty with economy," no expense seems to have been spared. Plutarch (*Life of Pericles* 12.2) wrote of an ancient debate as to whether it was right for Pericles to "rob" Athens's allies in order to gild and bedizen the city, which, "for all the world like a wanton woman, adds to her wardrobe precious stones and costly statues and temples worth their millions." Although recent research has challenged the notion that funds transferred from the Delian League to Athens in 454 B.C. provided substantial direct funding for the Parthenon, allied tribute certainly met other expenses and thus freed up local moneys for construction. Moreover, there is good evidence that the Athenians made alterations mid-course to make the building still more sumptuous.

Construction began in 447 B.C. and was substantially completed by 438, when the chryselephantine *Athena* was dedicated, though the last of the temple's pedimental sculptures were not hoisted into place until 432. Built almost entirely of local marble, some 20,000 tons quarried from Mt. Pentelikon (about 10 miles northeast of the Acropolis), the Parthenon was adorned with more architectural sculpture than any other Greek temple: 92 metopes carved in high relief; two pedimental compositions, each containing more than 20 over-life-size figures in the round; and the now famous low relief frieze, some 160 meters (525 feet) long. All of this, and some of the architecture too, was painted and gilded, while drill holes provide evidence for the addition of metal attachments, probably gilded bronze, in order to render such accouterments as spears, swords, bridles, et cetera.

The Parthenon's size, to some degree, was determined by its unfinished predecessor, destroyed by the Persians, but its architects, Iktinos and Kallikrates, changed the proportions. Throughout the building they employed a 4:9 ratio ($n:2n+1$; or $2^2:3^2$): this formula determined the ratio of column diameter to intercolumniation, interaxial space to column height, height to width, width to length, and so forth. Such unities contributed to the harmonious appearance of the temple – the freshness noted by Plutarch – and were probably explained in the architects' now lost treatise (mentioned by Vitruvius, 7 praef. 12). Such concerns are also evident elsewhere in contemporary thought. A few years after completion of the temple, for example, Plato commented that "measure and commensurability are everywhere identified with beauty and excellence" (*Philebus* 64e). Although they departed from the plan of the pre-Parthenon, Iktinos and Kallikrates made a virtue of the need to reuse its column drums and other material not entirely ruined by the Persians. They provided their building with a wider, eight-columned façade that simultaneously gave the Parthenon greater grandeur than its predecessor and other mainland temples that had only six columns on the short sides, and also recalled the octastyle façades of the imposing Ionic temples of Asia Minor, while providing a broader interior space for Pheidias's statue. Other innovations in plan were the Parthenon's shallow, prostyle porches (which were originally closed off by floor-to-ceiling grates) and the large back room, the ceiling of which was supported by four tall Ionic, or perhaps Corinthian, columns (the capitals do not survive).

Another exceptional feature of the temple is its many architectural refinements (Figure 16). Most of these deviations from straight horizontals and verticals, though perceivable by the naked eye, are not readily apparent. The platform of the temple, for example, is actually domed, rather than flat, and such upward curvature is also present in the entablature. The tapered columns, too, are curved, rather than straight, and although this slight swelling, or *entasis*, occurred in earlier Greek architecture, it is exceptionally subtle here. All of the columns tilt inward, the corner columns doubly so. The corner columns are also slightly larger in diameter than the others, because, according to Vitruvius (3.3.11), "they are sharply outlined by the unobstructed air around them, and seem to the beholder more slender than they are." This combination of refinements is unequaled, and scholars struggle to explain all of them. Vitruvius, writing some 400 years after construction, but with access to the treatise of Iktinos and Kallikrates, explains that they were designed to correct possible optical illusions: not only would the corner columns appear thinner if not thickened, but also horizontal lines might appear to sag if not curved upward. Whether or not such illusions actually occur matters less than whether they were thought to occur by the ancients, and thus needed to be corrected. Modern scholars, moreover, have observed that the temple's intentional deviations from the norm also impart vitality by creating a disjunction between what the viewer expects and actually sees. Thus, typical of its age, the grandeur and beauty of the Parthenon is based on the imposition of theoretical precepts, minute mathematical accuracy, and no small degree of illusionism.

Although damaged in antiquity, and later converted into a church and, following the Turkish conquest of Athens in A.D. 1456, a mosque, the structure of the Parthenon remained relatively well preserved until Venetian artillery ignited a powder magazine inside the temple, blowing out its center, on 26 September, 1687. Most of the carved metopes, however, had already been damaged by early Christian iconoclasts. The themes of these panels, however, can still be recovered. Those on three of the four sides of the building echoed the subsidiary decoration of Pheidias's *Athena Parthenos*: Gigantomachy (on the east), Amazonomachy (west), and, best preserved, Centauromachy (south). The *Ilioupersis* (Fall of Troy) on the north, meanwhile, seems not to have been depicted elsewhere on the Parthenon, but, as mentioned above, was one of the significant themes represented in the Painted Stoa. This imagery all alluded to the triumph of civilization over barbarism, but rather than depicting easy triumphs, the Amazonomachy and Centauromachy include fallen Greeks as well as defeated enemies (Figure 17). Thus these scenes simultaneously convey the cost, and increase the glory, of the ultimate victory. The Trojan series, meanwhile, is ideologically more complex, for, so far as the battered reliefs can be read, they focus on the aftermath of the destruction of a once proud city, rather than the heat of battle, suggesting, perhaps, some sympathy for those whose city had been sacked, as the Athenians' had been by the Persians. Similar sentiments have also been discerned in Early Classical vase paintings.

The metopes were the first of the Parthenon sculptures to be carved. Slightly over four feet square, they were fashioned on the ground and hoisted into place before work began on the temple's roof in 442 B.C. Although thematically linked, they reveal differences in composition, style, and skill. To complete such a massive program, stone carvers were gathered from throughout the Greek world. Some of the best preserved south metopes resemble earlier statuary on the Temple of Zeus at Olympia (ca. 468–456 B.C.) in the exaggerated, masklike faces of the centaurs (Figure 18). Others have more human features. The rendering of musculature and drapery also varies, but the finest of the carvings, composed dramatically, contrast – indeed, counterbalance – the unbridled passion of the centaurs with the graceful control and directed power of the humans (Figure 19). *Sophrosyne* (moderation, restraint, avoidance of excess) was praised in contemporary literature, and the Greeks fighting the centaurs are immune to the violent emotions of their monstrous opponents. Their blank expressions are timeless. Temporary responses to the uncertainty of changing circumstances have no place here. Some scholars have sought to identify the hand of Pheidias in these panels, but he was surely engaged full time on the gold and ivory *Parthenos*. In fact, the names of only one or two workers have been found on the building itself. Recent restoration work has revealed ancient graffiti on the hidden faces of blocks of the northern entablature: *Xanthias Thrax* ("Blondie [the?] Thracian"). It is unclear whether this was written by a sculptor or a less skilled workman, but it clearly indicates the involvement of foreigners as well as Athenians.

Perhaps the most famous part of the Parthenon today, the 525-foot-long continuous frieze was the least visible sculptural feature of the temple, located behind the metopes, within the colonnade, high above the ground (Figure 20). Recent research indicates that it was not part of the original plan, but was added to make the building still more opulent. Like the other Ionic elements in this predominantly Doric temple, the frieze also seems to underscore Athens's strong links to the Cycladic islands and Asia Minor, for although located on the Greek mainland, the Athenians claimed kinship with Ionian Greeks and had, at least since Solon (frag. 28a), considered theirs to be "the eldest city of Ionia." Continuous Ionic friezes also appear on other late fifth-century Athenian Doric temples (i.e., the so-called Hephaisteion overlooking the Agora and the temple of Poseidon at Sounion), but that on the Parthenon entirely encircles the interior of the colonnade and seems to depict contemporary Athenians, rather than mythological events, although precisely what is represented remains a topic of intense controversy.

Visible today at eye level in photographs and museum galleries, the frieze, with multiple overlapping figures carved in shallow relief of no more than 2 3/4 inches, was invisible from a distance, and could only be seen at a sharp angle, interrupted by the external colonnade. Paint and added metal attachments made the figures easier to read from the ground, but visitors to the Acropolis would only glimpse its lowest portions, below the metopes, unless they ventured near the temple and strained their necks. The frieze is not mentioned by any surviving ancient author, and observant viewers, as they proceeded eastward, would have been surprised by its very existence, and then by its changing imagery. First, along the west, north, and south, long ranks of horsemen (Figure 21) and then chariots with *apobatai* (hoplites trained to leap on and off the speeding vehicles) galloped toward the entrance. Then, about three-quarters along the flanks, the procession slowed as elders, musicians, and men carrying water jars (Figure 22) and trays and leading sacrificial animals approached the eastern façade. Once the procession turned the corners, maidens appeared carrying ritual implements,

FIGURE 1. The Acropolis from the Museion (southwest). Photo: American School of Classical Studies at Athens, Alison Frantz Photographic Collection, AT 71.

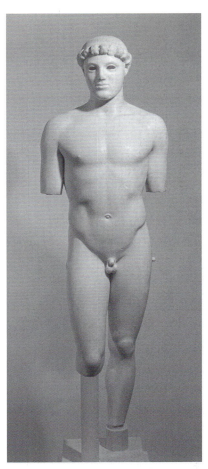

FIGURE 2. The Early Classical "Kritios boy" was erected as an offering on the Acropolis. The pose of the nude youth breaks from the stiff, symmetrical stance of Archaic Greek sculpture. The hollow eyes, originally inlaid, and wispy hair are technical innovations associated with bronzework. Ca. 480 B.C. Preserved height 85 cm. Athens, Acropolis Museum 698. Photo: American School of Classical Studies at Athens, Alison Frantz Photographic Collection, AT 334.

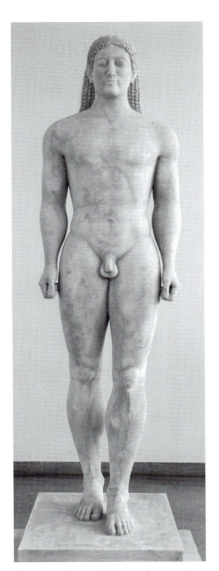

FIGURE 3. This *Kouros* (male youth), which served as an aristocratic funerary marker at Anavyssos in Attica, is one of the finest examples of the ideal male type popular throughout the Archaic Greek world prior to the development of the Classical style. Ca. 530 B.C. Height 1.94 m. Athens, National Archaeological Museum 3851. Photo: American School of Classical Studies at Athens, Alison Frantz Photographic Collection, AT 112.

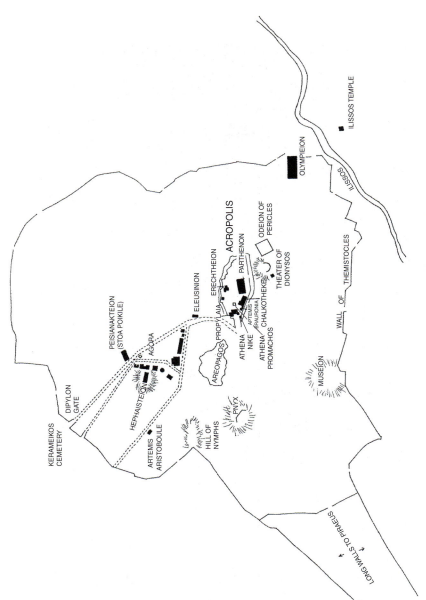

FIGURE 4. Athens in the late fifth-century B.C.

FIGURE 5. Black-figure prize amphorae (storage jars) like this, inscribed "from the games at Athens," contained olive oil awarded to victors in the Panathenaic Games. The reverse features the athletic event (here javelin throwers), while Athena, fully armed, is depicted on the obverse. On this example, produced after the restoration of the Athenian democracy in 403 B.C., the goddess's shield is decorated with a representation of the statues of the *Tyrannicides* by Kritios and Nesiotes. From Tocra in north Africa. Ca. 402 B.C. London, British Museum B605. Photo: © Copyright the Trustees of the British Museum.

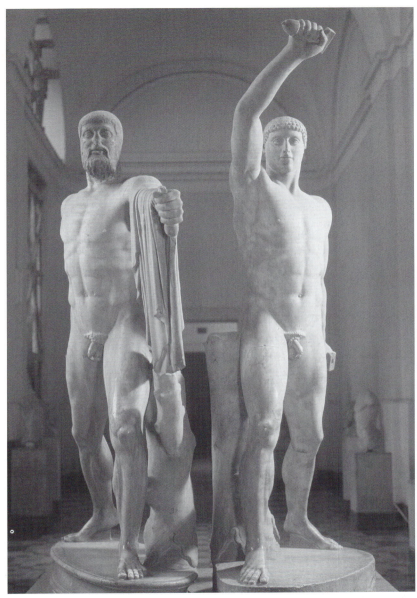

FIGURE 6. Roman marble copies of the *Tyrannicides* by Kritios and Nesiotes from the villa of the Emperor Hadrian at Tivoli, near Rome. The raised right arm of Harmodios (right) should be restored sharply bent (as in Figure 5). Early second century A.D. after bronze figures erected in the Agora of Athens in 477/6 B.C. Restored height 1.85 m. Naples, National Archaeological Museum 6009–6010. Photo: Alinari / Art Resource, NY, ART 55129.

FIGURE 7. "Mourning Athena" relief from the Acropolis. The goddess reads a stele, the precise meaning of which remains elusive. Ca. 460 B.C. Height 54 cm. Athens, Acropolis Museum 695. Photo: American School of Classical Studies at Athens, Alison Frantz Photographic Collection, AT 337.

FIGURE 8. Expanded view of an Attic red-figure calyx krater (mixing bowl) from Orvieto in central Italy. Scene uncertain, perhaps the mustering of heroes on the plain at Marathon or Theseus in the Underworld. Herakles, center, is recognizable by his club, lion skin, and bow; Athena is seen to the left. Variable ground lines and other compositional innovations have been associated with lost monumental wall paintings described by ancient authors. The other side depicts Apollo and Artemis slaying the children of Niobe. Name vase of the "Niobid Painter." Ca. 460 B.C. Paris, Musée du Louvre MNC 511, G341. Photo: after Furtwangler-Reichhold. Courtesy of the Getty Research Institute.

FIGURE 9. Gold-figured silver phiale (offering bowl) representing warriors on coursing chariots, from a Thracian tomb near Duvanli, Bulgaria. The style and effect resemble Attic red-figure vase paintings. Though few vessels of precious metal survive, many were recorded in Athenian temple inventories and other texts. Late fifth century B.C. Diameter 20.5 cm.; weight 428 g. Plovdiv Archaeological Museum 1515. Photo: The Art Archive / Archaeological Museum Sofia / Dagli Orti.

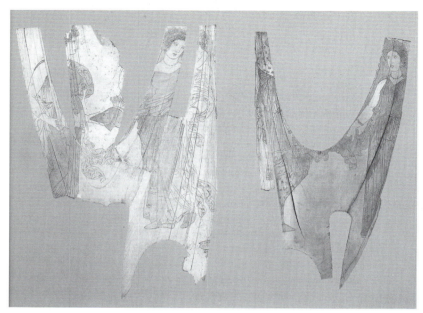

FIGURE 10. The Judgment of Paris (Athena holding a helmet, Aphrodite with Eros on her shoulder, Paris, and Hera) on a polychromatic incised ivory plaque that adorned a funerary couch. The calligraphic flourishes of drapery not surprisingly surpass those of the finest red-figure pots. From a Skythian burial in the Crimea. Ca. 400 B.C. Preserved height 20 cm. St. Petersburg, State Hermitage Museum K–O116. Photo: The State Hermitage Museum, St. Petersburg.

FIGURE 11. Impression of a red and yellow mottled jasper scaraboid intaglio said to have been found in a grave at Kara in Attica, inscribed "Dexamenos made [me]." Dexamenos is known from other signed gems to have been a native of Chios. This detailed but idealized image, which Arthur Evans optimistically identified as a portrait of Cimon, is an outstanding example of ancient gem engraving. 450–425 B.C. Length 2.1 cm.; width 1.7 cm.; thickness 0.6 cm. Boston, Museum of Fine Arts, Francis Bartlett Donation, 23.580. Photo: © Copyright 2007 Museum of Fine Arts, Boston.

FIGURE 12. Athenian silver tetradrachm featuring the head of Athena on the obverse, and, on the reverse, Pheidias's *Athena Parthenos* (447–438 B.C.) to the right of the goddess's owl, which is perched on an oil jar. First century B.C. London, The British Museum. Photo: © Copyright the Trustees of the British Museum.

FIGURE 13. Sculptor Alan LeQuire's full-scale steel and fiberglass re-creation of Pheidias's *Athena Parthenos* inside the Parthenon, Nashville, Tennessee. Height (including the base) 12.75 m. Photo: Gary Layda / courtesy of Wesley Paine, Metro Board of Parks and Recreation.

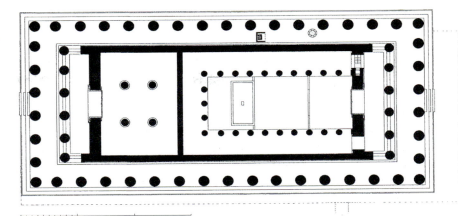

FIGURE 14. Plan of the Parthenon (447–432 B.C.) revised by M. Korres to reflect recent discoveries, including windows and a service stair in the east wall. The large rectangle in the center of the temple represents the base of Pheidias's *Athena Parthenos.*

FIGURE 15. The Parthenon from the northwest, as seen from the Propylaia. Photo: American School of Classical Studies at Athens, Alison Frantz Photographic Collection, AT 2.

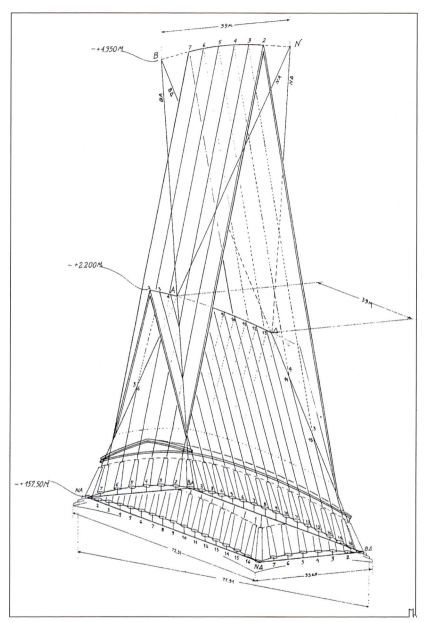

FIGURE 16. The refinements of the Parthenon exaggerated by M. Korres to show curvature of the stylobate and architrave as well as the thickening and inclination of the columns.

FIGURE 17. A victorious centaur exults over the wracked body of a defeated Greek. Parthenon south metope 28. Ca. 447–442 B.C. Height 1.33 m. London, The British Museum. Photo: © Copyright the Trustees of the British Museum.

FIGURE 18. A Greek and centaur lock awkwardly in battle. The cutting in the centaur's right arm is for an ancient join. Parthenon south metope 31. Ca. 447–442 B.C. Height 1.32 m. London, The British Museum. Photo: © Copyright the Trustees of the British Museum.

FIGURE 19. The cloak of a victorious Greek, which would have been picked out in paint, serves as a dramatic backdrop to this combat scene. Parthenon south metope 27. Ca. 447–442 B.C. Height 1.37 m. London, The British Museum. Photo: © Copyright the Trustees of the British Museum.

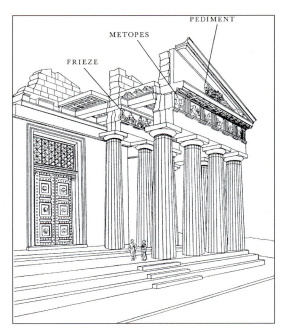

FIGURE 20. Cut-away view of the Parthenon showing the disposition of its sculptural decoration. With two pedimental compositions carved fully in the round, 92 high relief metopal panels, and a 160-meter-long low relief frieze, the temple was the most elaborate of its day. After S. Woodford, *The Parthenon*. Image: © Copyright the Trustees of the British Museum.

FIGURE 21. Idealized horsemen from the north frieze of the Parthenon. The multiple overlapping planes, which would have been enhanced by painted decoration, are carved in just 7 centimeters (2 3/4 inches) of shallow relief. Drill holes indicate the attachment of horse-trappings and weapons. Ca. 442–438 B.C. Height 1.06 m. London, The British Museum. Photo: Art Resource, NY, ART 21.

FIGURE 22. Four *hydrophoroi* (water carriers) and, at right, the hands and drapery of an *auletes* (pipe-player) from the north frieze of the Parthenon. Minor variations in pose and drapery enliven what might have been a repetitive, static scene. Ca. 442–438 B.C. Height 1.06 m. Athens, Acropolis Museum 864. Photo: American School of Classical Studies at Athens, Alison Frantz Photographic Collection, 161.

FIGURE 23. Poseidon, Apollo, and Artemis from the east frieze of the Parthenon. Idealized, like the humans on the frieze, the seated Olympians are larger in stature. Ca. 442–438 B.C. Height 1.06 m. Athens, Acropolis Museum 856. Photo: American School of Classical Studies at Athens, Alison Frantz Photographic Collection, 152.

FIGURE 24. Drawings of the west pediment of the Parthenon (carved ca. 438–432) made by Jacques Carrey (?) shortly before the explosion of temple in 1687. Paris, Cabinet des Médailles. Photo: Bridgeman-Giraudon / Art Resource, NY, ART 72677, 106583.

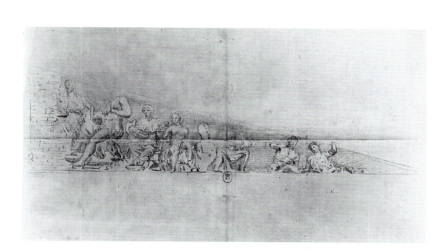

FIGURE 25. The Hestia (K), Dione? (L), and Aphrodite (M) from the east pediment of the Parthenon, ca. 438–432 B.C. (the letters are used conventionally to denote individual pediment figures). Preserved height (of K) 1.30 m.; length of group 3.15 m. London, The British Museum. Photo: Scala / Art Resource, NY ART 22872.

FIGURE 26. Watercolor reconstruction by Peter Connolly of the Acropolis, from the west, during the Panathenaic procession. Note that the symmetry of the Propylaia is illusory, so as not to impinge on the precinct of Athena Nike. Image: akg-images / Peter Connolly.

FIGURE 27. The Erechtheion, with its irregular plan and "Porch of the Maidens," was designed to accommodate multiple cults on an uneven site. (The foundations of the Old Temple of Athena are in the foreground.) Ca. 420–406 B.C. Photo: American School of Classical Studies at Athens, Alison Frantz Photographic Collection, AT 43.

FIGURE 28. The elegant temple of Athena Nike on the southwest bastion of the Acropolis. Ca. 435–420 B.C. Photo: American School of Classical Studies at Athens, Alison Frantz Photographic Collection, AT 8.

FIGURE 29. A Nike unbinding her sandal before approaching Athena, from the parapet around the Temple of Athena Nike. Ca. 420–405 B.C. Height 1.01 m. Athens, Acropolis Museum 973. Photo: American School of Classical Studies at Athens, Alison Frantz Photographic Collection, AT 136a.

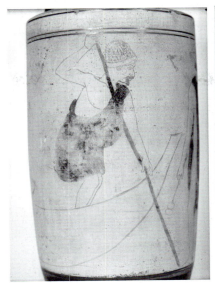

FIGURE 30. Charon, boatman of the dead, awaits a woman, led by Hermes to the Underworld. Minute souls (barely visible) flit about. The matte colors of the garments, added after firing, are relatively well preserved. Attributed to the "Sabouroff Painter." Ca. 440–430 B.C. Athens, National Archaeological Museum 1926. Photo: American School of Classical Studies at Athens, Alison Frantz Photographic Collection, AT 213–313.

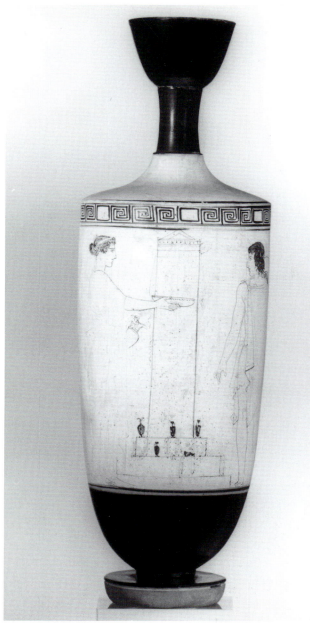

FIGURE 31. A woman makes an offering at the tomb of a warrior. Attic white-ground lekythos attributed to the "Bosanquet Painter." Ca. 440 B.C. Basel, Antikenmuseum Basel und Sammlung Ludwig Kä 402. Photo: Antikenmuseum.

FIGURE 32. A warrior takes leave of his wife on an Attic white-ground lekythos. A hair snood, mirror, and jug indicate a domestic interior. Matte pigment lost. Attributed to the "Achilles Painter." Ca. 440 B.C. Athens, National Archaeological Museum 1818. Photo: American School of Classical Studies at Athens, Alison Frantz Photographic Collection, AT 105.

FIGURE 33. Marble grave stele of Eupheros. Ca. 430 B.C. Height 1.47 m. Athens, Kerameikos Museum 1169. Photo: Deutsches Archäologisches Institut, Athens, Kerameikos 8516.

FIGURE 34. Marble grave stele of Ktesileos and Theano. Ca. 410–400 B.C. Height 0.93 m. Athens, National Archaeological Museum 3472. Photo: Scala / Art Resource, NY, ART 79323.

FIGURE 35. Marble grave stele of Hegeso. Ca. 400 B.C. Height 1.58 m. Athens,
National Archaeological Museum 3624. Photo: American School of Classical Studies at Athens, Alison Frantz Photographic Collection, AT 98.

FIGURE 36. A woman at her toilet on an Attic red-figure amphoriskos (perfume jar). Attributed to the "Eretria Painter." Ca. 420–410 B.C. Oxford, Ashmolean Museum 537. Photo: Ashmolean Museum, Oxford.

FIGURE 37. Naked *hetairai* (courtesans) entertain men at a symposion on an Attic red-figure kylix (drinking cup) from Tarquinia. Attributed to the "Tarquinia Painter." Ca. 470–460 B.C. Basel, Antikenmuseum Basel und Sammlung Ludwig Kä 415. Photo: Antikenmuseum.

FIGURE 38. A servant boy attends to a man who has had too much to drink: a cautionary tale on the interior of an Attic red-figure kylix (drinking cup) from Capua attributed to the "Dokimasia Painter." Ca. 480–460 B.C. Berlin, Staatliche Museen, Antikensammlung, Inv. F 2309. Photo: Johannes Laurentius, Bildarchiv Preussischer Kulturbesitz/Art Resource, NY, ART 190041.

FIGURE 39. Herakles prepares a sacrifice to Chryse at an open air sanctuary. Attic red–figure bell krater (mixing bowl) from Armento, Italy. Ca. 440–430 B.C. Vienna, Kunsthistorishes Museum 1144. Photo: Erich Lessing / Art Resource, NY, ART 53614.

FIGURE 40. Aigisthos kills Agamemnon on an Attic red-figure calyx krater (mixing bowl). Klytaimnestra, left, holds an axe in her right hand. The other side depicts Orestes killing Aigisthos. Attributed to the "Dokimasia Painter." Ca. 460 B.C. Height 51 cm.; diameter 51 cm. Boston, Museum of Fine Arts, William Francis Warden Fund, 63.1246. Photo: © Copyright 2007 Museum of Fine Arts, Boston.

FIGURE 41. The Valhalla, or German Hall of Fame and Honor, near Regensburg. Conceived by Prince Ludwig of Bavaria in 1807 to contain busts of the most eminent Germans, from Alaric and Theodoric in the middle ages to Mozart, Schiller, and Goethe. Designed by Leo von Klenze in 1821 and completed, on an artificial Acropolis above the Danube, in 1842. Athenian-inspired monuments have also been erected in London (to commemorate Wellington's defeat of Napoleon), Edinburgh, Munich, New York, Philadelphia, Washington, D.C., Buffalo, Nashville, and elsewhere. Photo: Erich Lessing, Art Resource, NY, ART 206758.

FIGURE 42. Athenian white-ground lekythos, ca. 450 B.C. View (left): a woman visits a tomb on which sits a small child, most likely representing the deceased son of the mourner (only the base of the tomb is visible). View (right): a female slave accompanies the mother to the tomb. Her hair and features indicate her identity; that she was the child's nurse is perhaps indicated by his looking toward her not his mother. Courtesy of the Michael C. Carlos Museum of Emory University.

FIGURE 43. Athenian red-figure hydria, ca. 450 B.C. Three women gather within a house or courtyard for a musical performance. The woman on the left holds a book roll for the performing musician in the center of the scene. Solow Art and Architecture Foundation, New York.

libation bowls, pitchers, and incense burners – some of the very objects mentioned in the temple's inscribed inventories. Then viewers would see older men, apparently the ten Eponymous Heroes, and beyond them, closer to the center, the Olympians themselves, seated, conversing with one another, paying but little attention to the procession of mortals (Figure 23). In the center of the east frieze, between two groups of deities who look in the opposite direction, a woman and two maidens busy themselves with stools and other cult paraphernalia while a man and a child fold a cloth. While this scene has engendered various interpretations, the traditional reading of the cloth as one of the *peploi* (elaborately decorated garments specially woven with costly purple dyes) that were regularly presented to the old wooden statue of Athena (not the *Parthenos*) at the Panathenaic procession has the most to recommend it. The bulk of the frieze, as well as its culmination above the entrance to the temple, however, focuses not so much on any specific activity or event, but rather on the people of Athens.

Because no previous Greek temple was ever decorated in this manner, modern scholars have searched for corresponding historical or mythological events, but Athenians walking alongside the temple would surely have seen in the long processional frieze some version of themselves, albeit physically perfect and highly idealized. Whether standing or walking, riding at a gallop or restraining their horses, the human figures on the frieze are expressionless, aloof, betraying no emotion, almost apotheosized. Like the *Tyrannicides*, they provided models for emulation: exemplary citizens of various ages in the service of their goddess and their *polis*. And for foreigners, whether allies, subjects, or rivals, the figures of the frieze advertised the qualities, material as well as spiritual, of the people whose empire and resources allowed the construction of so remarkable a monument.

The most visible components of the Parthenon's figural decoration, the pediments (Figure 24), proclaimed the Athenians' special relationship with their patron goddess. The east was damaged by the addition of an apse when the temple was converted into a church in the early middle ages: the center is lost, but Pausanias records that it depicted the miraculous birth of Athena. The subsidiary figures, carefully composed, indicate a centrifugal movement as word of this momentous event emanate from the apex of the triangle. Credit for the overall design of the Parthenon's sculptures has been given to Pheidias, whom Plutarch anachronistically calls the overseer (*epistates*) of the entire project, but although the master doubtless made a significant contribution to the overall program, he was accused of embezzlement, perhaps as part of an attempt to discredit Pericles, and apparently left Athens after completing the gold and ivory colossus in 438. In the years between the carving of the metopes and the frieze in the 440s and early 430s and the completion of the pediments in 432, the personal styles of individual marble sculptors were gradually leavened, and the pediments show a remarkable uniformity. The best preserved of the massive figures exhibit a powerful sensuality, even – or perhaps especially – the clothed deities, some of whose drapery defines and reveals their anatomy, an especially fitting trope for the reclining figure of Aphrodite, the goddess of physical love, splayed in her mother's lap (Figure 25), as yet oblivious to the birth of her half-sister and the dawning of a new age.

The west pediment, the first visible to anyone mounting the Acropolis, also depicted a significant moment in the life of Athena and the history of her city: the contest between the goddess and her uncle Poseidon. The notion that Olympians would vie with one another for patronage of the city has been cited as evidence of the Athenians' high communal self-regard. Athena offered the sacred olive, while Poseidon created a salt spring. Variant mythological traditions offer divergent accounts of how the goddess came to be judged the winner of the contest, but the prominent position of Poseidon in the dynamic, V–like composition (preserved in drawings made before the explosion of 1687, Figure 24), is significant, for the god embodies the divine underpinnings of Athens's maritime supremacy.[13]

The Parthenon was the first of the Periclean buildings on the Acropolis and the only one that Pericles lived to see completed. The Propylaia (Figure 26), begun in 437 B.C., was never finished. Work stopped in 432, apparently upon the outbreak of the Peloponnesian War, but the building was far enough along to fulfill its function as a ceremonial entryway: though it is not a temple, its pedimental façades sacralize the approach to the Acropolis. There is ample evidence that its architect, Mnesikles, had planned for the central, colonnaded entrance hall, which combines Doric and Ionic elements, to be flanked by four symmetrical wings, only one of which was completed, on the north. In the second century A.D. Pausanias saw old paintings there and called that part of the building a *Pinakotheke*, but the off-center door of the inner room strongly suggests that it was used for ritual dining, which regularly followed animal sacrifice, the key event of Greek religious rituals. The corresponding south wing of the Propylaia, meanwhile, was truncated in order not to impinge on the precinct of Athena Nike, but Mnesikles nonetheless installed columns and a false pier, creating the appearance of symmetry. Other innovations were the irregular spacing of the Doric frieze over the extra-wide central doorway and the double pediment. Throughout this and other Periclean buildings, the "rules" of Classical architecture were not a straitjacket (as they often were subsequently), but rather an adaptable system that could be employed variously to solve problems presented by site and function.

Such problems were nowhere more apparent than in the temple erected on the north side of the Acropolis, the so-called Erechtheion, best known today for its south porch, supported by marble maidens instead of columns (Figure 27). This porch overlaps the foundations of the Archaic temple destroyed by the Persians, and the new temple seems to have taken on some the functions of that building, though part of the ruined Old Temple may have been left standing as a memorial to Persian barbarity.[14] The Erechtheion housed some of the city's most sacred sites, and faced with the demands of multiple cults, as well as uneven ground, its unknown architect designed a highly ornate Ionic structure that, in contrast to the Parthenon and more traditional temples, had four very different façades, including asymmetrical porches on its long sides. Vitruvius, in fact, wrote that it had "all the features which are customarily on the front transferred to the flanks" (4.8.4). The temple's finely carved moldings, column bases, and capitals were painted, gilded, and even inlaid with colored glass beads. Its disparate elements were tied together by a continuous frieze, whose separately carved marble figures, approximately two feet tall, were doweled to a dark background of blue Eleusinian limestone. Building inscriptions record that work proceeded on and off during the Peloponnesian War, and one fragment dating to 408/7 B.C. indicates that the standard payment for carving individual human figures on the frieze was 60 drachmas (approximately two months' wages for an average workman). Of the surviving statuary, most figures are too fragmentary to identify, but the frieze may well have depicted myths of early Athens. The famous maidens of the south porch (called *korai* in the inscriptions, "Caryatids" only later) are better preserved. Lord Elgin's agents removed one in 1803, and the others were placed in the Acropolis Museum in the 1970s to protect them from further damage from acid rain. They stand with one leg flexed, while the heavy, almost fluted drapery over the other is well suited to their architectural function. Ancient Roman copies indicate that they held ritual offering bowls and in this as well as their fine garments they resemble the girls on the east frieze of the Parthenon, across the way. They must also have alluded to the young women of

Athens who regularly processed between the two temples on the way to make offerings at Athena's altar.

The fourth "Periclean" building on the Acropolis also replaced an earlier shrine on the same site. Probably constructed not long after Pericles' death in 429/8, the small, ornate Ionic Temple of Athena Nike atop the bastion protruding beyond the southwest wing of the Propylaia (Figures 26, 28) lacked the peripteral colonnade of the Parthenon, but its profuse architectural sculpture also propounded the theme of victory through myth, history, and allegory. Its sculpted pediments featured Amazonomachy and Gigantomachy; its continuous Ionic frieze depicted the assembly of the gods on the east, and historic battles of Greeks against Persians (apparently Marathon) and Greeks against Greeks (perhaps the Peloponnesian War?) on the other sides. The parapet presented processions of winged victories (who also appeared as *akroteria* at the apex and corners of the pediments) leading sacrificial animals to the goddess and erecting trophies in her honor. Much of this program alluded to the decoration of the Parthenon, and the rich carving of the parapet, like that of the Parthenon pediments, is virtuosic, stressing grace with elegant flourishes of drapery over soft, seductive flesh (Figure 29). The garment of the famous Nike *un*binding her sandal as she approaches Athena slips suggestively from her right shoulder, like that of Aphrodite on the Parthenon (see Figure 25), while her drapery, appearing wet and thin over the body, reveals the attractive female body it is ostensibly meant to conceal. Elsewhere, billowing drapery unrealistically thickens and takes on a life of its own in exuberant calligraphic folds, the deep cutting of which would have created vibrant contrasts of light and shadow in the bright Athenian sun. This highly mannered style, also evident in late fifth-century vase-painting (see Figure 36), parallels that of contemporary rhetoric, which is marked by antithesis, assonance, repetition, rhyme, et cetera. Some modern critics have seen such florid prettiness as undemandingly pleasant and even escapist, carved, as it seems to have been, during the dark years of the late fifth century, but the undeniable eroticism of the Nike Temple parapet is certainly appropriate for depiction of something all Greeks keenly desired to possess: victory. In the midst of the Peloponnesian War, the Athenians represented the idea of victory here, repeatedly, like a mantra, hoping to win a war they were destined to lose.[15]

A number of other temples dedicated to various divinities were erected in the lower city of Athens and the Attic countryside under Pericles and his successors, and so were important civic buildings, all of which demonstrated not only the piety of the Athenians, but also the wealth and power that were the fruits of their empire. These monuments cannot be discussed here, but their collective cost was enormous. Thucydides (2.13.3) reports that by 431 B.C. Pericles' building program, along with the siege of Potidaea, had reduced the silver reserves on the Acropolis from 9,700 to 6,000 talents. Nonetheless, construction continued on and off throughout the Peloponnesian War.[16]

Like state commissions, more modest objects fashioned for individuals were made to be exhibited in public, or at least semipublic, contexts, and they too served to enhance the status of their patrons and reinforce prevalent ideologies. Thus calling them "private" artworks is misleading, especially since they too frequently embodied and projected collective values. This is, perhaps, most evident in the large body of surviving funerary monuments and painted pots intended for the all-male drinking party, the *symposion*.

Offerings to the dead are among the earliest preserved works of Athenian art, and pottery deposited in and on tombs provides a continuous record of stylistic development throughout the first millennium B.C. Some of these vessels were decorated with funeral scenes: the deceased on a bier surrounded by mourners and/or mourners at the tomb. But although funerary art naturally sheds light on burial practices and a society's beliefs about death, it is essentially produced to serve the living. Apart from depictions of rituals associated with death and images of Hermes and/or the boatman Charon leading the deceased to the Underworld (Figure 30), the funerary art of Archaic and Classical Athens tended to be retrospective, rather than prospective. Idealized *kouroi* and *korai* were not only dedicated to gods in sanctuaries, but also erected over tombs. They embodied aristocratic values of beauty, strength, and wealth to be attributed to the departed, characterizing (even falsifying) the lives they lived, rather than some ideal life in the hereafter. They also simultaneously asserted the status of families that could afford to commission them. Far from portraits in the modern sense, these generic statues were personalized by inscriptions. Meanwhile, tall, narrow stelai, often surmounted by florals or protective sphinxes, also presented idealized images of the dead. Less expensive than carvings in the round, funerary reliefs frequently contained additional visual, as well as verbal, information to further individualize the deceased, even though he or she was depicted within only a limited number of accepted, normative types: men were given attributes of warriors, athletes, or priests; women (who seem to have been commemorated less frequently) were depicted as wives, brides, mothers, daughters, and sisters.

The production of costly marble funerary markers ceased in Attica around the time of the Persian Wars – perhaps on account of sumptuary laws aimed at restricting the expenditure of aristocrats, the redirection of resources following the sack of Athens, or recognition of the symbolic capital of restraint. Whatever the case, it did not resume until a decade or two after the middle of the fifth century, at which time Parthenonian stylistic traits are evident in the new series of grave reliefs. In the interim, the Athenian state financed public funerals of those who died in its service, and families commemorated their dead with modest *lekythoi* (ceramic oil jars) bearing polychromatic paintings on a white ground. The choice of vessel was appropriate because Greeks anointed the bodies of the dead before cremation and burial and subsequently offered perfumed oils at graveside rituals. Among other scenes, Classical lekythoi frequently bear images of family members, usually women, visiting, or preparing to visit, the grave; the deceased, too, sometimes appears, apparently unseen by the living (Figure 31). Other lekythoi bear quiet images of the dead interacting with the living in domestic contexts, as if still alive (Figure 32). These tranquil, intimate moments are extremely affecting by virtue of the dignity and elegance of the figures and the absence of openly expressed emotion. Their restraint poignantly conveys the pain of loss, but for all their serenity, they are more than personal monuments. Like the Athenians on the Parthenon frieze, the figures on the lekythoi are, for the most part, young and beautiful. They are ideal types that embody normative values: the strong, handsome men who willingly left their wives and homes to fight, and die, for the *polis*; the beautiful, elegant women who stayed behind as mainstays of the household. Personal loss is to be borne. What is new here is not so much the values embodied – indeed espoused – by the figures, but rather the emphasis on their relationship as family members and the public demands placed on those more intimate relationships.

When stone funeral reliefs reappear in Athens, ca. 430 B.C., stylistic and technical similarities to the sculptures of the Parthenon suggest that carvers of the Acropolis monuments found new work for private patrons during the Peloponnesian War. Like their Archaic counterparts, some of these reliefs glorify the deceased, presenting males as warriors, hunters, and athletes, but they also appropriate the iconography of state monuments. Eupheros (Figure 33), for example, not only carries the hooked strigil that identifies him as an athlete, but also is draped like the men on the Parthenon frieze and displays no emotion. Found near the grave of a boy about 15 years old, this relief projects onto the deceased the attributes of the ideal male: the citizen-athlete. Enclosed in a small temple-like frame, moreover, this monument, like many others of the period, seems to sacralize the dead.

Many Classical reliefs are wider than their tall, thin Archaic predecessors, with multifigure groups that invite the viewer to read implied narratives. The figures, moreover, frequently overlap the margins of their architectural setting, making them appear still more present to the viewer (paint would have enlivened them further). The gravestone of Ktesileos and Theano (Figure 34) depicts a bearded, draped male, fingers intertwined, legs crossed, leaning on a staff resting in the crook of his right arm. This is the dress of the Athenian citizen male, but here the man is depicted in the domestic sphere, gazing at his wife, elaborately draped, modestly raising her veil. It is unclear which of the figures is dead, or who commissioned the relief for whom. And in the end it does not matter, for the stone ultimately commemorates both. Indeed, it focuses not on some glorious accomplishment of either, but rather on their relationship. Marriage, however, was far from a personal matter in fifth-century Athens, and this intimate moment, like all scenes depicted on Attic gravestones, was displayed publicly in the cemeteries alongside public roads just outside the city gates.

One of the best-known stelai (Figure 35), that of Hegeso, the daughter of Proxenos, is variously dated by scholars. It depicts the deceased in fine, flowing robes, veiled, seated on a high-backed chair, her sandaled feet on a footstool. She selects an item, evidently a necklace (originally rendered in paint, as were her sandal straps), from the open jewelry box presented by a slave girl, smaller in stature, who wears a plain, long-sleeved garment. This quiet scene might strike a modern viewer as a mournful commentary on the fleeting pleasures of life that bring joy no more, and ancient Athenians, too, might have been struck by its almost tender alienation. But this is no more a scene of "everyday life" than the other images fashioned in ancient Greece. Retrospective funerary art offers an opportunity to articulate *ideals* of life, acting not so much as a memorial to an individual, but as the celebration of an ideal and an ideology of social living.[17] Hegeso, who presumably died before marriage, is presented as a respectable young woman – a potential bride, had she lived – by her calm and dignified demeanor, and also by her beauty and wealth. In fact, her wealth, in the form of the jewelry that would have constituted her dowry, literally enhances her beauty. This and other stelai that visually construct identities to suit a variety of social circumstances present the potential virtue of every citizen who willingly conforms to the expectations of the community. Such imagery was also adopted by prosperous noncitizens, such as foreigners and freed slaves.

The styles and motifs of sculptural monuments and more sumptuous items can also be found on more modest painted pots. Tens of thousands of these survive, for although they can be broken they are virtually indestructible, and thus fill modern museum galleries and storerooms. The red-figure technique, which was invented in Athens around 530 B.C., did not supplant black-figure until the early years of the fifth century and never wholly replaced it. Red-figure, however, was the medium of preference for Athenian fineware throughout the fifth century, and its production, like that of black-figure, was centered in the *Kerameikos* district west of the Agora, hence our term *ceramic*. Skilled potters produced a wide variety of shapes suitable for specific functions, and painters (sometimes, but not always, the same individuals) decorated them with figures and scenes that were sometimes closely linked to their function. Thus, for example, a small perfume jar depicts a woman in fine robes holding a mirror (Figure 36), a scene that also appears on Classical funerary reliefs.

Despite a wide range of painters, subjects, and shapes, most painted pots seem to have been produced for the symposion, the all-male drinking party in which women took part only as servants, musicians, dancers, and providers of other pleasures alongside boys. Thus, like their Archaic counterparts, Classical Athenian pots frequently bear images of Dionysos and his circle, or of the symposion itself (Figure 37). Subjects seemingly unrelated to their use, such as hunting, athletics, battle, and various myths, also appear regularly, just as they had in the Archaic period, for the symposion played a key role in the socialization of citizens, and the images on pots proffered examples, positive and negative, of qualities to develop and behaviors to be emulated and avoided. Thus drinking cups were adorned with the heroic youthful deeds of Theseus, as well as men unable to hold their wine (Figure 38). Two-handled wine storage jars (amphorae) depict warriors taking leave of their families (as on lekythoi) or in battle – often without the protection of armor! And mixing bowls represent preparations for sacrifice (Figure 39). Myth (often identified only through painted inscriptions) blurs with "everyday" life, reinforcing collective values. Mythological scenes, moreover, are rarely illustrations of texts. Indeed, they often pre-date surviving literary sources. Rather, they are retellings of well-known stories, represented according to the conventions of the medium and the needs of the artist. Thus, for example, it is Aigisthos, not Klytaimnestra, who slays Agamemnon on a red-figure krater (Figure 40).

Widely exported in antiquity, Athenian pots also supply valuable information about the extent of Athenian trade, though the precise mechanisms of exchange remain unclear. In the wake of the disaster of 404 B.C., however, Athenian potters and painters seem to have set up workshops abroad and to have engendered vibrant local "schools" (to use an anachronistic term) in Sicily and southern Italy. In sculpture, meanwhile, carvers trained on Periclean projects spread the styles inaugurated there. It was, however, the adoption of Athenian classicism by the Romans, more than anything else, that made it the standard by which later European art has been judged – at least until the late nineteenth century. The emperor Augustus and others recognized the success of Pericles and his fellow citizens in creating a visual language and a physical setting that both symbolized and embodied civic greatness, and thus they adopted and adapted the forms and styles of Periclean monuments. Democracy, per se, was not widely praised and seems not to have been of great concern. Rather, the art and architecture of ancient Athens have served later generations, as they did Pericles and his fellow citizens, as potent expressions of high ideals and imperialistic nationalism (Figure 41).

SUGGESTIONS FOR FURTHER READING

The bibliography of works on Greek art, and on Classical Athens in particular, is vast. C. M. Robertson, *A History of Greek Art*, 2 vols. (Cambridge: Cambridge University Press, 1975) remains unsurpassed. M. D. Fullerton, *Greek Art* (Cambridge: Cambridge University Press, 2000) is a shorter overview that profitably raises issues of reception and interpretation. J. J. Pollitt, *Art and Experience in Classical Greece* (Cambridge: Cambridge University Press, 1972), eloquently examines the monuments in light of contemporary literature and philosophy; the same author's *The Art of Greece: Sources and Documents*, second edition (Cambridge: Cambridge University Press, 1990), gathers passages from ancient authors in translation. E. D. Reeder et al., *Pandora: Women in Classical Greece* (Baltimore: The Walters Art Gallery, 1995), is an exhibition catalog with several illuminating essays. For Athens recent treatments include J. M. Camp, *The Athenian Agora: Excavations in the Heart of the Classical Athens* (London: Thames and Hudson, 1986) and *The Archaeology of Athens* (New Haven: Yale University Press, 2001); D. Castriota, *Myth, Ethos, and Actuality: Official Art in Fifth-Century B.C. Athens* (Madison: University of Wisconsin Press, 1992); and J. M. Hurwit, *The Athenian Akropolis* (Cambridge: Cambridge University Press, 1999) and *The Acropolis in the Age of Pericles* (Cambridge: Cambridge

University Press, 2004). For individual monuments see A. Stewart, *Greek Sculpture: An Exploration* (New Haven: Yale University Press, 1990); J. Boardman, *Greek Sculpture: The Classical Period* (London: Thames and Hudson, 1985); J. Boardman, ed., *The Oxford History of Classical Art* (Oxford: Oxford University Press, 1997); C. C. Mattusch, *Greek Bronze Statuary* (Ithaca, NY: Cornell University Press, 1988), and *Classical Bronzes* (Ithaca, NY: Cornell University Press, 1996); K. D. S. Lapatin, *Chryselephantine Statuary in the Ancient Mediterranean World* (Oxford: Oxford University Press, 2001); D. Harris, *The Treasures of the Parthenon and Erechtheion* (Oxford: Oxford University Press, 1995); D. Williams and J. Ogden, *Greek Gold: Jewelry of the Classical World* (New York: Abrams/Metropolitan Museum of Art, 1994); J. Boardman, *Greek Gems and Finger Rings* (London: Thames and Hudson, 1970); P. Tournikiotis, ed., *The Parthenon and its Impact in Modern Times* (Athens: Melissa, 1994); J. Neils, *The Parthenon Frieze* (Cambridge: Cambridge University Press, 2001); C. Clairmont, *Classical Attic Tombstones*, 9 vols. (Kilchberg: Akanthus, 1993); I. Morris, "Everyman's Grave," in A. L. Boegehold and A. C. Scafuro, eds., *Athenian Identity and Civic Ideology* (Baltimore: Johns Hopkins University Press, 1994), pp. 67–101; R. Leader, "In Death Not Divided: Gender, Family, and State on Classical Athenian Grave Stelae," *AJA* 101 (1997): 683–99. For painted pottery see, e.g., P. E. Arias, M. Hirmer, and B. B. Shefton, *A History of Greek Vase Painting* (London: Thames and Hudson, 1962); J. Boardman, *Athenian Red Figure Vases: The Classical Period* (London: Thames and Hudson, 1989); C. Bérard et al., *A City of Images: Iconography and Society in Ancient Greece*, trans. D. Lyons (Princeton: Princeton University Press, 1989); F. Lissarrague, *The Aesthetics of the Greek Banquet: Images of Wine and Ritual*, trans. A. Szegedy-Maszak (Princeton: Princeton University Press, 1990); T. Rasmussen and N. Spivey, eds., *Looking at Greek Vases* (Cambridge: Cambridge University Press, 1991); and M. Robertson, *The Art of Vase-Painting in Classical Athens* (Cambridge: Cambridge University Press, 1992). For the spread of Classical Athenian sculptural styles in antiquity see, e.g., B. S. Ridgway, *Fourth-Century Styles in Greek Sculpture* (Madison: University of Wisconsin Press, 1997).

NOTES

1   Translations of Plutarch are those of J. J. Pollitt, *The Art of Ancient Greece: Sources and Documents*, second edition (Cambridge: Cambridge University Press, 1990). See also P. A. Stadter, *A Commentary on Plutarch's Pericles* (Chapel Hill: University of North Carolina Press, 1989). For fourth-century B.C. Athenian authors' comments on the Acropolis monuments see, e.g., Isokrates 7.66, 15.234; and Demosthenes

22.13, 76; for the later reception of the Parthenon see, e.g., M. Pavan, *L'avventura del Partenone* (Florence: Sansoni, 1983); P. Tournikiotis, ed., *The Parthenon and Its Impact in Modern Times* (Athens: Melissa, 1994); E. Yalouri, *The Acropolis: Global Fame, Local Claim* (Oxford: Berg, 2001); M. Beard, *The Parthenon* (Cambridge, MA: Harvard University Press, 2003); and J. Neils, ed., *The Parthenon: From Antiquity to the Present* (Cambridge: Cambridge University Press, 2005). See also R. Jenkyns, *The Victorians and Ancient Greece* (Cambridge, MA: Harvard University Press, 1980).

2 Kritios Boy (Acropolis Museum 698): J. M. Hurwit, *The Athenian Akropolis* (Cambridge: Cambridge University Press, 1999), p. 147; J. Boardman, ed., *The Oxford History of Classical Art* (Oxford: Oxford University Press, 1997), p. 87.

3 Arguments for and against the historicity of the "Oath of Plataia" are assessed by P. Siewert, *Der Eid von Plataia* (Munich: Beck, 1972). More recently, G. Ferrari argues that the Old Temple of Athena was neither entirely destroyed by the Persians, nor rebuilt, but continued to function, as a partial ruin, throughout the fifth century B.C. and beyond: "The Ancient Temple of the Acropolis at Athens," *AJA* 106 (2002): 11–135. For early fifth-century building elsewhere in Athens see J. M. Camp, *The Archaeology of Athens* (New Haven: Yale University Press, 2001), esp. pp. 59–73.

4 Tyrannicides: C. C. Mattusch, *Greek Bronze Statuary* (Ithaca, NY: Cornell University Press, 1988), pp. 119–27 with references to earlier literature, and *Classical Bronzes* (Ithaca, NY: Cornell University Press, 1996), pp. 58–62; J. Boardman, *Greek Sculpture: The Classical Period* (London: Thames & Hudson, 1985), pp. 24–5 and (n. 2), pp. 92–3. Quotations: Thucydides 6.57, cf. 1.70; Simonides, frag. 76D. See also Aristotle (?) *AP* 17.3–19.1. M. W. Taylor, *The Tyrant Slayers: The Heroic Image in Fifth Century B.C. Athenian Art and Politics*, second edition (Salem, NH: Ayer, 1991), includes a chapter (VI) treating "The Reaction Against the Tyrannicides;" L. J. Samons, "Democracy, Empire, and the Search for the Athenian Character," *Arion* 8.3 (2001): 141 with n. 27 questions the democratic message of the group, as does J. Ober, "Tyrant-Killing as Therapeutic Stasis: A Political Debate in Images and Texts," in K. A. Morgan, ed., *Popular Tyranny. Sovereignty and Its Discontents* (Austin: University of Texas Press, 2003), pp. 215–50.

5 Eponymous Heroes: Mattusch *CB* (n. 4), pp. 38–53.

6 Mourning Athena (Akropolis Museum 695): Hurwit (n. 2), p. 150.

7 Bronze Athena *Promachos*: Mattusch, *GBS* (n. 4), pp. 168–72; Hurwit (n. 2), pp. 151–3; Pollitt (n. 1), pp. 62–3. Equivalent costs: J. W. Roberts, *City of Socrates* (London: Routledge, 1984), p. 45. For estimated trireme costs (which have ranged from 1–3 talents per vessel) cf. also V. Gabrielsen, *Financing the Athenian Fleet* (Baltimore: Johns Hopkins University Press, 1994), pp. 139–42.

8 *Stoa Poikile, Theseion*, Polygnotan painting, and Agatharchos: Pollitt (n. 1), pp. 126–46; J. M. Camp, *The Athenian Agora: Excavations in the Heart of Classical Athens* (London: Thames & Hudson, 1986), pp. 66–71, and *The Archaeology of Athens* (n. 3), pp. 65–6, 68–9; D. Castriota, *Myth, Ethos, and Actuality: Official Art in Fifth-Century B.C. Athens* (Madison: University of Wisconsin Press, 1992); M. D. Stansbury-O'Donnell in *AJA* 93 (1989): 203–15 and 94 (1990): 213–35. For related work on pots see, e.g., M. Robertson, *The Art of Vase-Painting in Classical Athens* (Cambridge: Cambridge University Press, 1992), esp. pp. 180–85; and P. E. Arias, M. Hirmer, and B. B. Shefton, *A History of Greek Vase-Painting* (London: Thames & Hudson 1962), pp. 354–7.

9   See, e.g., Plato *Ion*; Aristotle *Nichomachean Ethics* 1180b20; and D. Roochnik, *Of Art and Wisdom: Plato's Understanding of Techne* (University Park: Pennsylvania State University Press, 1996).

10   On the status of ancient craftsmen see, e.g., Xenophon *Oeconomicus* 4.2–3 (quoted); Aristotle *Politics* 3.5.5, 1277b; Lucian *The Dream* 7–9; Plutarch *Life of Pericles* 1.4–2.2; and A. Stewart, *Greek Statuary: An Exploration* (New Haven: Yale University Press, 1990), esp. pp. 65–72.

11   Reception of ancient sumptuous arts: M. Vickers and D. Gill, *Artful Crafts: Ancient Greek Silverware and Pottery* (Oxford: Oxford University Press, 1994); K. Lapatin, "The Fate of Plate and Other Precious Materials: Towards a Historiography of Ancient Greek Minor (?) Arts," in A. A. Donohue and M. D. Fullerton, eds., *Ancient Art and Its Historiography* (Cambridge: Cambridge University Press, 2003), pp. 69–91.

12   For the *Athena Parthenos* and the chryselephantine technique in general see K. D. S. Lapatin, "Pheidias elephantourgos," *AJA* 101 (1997): 663–82 and *Chryselephantine Statuary in the Ancient Mediterranean World* (Oxford: Oxford University Press, 2001).

13   For the Parthenon, its treasures, and its sculptures, see *Suggestions for Further Reading* and, on finance, L. Kallet, "Did Tribute Fund the Parthenon?" *CSCA* 8 (1989): 252–66 and L. J. Samons, "Athenian Finance and the Treasury of Athena," *Historia* 42 (1993): 129–38; J. J. Coulton, *Ancient Greek Architects at Work* (Ithaca, NY: Cornell University Press, 1977), esp. pp. 108–17, and L. Haselberger, ed., *Appearance and Essence: Refinements of Classical Architecture* (Philadelphia: University Museum Press, 1999), and in Neils (n. 1), pp. 101–57, on refinements; J. J. Pollitt, *Art and Experience in Classical Greece* (Cambridge: Cambridge University Press, 1972), pp. 72–5, for philosophical implications; H. W. Catling, "Archaeology in Greece 1988–89," *Archaeological Reports* 35 (1989): 9, for *Xanthias Thrax*; and J. Neils, *The Parthenon Frieze* (Cambridge: Cambridge University Press 2001), for the frieze controversy.

14   See Ferrari (n. 3).

15   Hurwit (n. 2), pp. 213–15; Pollitt (n. 13), pp. 115–25. See also I. S. Mark, *The Sanctuary of Athena Nike in Athens*, Hesperia Supplement 26 (Princeton: American School of Classical Studies at Athens, 1993); A. F. Stewart, "History, Myth, and Allegory in the Program of the Temple of Athena Nike at Athens," in Herbert L. Kessler and Marianna Shreve Simpson, eds., *Pictorial Narrative in Antiquity and the Middle Ages. Studies in the History of Art*, vol. 16, (Washington, DC: National Gallery of Art, Washington, 1985), pp. 53–74.

16   See, e.g., Camp (n. 3), pp. 100–137.

17   R. Leader, "In Death Not Divided: Gender, Family, and State on Classical Athenian Grave Stelae," *AJA* 101 (1997): 685.

6: Other Sorts: Slaves, Foreigners, and Women in Periclean Athens

Cynthia Patterson

When Pericles son of Xanthippos rose to speak in honor of the Athenian dead from the first year of the Peloponnesian War, coming "forward from the tomb and standing on a high platform, so that he might be heard by as many people as possible in the crowd" (Thucydides 2.34),[1] he stood as a privileged and powerful representative of the strong side of three social polarities in ancient Athens: he was free not slave, citizen not foreign, and male not female. These "either/or" contrasts were part of the basic Athenian – and indeed Greek – political and social vocabulary, but they did not create a simple bipolar society of one united "us" versus one excluded "other." Rather, the three sets of polarities combined to create a complex set of identities and a community in which male and female members of citizen households lived side by side with free and enslaved foreigners, male and female. Representatives of this complex community stood together in the Kerameikos to hear the words of Pericles on that day in 431 – just as they stood (willingly or unwillingly) behind the energetic and creative achievements of the Periclean era.

In this chapter I discuss the ways in which the categories of slave, foreign, and female combined in Periclean Athens to create multiple "other" identities, sharing, we could say, a common identity as "not-Pericles" but otherwise with often dramatically different roles and status. Pericles' Funeral Oration (as well as Thucydides' *History* as a whole) provides one source for unraveling and understanding the strands of the larger Athenian society that was Pericles' audience. Contemporary drama – tragedy and comedy – provides another. Produced by the male citizen elite for a larger audience of slave and free, citizen and foreigner, and male and female,[2] Athenian drama often mirrors that larger audience in its plots and characters. A third major source for understanding Athenian society is material evidence, such as grave reliefs, inscribed decrees, or painted pottery. Finally, an important if not quite "primary" source for the character of Periclean society is Plutarch's life of Pericles, a text written some 500 years after Pericles' death and informed by Roman as well as Greek experience, but one nonetheless rich in contemporary anecdotes and illuminating detail of Athenian "other sorts."[3]

Aristotle – 100 years after Pericles – insisted that the name "citizen" be reserved for adult male holders of political and judicial rights and not be given to all those "necessary for the existence of the state" (*Politics* 1278a). Among the latter he included resident aliens as well as children, oddly leaving women of any sort (free, foreign, or slave) in a curious silent limbo, and putting slaves as a whole into another category all together – that of human property. Adopting (and adapting) Aristotle's notion of "necessary" members, I discuss in this chapter three categories of "other" that were in a real sense "necessary conditions" of the historical Athenian polis: the slave, the foreigner, and the female. Periclean Athens was much more than the sum of its male citizens.

THE SLAVE

"Make up your minds that happiness depends on being free," Pericles exhorted his audience on the occasion of the public funeral for the war dead in the first year of the Peloponnesian War (Thucydides 2.43). On the eve of the war, he had urged the Athenian assembly that it would be slavish to give in to Spartan demands (1.141); and later, after the devastation of the plague, he reiterated that the choice facing Athens was "submission and immediate slavery or danger with the hope of survival" (2.61). Similarly, in Aeschylus's *Persians*, a play written some forty years earlier and "produced" by the young Pericles,[4] freedom provides the rallying cry of Greek resistance to the Persian invasion. As narrated by a Persian herald (in reality, of course, a Greek actor speaking in Greek to the theater audience), the battle of Salamis began with a unison chorus from the Greek oarsmen:

> O Greek sons, advance! Free your fathers' land,
> Free your sons, your wives, the sanctuaries
> Of paternal gods, the sepulchers

of ancestors. Now the contest's drawn:
All is at stake!

(401–6, tr. Benardete)

As freedom's antithesis, slavery was a highly charged political concept and moral principle as well as an economic institution in Periclean Athens. Moses Finley argued almost half a century ago that ancient Greece was a slave society, not just a "society with slaves," because of the way the slave was taken for granted in almost all aspects of daily life and the presumption that his or her existence was inevitable or necessary – even if it was, to some minds at least, "contrary to nature."[5] In addition, the expansion of the master/slave relationship to moral, social, and political relationships, whereby the lack of political self-rule was a form of slavery and the lack of self-control the mark of a slavish nature, is a strong indication of slavery's profound significance for the character of ancient society – and for ancient Athenian society in particular. Finley ends his article with the observation that "the cities in which individual freedom reached its highest expression – most obviously Athens – were cities in which chattel slavery flourished" and concludes that "one aspect of Greek history . . . is the advance, hand in hand, of freedom and slavery."[6] The implications and ramifications of that conclusion are still the focus of active discussion, but there is no debate that the slave is the preeminent "other" in the Athenian social universe and the proper starting point of this discussion.

As Finley noted, the seemingly paradoxical connection between the development of democracy and of chattel slavery in ancient Greece is best expressed in the history of Athens, where Solon, the "father of democracy," was the author of the *seisachtheia* or "throwing off of [debt] burdens" and the prohibition of any future enslavement of Athenians through debt. Despite the difficulties inherent in understanding the precise nature of the crisis Solon faced at the beginning of the sixth century, his articulation of the principle of a privileged free citizenry seems clear: Athenians are not slaves and slaves are not Athenians. Protection of the citizen's person emerges as key to the evolving status of citizen: after the prohibition of debt slavery, other protections – against rape, abuse, corporal punishment, or torture – emerged as fundamental to citizen status. For the slave, in contrast, the body (with the service it could provide) was essentially his or her identity – or indeed *"its identity"* as suggested by the remarkable coinage of the term *andrapoda*, a neuter plural for "slaves" reminiscent of the word for cattle, *tetrapoda*. In fact, vulnerability to corporal punishment, torture, and

155

cattle-like treatment was generally the mark of the slave in Athenian society.

In the century and a half from Solon to Pericles, the privileges, protections, and perquisites of citizen status grew (even under the tyrant Pisistratus) – along with a resulting need for legal distinctions between those with and those without citizen status. For example, rules requiring that slave evidence be "given" under torture and forbidding slaves to exercise in the palaestra are important features of the articulation of slave and citizen as legal and ideological opposites within the Athenian polis.[7] In reality the lines could be difficult to draw or maintain: the slave was in fact a person and might in fact be visibly indistinguishable from a citizen; at times he (or she) might take on roles and responsibilities that were similar if not identical to those of citizens.[8] Nonetheless, it remains true that the most basic antithesis in Athenian society was between slave and citizen.

The quantitative presence and importance of slaves in democratic (and Periclean) Athens, however, is less certain. Overall, Moses Finley's judgment that classical Athens was a slave society because of the way slaves were engaged in and considered essential for all varieties of economic activity – from mining and agriculture to manufacture and banking – has been confirmed and upheld in the years since he first published his essay. Slave labor was essential to the productive economy of Athens, with slaves supplementing rather than replacing free labor in almost all of the activities in which they were engaged. The actual size of the Athenian slave population, however, is uncertain – and perhaps unknowable. The one specific figure for total slave numbers from any era – Athenaeus's report of 400,000 slaves counted in the census of 317 B.C.E. – is wildly impossible, making guesses/estimates based on more reliable partial figures (e.g., Thucydides' report that 20,000 Athenian slaves fled during the Spartan occupation of Decelea) our only option. At present, the consensus seems to be that the slave population of Periclean Athens was probably at least equal to the adult male population (or ca. 50,000), with most citizen households owning at least one slave. The specific issue generating most debate in recent years is not the overall number of slaves in Athens but rather the number used in agriculture and the significance of their labor for the character of Athenian democracy. In 1959 Finley touched briefly on the question, realizing that the role of slavery in agriculture, clearly a "basic economic activity," was important for his argument. For Finley, a significant piece of evidence was the late classical report of Philochorus that at the festival of the Kronia "the heads of families ate the crops and fruits at the same table with the slaves, with whom they had shared the labours of cultivation," suggesting for agricultural slaves a role generally recognized by ritual and religion. Still, Finley concluded somewhat cautiously that "slavery dominated agriculture insofar as it was on a scale that transcended the labour of the householder and his son."[9]

Some two decades later, Michael Jameson pursued the issue in more depth, arguing that the labor-intensive character of ancient Athenian agriculture (where the limiting factor was land, not labor) made household slaves, male and female, key contributors to the agricultural labor force.[10] *Oiketes* was a term for "household slave," and given that agriculture was the most common economic activity of the Athenian household, *oiketai* (male and female) would certainly have been assigned the most laborious agricultural tasks. Further, the presence and labor of one or two household slaves perhaps allowed the Athenian citizen to spend significant time away from his farm, in the political center and public life of the polis. Just how far down the citizen social ladder slaveholding extended is a question that is not in the end answerable. Nonetheless, a balanced assessment of the available evidence, including comparative argument as well as qualitative and anecdotal material, supports the idea that slave-holding was "vital to the political economy" of Athens.[11]

The general points made here can be supported by looking at a number of examples of Athenian slaves, historical and literary, who together reveal the diversity and significance of slavery within Periclean Athens.

Plutarch Pericles 16: *Evangelos, the Estate Manager*

In describing the imperviousness to corruption and private economic gain that was a hallmark of Pericles' character, Plutarch pauses to relate some details of Pericles' household economy, including his notable decision to sell each year's produce in the marketplace – and then buy back from the market as needed, in order "to ensure that his fortune should not be dissipated by neglect nor yet cause him much trouble or loss of time when his mind was occupied with higher things" (16). The story is important for the emerging theme of the separation or distinction of public and private spheres in Periclean Athens and for Pericles' contribution to that process. For present purposes, however, what comes next in Plutarch's account is even more significant:

> [Pericles] had one slave, Evangelus, who kept up all this meticulous accounting and who was either exceptionally

gifted by nature or else was trained by Pericles, so that he excelled everyone else in the science of domestic economy.[12]

Here we not only see an educated slave with a position of responsibility within the household, we also know his name. He is not an anonymous *andrapodon* ("man-foot") but a character with a name (and a role to play) in Plutarch's moral biography of Pericles. Within this story, the paradox of chattel slavery is particularly vivid: the slave is a piece of property (a "living tool," to use Aristotle's phrase) but Evangelos is also a man with the intelligence to learn the science of household management, including as a key element the management of slaves. In a society that embraced or considered as inevitable the enslavement of fellow human beings and their treatment as simple chattel, actual slaves might well display obvious human capabilities and talents. Indeed, the paradox was especially striking in Periclean Athens with its open, egalitarian style of living. Plutarch, however, distinguishes the science that Evangelos mastered as "domestic economy" — so underlining the way in which the higher public life to which Pericles devoted his life was unavailable to the slave (here *oiketes*).

The Workmen on the Acropolis

Slaves were also employed in the public economy, for example, as part of the labor force of the Periclean building program. Again Plutarch, in an often quoted chapter:

> [Pericles] was anxious that the unskilled masses . . . should not be debarred from the national income, and yet should not be paid for sitting about and doing nothing. So he boldly laid before the people proposals for immense public works and plans for buildings, which would involve many different arts and industries and require long periods to complete. . . . The materials to be used were stone, bronze, ivory, gold, ebony, and cypress-wood, while the arts or trades which wrought or fashioned them were those of carpenter, modeler, copper-smith, stone-mason, dyer, worker in gold and ivory, painter, embroiderer, and engraver, and besides these the carriers and suppliers of the materials, such as merchants, sailors, and pilots for the sea-borne traffic, and wagon-makers, trainers of draught animals, and drivers for everything that came by land. There were also rope-makers, weavers, leather work-ers, road builders and miners. Each individual craft, like a

general with an army under his separate command, had its
own corps of unskilled labourers at its disposal, and these
worked in a subordinate capacity, as an instrument obeys the
hand, or the body the soul, and so through these various
demands the city's prosperity was extended far and wide and
shared among every age and condition in Athens.

(*Per.* 12)

Despite the philosophical overtones, and perhaps Roman undertones,
of this passage, Plutarch's point – that "every condition" benefited from
and shared in the Periclean building program – is supported by the
inscribed building records of the Erechtheion, the temple of Athena and
Erechtheus completed ca. 408 as part of the rebuilding of the Acropolis
begun under Periclean leadership in the middle of the century and continued after his death. Of the 86 workmen whose status is identifiable,
24 are citizens, 42 are metics, and 20 are slaves; men of different status
seem to have worked side by side, just as their names are listed together
with the same wage for the same job.[13]

The Fugitive Slaves of Thucydides 7.27

Thucydides is less expansive than Plutarch in describing the prosperity
of Periclean Athens, but his emphasis on wealth and skill as the keys to
Athenian power and expectation of victory, makes the same point (see,
for example, 1.141–4; 2.13). And in the Funeral Oration, Thucydides'
Pericles proudly boasts of the economic benefits of empire for the people
of Athens: "the greatness of our city brings it about that all the good
things from all over the world flow in to us, so that to us it seems just as
natural to enjoy foreign goods as our own local products" (2.38). Pericles
does not refer to slaves here – the speech is of course a celebration of the
free citizenry of the polis – but slave labor was the unspoken condition
of the free citizen enjoyment of the resources of the empire.

When Thucydides does refer, much later in his history, to the
slave labor force of Athens, he gives a specific and impressively large
number; he also notes their skill and implies the importance of their
labor in the exploitation of Athenian natural resources. The context is
the Peloponnesian fortification of Decelea in central Attica in 413, the
last year of the Athenian campaign in Sicily. Unlike previous Peloponnesian incursions, says Thucydides, this occupation of Athenian land
was costly for the Athenians. In addition to the loss of the use of the
land and its livestock, "more than 20,000 slaves, the majority of whom

were skilled workmen, deserted" (7.27). Thucydides moves on without further comment to further events of the war, but the notice is dramatic in its implications. A significant number of these fugitive slaves were most likely mine-workers, working to extract Athens's most valuable natural resource, the silver of Laureion in southern Attica. Nicias, a man who was according to Thucydides "devoted to the study and practice of virtue" (7.86), owned 1,000 slaves that he hired out for gang labor in the mines.[14] The labor of mining slaves was the brutal foundation for the dominance of Athens's silver "owls" throughout the Aegean.[15]

The Slaves of Athenian Drama

The life expectancy and hope of manumission of the slave miners were low, and their lives may have been remote from the daily experience of most Athenians. But Athenians did live in close relationship, and close quarters, with their household slaves – a feature of life reflected in the representation of slaves in the popular theater of Dionysos. The plots and characters of tragedy are generally mythical and those of comedy often wildly fantastic, but the slave characters in both types of drama contribute substantially to an understanding of Athenian chattel slavery. Here I consider briefly the female slave chorus in Aeschylus's *Libation Bearers* (produced in 458) and then the male household slaves of Aristophanes' *Wasps* (422) as evidence of both realities and perceptions of slavery in Athens.[16]

The chorus of slave women (captives from the Trojan war) plays a notably active part in the middle play of Aeschylus's *Oresteia* trilogy and appropriately give the play its title, *Choephoroi* or *Libation Bearers*. From the opening scene, in which they convince Electra to subvert the intention of her mother's offerings at the grave of Agamemnon from appeasement to vengeance, through their provision of key support by telling Aigisthus to leave his bodyguard behind, to their triumphant yet anxious final lines after the deed is done, the chorus of female slaves is consistent in their loyalty to the house and household of Agamemnon, their master, and in their hatred of Clytemnestra and Aigisthus, whom they consider tyrannical usurpers of authority. Their devotion is recognized by Electra when she first addresses them:

> You servant women, who set the house in order,
> since you are here in this supplication
> to attend me, give me your counsel in this matter!
> What am I to say while I pour these funeral offerings?
> (84–7, tr. Lloyd-Jones)

They are key contributors to the welfare of this *oikos*,[17] which is to them their *oikos* as well. Hugh Lloyd-Jones judges that "the sex and station of the Chorus render it especially suited" to this supportive role.[18] Why that might be true perhaps deserves some support or justification. Not all slaves were loyal, either in literature or in life, but the ideological inclusion of slaves within the *oikos* was one way of arguing that they should be. In any case, the close and intimate relationship of the "libation bearers" with the members of Agamemnon's household – particularly its children, Electra and Orestes – and the trust that exists between them are striking and important for our understanding of the Athenians' own idea (or ideal) of the household and the place of slaves – here female slaves – within the household.

Athenian drama thus gave a finer articulation to the gender distinctions among slaves than did the Athenians' own frequently gender-neutral slave terminology or Aristotle's implicit assumption that gender only really exists among the free (*Politics* 1252b). In contrast, Aristophanic comedy is well-stocked with specifically male slave characters, again most often of the household sort but including as well the Scythian policeman of the *Thesmophoriazousae*.[19] In the representation of slaves in Aristophanes' *Wasps*, however, we see the inherent brutality of chattel slavery even within the intimacy of personal household relationships. Corporal punishment for the slave is taken for granted and routinely used as a source of comedy. When the two household slaves Xanthias and Sosias do not succeed in keeping the jury-crazed Philocleon indoors, his son Bdelycleon threatens to put them "in chains without dinner." The father in turn threatens them with the reminder of an earlier occasion on which he caught a slave stealing grapes, tied the thief to a tree, and beat him. The end of the play brings the violence on stage, apparently as a source of amusement, when Sosias enters battered and beaten, and expressing his envy of the turtle with his shell.[20]

Slaves on Painted Pottery

One final source of evidence for the character of Athenian slavery is painted pottery. Female slaves in particular are shown in a variety of roles, from household "maids" to prostitutes providing entertainment or sexual services to men. The latter scenes range in tone from suggestively romantic to graphically violent, and in composition from intimate scenes to "group sex," while the women depicted range in age from quite young to clearly middle-aged.[21] In Figure 42, a slave accompanies her mistress to the tomb of a child (with the deceased himself sitting on top of the funeral stele). The slave's features are clearly distinguished as servile; that she is the child's nurse might be indicated by the fact that he looks to her and not to his mother.[22]

In sum, there can be little doubt that slaves and slavery were an essential part of Periclean society and economy. They were the antithesis of the free citizen and freedom; slaves were bodies without the means of self-rule and self-control. But slaves were also co-workers and co-residents of the city and in households, and persons on whom Athenians relied for public order and private pleasure. Indeed Athenian slavery gave Athenian freedom a special intensity, and Athenian freedom, exercised at the expense of the slave, gave Athenians a distinctive perspective on the life of both the free and the nonfree.

THE FOREIGNER: *XENOI* AND *XENOI METOIKOI*

Slaves in Athens after Solon were by definition foreigners, but of course not all foreigners were slaves. In this section I discuss the status of the foreigner in Periclean Athens, with particular attention to the development in the fifth century of the special status of *metoikos xenos* or "resident alien." The reception and protection of the *xenos* as "guest" in Greek society is one of the oldest themes in Greek literature, for the rules of *xenia* or "hospitality" were the domain of Zeus himself. Athenian treatment of foreigners, as of slaves, directly reflects the development of citizenship and citizen identity. Although the focus here will be on the fifth century and the Periclean era, Athenian tradition again attributed to Solon a role in the articulation of the status of the foreigner with a law that Plutarch cites to his own puzzlement. Solon's law about "new citizens," says Plutarch, required that citizenship should *not* be given *except* to those who were in exile from their homeland or who came to Athens with their whole household in order to practice a craft (*Solon* 24).

Modern commentators have also been puzzled by this story, generally because the law seems to suggest a more open policy of naturalization than is typically associated with Athens. At this early point in Athenian history, citizenship was apparently not yet tightly defined by birth. The options for free status in Athens at this time were simply citizen and foreigner, with the understanding that a foreigner who established permanent residence and a craft would no longer be considered foreign.[23] By the fifth century, however, with the growth of Athens into an imperial power, such a flexible and inherently porous system was no longer practicable or in keeping with Athenian self-interest as Athenians perceived it. One of the few decrees that we know Pericles proposed in his own name (perhaps indeed an indication of the seriousness of the problem) was his law on polis membership from the year 451/0, generally referred to in modern literature as his citizenship law: "any one not born of two *astoi* ['citizens'] should not have a share in the polis" (*AP* 26.4), or, as Plutarch paraphrased it much later, "Athenians are those born from Athenians" (*Per.* 37). The development of corresponding rules on the status of the foreigner and specifically the resident foreigner cannot be tied to any such specific enactment, but most likely belong to the same general time period, i.e., the first half of the fifth century.[24] From the perspective of both internal and external (domestic and foreign) pressures, these were crucial decades for the emergence of Athenian rules on citizen and foreign status. From Cleisthenes' "establishment" of democracy to its radical expansion under Pericles, and from the Persian War victories to the emergence of "imperial" Athens, the distinctions in status between Athenians and alien residents became increasingly articulated in law and practice.

In many ways, Periclean Athens was a remarkably open society – welcoming all sorts of foreign ideas, goods, and persons into its community; but just as famously perhaps, Athens securely (some would say jealously) guarded its citizen boundaries and established citizenship as the "family" privilege of those born into it. Athens welcomed – and at times even required – foreign participation in its society. Foreigners participated in Athenian festivals, petitioned in Athenian courts, and traded in Athenian markets (and were, eventually, by decree required to use Athenian currency). Around its citizen family, however, Athens drew a firm and clear line.

The status of the foreigner in Athens was thus a mixture of privilege and disability, with the result that the evaluation of its overall quality has been mixed, especially in the case of the resident foreigner, the *xenos metoikos* or "metic." The essential legal features of foreign status in Athens were as follows:

1. inability to own or inherit land[25]
2. inability to vote or hold any political or judicial office
3. vulnerability to summary arrest and sale into slavery for serious crimes; but also
4. ability to bring suit in the Athenian courts (where jurisdiction over foreign cases was given to special courts and officials)

5. ability to do business in Athens – including businesses that required the leasing of property, such as brothels or hotels.
6. opportunity to participate in and enjoy Athenian public festivals.

Metic (resident alien) status added some additional features:

7. requirement of a citizen sponsor or patron (*prostates*)
8. annual payment of an individual tax of 12 drachmae for a man, 6 for a woman
9. mandatory military service for the male
10. requirement to provide some "liturgies" (public works such as producing dramas)
11. special status within "foreigners'" court, with respect to protection of family and property
12. recognition of special "guest-friend" position with special clothing or group activities such as the wearing of red robes in the annual *pompe* ("procession") of the City Dionysia.[26]

As these facts make clear, the status of foreigner in Athens, and especially the status of metic or resident foreigner, was a mixed blessing. The metic was a foreigner over whom the polis had more control than it had over the itinerant foreigner – and also a foreigner to whom it gave more recognition and responsibility. Although some scholars have considered metic status a kind of "quasi-citizenship,"[27] in fact metic status did not overcome the well-guarded boundary between citizen and foreigner: the metic could not own land or marry into the Athenian citizen "family," and his or her legal protection did not include the significant protection of the body and freedom from corporal punishment or enslavement that was one distinguishing mark of citizen status. Although by the fourth century bits and pieces of citizen privilege might on occasion be given as rewards to outstanding benefactors of the Athenian polis (and the whole of citizenship could of course be given as the supreme prize to the deserving foreigner), metic status as such remained a foreign status. Its origins in the early fifth century were rooted in a need to distinguish and also control the free resident alien population.

That alien population, moreover, was hardly one united class or interest group; i.e., "metic" denoted a legal status but not necessarily a social or economic class. It should be noted that whether or not a particular foreigner appearing in the historical record was in fact enrolled as a metic is not always clear – in part perhaps because the label "metic" was not one that a man or woman seems to have been proud to append to his or her name.[28] Often the evidence for metic status is indirect or assumed. One well-known metic (both to us and to the Athenians) was Cephalus, the rich arms manufacturer in whose Piraeus house the discussion of Plato's *Republic* takes places. But Leptines the cook and Epameinon the donkey driver, honored with citizenship in a decree of 401, were apparently metics at the time, as was a certain Teucros when he testified against those who parodied the mysteries in 415.[29] But we would hardly expect Cephalus and Leptines to be guests at the same symposion or oarmates in the Athenian navy.

Thus, a consideration of the metic population in Athens reinforces the image of the complexity of Athenian society, in which social, economic, legal, and political status were not necessarily congruent. This general picture of the foreigner in Athens can now be illustrated with some specific examples, including Cephalus and Leptines as well as a few others of note.

The Visiting Philosophers: Anaxagoras and Protagoras

We begin with the high end of the social scale and with two foreigners with whom Pericles himself seems to have spent a significant amount of time, the philosophers Anaxagoras of Clazomenae and Protagoras of Abdera. According to Plutarch, Pericles admired the visiting philosopher Anaxagoras and spent enough time with him to "steep" his mind in speculative philosophy and to acquire a lofty bearing and public demeanor (*Per.* 5). The length of time Anaxagoras spent in Athens is unknown; Diogenes Laertius, the considerably later biographer of the philosophers, suggests that he stayed thirty years (2.7), and Plutarch's story of a chagrined Pericles at the height of his career visiting the old and now neglected philosopher – who with no one to take care of him had set about to starve himself to death (*Per.* 16) – implies at least a substantial stay. Pericles' association with Protagoras was, again according to Plutarch, the source of considerable friction with Pericles' son Xanthippos, who objected to his father's spending a full day in philosophical discussion about the issue of guilt in a case of accidental homicide (36). Plato, however, presents the same Xanthippos as one of the young Athenians who flocked to hear Protagoras at the house of the wealthy Athenian Callias (*Protagoras* 315a). Other sources confirm Protagoras's presence and popularity in Athens; he was, we are told, chosen to design the new city of Thurii;[30] but later, according to Plutarch in his life of Nicias, the Athenians turned against the visiting philosopher and sent him out of the city.[31] Being a foreigner in Athens could be a risky business.

The Arms Manufacturer: Cephalus of the Piraeus

Whether or not Anaxagoras and Protagoras were officially enrolled as metics (with Pericles as their *prostates* perhaps) is not clear. In the case of Cephalus, however, the rich manufacturer in whose Piraeus house Plato sets the dialogue of the *Republic*, there seems little doubt that he and his family – including his son the orator Lysias – were *metoikoi xenoi*. Although the *Republic*'s discussion quickly leaves the old Cephalus behind as he goes off to attend to a household sacrifice, Plato's portrait of the metic is notably gentle. Here is a resident alien who has made his fortune in the production of weapons in the midst of a long and devastating war, yet he is clearly the object of affection not resentment. He and his sons are quite comfortable in the company of Socrates and his young Athenian friends (including Plato's brothers Glaucon and Adeimantus), as are the Athenians with the family of Cephalus.

The Democratic Partisans and Informers: Leptines and Teucros

Plato's portrait of the cultivated family of Cephalus, however, should not obscure the probable reality that most resident aliens in Athens were positioned closer to the lower end of the social spectrum. Their loyalty and interests were often with Athenians of comparable class and background. So we find, as noted earlier, a metic cook and a metic donkey driver rewarded with citizenship for coming to the aid of the Athenian democracy in 403. Earlier in the war, the metic Teucros offered information in the prosecution of those who "profaned" the Eleusinian mysteries, among whom were quite a few members of the Athenian elite, including some who make appearances in Plato's dialogues.[32]

The "Mistress" of Pericles: Aspasia

So far we have considered only foreign men who found a place for themselves in Athenian life and society. Foreign women, however, also came to live in Athens, either with families or on their own. As noted earlier, a foreign woman became a metic in the same way as did a foreign man. Her *metoikion* (metic tax) was less (6 rather than 12 drachmas in the fourth century) and military service was not required. But she did need to have a citizen representative or *prostates*, and she did have a recognized legal identity as *metoikos xene*. One such woman was Aspasia, the woman with whom Pericles lived after divorcing his Athenian wife. Plutarch reports that Pericles was visibly devoted to Aspasia – that he regularly and openly kissed her upon returning home (*Per.* 24), and that he broke down in tears when she was put on trial for impiety (*Per.* 32). The very fact (if it was one) that she was so prosecuted is indicative of her paradoxical metic status, which gave her independent public visibility – and also personal vulnerability.[33]

The Divine metoikoi: Aeschylus's Eumenides

I end this discussion of the resident foreigner with a group of resident divinities, the Eumenides, who lived as guests in Athens on the invitation of Athena herself after they had lost their case against Orestes in the court of the Areopagus. Now, as kindly but still awe-inspiring deities – and as *metoikoi* (*Eumenides* 1011) – they will bring prosperity to Athens and ward off destruction. Indeed, these divine "guests" seem to have a status analogous to the human metic: their presence and good will is necessary for the well-being of the polis, but they themselves remain marginal, isolated figures, accentuated in their depiction by Aeschylus as old, unmarried, and childless.

THE FEMALE: SLAVES/FOREIGNERS/METICS (A REPRISE) AND CITIZENS

Finally, we come to our third and last category of "other" – the women of Athenian society. Of course we have already encountered women among the slaves and the foreigners in Athens, and it should require no further argument to show that the female and the other "others" in Athens did not form one coherent group. Indeed, one of the most common and misleading errors of recent discussions of women in Athens is that "women" are a single, unified class, status, and interest group – a single entry in the index. But although some women were slaves and some metics, other women in Athens belonged to the elite "family" of citizens – as *astai* (citizens) who were shareholders in the polis and beneficiaries of its prosperity. Of course, voting and office-holding, as well as military service, were and remained prerogatives and responsibilities of male citizens in Athens (and elsewhere until quite recently), just as, for example, burial ritual and lament for Athenian family members were the responsibility of Athenian women.[34] Plato's revolutionary ideas granting women political privilege in Book V of the *Republic* were indeed utopian. Still, Plato emphasized the overall superiority of men to women, especially in physical strength, and it is true that female citizens, like other females, were subject to male rule and were possible victims of male scorn or abuse. But the fact remains that there was such a thing as a female "citizen," a female "insider" and member of an Athenian family and the Athenian community, who had privileges and responsibilities distinct from those of female slaves or female metics. When Pericles celebrated the Athenian character as loving beauty and wisdom (Thuc. 2.40) and boasts of Athenian enjoyment of public festivals and imported luxuries, he is not speaking only of men. Again, vase painting offers evidence of Athenian women's enjoyment of the arts (Figure 43),[35] and Plato in the *Laws* (658d) suggests (although not with approval) that "cultivated women" might particularly enjoy tragic performance.

Let us examine, therefore, the free, citizen women of Periclean Athens. How do we understand their status? As reported in the *Athenaion Politeia* (and noted above), in the year 451/0 the Athenians voted on the proposal of Pericles himself that whoever was "not born from two *astoi* should not share in the polis." Many things could be said about this law (or decree), generally referred to as the Periclean citizenship law, and about its place in Athenian history.[36] Pericles' law will serve as a useful starting point for discussion of the status of female citizen in Periclean Athens and the concluding section of this chapter.

If Pericles' decree was a citizenship law, then it would seem that there were such people as female citizens in Athens, since the mother's status (as *aste* or, according to Plutarch, as one of the *Athenaioi*) is essential to her children's citizen status. Interpretations that deny this fact – such as the notion that what Pericles really meant was "born from an *astos* and the daughter of an *astos*" – do not convince,[37] but rather show how deeply entrenched is the Aristotelian and modern way of configuring citizenship or *politeia* as male legal and political privilege. It would be better to begin by considering the actual language of the law and its implications for the Athenian conception of polis membership. First, the expression "to share in the polis" reveals the way in which citizenship was conceived as active participation in the polis community, rather than as individual legal status or privilege. Second, the term *astos* (feminine *aste*, inclusive plural *astoi*), is the favored Athenian term for "insiders" opposed to the "outsider," the *xenos*. *Astoi* called to mind, at least implicitly and very often explicitly, their opposite, the *xenoi*. So, on the occasion with which this chapter began, Thucydides notes that "everyone who wishes to, both *astoi* and *xenoi*," participated in the public funeral procession for the war dead (Thucydides 2.24). The word *astoi* has a communal sense, like that of "sharing in," and draws a line around the community as a whole. *Polites*, on the other hand, generally has a more specific individual and political reference, and is the term used by Aristotle in his discussions of citizenship or *politeia* – defined as the right to hold the offices of juryman and assemblyman (*Pol.* 1275a–b). Nonetheless, the feminine form, *politis*, did occur, and in fact seems to have been coined in Athens. The first surviving use is by Sophocles in the *Electra* (1227) – used by Electra to address the female chorus of fellow Mycenaean free women.

On the other hand, the use of *astoi* does not *exclude* reference to political or legal roles.[38] In Aristophanes' *Ecclesiazousae* (458–9), for example, when Blepyros asks, "has everything been assigned to them [the women] which was the concern of the *astoi*?" he specifically means such things as assembly and jury duty. For emphasis, perhaps, he puts women, who ordinarily did not concern themselves with such things, in a separate category by themselves.[39] In contrast to the dominant view that considers Athenian citizenship as essentially male, the Athenian conception of citizenship as "sharing in the polis" had both a male and a female aspect; the shares of men and women were different but nonetheless shares, distinguishing those who held them, both men and women, from the nonshareholders, the noncitizens and *xenoi*. That citizenship – i.e., community membership – was gendered in Periclean Athens should come as no surprise; few social ideas or institutions were not.

What then were the distinguishing marks of female citizenship in Periclean Athens? Modern discussions have tended to emphasize the female's exclusion from political life, qualifying the idea of women's citizenship if not denying it entirely. One recent account of women's position in Athens puts it this way: "for Athenian women 'citizenship' meant only that they had a share in the religious, legal, and economic order of the Athenian community."[40] Given, however, that religion, law, and property/inheritance were key areas of public life in which insider status made a significant difference, the "only" in this statement is puzzling. We can in fact use these three categories to consider the meaning of female Athenian citizenship.

First, the important and prominent part Athenian women played in Athenian religion is readily acknowledged and emphasized by almost all commentators. The importance of the religious role is sometimes dismissed as an "exception" with the implication that religion is not truly public or political, an argument that holds no force in a Greek context.

Second, the legal privilege and protection given an Athenian woman under Athenian law is significant. An Athenian woman had the legal status of an Athenian in that her person was protected by the same rules and procedures as that of the Athenian man: an Athenian woman could not be enslaved in Athens; an Athenian woman was not tortured when giving evidence; and the murder of an Athenian woman was tried by the same procedures and in the same court as that of an Athenian man.

Robin Osborne has recently reasserted the traditional position that women were not citizens in Athens on the grounds that they did not participate in their own right or on their own behalf in the lawcourt; their evidence (e.g., their oaths) could only be reported as evidence by men – just as the "evidence" provided by slaves under torture was also reported.[41] The courts, suggests Osborne, were the competitive arena of the (male) citizens, and "to allow children, women, or slaves into courts as witnesses would be to allow them shares of honour, setting up differential honours in the juvenile, servile or female community, and to allow them a part in sharing out honour to men."[42] As will be seen in the discussion to follow of specific Athenian women, however, the Athenians did in fact allow women shares of gender-specific honor. Perhaps we should consider the possibility that actual court appearance, as distinguished from protection of the laws, was not in fact always considered a "privilege" or source of honor. Does the fact that the metic woman could apparently sue and be sued in court really mean that her status was more privileged or honored than – or preferable to – that of the citizen woman?

Finally, the place of the female Athenian in the property and inheritance system was important and substantial. Again, the traditional view is that Athenian women were excluded from property and inheritance in a system that was rigorously male-dominated and patrilineal. The view is deeply rooted in Anglo-American scholarship; here I will offer not a complete discussion, but introduce in evidence a number of issues and examples that may serve at least to fuel debate.[43]

First, despite the frequency with which it is asserted that Athenian inheritance was patrilineal, inheritance in Athens was based on a bilateral kindred extending to the children of cousins on both paternal and maternal sides, a web of relatives termed by the Athenians the *anchisteia tou genos* (the "nearest in birth or family") or simply the *anchisteia*. The order of succession within this group moved from male to female within each degree of relationship. This means, simply put, that children could inherit from both their paternal and maternal grandfathers, and that daughters followed their brothers in inheritance claim, but preceded their nephews. One peculiar feature of the system to modern eyes is the exclusion of the wife herself from the *anchisteia* of her husband. Since she remained, however, part of her own father's *anchisteia* (and might produce children who were his potential heirs), the Athenian system has its own consistency. The Athenian sense of family as bilateral can also be seen in the common practice of naming the first son after the paternal grandfather and the second after the maternal grandfather.

At this point, the response might be made that women within the *anchisteia* are simply "place-holders" to be called upon when no male heir is available and that they themselves are not true heirs or owners of anything. This objection can be countered in a number of different ways, by emphasizing (a) the role the dowry played as a "pre-mortem" inheritance for the daughter; (b) the substantial reality of female ownership in the case of the heiress or widow; and (c) the problematic nature of ownership in general in ancient Athens, where the use and management of property, in which women shared, could be as important as legal ownership or ability to alienate.[44] Instead, however, of arguing each of these technical legal points (a task that would take us into a broader consideration of Athenian law than is possible here), I end this section and the chapter as a whole with a consideration of the responsibilities and interests of some particular female citizens from the Periclean era.

The Women of Pericles' Audience

In describing the public funeral for the war dead that preceded Pericles' Funeral Oration, Thucydides says, "the women who are related to the dead are there to make their laments at the tomb" (2.34). So both Pericles' democratic city and its historian acknowledge one of the oldest responsibilities of women within both the household and the polis: burial and lament. There seems no reason to deny that female Athenians were among the "*astoi* and *xenoi*" who participated in the funeral.[45] Among the women in attendance one group receives special notice and pointed advice: "to those of you who are now widowed," says Pericles, "I can say all I have to say in a short word of advice. Your great glory is not to be inferior to your own nature, and the greatest glory of a woman is to be least talked about among men, whether in praise or blame."[46] Although this passage is generally taken to indicate the way in which Periclean democracy excluded women from public life, the language in fact suggests something quite different. Pericles distinguishes the public reputation the women will have as widows of the war dead, as long as they do not allow themselves to be the object of gossip (praise or blame) among male members of the community.[47] Gossip and slander were out of place in the sphere of public honor and esteem. It may thus be possible to think that Pericles is saying something positive to the Athenian widows, even if it is not what we in the twenty-first century might want him to have said.

Elpinice, Sister of Cimon

Plutarch relates an interesting anecdote about an earlier funeral oration delivered by Pericles ca. 440 after the defeat of the "rebellious" ally, Samos. According to Plutarch, as Pericles

> stepped down from the rostrum, many of the women of Athens clasped his hand and crowned him with garlands and filets like a victorious athlete. Elpinice, however, came up to him and said: "this was a noble action, Pericles, and you deserved all these garlands for it. You have thrown away the lives of these brave citizens of ours, not in a war against the Persians or the Phoenicians, such as my brother Cimon fought, but in destroying a Greek city which is one of our allies." Pericles listened to her words unmoved, so it is said, and only smiled and quoted to her Archilochus's verse: "why lavish perfumes on a head that's grey?"
>
> (*Per.* 28)

Elpinice and Pericles appear together in another anecdote earlier in the life on the occasion of the trial of Elpinice's brother Cimon on the charge of treason, a trial in which Pericles served as a public prosecutor. "The story goes," says Plutarch, "when she came and pleaded with him, Pericles told her with a smile, 'Elpinice, you are too old, much too old, for this kind of business.'" "However that may be," Plutarch goes on, "Pericles made no more than one speech by way of formally discharging his commission, and in the end did Cimon less harm than any of his other accusers" (*Per.* 10).

Elpinice was apparently a woman of some determination and influence. Her entry into public affairs (and the public eye), however, came at some cost to her reputation, as Pericles' quotation of Archilochus suggests and other contemporary "gossip" recorded by Plutarch reveals as well. Elpinice's devotion to her brother and forthright approach to Pericles (and public issues) translated into popular tales that she was a "loose woman," who carried on an incestuous relationship with Cimon

(Plut. *Cim.* 4). And Cimon himself was attacked with the same sort of suggestion of impropriety in the story that the mother of his children was "a woman of Cleitor" (*Cim.* 16). Here perhaps we see some of the social background for Pericles' general advice to women, but also the possibility of female interest in both politics and law.

Myrrhine and Lysimache, Priestesses of Athena Nike and Athena Polias

Some twenty years after Pericles' famous (Thucydidean) Funeral Oration, when the Peloponnesian War was not going well for Athens (and Pericles was no longer at the helm), Aristophanes produced his comedy *Lysistrata*. Behind the comic heroine and her "right-hand woman" Myrrhine there were, it seems, some real Athenian women – just as there were behind many of Aristophanes' male comic characters. At the time the play was produced in the spring of 411, the priestess of Athena Nike was very likely a woman named Myrrhine and the priestess of Athena Polias a woman named Lysimache.[48] The importance of this "coincidence" for our understanding of the play should be clear, but there is yet another dimension to the public identity of the two women. In the late fifth century both Myrrhine and Lysimache were honored with public monuments. For the one, an inscribed epigraph announces that

> This far-seen tomb is that of the daughter of Callimachus,
> Who was the first to tend the temple of Nike;
> Her name shared in her good fame, for by divine
> Fortune she was called Myrrhine. Truly
> She was the first who tended the statue of Athena Nike
> Chosen by lot out of everyone, Myrrhine, by good Fortune.[49]

Although not found in the same location, a marble lekythos showing a woman labeled as Myrhhine being led away by Hermes may be part of the same grave monument.[50] For Lysimache, the Athenians erected a bronze statue for which the marble base with a fragmentary dedicatory inscription is all that remains.[51]

Myrrhine and Lysimache were not alone in the honor they received after death; one of the notable features of fifth-century Athenian funerary monuments is the prominence they give to women, perhaps reflecting the democracy's emphasis on legitimate family membership as the basis of citizenship.[52] The connection of these two prominent

Athenian women with the social and political themes of *Lysistrata*, the destructiveness and senselessness of Greek "civil war," is hard to ignore. Women do have something to say about the public good. It is also difficult to find a better conclusion for this chapter than the image offered by Lysistrata of free Athenian society as a complex fleece that needs to be cleaned and combed: "Then card the wool into the work-basket of union and concord, mixing in everyone; the metics, and any *xenos* who's friendly to you . . . " (579–80, Sommerstein). Behind that image of "union and concord" rests the reality of slavery, the inhuman nature of which no Athenian source denies – perhaps just because it was a fate to which in the end no Athenian could claim to be invulnerable. "War," said the fifth-century philosopher Heraclitus, "is father of all, king of all. Some it makes gods, some it makes men, some it makes slaves, some free." Fifth-century Athens was a city more often at war than not. The wars for which male Athenian citizens voted, and in which they fought, had powerful consequences not only for themselves but also for the many others or "other sorts" in Periclean society.

Suggestions for Further Reading

Athenian social and gender history is an active and fast-moving field, in which important contributions often appear in journals or anthologies. Among the latter, V. Hunter and J. Edmondson, eds., *Law and Social Status in Classical Athens* (Oxford: Oxford University Press, 2000), is particularly relevant for the issues of this chapter. P. Cartledge, E. Cohen, and L. Foxhall, eds., *Money, Labour and Land: Approaches to the Economies of Ancient Greece* (London: Routledge, 2002), and A. Lardinois and L. McClure, eds., *Making Silence Speak: Women's Voices in Greek Literature and Society* (Princeton: Princeton University Press, 2001), also contain important essays (and bibliographies). A different perspective on Athenian women is offered in C. Cox, *Household Interests: Property, Marriage Strategies, and Family Dynamics in Ancient Athens* (Princeton: Princeton University Press, 1998); C. B. Patterson, *The Family in Greek History* (Cambridge, MA: Harvard University Press, 1998); and E. Fantham et al., *Women in the Classical World* (New York: Oxford University Press, 1994), chapter 3: "Women in Classical Athens: Heroines and House-wives." Among older studies, M. I. Finley's *Ancient Slavery and Modern Ideology* (New York: Viking Press, 1980), and D. Whitehead, *The Ideology of the Athenian Metic* (Cambridge: Cambridge University Press, 1977), remain fundamental. For general reference, see S. Todd, *The Shape of Athenian Law* (Oxford: Oxford University Press, 1993).

NOTES

1   Unless otherwise noted, quotations from Thucydides are from the translation of R. Warner: Thucydides, *The Peloponnesian War* (London: Penguin, 1972).

2   See R. Rehm, *The Play of Space* (Princeton: Princeton University Press, 2002), p. 50 (with references): "Based on the surviving evidence and testimonia, most scholars agree that the theater audience included anyone who could afford a ticket: men, women, children, metics, slaves, prisoners (released on bail especially for the festival), foreigners, Athenians and non-Athenians, citizens and noncitizens alike. This openness reflects the nature of Dionysiac cult generally, and the particular pan-Athenaic flavor of the City Dionysia." See also Henderson in this volume, pp. 183–4.

3   This is not intended as an exhaustive list of sources for Periclean Athens, but just a useful selection for this essay.

4   Pericles served as *choregos* for the play, providing funds for its production.

5   M. I. Finley, "Was Greek Civilization Based on Slave Labour?" in M. I. Finley, ed., *Slavery in Classical Antiquity* (Cambridge: Heffer & Sons, 1960), pp. 53–72. The distinction between slave society and "society with slaves" is made by Paul Cartledge in his summary of Finley in "The Political Economy of Greek Slavery," in P. Cartledge, E. Cohen, and L. Foxhall, eds., *Money, Labour and Land: Approaches to the Economies of Ancient Greece* (London: Routledge 2002), pp. 156–66. Aristotle (*Politics* 1253b20–23) is our source for the antislavery argument; his own argument is notoriously difficult and unsatisfactory. Aristotle argued for the existence of "natural slaves," who are not capable of rational decision making or action, while admitting that in practice not all of those enslaved are natural slaves, or vice versa.

6   Finley (n. 5), p. 72. American history of course offers a similar sort of paradox.

7   See Antiphon 5; Aeschines 1.138. On the difficult issue of judicial torture of slaves, see David L. Mirhady, "The Athenian Rationale for Torture," in V. Hunter and J. Edmondson, eds., *Law and Social Status in Classical Athens* (Oxford: Oxford University Press, 2000), pp. 53–74.

8   For the (admittedly politically charged) report that in appearance slaves in Athens were indistinguishable from citizens, see the [Xenophon] *Constitution of the Athenians* 1.10; for the employment of slaves in crafts alongside free men, see the Erechtheion building accounts (*IG* i³ 476), and further below.

9   Finley (n. 5), p. 57.

10   M. H. Jameson, "Agriculture and Slavery in Classical Athens," *CJ* 73 (1977): 122–45. See also Victor Hanson, *The Other Greeks: The Family Farm and Agrarian Roots of Western Civilization* (New York: Free Press, 1995).

11   M. H. Jameson, summing up the position of Paul Cartledge in "On Paul Cartledge, 'The political economy of Greek slavery,'" in Cartledge et al. (n. 5), p. 168.

12   I. Scott-Kilvert, trans., modified: *The Rise and Fall of Athens: Nine Greek Lives*, (London: Penguin, 1960).

13   *IG* i³ 476. On the Erechtheion accounts see R. H. Randall, "The Erechtheum Workmen," *AJA* 57 (1953): 199–210; in general on wages and labor in Athens see

W. T. Loomis, *Wages, Welfare Costs and Inflation in Classical Athens* (Ann Arbor: University of Michigan Press, 1998).

14　Xenophon *Poroi* 4.114–15. In this fourth-century text, Xenophon looks back to the fifth century for ideas on how the city could more profitably take advantage of its resources.

15　For the fiscal management of Athens's empire, see L. J. Samons, *Empire of the Owl: Athenian Imperial Finance* (Stuttgart: Steiner, 2000).

16　Orlando Patterson, *Freedom: Freedom in the Making of Western Culture* (New York: Basic Books, 1991), chapter 7, "A Woman's Song: The Female Force and the Ideology of Freedom in Greek Tragedy and Society," discusses the way in which the female characters, particularly the female slaves, of Athenian tragedy offer critical perspective on the slave experience. His reading, however, seems to go too far in suggesting that slaves in tragedy are actually struggling for their own freedom, that the *Libation Bearers* "is a play about a slave rebellion" (p. 115). On issues of female "voice" see J. Blok, "Virtual Voices: Toward a Choreography of Women's Speech in Classical Athens," in A. Lardinois and L. McClure, eds., *Making Silence Speak* (Princeton: Princeton University Press, 2001), pp. 95–116.

17　The Greek word here is *domata*, a frequent Aeschylean synonym for *oikos* or *oikia*.

18　H. Lloyd-Jones, *The Libation Bearers* (Englewood Cliffs, NJ: Prentice-Hall, 1985), p. 3.

19　That Athenians used public slaves as police and in other roles is one of the (from a modern perspective) odder features of its democracy. See Virginia Hunter, *Policing Athens* (Princeton: Princeton University Press, 1984), pp. 145–9.

20　See also the recommendations for slave discipline in Xenophon *Memorabilia* 11.1.15–17.

21　For general discussion of the full range of such scenes, see Eva Keuls, *The Reign of the Phallus* (New York: Harper and Row, 1985), chapter 6, pp. 153–86.

22　For discussion of the slave image in art and literature, see Kelly Joss, *Re-constructing the Slave: An Examination of Slave Representation in the Greek Polis* (Ph.D. dissertation, University of St. Andrews, 2006).

23　For Edward Cohen's argument (*The Athenian Nation* [Princeton: Princeton University Press, 2000]) that this openness continued into the classical era (fifth and fourth centuries), see below.

24　See David Whitehead, *The Ideology of the Athenian Metic* (Cambridge: Cambridge University Press, 1977).

25　This disability would clearly have consequences within the larger Athenian inheritance and kinship structures – e.g., if an Athenian man married a non-Athenian woman, could his children's maternal relatives ever make a claim on the property? By the fourth century, this issue or ambiguity was settled with laws specifically excluding marriage between Athenian and foreigner. See [Demosthenes] 59, *Against Neaira* 16; also A. Boegehold, "Perikles' Citizenship Law of 451/0," in A. Boegehold and A. Scafuro, eds., *Athenian Identity and Civic Ideology* (Baltimore: Johns Hopkins University Press, 1994), pp. 57–66, and C. Patterson, "The Case Against Neaira and the Public Ideology of the Athenian Family," ibid., pp. 199–216.

26　In addition to Whitehead (n. 24), see the discussions of S. Todd, *The Shape of Athenian Law* (Oxford: Oxford University Press, 1993), chapter 10, "Personal Status;" M. H. Hansen, *The Athenian Democracy in the Age of Demosthenes*, trans. J. A. Crook

(Oxford: Blackwell, 1991), and V. Hunter, "Status Distinctions in Athenian Law," in Hunter and Edmonson (n. 7), pp. 1–29.

27 See Whitehead (n. 24) for a thorough critique of this idea. Recently, Edward Cohen (n. 23), chapter 2, has revived the idea by way of the notion that the term *astoi* could include *metics* – and so *metics* had a kind of citizenship that could be passed on to their children. The idea, however, does not hold up in a full examination of the meaning and use of *astos* and is a fundamental flaw of Cohen's book. Cf. Patterson, "Athenian Citizenship Law," in D. Cohen and M. Gagarin, eds., *The Cambridge Companion to Greek Law* (New York: Cambridge University Press, 2005), pp. 267–89.

28 Whitehead (n. 24), p. 38; see also Patterson, "The Hospitality of Athenian Justice: The Metic in Court," in Hunter and Edmondson (n. 7), pp. 93–112.

29 *IG* ii² 10; Andocides *On the Mysteries* 15.

30 Diogenes Laertius 9.8.10.

31 *Nic.* 23. In the same chapter – but not necessarily referring to the same time – Plutarch asserts that Anaxagoras was thrown in prison, from which Pericles rescued him. For the doubtful historicity of these stories, see R. W. Wallace, "Private Lives and Public Enemies: Freedom of Thought in Classical Athens," in Boegehold and Scafuro (n. 25), pp. 127–55.

32 For example, Phaedrus and Charmides. For a complete list, see *HCT* IV.277–80.

33 On Aspasia, see M. Henry, *Prisoner of History: Aspasia of Miletus and Her Biographical Tradition* (New York: Oxford University Press, 1995), and C. W. Fornara and L. J. Samons, *Athens from Cleisthenes to Pericles* (Berkeley: University of California Press, 1991), pp. 163–5, who argue that Pericles and Aspasia were married and question the authenticity of her trial. On the legal position of metics – and their frequent isolation within the legal system – see Patterson (n. 28).

34 Specifically, the washing and laying out of the body and the formal lament of the corpse. Men, too, had responsibilities in burial (e.g., the actual physical act of burial), and sometimes – because of special need or circumstance – these burial roles might be exchanged. For example, Antigone herself "buries" the body of her brother in Sophocles' *Antigone*, and Theseus washes the bodies of the Argive dead in Euripides' *Suppliant Women*.

35 For a persuasive argument that these female musicians represent "proper" citizen women, see S. Bundrick, *Expressions of Harmony: Representations of Female Musicians in Fifth-Century Athenian Vase Painting* (Ph.D. dissertation: Emory University, 1998), and *Music and Image in Classical Athens* (New York: Cambridge University Press, 2005).

36 And many things have been said; since my discussion in 1981 (*Pericles Citizenship Law of 451/0 B.C.* [New York: Arno]), see A. Boegehold, "Pericles' Citizenship Law of 451/0," in Boegehold and Scafuro (n. 25), pp. 57–66, and especially Todd (n. 26), for discussion and bibliography. E. Cohen (n. 23) presents a radically different view from the *communis opinio* that is not, however, persuasive on this topic.

37 So N. Loraux argues in *Children of Athena*, trans. C. Levine (Princeton: Princeton University Press, 1993), pp. 119–20.

38 The definition of H. G. Liddell, R. Scott, and H. S. Jones, *Greek Lexicon* (Oxford: Oxford University Press, 1968) that the *astos* is one who has civil not political rights is not in fact supported by an examination of Athenian usage (see Patterson

[n. 36], Appendix 1). It is unfortunate that E. Cohen (n. 23), p. 61, uses the lexicon as "authority" for his own argument on this point.

39 Cf. *Thesmophoriazousae* 302–9 (the female chorus's prayer on behalf of the *demos ton Athenaion* and also *ton gunaikon*), and *Lysistrata*, which also emphasizes the "corporate" identity of Athenian citizen women.

40 Sue Blundell, *Women in Ancient Greece* (Cambridge, MA: Harvard University Press, 1995), p. 128.

41 "The words," says R. Osborne, "were separated from the person": "Religion, Imperial Politics, and the Offering of Freedom to Slaves," in Hunter and Edmondson (n. 7), pp. 75–92, at p. 81.

42 Osborne (n. 41), p. 80.

43 For discussion of these issues and the position of women in Athenian property law, see C. Patterson, *The Family in Greek History* (Cambridge, MA: Harvard University Press, 1998). Also, L. Foxhall, "Household, Gender and Property in Classical Athens," *CQ* 39 (1989): 22–44; and Hunter (n. 19), pp. 19–42.

44 See Foxhall (n. 43).

45 *Pace* N. Loraux, *The Invention of Athens. The Funeral Oration in the Classical City*, trans. A. Sheridan (Cambridge, MA: Harvard University Press, 1986), p. 24.

46 Thuc. 2.46, trans. Warner, modified.

47 See Lisa Kallet-Marx, "Thucydides 2.45.2 and the Status of War Widows in Periclean Athens," in R. Rosen and J. Farrell, eds., *Nomodeiktes. Greek Studies in Honor of Martin Ostwald* (Ann Arbor: University of Michigan Press, 1993), pp. 133–44. Cf., in the same volume, Paul Cartledge, "The Silent Women of Thucydides: 2.45.2 Re-Viewed," pp. 125–32. The way in which Pericles' advice is generally transformed from "not talked about" to "not talking" is remarkable. There is no reason to think that Pericles is telling Athenian women not to talk.

48 See D. Lewis, "Who Was Lysistrata?" *ABSA* 50 (1955): 1–12.

49 *SEG* 12.80, trans. in M. Dillon and L. Garland, eds., *Ancient Greece: Social and Historical Documents from Archaic Times to the Death of Socrates* (New York: Routledge, 2000).

50 C. Clairmont, "The Lekythos of Myrrhine," in G. Kopcke and M. Moore, eds., *Studies in Classical Art and Archaeology: A Tribute to Peter Heinrich von Blanckenhagen* (Locust Valley, NJ: J. J. Augustin, 1979), pp. 103–10.

51 Lewis (n. 48): 4–6.

52 See E. A. Meyer, "Epitaphs and Citizenship in Classical Athens," *JHS* 113 (1993): 99–121; K. Stears, "Dead Women's Society: Constructing Female Gender in Classical Athenian Funerary Sculpture," in N. Spencer, ed., *Time, Tradition and Society in Greek Archaeology* (London: Routledge 1995), pp. 109–31; R. Leader, "In Death Not Divided: Gender, Family, and State on Classical Athenian Grave Stelae," *AJA* 101 (1997): 683–99.

7: DRAMA AND DEMOCRACY

Jeffrey Henderson

I n fifth-century Athens tragedy, satyr drama, and comedy, together
with the largely choral dithyramb, achieved distinct generic forms
and a level of artistic refinement and portability that ensured their
continuing vitality and popularity throughout the Greco-Roman world
to the end of antiquity and, in the case of tragedy and comedy, into our
own world. While we admire the artistic qualities of Athenian drama, it
is worthwhile also to ask in what ways its development and success can
be related to the simultaneous development of democracy, particularly
during the age of Pericles and the Athenian empire, for exploring the
relationship between these principal artistic and political products of
fifth-century Athens cannot but enhance our understanding of each.

In Attica, drama at the polis level was attached to two annual, state-
organized Athenian festivals for Dionysus: the spring City or Greater
Dionysia as early as ca. 501 and from ca. 440 the winter Lenaea as
well; drama was also performed locally in the deme-organized Lesser or
Rural Dionysia. But drama was hardly confined to democratic Athens:
each of its dramatic forms (tragedy and satyr drama, comedy, and the
dithyramb) is attested before the democracy as well as in other Greek
locales. Although a reliable record of drama at the Dionysia begins only
ca. 501, at least tragedy seems to have become significant under the
(comparatively populist) tyranny of Peisistratus in the sixth century;[1]
whether and in what ways the organization of the dramatic festival(s)
figured among Cleisthenes' reforms cannot now be determined.[2] And
clearly there were theatrical publics beyond Athens, not only for comedy, which early in the fifth century was enjoying robust development
in western Greece by composers such as Epicharmus: non-Athenian
tragic poets occasionally competed at Athens, and in dithyramb non-
Athenian composers in fact won most of the prizes. As early as the

mid-fifth century such prominent composers as Aeschylus were being invited to produce tragedy/satyr drama abroad, and Ar. *Clouds* 520–25 implies that foreign production was also an option for comic poets. Nor was the relationship of drama with Dionysus essential: elsewhere we find drama associated with other gods or with heroes, for example, at Delphi with Apollo, despite the availability of Dionysus there; and although religion and the gods are ever-present in Athenian drama, Dionysus is comparatively seldom featured except in satyr drama, whose satyr-chorus was frequently (though not exclusively) associated with him.[3] In general, fifth-century Athenian cult and religion were based more in Panhellenic and polis traditions than in democratic institutions.

Nevertheless, drama in the fifth century was nowhere more energetically pursued than in democratic Athens, so that in subsequent ages the Athenian forms eclipsed all others and professional dramatists everywhere styled themselves "artists of Dionysus." In the fifth century alone, members of a citizen body no larger than 30,000–50,000 supported the production of some 2,000 dithyrambs, 1,250 tragedies, and 650 comedies.[4] The dramatic festivals were among the Athenians' most spectacular and expensive undertakings, and involved a significant number of organizers, stagehands, ticket distributors, theater managers, and performers, including for each City Dionysia some 28 poets and 28 producers (*choregoi*), 24 principal actors, 1,165 dancers, and a substantial number of musicians. The theater of Dionysus, which accommodated at least 17,000 spectators, concentrated much more of the Attic populace in one place at the same time than any other public event; the assembly, which met on Pnyx Hill, could accommodate only 6,000.

The development of Athenian drama seems to intersect the development of democracy following the Cleisthenic reforms at significant points. The history of comedy, a genre often critical of elites, suggests an especially close synchrony with the democracy, as it perhaps does outside of Athens as well.[5] Comedy entered the Dionysia in the reform year 487/6, when archons were first allotted (by then drawn from the second as well as the first census class) and just after the first known ostracism.[6] Comedy's most intensely political phase coincided with the ascendancy of Pericles (the era of full popular sovereignty that began with Ephialtes' reforms of 462/1 and lasted until the end of the Peloponnesian War in 404), tapered off after the reforms of 403, disappeared entirely during the oligarchic regime begun in 322 (the era of the entirely apolitical "New Comedy"), but reappeared during two democratic restorations;[7] contrast the west Greek court-comedy of Epicharmus (early to mid-fifth century), which was entirely apolitical.[8]

Conversely, we encounter topical tragedies before the reforms of 462/1 but not after Aeschylus's *Eumenides* of 458, which focused on the Areopagus council just after Ephialtes had reduced its powers.[9] During the fifth century, the remarkable autonomy of expression in Athenian drama was occasionally constrained by lawsuits or by such actions of the assembly as the fine imposed on the tragic composer Phrynichus in the 490s for his *Sack of Miletus*, which reminded the Athenians of "troubles close to home" (Hdt. 6.21), and the decree of Morychides' archonship (440/39), which coincided with Pericles' controversial action against Samos and with the appearance of drama (principally comedy) at the Lenaea.[10] Such constraints appear to have been motivated much more by civic than by religious or cultic considerations. Under the oligarchy of 322, the system of patronage by producers (*choregia*) and the subsidy for theatrical attendance (*theorikon*) were abolished. Writers critical of democracy, for example, the "Old Oligarch" ([Xenophon] *Athenian Constitution*) and Plato, are typically hostile toward all dramatic festivity and consistently link it to such democratic features as egalitarianism, freedom of speech, moral and political relativism, godlessness, and oratory.

In its institutional framework, too, Athenian drama adapted to democratic institutions traditional practices inherited from the Peisistratean era and/or characteristic of Greek poleis generally.[11] It is important to bear in mind that democracy in Athens was a process, not a revolution: Pericles and his allies radicalized government not through violence or tyranny but by votes of the Athenian assemblymen, so that wealthy elites were not killed, exiled, or stripped of their culture or privileges but rather accommodated in the new system along with everyone else. As in many other Attic festivals, Athenian drama was agonistic, a contest of honor and prestige involving state-regulated competition first among wealthy producers (*choregoi*) and poets and soon among actors and musicians as well. Such competitions served to channel elite rivalries to civic/democratic instead of tyrannical purposes, and though it would not be surprising to discover that drama was agonistic elsewhere in Greece, the "Old Oligarch" could single out the Athenian competitions for the complaint that "the rich perform *choregiai* while the *demos* is the beneficiary of *choregiai*."[12]

Athenian drama was in fact a traditional elite activity harnessed by the democracy for the enjoyment of the people, for the personnel of the dramatic competitions were necessarily drawn from the wealthy and cultivated strata of Athenian society. In being institutionally selected and privileged, they were a distinct cadre more like officeholders than the ordinary citizens who might seek a public platform, say by choosing to rise in the assembly or to bring an action in court, and in competing for individual honor they preserved a distinctly aristocratic heritage.

This was especially the case for producers of drama, the *choregoi*. *Choregia* was a particularly expensive, time-consuming, and socially demanding "liturgy" (required contribution to the state). *Choregoi* were appointed by the appropriate public official from a list of men wealthy enough to undertake the role; Pericles, for example, served as *choregos* for Aeschylus's *Persians* in 473/2. The *choregos*'s role (which could not be refused, though it could also be volunteered) was to recruit, house, and train a chorus (12 or 15 dancers for a tragic tetralogy, 24 for a comedy, and 50 for a dithyramb), whose members he could compel to perform and who were exempted from military service to do so.[13] A poet wishing to compete applied to the same public official for a chorus, and if selected was assigned a chorus and received from the state a stipend in an amount subject to modification by the assembly (Ar. *Frogs* 367–8, alleging the motivation of revenge for comic criticism); for the dithyramb, however, which was tribally organized, each *choregos* in an allotted order chose his own poet.[14] Initially the poets chose their own actors, and could also act in their own plays, but by the fourth century actors were assigned to poets by lot. The judges too were allotted, each of the ten Cleisthenic tribes submitting candidates, though the short list was selected by the council of 500 in consultation with that year's *choregoi*.

Although all civic institutions were inactive during the week of the Dionysia, the festival was not a complete suspension of civic activity in favor of religion and drama, but extended some civic activity into the theater of Dionysus. In addition to the dramatic competitions themselves, the Dionysia was an occasion for both religious ceremonies (prayers, processions, sacrifices, libations offered by the generals, ritualized revelry) and more straightforwardly civic (though not self-evidently democratic) displays: the commissioning of war orphans, who had been raised at state expense; the presentation by allied states, in the time of the Delian League (after 454/3), of their annual tribute; the proclamation of honors voted to distinguished Athenians and foreigners; and other civic business deemed appropriate for the occasion.

It is nevertheless unclear whether and in what ways either the civic or the religious ceremonies that preceded the dramas at the Dionysia were related to the dramas themselves.[15] Athenian drama does not particularly feature Dionysus or appear to be intrinsically Dionysiac; typically represented a far broader and more traditional world than that of the politically enfranchised citizenry; and as far as we know neither referred to the preplay ceremonies nor (at least overtly) addressed whatever religious or civic/democratic themes they may have embodied. Furthermore, we know of no such preplay civic ceremonies at the Lenaea, which was held in the winter when only Athenians could attend.[16] The reason for the inclusion of the preplay ceremonies at the Dionysia could well be that this festival, which fell in the late spring and attracted a uniquely large and international audience, was the most suitable venue for them.

The theatrical experience itself also suggests that the dramatic festivals were not civic but rather supracivic occasions when the horizons of the polis transcended those of its democratic executive, the corporation of *politai* (citizen males 18 years and older) that composed the *demos*. By the mid-fifth century, the plots of tragedy and satyr drama were set in the mythical past mostly in places other than Athens, focused almost exclusively on the concerns of the family and the whole polis community, only seldom portrayed any political class or any individual resembling an Athenian citizen, and hardly ever alluded to Athenian civic concerns, least of all democracy.[17] Tragedy and satyr drama differ from epic, from which they largely draw their myths, chiefly by involving polis, but not specifically Athenian, life in their choice of themes and emphases; they seldom treated Attic myths (despite some attempts to amplify the myths about the Attic hero Theseus) because there were so few Attic myths to treat and because audiences (in Athens as elsewhere) preferred myths of traditional Panhellenic stature and universal appeal. Even in comedy, which was often topical, civic subjects appear only in a relatively small "political" subgenre pursued by a subset of poets (principally Cratinus, Eupolis, and Aristophanes) and then almost exclusively during those periods of the Peloponnesian War era in which "demagogic" politicians, beginning with Pericles, achieved a certain ascendancy and drew comic attacks (the 430s–420s, 411–405, the 390s).

The audience that watched the plays was correspondingly heterogeneous. Unlike civic assemblies proper, attendance was not exclusive, and we hear of no attempt to debar any class of residents or even foreigners.[18] The *demos* was present as host, bestower of civic honors, regulator, and notional audience, and when performers speak of or to the audience they almost always address it as the *demos* or some subset of it.[19] But alongside the *demos* sat as many of those otherwise debarred from civic assemblies as could purchase seats: children, slaves, metics (i.e., resident aliens, who could also perform as dancers at the Lenaea), visiting foreigners, and very probably women as well.[20] These categories of people, normally invisible from the vantage point of civic assemblies, were also the typical characters in the dramas.[21] Although the competition witnessed by this inclusive audience was democratically managed and accountable to the *demos*, it was not contested between political units, the Cleisthenic demes, or (except for the dithyramb) the tribes. And unlike properly civic voices, who could address only the *demos* and appeal only to democratic laws and procedures, the dramatists composed for the polis-world at large and could appeal to older cultic and poetic traditions, as well as to a more universal ethical code.[22]

While it is safe to say that the audience was not exclusively made up of citizens, the question of women's attendance remains open: although there is no evidence for their exclusion from the theater, the evidence for their attendance is (or has been made to sound) ambiguous. Since the late eighteenth century (but not earlier), it has been generally argued that women must have been excluded, first on the assumption that attendance would have compromised their propriety, and then on the more modern assumption that civic space (theoretically defined as any space where citizen males congregated) was gendered space and therefore off limits to women.[23]

But even if we leave aside the resulting misalignment of audience with the characters and themes of drama, where women and the household are very prominent (the fact of all-male performers being a matter of convention and therefore irrelevant),[24] we must ask whether the theater was gendered space when it was the venue for dramatic festivals honoring Dionysus, whose cult was otherwise so inclusive and so intimately associated with women. Here modern gender theory should acknowledge that in any society most spaces public and private are marked for status or gender not absolutely but by their function on given occasions. If during the dramatic festivals the theater was accessible to anyone who wanted to attend, then the situation of civic males in the theater would merely reflect their situation in the polis at large as well as in the plays. It should not surprise us if Greek drama, a festive tradition that preceded and would long outlive the Athenian democracy, played to a fully inclusive audience and pursued themes reflecting the whole polis and not merely its political subset.

Furthermore, while the audience at the dramatic festivals was inclusive and not apparently disposed by deme or tribe, its organization did not follow wholly egalitarian principles. There was privileged seating for Athenian councilmen and other officials, major priest(esse)s, foreign dignitaries, and certain honorands, and some evidence suggests that women and slaves sat by themselves in the rear sections. And there was a charge for admission, an arrangement unique to the theatrical festivals. Since attendance was not restricted, the charge for admission was presumably instituted (date unknown) to control a demand that exceeded supply, and this could well have excluded the poorest citizens from attending the theater, an arrangement not incompatible with democracy if participation was not considered a civic right or duty, as for juries and assemblies, where pay for service (an idea attributable to Pericles) was introduced respectively in the 450s and 390s. A subsidy for attendance (*theorikon*), first attested in the mid-fourth century, was paid in the form of a grant to each deme on the basis of its register of citizens, but it is not known when this subsidy was introduced or how the grants were converted into tickets. It is possible that the subsidy was intended to assist the poor, but it could equally well have been a way to reserve more tickets for citizens.[25]

The foregoing considerations suggest that the Athenian *politai*, in administering the polis by democratic rules and ideology, deferred to traditional practices in the case of the dramatic competitions even during the Periclean era, when Athens distinguished itself from the rest of Greece in important ways. The dramatists preserved older traditions and addressed themes and audiences representing the whole polis, and in the case of tragedy and satyr drama, the polis mostly in its Panhellenic rather than peculiarly Athenian character. This supracivic character of Athenian drama is unsurprising, since participation in Athenian political life was restricted, and politics hardly pervaded the whole of society,[26] which otherwise retained traditional practices, traditions, institutions, and values that stood at some remove from, and could even come into conflict with, democratic practices and goals. The goal of Athenian society was not democratic life, much less democratic politics, nor was the demotic will identified with normative goodness. It was rather through the household (*oikos*) in its varied formations that every Athenian was connected to the polis, and the politically unenfranchised majority – women, children, foreigners, and slaves – were prominent within their own multiple realms, especially the religious and economic realms.[27] And it was the polis composed not of political units but rather of households that formed the world of drama. Drama focused on the tensions that divided the members of households, that complicated the relationships of households or individuals to the polis, or that created enmity between poleis. Only in a small subset of "political" comedies was the democratic polis a focus of drama, and then only against the backdrop of more inclusive and universal polis values.

Nevertheless, the development of democratic culture surely fostered and conditioned the development of Athenian drama during the fifth century. The vitality of the democratic polis depended on the ability of every citizen male to participate in creating and living by its rules and laws, written and unwritten, in understanding them, and in making them work, so that all members of the polis had to have a voice in deliberation, debate, or critique, in other words to have *parrhesia*, the freedom to speak the truth as one saw it for the benefit of the polis. Citizens exercised this freedom in civic fora either directly or indirectly through the male heads of their households, but the outlook and views of the unenfranchised members of the polis could also be represented vicariously in the dramatic festivals, through their portrayal in drama.[28]

The dramatic performances themselves resembled legal trials and assembly meetings[29] in that the audience responded to the portrayal of individuals in situations requiring the mediation of conflicting social values and the resolution of personal or civic conflicts.[30] Like the orators, and like all Greek poets before them, the dramatists were expected to inform, to instruct, and within certain bounds even to castigate their audiences.[31] Like lawcourts and assemblies, the dramatic festival exemplified, and devoted much of its attention to, the dissonance between the two major themes of democratic polity: egalitarianism and elitism.[32] And like lawcourts and assemblies, civic theater served to temper the understanding, the critical capacity, and the confidence of a citizenry now fully in charge of its own destiny. Like any other institution of the democracy, civic theater was predicated on the theory of the ultimate wisdom, and trainability in wisdom, of the citizenry. Thus it could not but serve and strengthen the vitality of democratic life, and that is why critics like Plato attacked drama in the same terms as they did oratory and free intellectual debate.

But the concerns expressed in the dramas significantly transcended the range of problems specific to the executive worlds of lawcourt and assembly, for they treated the ethics of family and private life, the lives of people as individuals as opposed to civic categories, the discontinuity or conflict between the political and the larger society, and the wider world beyond Athens, including the gods, heroes, and religious life of other societies. And the dramatic festivals, being in certain respects privileged extensions of civic life and thus, unbound by its rules, could shelter expressions of dissent from the "state truth" of politics. And so drama became the principal communal outlet for portraying the polis in all its diversity and social hierarchies; for reconsidering traditions and norms, airing concerns, examining problems, and testing solutions that affected the democratic culture as a whole but had no other public outlet.

As theatergoers, people debarred from other venues of civic discourse and publicity, especially women,[33] could experience the role of democratic audience. Community knowledge, from popular gossip to the concerns of the political class, could be aired and diffused. People whose suggestions, concerns, or complaints had not been, or could not be, presented to the executive *demos* might expect the poets to raise them on their behalf. Such people would include such civic minorities as the "quiet" members of the elite and the "little people" who were rarely able to attend civic meetings, let alone likely to rise in the assembly or to litigate, such as farmers from distant demes or the very poor. In these ways the dramatic festivals served both as the voice of, and as a window into, household and private life; a platform for experimental politics; an opportunity to air, and perhaps to mend or at least paper over, significant rifts in the body politic, and to act as a counterweight to the public and strictly political realms of polis life.

While democracy may thus have been a precondition of fifth-century Attic drama, democracy never became an ideological theme or a normative/didactic project of the plays, least of all tragic plays. In contrast to comedy, the representation of the polis in tragedy, resonant as it may have been with its democratic environment, was through universals rather than topical particulars. As the Periclean era set in following the reforms of Ephialtes, the tragic poets restricted themselves to mythological scenarios (stories about kings, tyrants, heroes, and their families) and to timeless themes explored at a high level of generality, avoiding either references to the contemporary world or direct engagement with issues of the day. That is why Attic tragedy speaks to audiences in any time or place, why its myths can illuminate the particulars of any era,[34] and why our responses are various, complex, and ambivalent.

Sophocles' *Antigone*, for example, raises the issue of the relative claims of gods, family, and political community, arguably with particular meaning for the Athenian democracy in the age of Pericles, which by adopting the citizenship law of 451 went farther than other polis regimes in defining the role of women,[35] which restricted the private burial of war dead, and which was notoriously open to (though not always tolerant of) debate about the relative claims of human and divine law. But nowhere is there a particular reference to Athens or to democratic politics or life; the play treats issues and practices that were hardly unique to democratic Athens, so that it would have been meaningful in any other constitutionally governed polis; after all, Antigone's story was Theban, and the play went on to become a staple of the theatrical repertory everywhere.

Of general importance in Attic tragedy is "the contradiction between tyranny and the polis, of which the saving of the city through the self-destruction of the ruling family is one aspect."[36] This tragic theme surely resonated with mid-fifth-century Athenians, preoccupied as they were with tyranny: they associated the birth of their democracy with liberation from tyranny, and regarded tyranny both as the antithesis of democracy and as a threat requiring constant vigilance, even if we now see the historical unreality of this historical construction.[37] And yet it is difficult to find a straightforwardly democratic moral in the portrayal of a given tragic tyrant. Neither Creon nor Antigone makes an indisputably right or wrong case, and if the Oedipus of *Oedipus Tyrannus*, who is in most respects a typical tyrant, somehow embodied Pericles or even democratic Athens, as has been suggested,[38] then the play's ideological moral is ambivalent. And of course tragic tyrants were equally intelligible within the ideological framework of the Greek polis generally.

Fifth-century (Old) Attic comedy, by contrast, did not restrict itself to mythological subjects or maintain dramatic illusion but was often highly topical, sharply portraying Athens and its people and engaging in focused debate on a wide range of political, social, and cultural issues of the day. The characteristic outspokenness of Old Comedy is unexampled elsewhere in Greece or even in Athens during nondemocratic eras, so that this dramatic genre has a fair claim to be a phenomenon related to democracy, especially to the *parrhesia* that encouraged other forms of intellectual debate during the Periclean age. That Old Comic satire was not always mere foolery but could engage with controversial issues is indicated by the occasional lawsuits and decrees seeking to limit (or in the case of Aristophanes' *Frogs*, to reward) its outspokenness,[39] by its respect for the laws governing slander and other utterances harmful to the polis,[40] and by its evidently partisan tendencies.[41] Politically engaged comedy thus resembles oratory in voicing criticism and advice pitched within, and subject to, the rules governing public speech. Instances of comic censorship seem to become less rather than more frequent during the fifth century, probably because they were largely unsuccessful, the public apparently preferring to allow the comic poets wide latitude, while the tragic poets stayed above the fray.

As political voices, however, Aristophanes and his rivals (to judge from the fragmentary remains of their plays[42]) show a consistent tendency to espouse the social, moral, and political sentiments not of the *demos* at large but of landowning conservatives, that is to say the opponents and not the supporters of men like Pericles. The wealthy as a class are never criticized, whereas the poor often are (though this attitude changes by the early fourth century). There is nostalgia for the good old days of the early democracy, before the reforms of Ephialtes, before Pericles eclipsed Cimon, and before the rise of "demagogues" such as Cleon.[43] According to the comic poets, in those days the people were united and deferred to men from the traditional ruling families, and so had been able to repel the Persian invaders, win a great empire, and lift Athens to unprecedented heights of prosperity; but the following generations had chosen base leaders and thus precipitated Athens's decline. There is disapproval of the popular intellectual movements associated with the "sophists" (including Socrates)[44] and of such "vulgar" novelties in poetry and music as those of Euripides (never Sophocles) and the new dithyrambists. There is hostility to the populist policies of Pericles and the new breed of leaders (like Cleon) who had emerged after his death in 429, such as the subsidy that enabled the poor to serve on juries (but not the equipment subsidies paid to the wealthy Knights). There is criticism of the way the council, the assembly, and the courts exercised their authority, particularly when private wealth in Athens and the empire was thereby threatened. And there is disagreement with the rationale behind, and the leadership of, the Peloponnesian War, because it had ended the Cimonian dream of joint Athenian-Spartan hegemony and pitted Greek against Greek; because it encouraged renewed barbarian aggression; and because it furthered the selfish and dangerous ambitions of demagogues. But significantly, we hear such disparagement of the war only when current policy exposed the Attic countryside, and thus the landowners, to enemy invasion and devastation; at other times the plays either say nothing about the war or positively support it, for example in *Birds* of 414.

The comic poets also show consistent bias in their choice of political figures to vilify. All of their political targets were "radical" democrats such as Pericles and his successors, whereas conservatives such as Nicias, Laches, Alcibiades, those implicated in the scandals of 415, and the oligarchs disenfranchised after the *coup d'état* of 411 – potential satirical targets at least as obvious as Pericles and Cleon – are entirely spared, and occasionally even defended. This bias cannot be satisfactorily explained as merely an automatic comic response to the political predominance of radical democrats during the era of political comedy, on the theory that political comedy tends to attack the powers that be whatever their political stripe, because the poets also mention other political figures favorably, all of them opponents of the radical democrats; they not only ridicule radical policies but also champion conservative policies on their merits; and during periods when the radicals are in eclipse they continue to attack them while sparing currently ascendant conservatives.

At the same time, however, the comic poets were egalitarian in their sympathies, consistently adopting the vantage point of typical rather than elite Athenians. The hero(in)es and other sympathetic characters of Old Comedy exclusively represent both ordinary or "quiet" people and people (like women and slaves) who were otherwise debarred from public life, and the poets offered advice and criticism exclusively on their behalf.[45] It is significant that comic hero(in)es are always fictitious creations, whereas their opponents represent real individuals and groups holding power or celebrity in the polis. The comic vantage point is essentially that of the ordinary citizen looking into the arena of civic power and faulting those who dominate it, while the ordinary citizens themselves are spared criticism. The illusion of demotic righteousness versus elite chicanery is reinforced by comic avoidance of praise: all good ideas come from comic hero(in)es, even when in actual life they could be attributed to actual people, for example, the Peace of Nicias of 421, attributed in Aristophanes' *Peace* to the vintner-hero Trygaeus without mention of Nicias.

Comic hero(in)es thus gave the majority of spectators vicarious pleasure in the triumph of the insignificant over the great, or the politically excluded over the political class; their complaints might well have served as a safety valve for unofficial discontent before it became politically or socially disruptive. In short, by frankly criticizing the powerful, the comic hero(ine) did what *isegoria* and *parrhesia* ideally allowed but could not fully provide for. By calling attention to social and political problems and controversies, comedy supplemented the police functions of assembly and court, using negative publicity as a substitute for legal sanctions. Under the democracy, leadership required dignity and was easily undermined by popular suspicions, and even private misbehavior could become the basis for legal action if someone could show that it harmed the polis, as happened, for example, in the case of Socrates, who blamed his prosecution on popular prejudices originally created by comedy.[46] It was the potential for such impact on the real world that kept comic speech from being exempted from the rules governing *parrhesia*.

But the comic poets did not confine themselves to griping on behalf of ordinary people. Being citizens as well as poets, they often had their own axes to grind, and they expected to have an impact beyond the festival. When Aristophanes claims that his plays serve only the public interest and not his own (e.g., *Wasps* 1023–8) he is, like an orator, defending himself against plausible suspicions to the contrary, even if disingenuously. When the demos officially crowned and commended him for the advice he had offered in the *parabasis* of *Frogs* (686–705) and decreed a reperformance of the play, there is reason to suspect a political motivation and a behind-the-scenes *quid pro quo* arrangement with the enemies of the popular politician Cleophon.[47] It is not unlikely that Hermippus's attack on Pericles' war-policy in his *Moirai* of 430 (cf. fr. 47) was politically motivated as well.[48]

But though the comic poets often castigated the *demos* for poor judgment, they neither questioned the essential rightness of democracy and its institutions nor called for a change of regime: even the new order in *Assemblywomen* is democratically legislated. No less than orators, comic poets were free to criticize the *demos* and its various subsets, e.g., assemblies and juries, but they were always careful to blame the *demos*'s shortcomings on particular leaders or a cadre of selfish and untrustworthy citizens.[49] They seem to have taken the same line about the empire, which Pericles and his successors thought so critical to maintaining the power and prestige of the democracy, in that they criticized Athenian leaders for imperial mismanagement and corruption but never questioned the justification for empire. They warn the *demos* against the flattery and dishonesty of its leaders, exhort it to reclaim its own rightful sovereignty, and urge it to choose better leaders; they urge the *demos* to reclaim the strength and success that characterized the democracy of an earlier era; and on important current issues they offer advice that would plausibly strengthen Athens and might be democratically enacted. In all this they both parallel the orators and stand in contrast to private critics such as Thucydides and Plato.

By way of conclusion, we may say that in developing their democracy, the mid-fifth-century Athenians accommodated the traditional dramatic genres with spectacular energy and creativity while at the same time deferring to drama's traditional Panhellenic scope, traditions, and focus on universal polis life. While the dramatic festivals were showcases for the power and sophistication of the democratic community, their organization preserved elements of the aristocratic past, with elite producers, poets, and performers competing for individual prestige, and attendance was restricted not by any civic or religious criterion but only by the unique charge for admission. Although drama was held to the rules governing all public discourse, its unlimited range of characters both mythical and topical could voice issues, concerns, and arguments that ranged beyond what was possible in other public venues or for which there was no other public outlet at all. While the Periclean democracy championed a public and egalitarian ideology, and kept the private and family worlds as much as possible out of sight, drama focused on households and individuals, who moreover were often sympathetically at odds with the collective polis or its leaders; comedy in particular could voice criticism and advice that was both topical and sharply partisan. And while the democracy prized, and indeed depended on, rationality, self-sufficiency, progress, and novelty, drama in the name of the gods and tradition cast all these into question. But in the end, it is hard to imagine that Athenian drama could have flourished as it did under any other system.

SUGGESTIONS FOR FURTHER READING

The relationship between drama and democracy in classical Athens has been a topic interesting to scholars since antiquity. Good contemporary treatments are the essays in J. J. Winkler and F. I. Zeitlin, eds., *Nothing to Do with Dionysos? Athenian Drama in Its Social Context* (Princeton: Princeton University Press, 1990), D. Boedeker and K. Raaflaub, eds., *Democracy, Empire, and the Arts in Fifth-Century Athens* (Cambridge, MA: Harvard University Press, 1998), and M. S. Silk, ed., *Tragedy and the Tragic: Greek Theatre and Beyond* (Oxford: Oxford University Press, 1996); the comprehensive account of fifth-century Athenian cultural and constitutional history by M. Ostwald, *From Popular Sovereignty to the Sovereignty of Law* (Berkeley: University of California Press, 1986); and the survey of sources for ancient drama by E. Csapo and W. J. Slater, *The Context of Ancient Drama* (Ann Arbor: University of Michigan Press, 1995).

NOTES

1 P. J. Rhodes, "Nothing to Do with Democracy: Athenian Drama and the *Polis*," *JHS* 123 (2003): 106–7; for reservations, S. Scullion, "Nothing to Do with Dionysus: Tragedy Misconceived as Ritual," *CQ* 52 (2002): 102–37.

2 Rhodes (n. 1): 107. W. R. Connor, "City Dionysia and Athenian Democracy," *Classica et Mediaevalia* 40 (1989): 7–32 = W. R. Connor, et al., eds., *Aspects of Athenian Democracy* (Copenhagen: Museum Tusculanum Press, 1990), pp. 7–32, argues that the Dionysia was newly created with the reforms of Cleisthenes as "a celebration of civic freedom" (p. 23), but for reservations cf. C. Sourvinou-Inwood, "Something to Do with Athens: Tragedy and Ritual," in R. Osborne and S. Hornblower, eds., *Ritual, Finance, Politics: Athenian Democratic Accounts Presented to David Lewis* (Oxford: Oxford University Press, 1994), pp. 275–6, and F. Quass, Review of W. R. Connor et al., eds., *Aspects of Athenian Democracy* (above), *Gnomon* 67 (1995): 28–9.

3   Hence the traditional Athenian complaint, "Nothing to do with Dionysus!" For cultic and ritual drama in the eastern Mediterranean generally see I. Nielsen, *Cultic Theatres and Ritual Drama: A Study in Regional Development and Religious Interchange between East and West in Antiquity* (Aarhus: Aarhus University Press, 2002).

4   For productivity cf. R. Kannicht, "Dikaiopolis. Von der Schwierigkeit, ein rechter Bürger zu sein," in W. Barner et al., eds. *Literatur in der Demokratie. Für Walter Jens zum 60. Geburtstag* (Munich: Kindler, 1983), pp. 246–57; for population statistics cf. E. Cohen, *The Athenian Nation* (Princeton: Princeton University Press, 2000), pp. 17, 65.

5   As Aristotle *Poetics* 1448a28–40, on sixth-century Megara (cf. E. Csapo and W. J. Slater, *The Context of Ancient Drama* [Ann Arbor: University of Michigan Press, 1995], p. 174); note also 1461b26–62a4, where the treatment of tragedy as vulgar in comparison with epic points to an assumption that it also was associated with democracy.

6   See [Aristotle] *AP* 22.5, with P. J. Rhodes, *A Commentary on the Aristotelian Athenaion Politeia* (Oxford: Oxford University Press, 1981; revised reprint, 1993); on ostracism and comedy see M. Christ, "Ostracism, Sycophancy, and the Deception of the Demos: [Arist.] *Ath Pol.* 43.5," *CQ* 42 (1992): 336–46, and Rhodes, "The Ostracism of Hyperbolus," in Osborne and Hornblower (n. 2), pp. 85–98.

7   See Csapo and Slater (n. 5), p. 166.

8   For Epicharmus generally see R. Kerkhof, *Dorische Posse, Epicharm und attische Komödie* (Munich and Leipzig: Saur, 2001).

9   The polarities between comedy and tragedy are discussed by O. Taplin, "Fifth-Century Tragedy and Comedy: A *Synkrisis*," *JHS* 106 (1986): 163–74; that no poet composed both tragedy/satyr drama and comedy indicates their inherited generic distinction.

10   See most recently A. H. Sommerstein, "Harassing the Satirist: The Alleged Attempts to Prosecute Aristophanes," in I. Sluiter and R. M. Rosen, eds., *Free Speech in Classical Antiquity* (Leiden: Brill, 2004), pp. 145–74; for Pericles' likely involvement cf. R. Wallace, "The Athenian Laws against Slander," in G. Thür, ed., *Symposion 1993* (Cologne: Böhlau, 1994), pp. 109–24.

11   For the institutional framework see in general Csapo and Slater (n. 5).

12   [Xenophon] *AP* 2.13.

13   The relationship of *choregia* to democracy is discussed by P. Wilson, *The Athenian Institution of the Khoregia* (Cambridge: Cambridge University Press, 2000), pp. 144–97, though he overstates the case by claiming for Athenian democracy features that were also characteristic of polis organization generally; cf. Rhodes (n. 1).

14   For the social background of the poets see J. Henderson, "The *dêmos* and the Comic Competition," in J. Winkler and F. Zeitlin, *Nothing to Do with Dionysos?* (Princeton: Princeton University Press, 1990), pp. 291–2. The frequent association of Aristophanes with Callistratus and Philonides as *choregoi* suggests that *choregoi* had some say in the assignment of poets.

15   For the issues see S. Goldhill, "The Great Dionysia and Civic Ideology," in Winkler and Zeitlin (n. 14), pp. 97–129, and Rhodes (n. 1): 111–13.

16   Cf. Aristophanes *Acharnians* 504–6.

17   Such explicit references to democracy as in the *Suppliant Women* tragedies by Aeschylus (line 604) and Euripides (lines 395–462) are rare and abstract, as also

the characterization of other poleis, e.g., Argos in the *Oresteia*. See further L. J. Samons, "Democracy, Empire, and the Search for the Athenian Character," *Arion* 8.3 (2001): 128–57, especially 151–2.

18 Foreigners did not attend the Lenaea because it was held in winter, not because they were debarred.

19 For the concept of notional versus actual audience see J. Henderson, "Women and the Athenian Dramatic Festivals," *TAPA* 121 (1991): 133–47.

20 For the audience generally see Csapo and Slater (n. 5), pp. 286–90; for women Henderson (n. 19).

21 In Aristophanes *Frogs* 948–52 the broad range of characters that were given expression in drama is taken as democratic, but also, for the old-fashioned Aeschylus, as improper to good tragedy.

22 O. Taplin, "Comedy and the Tragic," in M. S. Silk, ed., *Tragedy and the Tragic. Greek Theatre and Beyond* (Oxford: Oxford University Press, 1996), pp. 200–201 n. 21, calls the claim that in the theater "citizen males may have been surrounded, perhaps even outnumbered, by the 'others' on whose behalf they ran the polis" (Henderson [n. 19]: 145) "surely a wild exaggeration." But after all, this was true of the polis itself and so could also have been true of the theater. For *politai* in their proper demographic perspective see Cohen (n. 4). Aristophanes implies that politicians who move to reduce poets' stipends are interfering with "the ancestral rites of Dionysus" (*Frogs* 367–8).

23 See, e.g., Goldhill, "Representing Democracy: Women at the Great Dionysia," in Osborne and Hornblower (n. 2), pp. 347–69.

24 Among all our extant tragedies, only Sophocles' *Philoctetes* lacks at least one female character or chorus, and these were clearly intended and understood to represent real-life counterparts.

25 For the *theorikon* see Csapo and Slater (n. 5), pp. 420–21.

26 Recall Pericles' distinction between civic duties and private freedoms, Thucydides 2.37.

27 For the economic primacy of the *oikos* and the importance of its members of both sexes cf. Cohen (n. 4), pp. 40–45.

28 In Ar. *Frogs* 951–2 Euripides thus claims to have composed "democratically" in giving speaking parts to a broad range of characters.

29 And vice versa in some respects: for the theatricality of speeches cf., e.g., Aeschines *Against Ctesiphon* 153, 156, and in general S. Halliwell "The Uses of Laughter in Greek Culture," *CQ* 41 (1991): 293–4.

30 See J. Ober and B. Strauss, "Drama, Rhetoric, and the Discourse of Athenian Democracy," in Winkler and Zeitlin (n. 14), pp. 237–70.

31 For elements of the traditional role of lone advisor, moralizer, and castigator of the group that were shared by poet and orator see K. J. Dover, *Greek Popular Morality in the Time of Plato and Aristotle* (Berkeley: University of California Press, 1974), pp. 23–33.

32 For this dissonance in tragedy see M. Griffith, "Brilliant Dynasts. Power and Politics in the *Oresteia*," *CA* 14 (1995): 62–129.

33 Male control of the public image of women is explicitly protested in, e.g., Aristophanes *Lysistrata* and *Women at the Thesmophoria*, and Euripides *Medea* 410–30.

34 Euripides' *Telephus* of 438, for example, treated an episode from the Trojan War against the backdrop of the contemporary Samian War and then was rechanneled in Aristophanes' *Acharnians* of 425 to criticize the Peloponnesian War.

35 The play was associated by ancient scholars with Sophocles' generalship in 441/0, but there are reasons to believe that it was earlier, e.g., the statement in Hypothesis 1.15 that it was the thirty-second of Sophocles' ca. 120 plays, and such stylistic features as the absence of *antilabe*: see Scullion, "Tragic Dates," *CQ* 52 (2002): 81–101.

36 R. Seaford, "The Social Function of Attic Tragedy: A Response to Jasper Griffin," *CQ* 50 (2000): 42.

37 J. Griffin, "The Social Function of Attic Tragedy," *CQ* 48 (1998): 51–2, points out that oligarchy/aristocracy was the real threat, so that the tragic emphasis on tyrants did not engage with democratic ideology. But the Athenians did not see it that way: Henderson, "Demos, Demagogue, Tyrant in Attic Old Comedy," in K. A. Morgan, ed., *Popular Tyranny: Sovereignty and Its Discontents in Ancient Greece* (Austin: University of Texas Press, 2003), pp. 155–79.

38 B. Knox, *Oedipus at Thebes: Sophocles' Tragic Hero and His Time* (New Haven: Yale University Press, 1957).

39 Sommerstein (n. 10).

40 J. Henderson, "Attic Comedy, Frank Speech, and Democracy," in D. Boedeker and K. Raaflaub, eds., *Democracy, Empire, and the Arts in Fifth-Century Athens* (Cambridge, MA: Harvard University Press, 1998), pp. 255–73, 405–10.

41 A. H. Sommerstein, "How to Avoid Being a Komodoumenos," *CQ* 46 (1996): 327–56.

42 In general see D. Harvey and J. Wilkins, eds., *The Rivals of Aristophanes. Studies in Athenian Old Comedy* (London: Duckworth and the Classical Press of Wales, 2000).

43 For "demagogue-comedy" see A. H. Sommerstein, "Platon, Eupolis and the 'Demagogue-Comedy,'" in Harvey and Wilkins (n. 42), pp. 437–51.

44 See C. Carey, "Old Comedy and the Sophists," in Harvey and Wilkins (n. 42), pp. 419–36.

45 See in general J. Henderson, "Comic Hero versus Political Elite," in A. H. Sommerstein et al., eds., *Tragedy, Comedy and the Polis* (Bari: Levante Editori 1993), pp. 307–19.

46 Plato *Apology* 18b–d, 19b–c, 23c–d.

47 D. M. MacDowell, *Aristophanes and Athens* (Oxford: Oxford University Press, 1995), pp. 299–300.

48 Plutarch *Pericles* 32 connects Hermippus also with the prosecution of Aspasia.

49 For this line see, e.g., Demosthenes 3.30–31.

8: THE BUREAUCRACY OF DEMOCRACY AND EMPIRE

J. P. Sickinger

Sometime in the second half of the fifth century the Athenians ratified a decree, proposed by a citizen named Kleinias, setting out stricter regulations for the collection and delivery of tribute to Athens (*IG* i³ 34). Although the decree cannot be dated precisely (suggested dates range from ca. 448 to ca. 424), its provisions provide important insights into Athenian imperial administration.[1] They also testify to the official, administrative role that written texts played in fifth-century Athens. The decree requires subject cities to send to Athens, together with tribute payments, sealed tablets recording the amounts they are sending (lines 6–16). These tablets are to be opened at Athens and read out to the *boule* as payments are delivered (lines 16–18). Further texts are created at Athens itself. The *hellenotamiai* are instructed to report to the assembly which cities have paid their tribute in full, and which cities have not (lines 18–22). Then a commission of four men is to draw up a written list of the names of defaulting cities, copying that information from the earlier report (also presumably written) of the *hellenotamiai* (lines 22–8). This written list of cities in arrears will serve as the foundation of the commissioners' work: their principal task is to collect balances of unpaid tribute from delinquent cities.

The contents of later sections of the decree are less certain, because the stone on which its text is preserved is fragmentary. But they too allude to documents, some of which concern legal proceedings. Some clauses appear to outline procedures against individuals interfering with the efficient delivery of tribute; such persons are to be liable to *graphai*, written indictments, lodged with the *prytaneis* (lines 31–41). The decree includes another mention of a *pinakion*, a writing tablet, perhaps one for displaying the tribute assessed of individual cities and the sums actually paid (lines 43–6). Further clauses seem to establish a process for cities to appeal charges that they have not paid *in toto*, and at least one additional reference to a *graphe* occurs (line 67), and perhaps yet another to a writing tablet, a *pinax* (line 72).

These provisions offer tantalizing hints at the variety and number of documents produced in the conduct of public business at Athens in the second half of the fifth century. Although the decree survives in a single stone copy, it had the potential for generating hundreds of documents each year, if its provisions were faithfully executed. More than 150 cities paid tribute to Athens; consequently, just as many records of tribute payment, written on tablets, made their way into Athens from allied cities after the decree's enactment. Additional documents were created in Athens itself, in the form of records of tribute payments, lists of cities in arrears, and written indictments associated with legal proceedings arising from irregularities in payment and delivery. These texts on writing tablets have not survived. But the sheer number mentioned or alluded to in this one decree should serve as a powerful reminder of the volume of documents that once existed, and of the role they played in the running of the Athenian empire and of the Athenian democracy itself.

And yet the tendency in recent scholarship has been to downplay and minimize the functions of writing in classical Athens, at least before the late fifth century. Without question the written word was serving new functions and finding new civic applications in the fifth century, but the number of documents and their impact are sometimes said to have been limited. The Athenians, we are told, never came close to achieving mass literacy, and they possessed very ambivalent attitudes toward the written word, attitudes often at variance with modern, Western assumptions about writing as a tool of rational thought and progress.[2] Moreover, they failed to deploy writing in ways that some scholars expect. Athens lacked both a centralized list of citizens and a property census, and the Athenians first established a centralized archives building in the last decade of the fifth century; only in the fourth century did they become more "document-minded."[3] Study of surviving inscriptions has played no small role in framing these views. C. Hedrick, for example, has claimed that for the first century of its existence, down to the last decade of the fifth century, the Athenian democracy systematically made texts public only in monumental form.[4] R. Thomas goes further. According to her, "public, exemplary, and monumental inscriptions were probably the most characteristic public use of the written word in the service of the classical city-state." These inscriptions, however, "were often thought of primarily as symbolic memorials" of decisions rather than as documents to be used for administrative purposes.[5] Writing, it appears, was primarily a symbolic tool, one that played little role in the actual running of Athenian government.

Hedrick, Thomas, and others allude to the existence of nonlapidary Athenian documents, but they devote little discussion to their numbers or functions. This lack of emphasis in favor of stone inscriptions is perhaps natural, because only documents on stone remain in any meaningful quantity. Official, public writing in fifth-century Athens extended far beyond the laws, treaties, and other documents displayed in monumental, lapidary form. Nonlapidary texts, like many of those alluded to in the decree of Kleinias, were also produced, and their functions expanded significantly during the fifth century. This growth resulted from the increasing volume of business handled by the Athenian state and its component parts, a development sparked by the democratic reforms of Ephialtes and the expansion of the Athenian empire, and it is manifest in the relatively large number of inscriptions on stone preserved from the fifth century. But inscriptions tell a very small part of the story of Athenian bureaucratic practice; far more important for administrative purposes were the vast numbers of texts written on other materials, most commonly wooden tablets and sheets of papyrus. Documents made from these materials seldom survive, but literary and epigraphical sources attest to the variety and quantity of nonlapidary texts. This chapter offers a brief survey of their functions in fifth-century Athens. It begins with a short review of the civic uses of writing at Athens from the archaic period into early classical times, with specific attention to the practice of inscribing documents on stone – a relatively late and limited phenomenon. It then turns to some areas of Athenian government – its military, lawcourts, financial administration, and empire – and explores how written texts increasingly played a role in administration.

The earliest official, public use of alphabetic writing at Athens appears to have been for the publication of laws. Around 620 the lawgiver Drakon published some rules governing homicide and probably a few other offences. Early in the sixth century Solon repealed most of Drakon's laws, except for those on homicide, and replaced them with new, more extensive laws of his own. Solon's laws, like those of Drakon, were recorded on *axones*, objects made from wooden boards or planks on whose surfaces individual statutes were written. The extent of Solon's legislation is uncertain, but a law recorded on a sixteenth *axon* is attested (Plut. *Sol.* 23.4), suggesting a fairly extensive body of texts. Some sources also speak of objects called *kyrbeis* on which the laws of Solon, and possibly those of Drakon (*AP* 7.1; Ar. *Birds* 1352–7), were recorded. But the form and content of these objects, and their relationship to the *axones*, are very uncertain.[6] The factors driving the publication of laws are also controversial. Recent studies have emphasized the monumental quality of early laws: setting down texts in writing gave them physical form and imbued them with a greater degree of authority than traditional customs and practices. But practical goals ought not to be overlooked. The term *axones* means literally "axles," which suggests that these objects could be rotated, certainly for reading and consultation.[7]

Despite the tradition that the Athenians possessed written laws from the end of the seventh century, few stone inscriptions recording laws, decrees, or other legislative acts survive from before the middle of the fifth century. The sixth century has yielded two sacred laws on stone from Eleusis (*IG* i³ 230, 231), and a third (*IG* i³ 232) dated to the period 510–480. The earliest Athenian decree on stone (*IG* i³ 1) concerns settlers on the island of Salamis and is likewise dated to the last decade of the sixth century. An inscription from Marathon records two measures (*IG* i³ 2, 3) related to the sanctuary of Herakles at Marathon belonging to the early fifth century, while the Hekatompedon decrees, which record regulations concerning the Acropolis (*IG* i³ 4A, B), date from 485/4. A few more inscriptions are dated to the first half of the fifth century, but only in the 450s does the number of inscribed decrees start to rise significantly. This apparent paucity of inscribed texts in earlier times can be explained in a variety of ways. Many inscriptions may have been destroyed in the Persian sacks of Athens in 480 and 479. The Athenians also occasionally took down stelai when the regulations engraved on them became obsolete in light of more recent legislation (see *IG* ii² 6, 43, 116; *AP* 35.2; Philoch. *FGrHist* 328 F55a, b). But Athenians may not have inscribed all new laws and decrees in monumental form: before the mid-fifth century, publication of laws and decrees on stone was probably quite rare, with wood – the material of Drakon's and Solon's *axones* – being the material of choice for recording and displaying legislative decisions.[8]

This hypothesis finds support in the publication practices of the second half of the fifth century, when monumentalization of legislation in lapidary form remained far from universal. The number of stone inscriptions preserving decisions of the Athenian assembly starts to climb in the 450s, and more than 200 laws and decrees survive from the half century before 403/2. Their distribution by type, however, is telling. Decrees honoring foreigners are the most numerous; decrees related to foreign affairs and the administration of the Athenian empire follow closely in number. Slightly fewer are laws and decrees concerning sacred and cultic matters. Laws and decrees concerning nonsacred, domestic issues, however, are relatively rare.[9] This dearth is not the result of legislative inactivity; the fifth century was a period that saw significant reforms of Athenian government and civic life. Different sources speak of the opening of the archonship to *zeugitai* around 457/6 (*AP* 26.2), the creation of deme judges in 453/2 (*AP* 26.3), the redefinition of requirements of Athenian citizenship in 451/0 (*AP* 26.4), a review of citizen rolls in 446/5 (Philoch. *FGrHist* 328 F119), limits on personal attacks by comic poets in 440/39 (schol. Ar. *Acharn.* 67; [Xen.] *AP* 2.18), and the establishment of sectional seating for councilors in 410/9 (Philoch. *FGrHist* 328 F140). Undated legislation also established pay for dikastic service and public office, among other things (*AP* 24; Arist. *Pol.* 1274a8; schol. Ar. *Wasps* 300; Plut. *Per.* 9.1–3). And yet none of these measures is represented in the surviving corpus of fifth-century Attic inscriptions, nor, more significantly, do we see inscriptions with similar contents. Publication of the city's laws in monumental form first became a concern only in the last decade of the fifth century. Officials called *anagrapheis* ("recorders") spent several years reviewing Athens's existing laws, apparently to determine which laws were still valid and which ones had been superseded by later legislation. These officials published some measures on individual stelai, and the goal of their work may have been full-scale publication of all valid laws in the Royal Stoa. But it is not clear that they were successful, and the inscriptions associated with this legislative review are focused primarily on a calendar of sacrifices and a few other measures concerned with state finance.[10]

The absence of laws and decrees related to the inner workings of the democracy from the epigraphical record of the fifth century should raise questions about assertions that documents were made public only in monumental form for the first century of the democracy, that inscriptions were the principal documents of Athenian society, and that laws were normally displayed on stone stelai in the fifth century. It is inconceivable that fifth-century Athenians failed to keep written records of legislative measures establishing new state officials, changing the requirements of citizenship, or creating pay for public office, all the more so since they had a tradition of written laws reaching back almost two centuries. They simply recorded, preserved, and displayed many, if not the majority, of their new laws on materials other than stone. Publication of such acts in lapidary form was not automatic; the inscribing of laws or decrees on stone stelai was a privilege reserved initially for certain types of documents, specifically ones granting honors to foreigners, creating treaties with foreign states, or regulating state cults and their finances. It could be argued that laws on certain topics were inscribed but have been lost without a trace; they might have been set up, for example, in locations not yet fully explored. Given, however, the large number of Athenian laws and decrees on specific topics that have survived, the most economical interpretation of the evidence is that Athenians did not routinely monumentalize every legislative enactment.[11]

The reluctance of the Athenians to inscribe every decision of the assembly onto stone should not be equated with a failure to recognize the value of the written word in political life; documents on other materials found frequent administrative uses. Indeed, already in the sixth century Athenians officials had turned to writing in the execution of their duties. Two inscriptions of the middle of the sixth century mention individuals who served other officials as *grammateis*, secretaries (*IG* i[3] 508, 509). Their duties are not specified, but they presumably functioned like later *grammateis*, who regularly served state officials by drafting various sorts of documents; later secretaries were especially involved in tracking the income and expenditures of state officials. A bronze plaque (*IG* i[3] 510) from the same period lists the names of several Athenian treasurers, followed by a further list of bronze objects that were evidently under their care. The form of the text – a list of objects – resembles that of the published inventories of items housed in Athenian temples that start in the 430s, and thus hints at the keeping of a rudimentary form of inventories already in the mid-sixth century. So too does a passage in one of the Hekatompedon decrees that requires treasurers to record bronze objects on the Acropolis; it dates from 485/4 (*IG* i[3] 4B, lines 1–4). Vase paintings also point to the use of writing tablets for some types of early documents. Three sculptures of seated scribes, each holding a writing tablet in his lap, survive from the late sixth-century Acropolis and seem to commemorate officials engaged in some type of record-keeping activity. Individuals with writing tablets are also depicted on two vases by the Dokimasia Painter of the late sixth and early fifth century; the scenes also show cavalrymen and their mounts, and they have been associated with a scrutiny or a registration of Athenian cavalrymen. The use of writing tablets for cavalry records is first attested in a speech of Lysias of the early fourth century (Lys. 16.6) and then in more detail in Aristotle's *Constitution of the Athenians* of the 320s (*AP* 49.1–2), but the vase depictions suggest that some form of written registration of cavalry members was practiced more than a century before the earliest literary attestation.[12]

If writing had already achieved some administrative role in sixth-century Athens, its uses only grew during the fifth century, as documents became an integral component of civic life. Take, for instance, the process of enrolling citizens for hoplite service. During the fifth century, the Athenians relied on a system of conscription employing written lists called *katalogoi* to summon citizens for infantry duty.[13] Registration of hoplites was the responsibility of Athens's generals, the *strategoi*, assisted by the regimental commanders, the taxiarchs. Once the assembly authorized the dispatch of hoplite forces, the generals might issue a call for volunteers, but their normal practice was to draft lists of citizens to serve on each campaign. One list was compiled for each of Athens's ten tribes, and the names of conscripts were displayed on wooden tablets according to their tribal affiliation at the monument of the Eponymous Heroes in the Athenian Agora.

The earliest direct reference to the display of the names of conscripted hoplites occurs in Aristophanes' *Peace* of 421, where Aristophanes lampoons the reaction of a citizen surprised to see his name posted (Ar. *Peace* 1183–4). Conscription *ek katalogou*, "by list," however, was older. Some sources indicate that *katalogoi* were in use already in the 460s and 450s (*AP* 26.1; Arist. *Pol.* 1303a8–10; Diod. 11.84.4–5). An origin or expansion of the practice in these decades is easily comprehensible. Military campaigns before the Persian Wars often involved brief expeditions close to home, like those against the Boiotians and Chalkidians around 506 (Hdt. 5.74, 77) or to Marathon in 490 (Hdt. 6.103–17). On these campaigns the Athenians often fought *pandemei*, with their full citizen body, and hoplites possibly mustered through simple oral proclamations directing all eligible citizens to appear for service at a particular time and place. After the Persian Wars, however, the nature of Athenian military campaigns changed. The Athenians now regularly undertook expeditions by sea and far from home. Rowers in the fleet now provided the bulk of Athens's fighting force, but hoplites continued to serve and fight, except that they did so in smaller contingents than before. Thus, Kimon brought 4,000 hoplites to assist the Spartans against the Messenians in 463 (Ar. *Lysistrata* 1143–4); Tolmides enrolled 1,000 hoplites for campaigns around Laconia around 456 (Diod. 11.84.3–4) and against the Boiotians in 447 (Thuc. 1.113.1); contingents of similar sizes campaigned in the Peloponnesian War (e.g., Thuc. 1.61.1, 64.2; 2.23.2, 56, 58, 79, etc.). Deployment of contingents smaller in size than the entire citizen body necessitated implementation of some mechanism to identify and inform those individual called on to serve. If the *katalogos* method of conscription was not already in use, it appeared in the 470s and 460s to satisfy the new necessities of Athenian hoplite warfare.

Public display of the names of hoplite conscripts was perhaps the most conspicuous application of writing in the *katalogos* system, but it was not the only one. Military authorities first had to identify which citizens were available to be called. Some scholars used to believe that the generals relied on a central register of all Athenian hoplites, from which they could select those citizens they wanted for a particular campaign. If that view is correct, conscription entailed consultation of an existing document, one that had to be reviewed and updated periodically, as happened with the register of Athenian cavalrymen in the fourth century (*AP* 49.1–2). More recently, however, others have questioned the historicity of such a register, and it seems more likely that the generals had to rely on other sources to find and identify eligible hoplites.[14] Personal knowledge of effective soldiers might have provided some names, but a reliance on memory alone can hardly account for contingents that numbered in the thousands; written documents will have played a role. The demes of Attica maintained membership lists called *lexiarchika grammateia*. Registration on these lists served as proof of Athenian citizenship, but the documents also appear to have had a military function. They noted which citizens were cavalrymen and probably which were hoplites (*IG* i³ 138, lines 1–7, from the 430s), and these designations would be useful in establishing a pool of eligible soldiers. Recourse to the *lexiarchika grammateia* for military purposes is implied by a fourth-century decree calling on the demarchs, the local officials who maintained these deme registers, to assist the generals in enrolling citizens to serve in the fleet (Dem. 50.6). The demarchs are presumably involved because they maintained the *lexiarchika grammateia*. Especially intriguing is a clause of the decree of Themistokles, an inscription of the third century that records a decree purporting to date from 480, that instructs the generals to resort to the *lexiarchika grammateia* for a similar purpose: they were to draft, from the demes' membership lists, marines (who were often hoplites) to serve on ship.[15] It is tempting to think that this order was grounded in a more standard procedure for enlisting hoplites for service on land campaigns. When a campaign was authorized, the demarchs provided the generals with lists of eligible hoplites based on information contained in the *lexiarchika grammateia*. The generals drew up the *katalogoi* based on these preliminary lists, and they displayed their results – lists with hundreds and perhaps thousands of names – for reading at the monument of the Eponymous Heroes (Ar. *Peace* 1183–4; cf. *Birds* 450).

Consultation of written documents, however, did not stop there. A draftee could appeal his inclusion on a *katalogos* on various grounds (e.g., Lys. 9.4, 15), so that the publicly displayed *katalogoi* would have to be examined and revised accordingly. And *katalogoi* were checked yet again when a hoplite force mustered. At that time, the taxiarchs examined the enrollment lists to make sure that those summoned actually appeared, and they noted the names of those who were missing (Poll. 1.118). Drafting, consulting, and reading written documents, none of which ever achieved monumentalization on stone, were thus involved in the conscription of hoplite forces from beginning to end.[16]

The Athenian legal system also saw an increase in its use of writing during the fifth century. The Athenians had possessed written laws in some form since the end of the seventh century, but legal proceedings retained an oral character throughout the classical period. Pretrial hearings involved litigants appearing before magistrates and lodging complaints orally. Opponents faced off against one another at trials through speeches they delivered before mass audiences of judges. Witnesses gave testimony orally and in person. Only a series of reforms dating from the early fourth century imposed on litigants a greater reliance on documents. Some time after 380 litigants began to submit written versions of the initial complaints and other pleadings to magistrates. The same period also witnessed enactment of a law requiring witnesses to submit testimony in writing before trial to prevent later alterations (Dem. 45.44); henceforth, witnesses did not speak at trial but simply affirmed the validity of testimony recorded earlier. The motivations for these reforms are unknown. A desire to simplify court administration may have been a factor, but they also suggest that a larger number of Athenians were comfortable with producing written texts.[17]

Whatever the causes of these fourth-century innovations, they were not the first administrative applications of writing in the legal process. Notices of pending suits were exhibited on wooden tablets at the monument of the Eponymous Heroes (Dem. 21.103) and at the offices of individual magistrates (Dem. 57.3–4). That practice, which gave public notice of cases to the reading public, is first attested explicitly in the fourth century, but references to *sanides*, wooden boards used as writing materials, in Aristophanes' *Wasps* of 422 (lines 349, 848) point to its existence already in the fifth century.[18] Judicial officials of the fifth century also kept administrative notes related to cases over which they presided. Strepsiades, the hero of Aristophanes' *Clouds*, at one point imagines himself "melting" away, by means of a sunbeam reflected in a mirror, the text of a suit brought against him as it was being written down by a court secretary (*Clouds* 759–74). The passage comments on the character of Strepsiades, but it is based on the real custom of court officials writing down charges and complaints on wax-covered, wooden tablets. These documents should be distinguished from the publicly displayed notices of lawsuits, which were routinely exhibited on whitened wooden boards; texts scratched into wax were unsuitable for outdoor display and were probably kept by magistrates themselves. Legal terminology offers some clues to the regularity of such note-keeping. A term associated with the initiation of legal proceedings in the fifth century is *graphesthai*, the middle form of the verb "to write." It appears already in plays of Aristophanes (Ar. *Clouds* 1482, *Wasps* 881, 894, 907, *Peace* 107) and speeches of Antiphon (Ant. 6.35, 49), but also in several fifth-century inscriptions, including some conventionally dated to the late 450s and 440s (*IG* i^3 19, 34, 46). The middle form carries the meaning "to have" or "to cause" someone "to be written down," and in judicial contexts it denotes that, at the start of legal proceedings, litigants had their opponents "written down" by court officials, probably in a process similar to the one lying behind Strepsiades' vision of melting a suit. The verb *graphesthai* is also related to the noun *graphe*, the term used by the Athenians to denote a procedure by which any citizen could bring suit on behalf of an injured party for certain offenses. Solon is credited with establishing that procedure, and the term *graphe* was probably applied to it because it was the first type of suit in which magistrates recorded complaints in writing. By the late fifth century, however, the verb *graphesthai* was being used for *dikai* as well (Ant. 1.2, 6.35–41 [passim]; Ar. *Knights* 1256, *Clouds* 759–74; Isoc. 18.12), and judicial officials were jotting down initial complaints in all types of suits.

What court officers did with these written complaints is nowhere explained, but the silence of our sources is not evidence that they went unused. Judicial magistrates, like other Athenian officials, were accountable for their conduct in office. Notes documenting the cases over which they had presided offered potentially valuable evidence of their activities in office, especially if they were faced with charges of dereliction, false prosecution, or some other form of misconduct. More basically, magistrates found notes and documents related to their caseloads valuable in the general administration of the court system. Trials passed through several stages, from an initial summons through preliminary hearing to the trial itself, and each step had to be scheduled and tracked. Simple documents recording the names of litigants, the charges involved, and other details assisted magistrates in tracking cases as they worked through the legal process. Indeed, the expansion of the *dikasteria* in the fifth century may have led officials to turn to documents even more. The reforms of Ephialtes, passed in 462/1, transferred to the *dikasteria* additional (but unspecified) powers, and the number of Athenian courts, together with the number of cases heard, grew in the decades that followed. The Athenians also required certain types of cases involving allied states to be heard in Athenian courts, a rule that can only have put further burdens on Athens's judicial officials.[19] Aristophanes' claim (*Wasps* 660–63) that the courts were in session 300 days each year is probably an exaggeration, but courts met frequently, and magistrates handled large numbers of cases.[20] Writing served as a simple, practical tool to help them manage their caseloads.

Athenian officials also documented in writing the moneys, treasures, and other public property they received, lent out, or disbursed. Inscriptions on stone reflect the detailed nature of some of these records, but they represent a mere fraction of the documents actually created, most of which were written on perishable materials.[21] One entry in the building accounts of the Erechtheion for the year 409/8 mentions the purchase of two wooden boards (*sanides*) onto which the officials supervising construction recorded their account (*IG* i[3] 476, lines 188–91). A later entry in the same year notes the purchase of two rolls of papyrus (*chartai*) for making copies (*IG* i[3] 476, lines 289–91), perhaps copies of the accounts for that prytany. The purchase of similar materials by other officials for record-keeping purposes is not attested, but all state officials who handled state funds were subject to review, and others too worked with documents made from the same or similar materials. Throughout the year they kept notes tracking the moneys or other goods they received, and then, at the end of their terms, they gathered up these texts, written on perishable materials, and submitted them to the *logistai*, the state auditors, for review. These documents, written on wood and papyrus, were the principal fiscal documents of the Athenian state and the means by which officials were kept in check.

The first of the so-called Kallias decrees, now dated to 433/2, illustrates another use of nonlapidary documents, in this case for records of debts.[22] The decree calls for the repayment of funds owed to the cults of various divinities. It instructs the *logistai* to calculate what is owed and the *prytaneis* to oversee repayment and erasure of all debt records, written on *pinakia* and *grammateia* (writing tablets), after they have made a search for them. Cult officials and others with any knowledge of these documents are also instructed to produce them. Note that the decree's instructions to collect and erase these locally controlled documents appear in conjunction with the repayment of the debts, not with the order to the *logistai* to calculate what was owed. That is, the search for debt records was not to establish debts but to cancel all noncentralized records of those debts in order to prevent future claims. Before repayment and cancellation of these debt notes, the *logistai* had already determined the amounts to be repaid based on calculations made from other texts, probably documents they themselves had drawn up or received when the loans were first made. We have no evidence that the *logistai* routinely published results of all their audits on stone, so they must have kept long-term records of past audits on nondurable materials. At least two sets of perishable documents recording the original debts, therefore, must have existed. What is more, although the decree called for the erasure of certain documents recording debts, those records were hardly ephemeral. The decree did not specify when the original loans were made, but several years might have passed between the making of the loans and repayment.[23] In short, the provisions of the first Kallias decree testify to the complex network of documents that tracked state funds and treasures, and to the exactitude of the Athenians in maintaining strict control over the whereabouts of these funds, possibly for periods of several years. This exactitude they exercised not through texts written on stone, but on the basis of impermanent but not necessarily ephemeral tablets of wood and papyrus sheets.

A large portion of the wealth flowing into fifth-century Athens derived from the city's overseas empire. Here too administration relied heavily on writing and documents, most of which were never exhibited in monumental form. The Athenians regularly passed decrees applying to individual states or to the empire as a whole. Some of these were published on stone in allied cities, and many more were announced by heralds appointed to disseminate news of new measures to subject cities.[24] In both cases, however, texts of imperial legislation reached allies by means of written texts. Aristophanes pokes fun at this practice in a passage of *Birds*, where an Athenian official comes on stage holding a copy of a decree, written on papyrus, which he reads out (lines 1024–5). The same play also depicts a decree-seller hawking Athenian laws and decrees to the play's utopian city of Cloudcuckooland, an apparent satire of the proliferation of Athenian decrees throughout the empire (lines 1035–57). *Birds* dates from 414, and its attention to documents may well reflect an increasing reliance on written texts that developed at the end of the fifth century. But the administrative demands of the empire were not new in the late fifth century, and nonmonumental texts played a role in its running from a much earlier time.

For example, the procedures of assessing and collecting tribute made extensive use of documents. Our best evidence for assessments comes from the decree of Thoudippos (*IG* i³ 71), passed in 426/5, which lays down procedures for assessing the tribute to be paid by Athens's subjects. Officials called *taktai* ("assessors") were to draw up preliminary lists of cities that were to pay tribute, and probably to recommend changes to the amounts they had paid before (lines 8–10). This preliminary list was almost certainly in writing.[25] Subject cities had the opportunity to appeal these preliminary recommendations in a court presided over by officials called *eisagogeis* ("introducers"). These officials were to be assisted by both a secretary and a co-secretary (lines 7–8); the appointment of not one but two secretaries all but proves that their work involved drafting, copying, and revising written texts. Eventually, the *boule* reviewed and ratified proposed assessments. Among other things, it was to ensure that no city paid less than it had before, unless special circumstances affected a city's ability to pay (lines 19–22); such a requirement necessitated some comparison of the newly proposed assessments for each city with assessments of previous periods, and, hence, consultation of written texts. Oral debate and discussion, sometimes quite vigorous, must have occurred in the courts where cities appealed their new assessments and perhaps even before the *boule* that had the final say. But these debates revolved around written texts, and the entire process involved compiling, comparing, and revising assessment figures that were only carved on stone when final decisions were made.

Payment of tribute also entailed drafting, consulting, and preserving nonmonumental texts. I began this chapter with a discussion of the decree of Kleinias (*IG* i³ 34), which instructed cities to record tribute payments on sealed tablets and Athenian officials to draw up lists of cities that had not delivered their full tribute. But recourse to documents was more pervasive. When payments were brought before the *boule*, that body or the *hellenotamiai* had to compare what was delivered not only with the amount specified in the sealed tablets sent by individual cities but also with the sums that cities had been assessed to pay; that is, consultation of the assessed quotas was required. The assessment of 425/4 was to be inscribed on two stelai, one in the Bouleuterion, the meeting place of the *boule*, and one on the Acropolis (*IG* i³ 71, lines 22–5). It is tempting to think that the Bouleuterion was chosen so that payments could be checked against assessments as allied tribute arrived. Once payment was made, the *hellenotamiai* recorded the sums paid by individual cities and whether or not they met the assessed quotas. This record of tribute payment also served as the basis of the list of cities in arrears, which provided the commissioners created by the decree with the names of those cities from which full payment was to be demanded (IG i³ 34, lines 22–8). Records of tribute payment were also published, but not in monumental form. Instead, wooden tablets exhibited the names of paying cities, cities in arrears, and cities failing to pay altogether (IG i³ 34, lines 43–6; IG i³ 68, lines 18–21).[26] These documents allowed interested citizens to inspect the state of imperial revenues, and they illustrate how nonlapidary texts served the valuable function of keeping Athenians informed of public business.

The date of the decree of Kleinias is, admittedly, uncertain. Scholars traditionally have put it around 448, but there are good grounds for dating it two decades later, perhaps as late as 424.[27] The decree of Thoudippos likewise dates from this period (425). These late dates might tempt us to interpret the nonmonumental, administrative texts implied or explicitly referred to in these inscriptions as phenomena of the late fifth century and of a newfound awareness of the value of the written word that, according to some scholars, characterizes this period. We ought to avoid succumbing to that temptation with diligence. The procedures by which the Athenians assessed and collected tribute in the early years of the Delian League are poorly attested, and the practices first mentioned in the 420s were hardly created *ex nihilo*. The decree of Thoudippos at one point seems to instruct the *boule* to assess tribute as it had before (IG i³ 71, lines 16–18), and *taktai* are attested already in the tribute quota lists of 430/29 (IG i³ 281, line 54). In addition, provisions that might appear innovative to us could easily reflect the systemization of long-standing practices. So, when the Kleinias decree requires allied cities to send to Athens sealed tablets documenting their tribute payments, we may not be witnessing a new, innovative procedure; rather, the instructions may make required of all allies a practice already exercised by some cities on an individual and informal basis. Earlier administrative practices were undoubtedly more rudimentary and more sparing in their use of written documents than those displayed in sources of the 420s. But nonmonumental, nonlapidary texts had played a significant role in administration long before the 420s, and it is difficult to imagine the empire ever having been run without their aid.[28]

In this chapter I have shown some of the practical functions served by the written word in the fifth century, and that documents recorded on perishable materials were instrumental in running several areas of

Athenian government. These documents do not survive, but their numbers were large and their functions various. From the registration of hoplite armies to the administration of the lawcourts and the empire, Athenian officials relied on written texts to keep track of information relevant to their duties and to inform the public of items of importance to them. Written texts satisfied many of the needs of administration, not because writing possessed some innately progressive, rational qualities, but because the Athenians recognized early on that written documents made useful administrative tools.

The use of documents for administrative matters was not without its drawbacks. Texts written on writing tablets, for example, were subject to manipulation and alteration. A young Athenian named Mantitheos complained at his scrutiny for membership in the cavalry that the list of cavalry members who served in the time of the Thirty Tyrants was inaccurate; some of those who had served were not listed, whereas the names of many men who were not even in Athens were included (Lys. 16.6–7). Likewise, Alkibiades, when a friend was facing prosecution for an unspecified charge, is once said to have entered the Metroon and, wiping with his finger, to have erased the text of the charge, thereby effectively canceling the suit (Athen. 9.72.407b–c). The anecdote's historicity is dubious, but it recalls Strepsiades' vision of erasing a suit against him in Aristophanes' *Clouds*, and the two vignettes probably play on a recognition on the part of Athenians that documents on nondurable materials were potentially unstable. And yet such weaknesses did not deter the Athenians as a whole from resorting widely to documents as they ran their government and their empire. Any ambivalence Athenians may have felt was more than offset by the practical gains offered by the written word.

Administration was not the only function served by documents, nor were documents on nondurable materials the only public form of writing. The Athenians also monumentalized many items of public business on stone inscriptions, as we have repeatedly noted. These lapidary texts had any of several functions. Interested parties consulted them, as many sources indicate, for a variety of reasons, but the dissemination of information was not their only value. Publication of an honorary decree on a large stone stele enhanced the abstract honors included in a decree and gave monumental form to honors that might otherwise possess no physical existence. The large number of fifth-century texts dealing with sacred matters and sacred funds suggests that religious motives as much as democratic principles informed the decisions to publish some documents on stone. And treaties and decrees regulating Athens's relations with its subject cities might be regarded as sources of pride for Athenians, or symbols of oppression for their subjects.

But publication of documents on stone was quite restricted, and stone inscriptions formed just a small part of the administrative apparatus of the age of Perikles. Nonlapidary texts existed in far greater numbers and served a variety of functions. True, many of these documents were destroyed after they had outlived their usefulness, but that practice is a sign of the practicality, not a failure to appreciate the potential, of written records. The complete loss of documents on wood and papyrus renders detailed knowledge of them impossible, but that is no reason for them to be ignored. Enough evidence survives, only a portion of it reviewed here, to show that their use was widespread, and that their numbers were overwhelming, certainly in the 420s, and probably from the 460s and 450s, if not before. Administrative, nonmonumental texts written on wood and papyrus were the most characteristic form of official writing in fifth-century Athens.

Suggestions for Further Reading

The best overview of ancient writing and its functions is W. V. Harris, *Ancient Literacy* (Cambridge, MA: Harvard University Press, 1989). The relationship between literacy and orality is the focus of R. Thomas, *Literacy and Orality in Ancient Greece* (Cambridge: Cambridge University Press, 1992). Thomas tends to emphasize the oral more than the literate and to downplay the practical in favor of the symbolic, but chapter 1 offers a good overview of previous scholarship. D. Steiner, *The Tyrant's Writ* (Princeton: Princeton University Press, 1994), examines representations of writing in Greek myth and literature but is over-simplistic on documents and practical applications of written texts. K. Robb, *Literacy and Paideia in Ancient Greece* (New York: Oxford University Press, 1994), includes some useful observations on written law in ancient Athens. The utility of all these works is limited by their incomplete control over the epigraphical material.

Several essays on the public uses of writing appear in M. Detienne, ed., *Les savoirs de l'écriture en Grèce ancienne* (Lille: Presses Universitaires de Lille, 1988). For a balanced discussion of Greek inscriptions and archives see P. J. Rhodes, "Public Documents in the Greek States: Archives and Inscriptions. Part I," *G&R* 48.1 (2001): 33–44, and "Public Documents in the Greek States: Archives and Inscriptions. Part II," *G&R* 48.2 (2001): 136–53. The use of documents in classical Athens is treated by R. Thomas, *Oral Tradition and Written Record in Classical Athens* (Cambridge: Cambridge University Press, 1989), chapter 1; for a different view, see J. P. Sickinger, *Public Records and Archives in Classical Athens* (Chapel Hill: University of North Carolina Press, 1999). On the relationship between inscriptions and Athens's democratic government, see C. Hedrick, "Democracy and the Athenian Epigraphical Habit," *Hesperia* 68 (1999): 387–439. The consultation of documents in drafting new legislation is examined by J. P. Sickinger, "Literacy, Orality, and Athenian Legislative Practice," in *Epea and Grammata. Oral & Written Communication in Ancient Greece*, edited by I. Worthington and J. M. Foley (Leiden: Brill, 2002), pp. 147–69. On the late fifth-century revision of Athens's laws, see, in addition to the works cited in the notes, P. J. Rhodes, "The Athenian Code of Laws, 410–399 B.C.," *JHS* 111 (1991): 87–100, and N. Robertson, "The Laws of Athens, 410–399 B.C.: The Evidence for Review and Publication," *JHS* 110 (1990): 43–74.

NOTES

1   For a recent discussion see L. J. Samons, *Empire of the Owl: Athenian Imperial Finance* (Stuttgart: Steiner, 2000), pp. 189–93; cf. also R. Meiggs and D. M. Lewis, *A Selection of Greek Historical Inscriptions to the End of the Fifth Century B.C.*, revised edition (Oxford: Oxford University Press, 1988), pp. 117–21. All dates are B.C. unless otherwise noted.

2   On levels of literacy see W. V. Harris, *Ancient Literacy* (Cambridge, MA: Harvard University Press, 1989), pp. 65–115; on images of and attitudes toward writing see D. Steiner, *The Tyrant's Writ* (Princeton: Princeton University Press, 1994).

3   For the absence of certain types of documents see Harris (n. 2), pp. 78–80; R. Thomas, *Oral Tradition and Written Record in Classical Athens* (Cambridge: Cambridge University Press, 1989), p. 82, and *Literacy and Orality in Ancient Greece* (Cambridge: Cambridge University Press, 1992), p. 138.

4   C. Hedrick, "Reading, Writing, and Democracy," in R. Osborne and S. Hornblower, eds., *Ritual, Finance, Politics: Athenian Democratic Accounts Presented to David Lewis* (Oxford: Oxford University Press, 1994), p. 173; see also C. Hedrick, "Democracy and the Athenian Epigraphical Habit," *Hesperia* 68 (1999): 387–439, for a long discussion of the Athenian practice of publishing documents on stone.

5   R. Thomas, *Literacy and Orality* (n. 3), pp. 84, 86; cf. also P. Vasunia, *The Gift of the Nile: Hellenizing Egypt from Aeschylus to Alexander* (Berkeley: University of California Press, 2001), p. 146, citing Thomas with approbation. According to B. Powell, *Writing and the Origin of Greek Literature* (Cambridge: Cambridge University Press, 2002), p. 25, writing found few administrative uses until the Hellenistic period.

6   On the *axones* and *kyrbeis* see especially R. S. Stroud, *The Axones and Kyrbeis of Drakon and Solon*, California Studies in Classical Philology 19 (Berkeley: University of California Press, 1979); J. P. Sickinger, *Public Records and Archives in Classical Athens* (Chapel Hill: University of North Carolina Press, 1999), pp. 14–34.

7   Thomas, *Literacy and Orality* (n. 3), pp. 65–73; cf. also K.-J. Hölkeskamp, "(In-) Schrift und Monument. Zum Begriff des Gesetzes im archaischen und klassischen Griechenland," *ZPE* 132 (2000): 73–96 and *Schiedsrichter, Gesetzgeber und Gesetzgebung im archaischen Griechenland* (Stuttgart: Steiner: 1999). On the question of consultation see Sickinger (n. 6), p. 31.

8   For Athenian documents and inscriptions in the archaic period see Sickinger (n. 6), pp. 35–61.

9   According to S. C. Todd, *The Shape of Athenian Law* (Oxford: Oxford University Press, 1993), p. 56, "laws were normally inscribed on stone *stêlai*." But see H. Immerwahr, *Attic Script* (Oxford: Oxford University Press, 1990), pp. 121–2, who notes the small number of laws on stone before the end of the fifth century; for preliminary quantification see J. P. Sickinger, "Literacy, Documents, and Archives in the Ancient Athenian Democracy," *American Archivist* 62 (1999): 242.

10 On the late fifth-century revision of the laws see Sickinger (n. 6), pp. 94–104; cf. also M. Munn, *The School of History. Athens in the Age of Socrates* (Berkeley: University of California Press, 2000), pp. 247–72.

11 On Greek publication practices see P. J. Rhodes, "Public Documents in the Greek States: Archives and Inscriptions. Part I," *G&R* 48.1 (2001): 33–44, and "Public Documents in the Greek States: Archives and Inscriptions. Part II," *G&R* 48.2 (2001): 136–53; for Athenian practice in the fifth century see Sickinger (n. 6), pp. 64–72.

12 On Athenian documents in the sixth century see Sickinger (n. 6), pp. 35–61; on writing more generally in the archaic period see Harris (n. 2), pp. 45–64. The Acropolis scribes are discussed by I. Trianti, "Παρατηρήσεις σε δύο ομάδες γλυπτών του τέλους του 6ου αιώνα από την Ακρόπολη in *The Archaeology of Athens and Attica under the Democracy*, ed. W. D. E. Coulson et al. (Oxford: Oxbow, 1994), pp. 83–6; on vases by the Dokimasia Painter depicting cavalrymen see G. Bugh, *The Horsemen of Athens* (Princeton: Princeton University Press, 1988), pp. 14–20.

13 On enrollment by *katalagoi* see now M. Christ, "Conscription of Hoplites in Classical Athens" *CQ* 51 (2001): 398–409; cf. also D. Hamel, *Athenian Generals. Military Authority in the Classical Period* (Leiden: Brill, 1998), 24–6.

14 For the debate, see M. H. Hansen, *Demography and Democracy: The Number of Athenian Citizens in the Fourth Century B.C.* (Herning: Systime, 1985), pp. 83–9.

15 ML pp. 48–9, no. 23, lines 24–6.

16 For these stages of conscription in the fifth century see Christ (n. 13): 398–408.

17 For an overview of the stages of procedure in Athenian trials see A. L. Boegehold, *The Athenian Agora*, vol. 28, *The Lawcourts at Athens* (Princeton: American School of Classical Studies at Athens, 1995), pp. 21–42; on oral and written pleadings see G. M. Calhoun, "Oral and Written Pleading in Athenian Courts" *TAPA* 50 (1919): 177–93; on written testimony see D. M. MacDowell, *The Law in Classical Athens* (Ithaca, NY: Cornell University Press, 1978), 242–3.

18 Boegehold (n. 17), pp. 236–7.

19 On the proliferation of courts see M. Ostwald, *From Popular Sovereignty to the Sovereignty of Law* (Berkeley: University of California Press, 1986), pp. 47–77. On jurisdiction in the Athenian empire see [Xen.] *AP* 1.16–18, Antiph. 5.47, and R. Meiggs, *The Athenian Empire* (Oxford: Oxford University Press 1972), pp. 220–23.

20 On the number of days on which the lawcourts met see M. H. Hansen, "How Often Did the Athenian Dikasteria Meet?" *GRBS* 20 (1979): 243–6.

21 On these nonlapidary texts see J. K. Davies, "Accounts and Accountability in Classical Athens," in Osborne and Hornblower (n. 4), pp. 201–12. For the limited publication on stone of Athenian financial documents see Samons (n. 1), pp. 312–17.

22 *IG* i³ 52A; for discussion see now Samons (n. 1), pp. 113–38.

23 The Logistai inscription (*IG* i³ 369), for example, records a series of loans made from various sacral treasuries in the years 426/4–423/2, and the interest accruing on these and other loans going back to 433/2; see ML, pp. 205–17, no. 72.

24 Publication in allied cities: *IG* i³ 37, 40, 75, 76; heralds announcing imperial policies: *IG* i³ 66, 68, 71, 78.

25 See *IG* i³ 71, line 9, where, according to a restoration, the *taktai* are required to publish a preliminary list of cities to be assessed.

26 For records of tribute payment on wooden tablets see B. D. Meritt, H. T. Wade-Gery, and M. F. McGregor, *The Athenian Tribute Lists*, vol. 3 (Princeton: American School of Classical Studies at Athens 1950), pp. 15–16.

27 See Samons (n. 1), pp. 173–93.

28 According to W. V. Harris (n. 2), p. 75, the Athenians could not have administered their empire without a "sizeable body of literate citizens" from as early as the 470s.

9: Plato's Sophists, Intellectual History after 450, and Sokrates

Robert W. Wallace

Plato's Sophists

Aseries of figures whom Plato called "the sophists" were among the most prominent intellectuals working in Athens during the second half of the fifth century.[1] By a traditional consensus based largely on his testimony,[2] the sophists were traveling wisdom professors for hire, especially in the art of rhetoric. Plato's principal sophists include Protagoras of Abdera, Gorgias of Leontini, Prodikos of Keos, Hippias of Elis, and Thrasymachos of Chalcedon. Less prominent sophists include the Athenians Antiphon, Kallikles, Kritias, the Chian brothers Euthydemos and Dionysodoros, and Polos of Akragas. Most of these figures are featured in Plato's dialogues, and some seven dialogues bear sophists' names. The sophists were among Plato's constant preoccupations, for reasons we shall see.

Plato and his followers sharply distinguish the sophists from the philosophers who worked before and after them. "Never before had such teachers been seen, never such teaching."[3] "Philosophers" – our sense of this term is also Platonic – investigated metaphysical, political, and ethical questions in search of the truth.[4] "Sophists" taught expository and argumentative techniques to those who sought success in public life (Pl. *Prt.* 316b, 319a). Rhetoric "brings freedom to men and to each man dominion over others," Plato's Gorgias proclaims. "Possessed of such power you will make the doctor and the trainer your slaves; your businessman will prove to be making money not for himself but for another, for you who can speak and persuade multitudes" (*Gorg.* 452d–e). As "the most obvious observation," Ostwald writes, "all sophists were primarily concerned with rhetoric and argumentation."[5] Contemporaries often described that concern in negative terms, as making the wrong or false seem right or true – "making the worse *logos* seem the better." According to Aristotle (*Rhet.* 1402a), Protagoras taught his students how to "make the lesser argument the stronger . . . wherefore men were justly disgusted with his promise; for it is a lie, not a true but an apparent probability."

In tandem with their interest in rhetoric, Plato's sophists rejected positive doctrine, absolute truth, and moral certainty (*Soph.* 231d). Politics was "identical to rhetoric or even inferior to it" (Arist. *NE* 1181a12–15). Only appearing to be wise, and understanding only appearances rather than realities, sophists taught pandering to the masses instead of the highest good (*Soph.* 233a, 268c–d).

Notoriously, Plato's sophists were professional teachers, often handsomely paid. Sokrates says that Protagoras "set up as a teacher of culture and virtue" and was "the first to claim payment for this service" (*Prt.* 349a). In *Soph.* 231d, Plato defines the sophist as "a paid hunter of the young and the wealthy." We hear of various fees, such as Prodikos's "fifty-drachma display [*epideixis*]" (*Crat.* 384b). Xenophon (*Mem.* 6.13) states, "those who sell [wisdom] to anyone for money are called sophists." For Aristotle, sophists argue for profit and publicity (*Soph. Elench.* 171b). They are "just like prostitutes" (ibid. 165a).

Finally, Plato's sophists were interested in a wide range of *technai*, skills or arts (although Plato is prepared to deny that these are true *technai*: *Gorg.* 462b–5c). With typical irony, Plato has the arch-sophist Protagoras complain that "the other sophists treat their pupils badly. These young men who have deliberately turned their backs on *technai*, they take and plunge into *technai* again, teaching them arithmetic and astronomy and geometry and music" (*Prt.* 318d–e).

Although Plato's concept of "the sophist" was adumbrated elsewhere in the later fifth century, his persuasive rhetoric proved decisive in defining that group. As many scholars now agree, however, that concept is fundamentally problematic and its consequences have been devastating.[6] These brilliant intellectuals were more complex, more diverse among themselves, and less distinct from others than he represents. They were not a school or even a movement, neither monopolizing nor limiting themselves to the topics that Plato attributes to them, sometimes in misleading ways. In fact, few if any intellectuals after 450 were "relativist" or amoral. That misrepresentation and the reproach that they were paid were intended to blacken them: their critics asserted that only students of fine moral quality should be taught, rather than anyone who could pay.[7] Plato both distorts and exaggerates their interest in rhetoric. Instead, the wide-ranging questions that engaged these intellectuals continue to rank among the most significant issues of philosophical debate. As cultural figures, Plato's sophists evolved from older types, and many of their ideas evolved out of older concepts. Before and after 450, sophisticated philosophical inquiry occurred widely in the Greek world. Even Plato's sophists worked mostly outside Athens. Born ca. 490, Protagoras came from Thracian Abdera; born ca. 485, Gorgias came from Sicilian Leontini; Prodikos, whose dates are unknown, came from the island of Keos; Protagoras's younger contemporary Hippias came from Elis in the Peloponnese. The "sophistic movement" began well before 450 and was Panhellenic.[8] In Athens, contemporaries including historians, dramatists, artists, and architects contributed to the conceptual advances often reductively linked with "the sophists." Before 430 many of these intellectuals proved useful in the democracy and were a positive force. After 430, intellectual developments as well as political and social change lent darker, more pessimistic colors to political and cultural analysis. Henceforth, most intellectuals in Athens worked outside politics.

Plato's use of the word "sophist" epitomizes these difficulties. With charming irony he himself notes that none of the sophists except Protagoras called themselves *sophistai*, and that Protagoras meant something entirely different by the term (*Prt.* 316–17). Other evidence bears Plato out. In 423 Aristophanes' *Clouds* represents Sokrates especially as an immoral teacher of rhetoric for pay (e.g., lines 98, 876). However, Aristophanes repeatedly calls him and other intellectuals *phrontistai*, "thinkers" (lines 75, 95, 101, 137, 142, 155, 181, etc.). That same year the comic poet Ameipsias staged *Konnos* – the name of Sokrates' music teacher – with a chorus of *phrontistai* (all the trendy intellectuals then in Athens: Athen. 218c) and much criticism of Sokrates. Aristophanes' *Birds* of 414 also ridicules a number of intellectuals (904–1035) including Prodikos (692), and the *nomos-phusis* contrast (753–68: see below), but nowhere uses the word "sophist." Until the end of the fifth century, *sophistes* remained a traditional, venerable epithet, often translated "expert" or "one skilled in an art," and used by many including poets, doctors, musicians, diviners, generals, and athletes.[9] Aristophanes himself says "I *sophizomai*" (*Clouds* 547). Even in the fourth century, some continued to use "sophist" differently from Plato. Isokrates called the philosophers Zeno, Melissos, Parmenides, and Empedokles sophists (*Antid.* 261–8, *Panath.* 26–9). The orator Aeschines (1.173) called Sokrates a sophist. Plato's "sophists" did not mark themselves off from their contemporaries. However, Plato's usage prevailed, narrowing, darkening, and distorting a term that had earlier included quite different cultural types.

To understand the intellectual life of fifth-century Athens, Plato's term "sophist" must first be discarded. A complex designation that he made inescapably pejorative, his "sophist" is a pastiche, a dazzling fabrication elaborated from social practices and philosophical views that he found inimical. He and other Sokratics successfully disseminated a homogenizing, only very recently pejorative sobriquet, to tar with one brush their most dangerous intellectual rivals. The stiff artificiality of his construction has often reduced scholars to despair, as to whether this or that intellectual was "a sophist." The fourth century began the age of definition, specialization, and professionalization, as philosophers, rhetors, playwrights, politicians, generals, and sometimes even sophists became distinct cultural categories. Fifth-century cultural roles were fluid and overlapping.[10] Any single designation for these men, including "sophist," is necessarily anachronistic and reductive. Fifth-century uses of *sophistes* are in turn too broad, including doctors and athletes. In addition, Plato's Protagoras tells us that intellectuals did not use it.

Finally, the exculpatory term "pre-Sokratic" must also be abandoned, because Sokrates does not provide a useful dividing line in Greek intellectual history. As we shall see, Plato's protean master was in many ways a typical albeit extraordinary intellectual and master teacher of the later fifth century. Sokrates and even early Plato were mostly quite at home among the "sophists." Later Plato drew decisively away from them, into a transcendent world of Forms, proclaiming that he knew the truth and bringing his ideal Sokrates along with him. Plato thus pulled off two coups. First, he discredited two generations of some of the world's most brilliant and innovative thinkers, largely because – like most modern philosophers – they declined to accept a transcendent reality and were aware of potential disjunctions between words and things. Secondly, he managed to smuggle his teacher out from amidst that group.

INTELLECTUAL PERSPECTIVES AFTER 450

Athens's intellectual culture after 450 was at once revolutionary, evolutionary, and driven by deep-seated Greek mentalities including competitiveness, innovation, and skepticism toward received traditions.

Best known in this period was the central importance of "the human," *to anthropinon* in Thucydides' term. Human questions had always been the principal concern of Greek poetry. Following the emergence of written prose, intellectuals continued to explore these questions in speech and dialogue. Their investigations also became wider ranging and more systematic, exploring various aspects of human culture including language, social customs (including comparative anthropology), ethics, politics, music, and literary criticism. How words come to designate or to mean, and how words are connected (if at all) with external realities, became – as they remain – fundamental issues of debate.[11]

Some of these intellectuals figure among Plato's sophists, others do not. Not considered "a sophist" although a contemporary, Demokritos of Abdera wrote on ethics, in favor of pleasure with moderation (68 B 189, 191, 207, 224, 231), and on law and politics, in support of democracy (B 248–56). "The atomist Democritus may be broadly classed with the sophists when he is concerned with ethical topics."[12] He also worked on language, speech, and elocution, publishing *Correct Language and Glosses*, *On Rhythms and Harmony*, and *On Euphonious and Harsh-Sounding Letters*, all topics commonly linked with "the sophists."

In tandem with their focus on the human, after 450 most intellectuals (including Thucydides, Euripides, and the Hippokratic medical writers) were critical of (or avoided) religion and the metaphysical. Their disregard of metaphysics was partly the result of broader evolutions within religion and philosophy. By mid century, facing numerous rival explanations of metaphysical phenomena and the mounting evidence of comparative religion (Hdt. 3.38), many intelligent Greeks had come to see that religious beliefs consisted only of what the faithful had been convinced to believe.[13] Protagoras (80 B 4) and some of Euripides' plays[14] decline to say what or even whether the gods might be. Thucydides discounts and ignores them, except as social institutions and superstitious fantasies. Although by no means new, criticism of inherited religion now characterized intellectual life and also became more extreme. Prodikos, Anaxagoras, Perikles, and Diagoras were probably atheists. Earlier skeptical, provocative contentions that only water, or air, or "is" exists, inspired Gorgias to conclude that "nothing exists."

These developments helped to promote the study of rhetoric, the art of convincing others. Rhetoric also had deep roots in Greek culture. Antilogies – opposing speeches – had always characterized assembly and courtroom debates. Vernant traced the origins of Greek philosophy to public debates over elections and other community decisions from the seventh century.[15] In the first half of the fifth century, the Sicilians Tisias and Korax ("Crow") were early students of rhetoric, developing especially the argument from likelihood (*eikos*).[16] After 450 rhetoric flourished. Antilogies were a central interest of Protagoras and Antiphon, and drive the themes of Thucydides' history. In Euripides, often subordinate characters – especially women (Hekabe, Medea) – deploy powerful arguments against men of weaker intellect and character. Gorgias and Hippias delivered impressive display speeches (*epideixeis*) at the Panhellenic games and elsewhere, and Hippias offered to speak extempore on a wide variety of subjects.

Fifth-century work on rhetoric has often been misjudged. Although contemporaries loved to satirize various rhetorical practices as immoral (*Clouds* 889–1113), no one is known to have advertised that he could make the worse cause seem the better. The liberal historian George Grote long ago observed that no great teacher has ever made such a proclamation.[17] Those allegations were a parody, mocking contemporary interest in exploring both sides of complex questions.[18] Several scholars have recently argued that the *techne* of rhetoric itself was a fourth-century invention; earlier rhetoricians confined themselves to display or sample speeches and practice in debate.[19] Finally, Plato and others wrongly tie rhetorical instruction to "the sophists." Even among Plato's sophists, Prodikos, Hippias, and Antiphon taught many other things; Damon is not known to have taught rhetoric; and rhetoricians such as Tisias and Korax are not called sophists.[20]

So far from promoting immorality, many of even Plato's sophists professed to teach *arete*, "virtue" or "excellence." In *Apology* 20b, Plato jokes that the obscure sophist Euenos professed to teach *arete* for 500 drachmas. He says that Protagoras "set up as a teacher of culture and *arete*" (*Prt.* 349a); in *Prt.* 320–24, Protagoras himself defends the teaching of *arete*. In *Gorg.* 519c, Sokrates tells Kallikles, "your sophists claim to be teachers of *arete*." In *Meno* 95c, Sokrates and Meno discuss how far the sophists taught *arete*. Although they deny that Gorgias made any such profession, an inscription at Olympia proclaimed, "no one ever found a better *techne* for training the soul for contests of *arete* than Gorgias" (82 A 8). Prodikos's myth of the Choice of Herakles (between virtue and vice) shows that Prodikos advocated virtue (Xen. *Mem.* 2.1.21–34).

Although Plato and others associate rhetoric with subjective relativism and the denial of external reality, no fifth-century intellectual can be shown to be a relativist, in the sense of reducing everything to a matter of subjective opinion.[21] Antilogies need not be grounded on the epistemological doctrine that anything may be true. Protagoras's claim (80 B 1) that each person must decide for himself what is real, meant that each person has his own experience, but as predicates of different substantive things. Gorgias's claim that nothing exists derived from the gap between language and reality; he accepted a distinction between true and false thoughts. First attested in Antiphon (see below), the distinction between "custom" (*nomos*) and "nature" (*phusis*) presupposes the existence of nature. The antilogic *Dissoi Logoi* takes as its goal "to understand the truth of things" (90.8.1).[22]

At the same time, the age was antidogmatic, skeptical, and relentlessly critical. If men sought the truth, they knew that truth was hard to attain. The (alternative?) title(s) of Protagoras's *Truth or Knock-Down Arguments* is symptomatic. Most scholars agree that this philosophical skepticism originated in the Eleatic school of Parmenides in the early fifth century. Parmenides called cosmology "deceptive": the senses cannot ascertain reality but only an image or appearance (28 B 8: 52).

Polymathy also was a contemporary trait. Hippias's specialties were astronomy and mathematics; he also worked on language, history, poetry, mnemonics, music, and archaeology. With a showman's flair for the practical applications of *technai*, he once visited Olympia wearing or carrying only things which he had made, including a ring, a seal, an oil can, his clothes, and his shoes (86 A 12). Antiphon composed model and other speeches, and also worked on mathematics, physics, metaphysics, and various social and political issues.[23] In addition to the works already mentioned, Demokritos wrote a practical book *On Farming* and numerous other texts including *On Medical Method* and *Voyage Round the World*.

Many of even Plato's sophists retained a keen interest in the physical world and cosmology. As noted, Hippias worked on astronomy and mathematics. Antiphon believed he had discovered how to square the circle (87 B 13). Protagoras thought that the physical world was in flux, accretions replacing emissions (80 A 14). In the second half of the fifth century, Anaxagoras, Diogenes, Leukippos, and Demokritos all continued the Milesian tradition of cosmology, while seeking to reconcile the perceptible world with Eleatic skepticism.

Plato correctly stated that work of this period often had a technical element, something he disliked. Among contemporary intellectuals, Aristophanes' *Clouds* ridicules not "doctors" (*iatroi*) but *iatrotechnai* (line 331). Protagoras analyzed the structure of sentences (80 A 1), and Damon the structures of music and meter (Pl. *Rep.* 400).

Many intellectuals now engaged in empirical research. Aristophanes' *Clouds* parodies this work, as measuring the length of a flea's jump (lines 144–52). Concrete experience and the use of *tekmeria*, "grounds for belief," characterized medical research, as the Hippocratic writers made close observation, not abstract reasoning, the basis of medical treatment.[24]

Many also worked to apply their research in the world outside their studies, where a number of them played an active role. Gorgias, Prodikos, and Hippias were ambassadors; Protagoras wrote a law code for Thurioi; Hippodamos laid out the town plans for Thurioi and Peiraieus.

These intellectuals shared and transmitted their research through lectures, seminars (by question and answer: Pl. *Soph.* 268b–c), small classes, and public speeches. Around the Greek world, the excitement they generated was palpable. Famous intellectuals often traveled and might command high fees. At the time of his eponymous dialogue, Plato's Protagoras has only recently arrived in Athens (*Prt.* 309d) and mentions a previous visit to the city a few years earlier (310e). Gorgias first came to Athens in 427 when he was around fifty; Isokrates (15.155) says he spent a good deal of time in Thessaly, "devoting himself to making money." Plato's Hippias claims that on a tour through Sicily, "although Protagoras was staying there and had a great reputation and was the older, . . . in a very short time I made more than 15,000 drachmas, and in one small place, Inykon [location unknown!], more than 2,000 drachmas" (*Hipp. Maj.* 282d–e; one drachma was approximately a worker's day wage). How far this testimonium is serious we do not know. The phenomenon itself cannot be doubted.

Although "rootless cosmopolitanism" detached these men from their native cities, the fact of travel – bringing wealth and fame – cannot be essential to a philosophical identity. The contrary argument was another of Plato's tricks to disassociate Sokrates from his contemporaries. Non-"sophists" also traveled, such as Anaxagoras and Demokritos. Plato himself traveled, and was wholly detached from Athens. Pay also is not essential. Other fifth-century philosophers were paid; Zeno received 100 *mnai* from Kallias (Pl.[?] I *Alcibiad.* 49a). Conversely, as Gagarin points out, these intellectuals were now more open, more democratic than older elite teachers.[25] "The sophists" were criticized as teachers because they disrupted the traditional forms and content of education.[26] Although their critics condemned the obligation to teach anyone who paid, it is doubtful how far any of these superstar intellectuals felt constrained to teach anyone just to pocket the fee. Thrasymachos, Kritias, and Damon are not known to have lectured or given classes or to have taken fees. By contrast, Stesimbrotos of Thasos, known to us as a historian of contemporary politics rather than a sophist, lectured in Athens in the 430s on Homeric criticism and charged for it.[27]

What was the goal of the new instruction? Ford stresses its liberal and impractical qualities – "to be polished at dinner parties" (*Clouds* 649).[28] Its practical uses were perhaps even more significant. According to Plato (*Theaet.* 166d–7c), the sophists were handsomely paid because they taught people the practical skills necessary to improve their cities. Thucydides was both a general and an intellectual; he proclaims his history's usefulness as a practical guide to the future (1.22.4, 2.48.3). Perikles applied what he learned from Anaxagoras and Damon to the task of managing Athens. In *Meno* 91a, Sokrates says that the sophists teach "the kind of wisdom and virtue which fits men to manage an estate or govern a city, to look after their parents, and to entertain and send off guests in proper style."

Although Plato sharply distinguished the "sophists" from the philosophers before and after them, these intellectuals continued older cultural patterns. Traveling wise men (sometimes called *sophoi* or *sophistai*) had long been educators and counselors of communities and their leaders.[29] These men were often poets, whose public role was to educate and benefit the polis.[30] Greeks had long valued foreign wisdom experts, importing knowledge to solve community problems. Epimenides of Crete arrived in late seventh-century Athens to resolve civil strife ([Arist.] *AP* 1). The early fifth-century Athenian poet Pratinas said that the Cretan Thaletas saved Sparta from a plague through music ([Plut.] *De mus.* 1146b). When in the later fifth century prose logic replaced poetic inspiration as the primary means of thought and communication,[31] intellectuals ceased to be poets and poetry's importance faded. Still, in oratorical performances to the demos and their counsel to community elites, these intellectuals might reincarnate older poetic types. Gorgias's florid rhetoric and purple rhapsode's robe (82 A9) were poetical. Although Plato saw the sophists as new and evil, in many ways these practical wisdom experts were an ancient type.

For the elite, the figure of community poet joined a second, older typology, the wise counselor to political leaders. According to Herodotos (8.57–8), Mnesiphilos of Phrearrioi suggested to Themistokles the strategy at Salamis. Plutarch says that Mnesiphilos "was not a *rhetor* nor a physical scientist, but a cultivator of what was then called *sophia*, although it was only political cleverness and practical sagacity" (*Them.* 2.6). In Xenophon (*Mem.* 4.2.2) someone asks Sokrates, "was it by constant association with some wise man or by natural ability that

Themistokles stood out among his fellow-citizens?" Sokrates replies that leaders require practical advice from competent teachers. It is not important whether these specific reports are historical. They indicate an early type of counselor, fulfilling one role of Plato's sophists.

INTELLECTUALS AND POLITICS AFTER 450

After 450, wealth, imperial power, and an ever more confident democracy energized Athens. Until 431, when Perikles provoked Sparta into war, optimistic confidence and creative innovation inspired work on many fronts, to master a broad range of technical, artistic, conceptual, and scientific problems. The Parthenon was built; political science was born; prose became a serious challenger to poetry for deep reflection, expanding critical thought and debate; intellectuals and politicians now applied their research to society and politics.

The Athenians and other Greeks were fully conscious of this revolution. Around 445 (according to one dating), *Prometheus Bound* (lines 442–506) celebrated human progress and Prometheus's gift of all *technai* to man. Ca. 442, Sophokles' *Antigone* proclaimed that "many things are wondrous, but nothing more wondrous than man"; man possesses "*technai* exceeding all expectation" (lines 332–3, 366). In the 430s, the Corinthians in Thucydides state that in politics as in any other *techne*, the new must drive out the old (1.71.3). Their description of the Athenians mirrors the restless intelligence of Sophokles' Oedipus.[32] Thucydides' Perikles tells the demos, "we are lovers of wisdom [*philosophoumen*] without sacrificing manly courage" (2.40.1). The demos welcomed Gorgias enthusiastically in 427 (Diod. Sic. 12.53.3). That same year Thucydides' Kleon (3.38.5) remarks that "overcome by the pleasure of listening," the assembly "is like an audience sitting at the feet of sophists." A positive, progressive spirit shines through a mid-fifth-century dedication: "it is a noble thing for wise men to be wise through *techne*, for he who possesses *techne* will have a better life" (*IG* i² 678).

In Athens before the war, many intellectuals were a positive, benevolent force. Their work suited the mood of progressive optimism, and the upper classes who patronized them continued to dominate city politics. Among these figures, Protagoras is best known because of Plato's portrait. Like *Prometheus Bound* and Prodikos's *Horai*, Protagoras, too, celebrated man's progress in *On the Original State of Man* (cf. Pl. *Prt.* 320c–22d). He also championed democracy. In one of antiquity's few justifications of popular rule (*Prt.* 323–5), he argued that because to some degree everyone shares in political wisdom and justice, everyone should share in governing. His concept that each person must determine reality for himself supported individual judgment and hence egalitarianism and democracy.[33] On questions of rhetoric and truth, if every situation admits of contrasting arguments there are nonetheless better and worse arguments, based on realities. If a sick man says his food tastes bitter, we should not try to convince him otherwise, but restore him to health. In Protagoras's conception as Plato represents it, the sophists seek to make everyone better by *logoi* (*Theaet.* 166d–67c). By teaching *euboulia*, "good counsel," he wished to "make men good citizens" and skilled managers of their domestic affairs (*Prt.* 318e–319a) and to make his students better every day (*Prt.* 316c, 318a). As I have noted, Protagoras was also active in civic affairs, writing a law code for Thurioi. These and other testimonia indicate a constructive, democratic, basically cheerful theoretician who sought to improve people's lives.

Born about 500 and heir to Athens's early music theorists,[34] Damon was active at least through the 420s. He was an important political counselor to Perikles and worked to expand the democracy, proposing the introduction of jury pay and formulating the democratic slogan "give the people their own" ([Arist.] *AP* 27; Plut. *Per.* 4). As with other contemporary intellectuals, some of Damon's research was purely scientific. He named, described, and categorized poetic meters and possibly also the *harmoniai*, musical scales (Pl. *Rep.* 400). His main areas of research were humanistic music theory and music's social and political applications (ibid. 424). As contemporaries studied the practical uses of rhetoric, Damon first studied the effects of different types of music on behavior and character. In similar ways, the Hippocratic *Airs Waters Places* (e.g., 12, 16, 23) evaluated the effects on character of geography and climate.

Perikles himself best illustrates the link between politics and advanced humanistic research. His philosophical interests were both intellectual and practical. According to Plutarch (*Per.* 36.2), he held philosophical meetings at his house. He was taught by Damon and Anaxagoras.[35] In Plato's *Phaedrus* (269e–70a), Sokrates claims that Perikles acquired from Anaxagoras the mental elevation and finished execution needed for success in rhetoric. "Most skilled at both speaking and taking action" (1.139.4), in Thucydides' portrait Perikles' chief quality is confidence in his intelligence. Indeed, he provoked Sparta into war because of his calculations regarding Athens's future. This combination of abstract thought and practical utility also appears in Perikles' association with Damon. Having studied music's behavioral effects, Perikles constructed the Odeion music hall, reorganized the musical component of the Panathenaic festival, and selected the musicians for the first competition (Plut. *Per.* 13). Olympiodoros later mentions "the songs which Perikles learned from Damon, through which he harmonized the city" (*In Plat. Alcibiad. comm.* 138.4–11).

Plutarch (*Per.* 15) well imagined Perikles' ideals, if not his city's historical realities:

> There were times when [the demos] bitterly resented [Perikles'] policy, and then he tightened the reins and forced them to do what was to their advantage, much as a wise physician treats a prolonged and complicated disease, allowing the patient at some moments pleasures which can do him no harm, and at others giving him caustics and bitter drugs which cure him. There were, as might be expected, all kinds of disorders to be found among a mass of citizens who possessed an empire as great as Athens's, and Perikles was the only man capable of keeping each of these under control. He achieved this most often by using the people's hopes and fears as if they were rudders, curbing them when they were arrogant and raising their hopes or comforting them when they were disheartened. In this way he proved that rhetoric, in Plato's phrase [*Phaedr.* 271c], is the art of working upon the souls of men by means of words, and that its chief business is the knowledge of men's characters and passions, which are so to speak the strings and stops of the soul and require a most skilful and delicate touch.

Perikles' death in 429 marked a turning point in intellectual history as well as in politics. Intellectuals came to be less involved with the democracy, and in many ways became a darker, more negative force. None of these later figures is known to have written laws for cities or worked on town planning. Returning from his ostracism in the late 430s, Damon continued his research and teaching, but did not engage in politics. This withdrawal from public life into darker, more private moods reflected three developments. Many elite citizens were themselves now alienated from politics; these were years of war and plague; finally, various theoretical positions evolved into more extreme, sometimes even offensive forms, as intellectuals sought fame or notoriety by bolder conceptual innovations. The recent histories of painting, photography, and music (Wagner, Stravinsky, jazz) offer parallels.

Antiphon of Athens (ca. 470–411) marked the transition between these two periods.[36] Antiphon is often thought to have "preached a thorough-going left-wing egalitarianism,"[37] denying any natural distinction between Greek and barbarian or between well- and low-born (80 B 44b, from *Truth*). "We give reverence and respect to the children of noble fathers: we neither reverence nor respect the offspring of a humble house. In this we have barbarised ourselves." According to [Plut.] *X Orat.* 833c–d, before Antiphon turned to speech-writing sometime in the 430s,

> he invented a method of curing distress, just as physicians have a treatment for those who are ill. At Corinth, fitting up a room near the marketplace, he wrote on the door that he could cure by words those who were in distress; and by asking questions and finding out the causes of their condition he consoled those in trouble.

Admittedly, the source for this early effort at psychiatry is of uncertain value. However, various scholars have shown how well it parallels contemporary research.[38] As Damon used music and Gorgias used rhetoric (as if "a drug") to affect emotions and character, so Antiphon attempted to help people through personal interrogation. Plato's Protagoras remarks, "in education a change must be effected from a worse condition to a better; but the physician produces a change by means of drugs, the sophist does it by *logoi*" (*Theaet.* 167a).

By 411, however, this brilliant intellectual and speech-writer had become a passionate conservative and oligarch (Thuc. 8.68.1). In *On Concord* (87 B 61) he wrote, "There is nothing worse for men than lack of rule. With this in mind men of old accustomed children to being ruled and to do what they are told so that when they became men they should not become confused in a great change." This passage echoes the conservative ideology of "returning to" a government modeled on a paternalist household, the so-called "forefathers' polity" first attested in 411 when Antiphon became prominent ([Arist.] *AP* 29.3).

The first attested distinction between *nomos* ("custom," "convention," "law") and *phusis* ("nature") also occurs in later Antiphon. His *Truth* argued that civic norms of justice are different from natural justice and much less effective and fair; because laws do not accord with nature, people should ignore them when they can do so undetected. Kallikles in Plato's *Gorgias* also defends the natural state, arguing that laws are devised by a weakling majority to shackle the strong. Thrasymachos in *Republic* I adopts a similar position, questioning why individuals should restrain themselves in the interests of others. These arguments were shocking, but can also be seen as an attempt to find a better form of justice, based on nature. Justice is also the goal of Plato's *Republic*, there resulting in a totalitarian regime. The excitement generated by the *nomos-phusis* distinction has been compared to Freud's discovery of the unconscious and infantile sexuality. In both cases, the potential for immorality was quickly seen. In Aristophanes' *Clouds* (1321–1446) Pheidippides argues at length that it is perfectly acceptable to beat one's father and even one's mother. He "scorns the established *nomoi*" (1400).

Following Thuc. 2.65, many have seen a sharp transition in politics from Periklean Athens to the so-called age of the demagogues, "living off the law courts and the assemblies."[39] Although many characteristics of post-429 politics occur in earlier years, no longer were age, military ability, and noble lineage required for political success. The main requirement was rhetorical skill. It is therefore paradoxical that post-Periklean Athens saw a reaction against intellectualism, especially on the part of progressive democrats. Although the sources for this development are almost all hostile to Athens's "new" politicians, their combined testimony carries weight.

Kleon is the best-known of these democratic politicians. His family was wealthy but not noble. Thucydides considered him a vulgar anti-intellectual and despised him. In 3.37 he has Kleon argue that ignorance with moderation is more beneficial than cleverness with license. "Base" men, distrusting their own intelligence, have better success at governing than the more intelligent, who wish to seem wiser than the laws and thus cause cities disaster. Aristophanes' *Knights* parodies similar attitudes, targeting Kleon and another demagogue, the "Sausage Seller." When told that he will become the greatest man in city, the Sausage Seller replies, "But my good man, I don't know anything about *mousike*, except the alphabet, and that just barely." Demos's slave responds: "That is your only drawback, that you know it, even 'just barely.' *Demagogia* [leading the people] is no longer for a cultured or well-behaved man, but for the ignorant and the obnoxious" (*Kn.* 188–92). As Connor points out, Old Comedy never ridicules Athens's new politicians for hyperintellectualism.[40] No democratic politician ever comes to hear the sophists in Plato's dialogues.

Another prominent democratic politician was Anytos. Plato (*Meno* 90a) describes Anytos's father as a self-made man, leaving his son a tannery and a shoemaker's business. When with typical irony Sokrates defends the sophists, Anytos remarks that people must be mad to pay any sophist or permit their children to study with them – cities should not even let them in! "I've never in my life had anything to do with a single one of them, nor would I hear of any of my family doing so" (*Meno* 92a–b). According to Xenophon (*Apol.* 29–32), Sokrates publicly berated Anytos for bringing up his son in the tannery trade.

> At one time I had a brief association with the son of Anytos, and I thought him not lacking in firmness of soul; and so I predict that he will not continue in the servile occupation that his father has provided for him. Rather, through want of a worthy adviser he will fall into some disgraceful propensity and will surely go far in a career of vice.

Anytos was one of Sokrates' prosecutors in 399.

Why did the new politicians reject intellectualism? One reason must relate to their lower social and economic status. In the later 410s the comic poet Eupolis remarked, "once upon a time our city's Generals came from the best families, first by wealth and first by birth. We used to pray to them as if they were gods – and so they were, and we prospered. But now we go on campaign at random, electing as our generals – garbage."[41] These politicians had limited experience with elite social and educational resources, including symposia, *hetaireiai* (aristocratic political clubs), and "worthy advisers." They were also suspicious of these resources as undemocratic (Plut. *Mor.* 806f).

Conversely, after 430 the upper classes retained their intellectual interests (as the scenes in Plato show), but withdrew from politics.[42] In [Pl.] *Ax.* 368d–9b Axiochos remarks, "I've had enough of the public platform." In Xenophon (*Mem.* 3.7.1–2), Sokrates says that Charmides is quite capable of serving in politics but is unwilling to do so. Barring the extraordinary exception of Alkibiades, what explains this phenomenon? Contemporary sources suggest two reasons: the demos no longer needed aristocratic leaders, and the aristocracy refused to play democratic politics with "inferiors." Euripides' Ion remarks, "if I make an effort to be in the first rank of the city . . . , we'll be hated by those of no ability. For superiority always rankles. But the upper classes and those who are capable of being *sophoi*, who keep quiet and do not hasten into public life, will treat me as a laughing stock and a fool if I don't mind my own business in a city filled with fear" (*Ion* 595–601). *Knights* and Thucydides'

Mytilenean debate (3.37–48) imply that only a hyper-Kleon like the Sausage Seller can defeat a Kleon.[43] Euripides' Hippolytos observes (*Hipp.* 986–9):

> I am unpolished in speaking to the mob,
> although among my age-group and among the few I am
>   rather *sophos*.
> That is as it should be. Those who are base
> among the *sophoi* are rather *mousikoi* in speaking before the
>   mob.

The demos's reaction to intellectuals was ambivalent. Old Comedy's mockery of ignorant "Kleons" presupposes that the demos did not automatically question a good education. We have noted their excitement at hearing Gorgias in 427, and Kleon's description of the assembly as "slaves of the ever unheard-of, and despisers of the familiar," as if "sitting at the feet of sophists," in Thucydides. Year after year people bought theater tickets to hear Euripides' characters proclaim newfangled theories and sometimes blasphemy.

At the same time, intellectual activity now attracted hostility, primarily because intellectuals had become more extreme, more isolated from the demos, and less sympathetic to the democracy. Comedy and other voices scorned their "idle prattling," "subtle quibbling,"[44] and immoral rhetoric (*Clouds* 889–1111). In *Clouds* 359, Sokrates is called "high priest of the most hair-splitting twaddle." A fragment of Aristophanes (506 KA) states, "a book has ruined this man, or Prodikos has, or at any rate one of the idle prattlers." Isokrates (*Busiris* 48–9) says that philosophy is hated because its practitioners defend shameful causes. Plato's Kallikles (*Gorg.* 482c ff.) defends the use of power for private ends. Thrasymachos in *Republic* I argues that justice is the interest of the stronger (338c). Paradigmatic of at least one contemporary perception of the debased moral climate is Thucydides' Melian Dialogue (5.85–111), placed in 416, a key thematic passage in his history. In this fictional drama the Melians argue for their lives on the basis of justice, the gods, kinship, and shame. The Athenians counter with expediency, self-interest, and superior power: "the strong do what they will, and the weak suffer what they must" (5.89). Thucydides traces what he regards as Athens's moral degeneration after the death of Perikles. The historian himself scorned Athens's democracy. His progressively dark pages contrast with Herodotos, working and lecturing in the Periklean period and perhaps even rewarded by the demos (Plut. *De mal. Hdt.* 26), not banished by them.

The force of intellectual momentum, as later theorists espoused ever more extreme positions, attracted Athens's embittered antidemocratic elite in a dangerous synergy. Their collaboration led to "the bloody lunacy of 411,"[45] an oligarchic revolution fueled by theory, and in 404 to the oligarchic junta called the Thirty, including Sokrates' students. Among other points, that deadly alliance between Athens's intellectual and social elites banned the teaching of rhetoric, presumably as a democratic *techne* (Xen. *Mem.* 1.2.31).

SOKRATES

Plato so artfully and persistently distinguished his teacher from "the sophists" that Gregory Vlastos, Sokrates' greatest modern student, could write his biography and mention the sophists only once – and only to note how different they were. However, Plato's Sokrates fits most of the characteristics of Plato's "sophist."[46] Plato's Sokrates primarily discusses ethics and politics, although Plato indicates wider interests, for example in music (*Euthyd.* 272c). Plato's Sokrates is quintessentially identified with debate and argument. His characteristic use of cross-questioning reflects his constant challenge to received opinion, eliciting contradictions and absurdities which he replaces not with positive doctrine but "uncertainty," *aporia*. He expounds no coherent set of beliefs. He held unconventional views about the gods. His entourage was a crowd of rich young Athenians. Like many of the later sophists, he hated democracy and stayed out of politics; otherwise, "I should have been put to death long ago" (*Apol.* 31d). In Plato, his relations with other sophists are often friendly. He refers students to sophists such as Damon and Prodikos[47] as a "match-maker" (*Theat.* 151b). He helps his young friend Hippokrates meet Protagoras (*Prt.* 316a).

The grounds on which scholars distinguish Plato's Sokrates from Plato's sophists are, first, that he did not accept pay. He was, however, often lavishly entertained, and his trademark, spartanizing filth was a provocation and a philosophical and political statement, like Diogenes the Cynic's. As I have said, pay cannot be essential to a philosophical identity. Plato's Sokrates also claimed not to teach. In fact, however, he taught all the time, and to judge from Plato was Athens's greatest teacher. He did not teach rhetoric; but others of Plato's sophists also did not. More important, his art of speaking by cross-questioning was "a sophist's" technique,[48] which his students widely imitated (*Apol.* 23c). Plato's Sokrates claimed no special expertise. That claim was deeply ironic. He argued that virtue cannot be taught. That argument also was meant to provoke; it reflected a debate at least as old as Pindar (2 *Olym.* 86–8), and above all, it defended Sokrates against the murderous outrages perpetrated by his students in 404. He did not travel, but he was profoundly alienated from Athens's democratic government.

Plato's most important distinction between Sokrates and the sophists is that his Sokrates professes to be deeply moral, seeking to comprehend truth and virtue. Many scholars have accepted this distinction. In his magisterial work, Guthrie claimed that "the essential difference" between Sokrates and the sophists was that for Sokrates, ethics was a field of knowledge whose purpose was to show universal ethical and political laws and truths; the sophists' skepticism and relativism reduced everything to matters of opinion.[49] As we have seen, however, Plato himself indicates that other "sophists" also professed to teach virtue and seek the truth. Sokrates was in this way typical – how skillfully Plato's silvery tongue has misled his readers. From another perspective, there is no evidence that even Plato's early Sokrates accepted any transcendent truths; he espouses no positive doctrine. Most scholars agree that Plato's later absolutism and transcendental Forms – dangerous fantasies – were not Sokratic.

How far was Sokrates a typical intellectual of his period? His contemporaries had no doubt that he was both typical and dangerous. Aristophanes' *Clouds* describes him as the archetypical "genus intellectual" (Dover's phrase); and Aristophanes knew Sokrates well. Ameipsias's *Konnos* criticized him as elitist, "the best of few men, and by far the most idle and foolish" (fr. 9 KA). Aristophanes' *Frogs* (lines 1491–9) also criticized him: "to spend one's time fecklessly on pretentious talk and nit-picking humbug is to act like a lunatic." The orator Lysias attacked "a pupil of Sokrates" who indulged in much "pretentious talk about justice and virtue" (fr. 1 Thal.). Thus, contemporary writers identified Sokrates as a worst offender among Athens's intellectuals. Although Plato spent a lifetime denying it, his own portrait reveals that Sokrates was very much part of the intellectual life of his time.

As Antiphon had done in 411, in 404 some of Sokrates' students helped overthrow Athens's democracy. They murdered some 1,500 citizens to steal their money, notwithstanding their teacher's longstanding claim – now patently outrageous – that he only advocated goodness and the highest virtue of the soul. As Hansen points out,[50] even after the Thirty were overthrown, Sokrates presumably went around Athens saying that democracy was a bad form of government and should be replaced (Pl. *Apol.* 29c: "I shall never stop philosophizing and elucidating the truth"; 30b–c: "I am not going to alter my conduct, not even if I have to die a hundred deaths"). In consequence, he was convicted of being an impious, anti-Athenian, and corrupting teacher of the type the demos had grown wary of since the 420s. He chose to die, offering only a perverse defense to the charges brought against him, and proposing no serious alternative to the death penalty his prosecutors sought. Was the judgment of his fellow citizens altogether unjust?

CONCLUSION

> Plato seems somehow to be always reviling the term "sophist," he seems the one who has especially attacked that term. The reason for this is his contempt for the masses and for those of his profession.
>
> Aelius Aristeides *Or.* 3.681 = LVI, vol. 2, p. 408 (Dind.)

Why did Plato label and target "the sophists"? Born in 427, he grew up in the more negative political and intellectual climate of the war years. His immediate intellectual predecessors were brilliant men of great acclaim and influence, who were interested not in transcendent truth but in human questions, words, the art of persuasion, government, and progress on many fronts. Then came defeat by Sparta; the disastrous, murderous oligarchic junta led by Plato's friends and relatives; and the execution of his beloved master. Plato's *Seventh Letter* (324b–6b) makes patent the profound effects these events had on him.

Plato left Athens for twelve years, and returned with new ideas. Conventional politics was impossible, rhetoric was dangerous, practical research was useless. Expert philosophers had to solve the world's problems by attaining knowledge of goodness and justice. Henceforth, part of Plato's project lay in explicating his solutions to the problems raised in the fifth century and by Athens's democracy. A second part lay in clearing the ground. A superb writer, Plato deployed all the skill of his formidable intellect especially against the more extreme views of his immediate predecessors.[51] No less important, his teacher had been executed as a dangerous intellectual. In his early and middle period, Plato never ceased in his effort to extract Sokrates from his contemporaries, whose views he had come to despise, and thus provide one more reason to condemn democracy. At least until recently, Plato's efforts to discredit the sophists and to distinguish Sokrates from them have been successful, although to the detriment of the history of fifth-century philosophy and the future of popular government.

SUGGESTIONS FOR FURTHER READING

The bibliography on Plato is enormous. R. Kraut, *The Cambridge Companion to Plato* (Cambridge: Cambridge University Press, 1992), includes a wide range of essays and lengthy bibliographies on Plato and contemporary philosophy. For a good conventional survey see W. K. C. Guthrie, *A History of Greek Philosophy*, vol. 4, *Plato: the Man and His Dialogues. Earlier Period* (Cambridge: Cambridge University Press, 1975). On the sophists, G. Kerferd, *The Sophistic Movement* (n. 1), is good but dated and overly conventional; cf. A. Nightingale, "Sages, Sophists, and Philosophers: Greek Wisdom Literature" (n. 4). On Socrates, see above all G. Vlastos, *Socrates, Ironist and Moral Philosopher* (Ithaca, NY: Cornell University Press, 1991). As I have mentioned (n. 6), Karl Popper's iconoclastic *The Open Society and Its Enemies*, fifth edition (Princeton: Princeton University Press, 1966; orig. ed. 1945), although dated, is still worth reading on Plato, Sokrates, and "the sophists."

NOTES

1   Except on intellectual history before 450, this essay supersedes R. W. Wallace, "The Sophists in Athens," in K. Raaflaub and D. Boedeker, eds., *Democracy, Empire, and the Arts in Fifth-Century Athens* (Cambridge, MA: Harvard University Press, 1998), pp. 203–22. Translations are adapted from standard versions. Pre-Platonic philosophers are cited by their numbers in DK. Two standard treatments of the sophists are W. K. C. Guthrie, *A History of Greek Philosophy*, vol. 3, *The Fifth-Century Enlightenment* (Cambridge: Cambridge University Press, 1969), and G. B. Kerferd, *The Sophistic Movement* (Cambridge: Cambridge University Press, 1981). Lowell Edmunds kindly commented on this paper.

2   On Plato's importance for standard reconstructions of the sophists, see, e.g., Kerferd (n. 1), p. 1 and *passim*, and G. Striker, "Methods of Sophistry," in *Essays on Hellenistic Epistemology and Ethics* (Cambridge: Cambridge University Press, 1996), p. 3.

3   J. de Romilly, *The Great Sophists in Periclean Athens* (Oxford: Oxford University Press, 1992), p. 4.

4   On the evolving concept of philosopher, see Striker (n. 2), pp. 3–6 and *passim*; A. Nehamas, *Virtues of Authenticity. Essays on Plato and Socrates* (Princeton: Princeton University Press, 1999), pp. 108–12 and *passim*; and A. Nightingale, "Sages, Sophists, and Philosophers: Greek Wisdom Literature," in O. Taplin, ed., *Literature*

in the Greek and Roman Worlds (Oxford: Oxford University Press, 2000), pp. 156–8, 179–85.

5   M. Ostwald, *From Popular Sovereignty to the Sovereignty of Law. Law, Society, and Politics in Fifth-Century Athens* (Berkeley: University of California Press, 1986), p. 242.

6   Although Plato's hostility to the sophists has long been recognized, systematic attempts to discount the effects of that hostility have only recently become common. Contrast "sophists" in the second (1971) and third (1996) editions of *The Oxford Classical Dictionary*, and see, e.g., S. Goldhill, *Reading Greek Tragedy* (Cambridge: Cambridge University Press, 1986), pp. 222–4, and G. E. R. Lloyd *The Revolutions of Wisdom. Studies in the Claims and Practice of Ancient Greek Science* (Berkeley: University of California Press, 1987), pp. 92–4 with n. 152. Even Guthrie (n. 1) and Kerferd (n. 1) are sometimes unduly influenced by Plato. G. Grote, *A History of Greece* (London: J. Murray, 1846–1856; London: reprint edition, 1869–1884), and Karl Popper's response to totalitarianism, *The Open Society and Its Enemies*, vol. 1, *The Spell of Plato* (London, 1945; fifth edition, Princeton: Princeton University Press, 1966), were pioneers: passionate, compelling attacks on Plato in defense of the sophists.

7   D. Blank, "Socratics vs. Sophists on Payment for Teaching," *CA* 4 (1985): 1–49.

8   Wallace (n. 1).

9   See Ar. *Clouds* 331, Xen. *Mem.* 3.1.1–3, G. B. Kerferd, "The First Greek Sophists," *CR* 1 (1950): 8–10, K. J. Dover, *Aristophanes Clouds* (Oxford: Oxford University Press, 1968), p. xxxv n. 1, and M. Ostwald "Philosophy, Rhetoric and Science," in *CAH* V².341–3.

10 R. W. Wallace, "Speech, Song and Text, Public and Private. Evolutions in Communications Media and Fora in Fourth-Century Athens," in W. Eder, ed., *Die athenische Demokratie im 4. Jahrhundert v. Chr.* (Stuttgart: Steiner, 1995), pp. 199–217.

11 Kerferd (n. 1), pp. 88–110.

12 A. W. H. Adkins, *Moral Values and Political Behaviour in Ancient Greece From Homer to the End of the Fifth Century* (New York: Norton, 1972), p. 103.

13 Cf. Striker (n. 2), p. 15.

14 *Bellerophon*: "Does any man say there are gods in heaven? No, there are none" (*TGrF* fr. 286); *Iph. at Aul.* 1034–5: "If there are gods . . . , but if there are not. . . . "

15 J.-P. Vernant, *Les origines de la pensée grecque* (Paris: Presses Universitaires de France, 1962), also published as *The Origins of Greek Thought* (Ithaca, NY: Cornell University Press, 1982).

16 Cic. *Brutus* 12.46–8. For a critical assessment (also rejecting "Crow"), see T. Cole, *The Origins of Rhetoric in Ancient Greece* (Baltimore: Johns Hopkins University Press, 1991), pp. 22–5. Tisias is never labeled a sophist, presumably as too distant from Plato and no competitor. Aristotle (*Soph. Elench.* 183b31ff.) mentions that these Sicilians were not the first students of rhetoric.

17 Grote (n. 6), vol. VIII (1869), p. 204.

18 A. Ford, "Sophists without Rhetoric: The Arts of Speech in Fifth-Century Athens," in Yun Lee Too, ed., *Education in Greek and Roman Antiquity* (Leiden: Brill, 2001), pp. 88–92.

19 See Ford (n. 18) and refs., e.g., to Cole (n. 16).

20 Lloyd (n. 6), pp. 92–4, nn. 152, 153.

21 Kerferd (n. 1), pp. 83–110; P. Woodruff, "Rhetoric and Relativism: Protagoras and Gorgias," in A. A. Long, ed., *The Cambridge Companion to Early Greek Philosophy* (Cambridge: Cambridge University Press, 1999), pp. 290–310.

22 "If it were not for Plato's insistence that a philosopher must settle for a definite doctrine, we might say that [the sophists] were philosophers after all – in our sense, not Plato's": Striker (n. 2), p. 21. In fact, many of these men maintained positive doctrines.

23 M. Gagarin *Antiphon the Athenian. Oratory, Law, and Justice in the Age of the Sophists* (Austin: University of Texas Press, 2002), p. 4.

24 See the Hippocratic *On Ancient Medicine*, and G. E. R. Lloyd, *Magic, Reason and Experience* (Cambridge: Cambridge University Press, 1979), pp. 126–225, "The Development of Empirical Research."

25 Gagarin (n. 23).

26 Goldhill (n. 6), p. 227.

27 Xen. *Symp.* 3.6, *FGrHist* 107 fr. 10a with Jacoby's comment on T2.

28 Ford (n. 18), pp. 88–94.

29 For a more detailed discussion of these early figures (including Simonides and Lasos of Hermione), see Wallace (n. 1).

30 See later Ar. *Achar.* 656–8, *Frogs* 1009–10, 1054–8, Pl. *Prt.* 325c-6c, and J. Henderson, "The *dêmos* and the Comic Competition," in J. J. Winkler and F. Zeitlin, eds., *Nothing to Do with Dionysos? Athenian Drama in Its Social Context* (Princeton: Princeton University Press, 1990), pp. 271–2, 297–307, 312–13. The "ancient quarrel" between poetry and philosophy is a Platonic myth.

31 Wallace (n. 10).

32 B. Knox, "Why Is Oedipus Called Tyrannos?" in *Word and Action. Essays on the Ancient Theater* (Baltimore: Johns Hopkins University Press, 1979), pp. 87–95.

33 J. V. Luce, *An Introduction to Greek Philosophy* (London: Thames and Hudson, 1992), p. 82.

34 Wallace (n. 1).

35 Isokr. *Antid.* 235, Pl. *Phaedr.* 269e–70a, Pl.(?) I *Alcibiad.* 118c, cf. [Arist.] *AP* 27.4. For a critique cf. P. Stadter, "Pericles among the Intellectuals," *Illinois Classical Studies* 16 (1991): 111–24.

36 On the "unity" of Antiphon "the rhetorician" and "the sophist," see Gagarin (n. 23).

37 Kerferd (n. 1), p. 50; see also Guthrie (n. 1), pp. 293–4.

38 E.g., Guthrie (n. 1), pp. 168, 290–91, Kerferd (n. 1), p. 51.

39 Isokr. 8.130; see Arist. *Pol.* 1320a4–6; W. R. Connor, *The New Politicians of Fifth-Century Athens* (Princeton: Princeton University Press, 1971).

40 Connor (n. 39), p. 166 n. 54.

41 *Demes* fr. 117, trans. W. G. Forrest, "An Athenian Generation Gap," *YCS* 24 (1975): 41–2.

42 See L. B. Carter, *The Quiet Athenian* (Oxford: Oxford University Press, 1986), pp. 52–75 (chapter 3: "Noble Youths").

43 Forrest (n. 41): 47; Adkins (n. 12), p. 145.

44 C. Natali, "*Adoleschia, Leptologia*, and the Philosophers in Athens," *Phronesis* 32 (1987): 232–41.

45 Forrest (n. 41): 49.

46 See Kerferd (n. 1), pp. 55–7, and *The Sophists and Their Legacy* (Wiesbaden: Steiner, 1981), pp. 4–5, and Nehamas (n. 4), p. 115 and *passim*.

47 *Lch.* 180c–d, 197d; D. Blank "Socratics vs. Sophists on Payment for Teaching," *CA* 4 (1985): 6–7.

48 Nehamas (n. 4), p. 110.

49 Guthrie (n. 1), p. 425.

50 M. H. Hansen, "The Trial of Sokrates – From the Athenian Point of View" (Copenhagen: Royal Danish Academy of Sciences and Letters, 1995), *Hist.-fil.-Medd.* 71: 1–31.

51 The older generation of "sophists" – Protagoras, Gorgias, and Damon – receive fairly benign treatment, although Plato never relented in pointing out their errors.

10: DEMOCRATIC THEORY AND PRACTICE

R. Sealey

The basic institutions of the Athenian republic, including the assembly, the council, election and sortition, and the courts, had been fashioned before Xerxes invaded Greece in 480. But the word *demokratia*, first attested in the work of Herodotos, was coined later, about the middle of the fifth century, and it soon came to be applied to Athens. Thereafter it figured prominently in discussions of political theory. Yet the average Athenian, admittedly an elusive person, did not concern himself much with theoretical discussion, if one may judge from the plays of Aristophanes, who offers the modern reader a closer approach to everyday life than any other writer of the fifth century. So it is advisable first to study the institutions of the Athenians in their historical development and then to ask what principles they imply. That is, one should proceed from practice to theory.

THE EMERGENCE OF THE POLIS

Modern understanding of the way society developed in Greece early in the historical period has changed radically in the last two decades. Previously it was believed that, after the collapse of the civilization of the Bronze Age (ca. 1200), migrating bands of people wandered until they found land to settle. Supposedly, when they did so, in the typical community hereditary kingship arose from the former leader of the migratory host, commanders of groups within the host became a council advising the king, and from the parade of all the warriors there arose an assembly of adult male citizens to decide issues by vote. On this view the political history of the emergent cities was to be reconstructed as a series of struggles between monarchy, aristocracy, and democracy. But this theory ceased to be tenable when the evidence for kingship in early Greece was re-examined and found to be inadequate. The traditions telling of early kings were fictions invented in the fifth and fourth centuries by ambitious families, who wished to boast of distinguished ancestry. The earliest stone buildings, erected late in the seventh century or later, were temples, not palaces.[1]

Instead of the old view, the new reconstruction supposes that after a long period of migration and disorder stable settlements arose. They drew their subsistence mainly from agriculture and fishing. Each settlement had a number of family-households varying in wealth and power. A wealthy household attracted dependents. Each household managed its own affairs in a patriarchal manner. Power, in short, was private; there were no public organs, although the head of a less powerful household would not wish to offend the head of a more powerful one. But although there were no public officers, sometimes tasks had to be performed for the benefit of the whole community. Tasks of two kinds, military and judicial, call for note. If the settlement was attacked by men from another settlement, the defenders went to fight and some followed the lead of others. The military leaders may have been men respected for prowess or for skill in strategic planning. But they were neither elected nor designated in any regular way. They were simply the men whom the others in fact followed. Again, if a dispute arose within the settlement and the disputants were so powerful and so embittered that their quarrel threatened to destroy the settlement, there was need for a third person who would try to resolve the conflict. He might come forward on his own initiative, or he might be invited by others not immediately involved, or he might intervene in response to a request from one of the parties.

The requirements of defense, sometimes scarcely distinguishable from attack, and of appeasing internal disputes were public tasks to be performed by private persons. Sometimes there were other tasks concerning the whole community, and they were performed in the same way. For example, if an epidemic broke out in the village, one could ascertain from a soothsayer or an oracular shrine which god had been offended and how to appease him with a sacrifice. Then a private person served as priest to offer the sacrifice for the general welfare. But religious tasks can be disregarded here. Only leadership in warfare and settlement of disputes were later to generate public institutions.

Conditions of the informal kind here reconstructed are reflected in the *Odyssey*. There is no public meeting in Ithaka for twenty years, because the head of the most powerful household has gone to Troy (2.26–7). In Phaiakia there are twelve *basileis* and Alkinoos is the thirteenth (8.390–91). Although *basileus* is often translated as "king," the *basileis* of Phaiakia were too numerous for the implications of that word. They were private heads of powerful households. Other words for a private person who could be relied on to perform a public task were *archon* and *prytanis* and were favored in some cities.

In and after the eighth century growth of wealth and population brought changes. Many cities became so large that the informal gatherings, which had met to resist attack or watch an internal dispute and perhaps participate, became differentiated into an assembly (*ekklesia*) and a council (*boule*). All adult men could attend the assembly. The council began as a meeting of powerful men. Likewise public tasks came to be carried out so frequently that men performing them were transformed into public officers. Usually the offices were collegiate, annual, and elective. These features of the offices were caused by jealousy among men of power. The early constitutional history of the Greek cities is the story, not of competition between rival forms of government, but of the emergence of public authority, including officers and other organs, where there had previously been only private power. The development was from prestate conditions to the state and the state was of the kind called the *polis* or Greek city.[2]

POLITICAL ORGANS

The emergence of the Athenian polis was a protracted process with many stages. Organs of two kinds arose from the need to perform public tasks of the two kinds outlined above. There were political organs to formulate communal policy and judicial organs to resolve disputes. The relationship between the political organs – the assembly, the council, and the offices – was shaped decisively by the reforms that Kleisthenes carried out in the last decade of the sixth century.[3] He assigned the citizens to new subdivisions with hereditary membership in the male line. The basic unit was the deme. This was a village or a ward of a town. Henceforth Attica consisted of 139 demes. By a complicated scheme Kleisthenes grouped the demes to form ten *phylai* (singular *phyle*, usually translated into English as "tribe" by reference to the *tribus* of the Roman Republic). The phylai served for distributing the burdens, such as military service, and the benefits of citizenship. Kleisthenes also instituted a council of 500 members. Each of the phylai supplied fifty councilors, and within each phyle each deme supplied a number of councilors approximately proportional to its size. Within the deme councilors were chosen by casting lots. Membership was annual. In the fourth century a citizen was allowed only two terms on the council; the rule current in the fifth century is not known. Furthermore, starting in 501, the Athenians elected ten generals (*strategoi*) each year to exercise command of operations on land and sea.

The character and effect of the measures of Kleisthenes are in some ways obscure and disputed, but two conclusions can be asserted with confidence. The first concerns their military purpose. The reforms enabled the polis to draw on its manpower for armed action far more effectively than before.[4] The Athenians of the fifth century engaged frequently in such operations. Judging from their activities, they believed the converse of the doctrine of Clausewitz; they thought that policy is a continuation of warfare by other means.

The second conclusion concerns internal strife and stability. Telling of the rise of Peisistratos to power in the middle part of the sixth century, Herodotos (1.59.3) says that there was *stasis* between ambitious rivals. Stasis was competition of an intensity that could easily issue in disruption. The notion was familiar to the audience whom Herodotos addressed, and so he did not need to explain it. Again, after narrating the overthrow of Hippias, the son and successor of Peisistratos, Herodotos (5.66.2) says that stasis arose between Kleisthenes and Isagoras. In short, a return to stasis as usual took place. But by carrying his measures Kleisthenes defeated his rival and after that there was no more stasis for a long time. Thucydides (1.107.4) mentions a subversive conspiracy of 457, but nothing came of it. At last revolutions were launched in 411 and 404, but they were prompted by major defeats in the Peloponnesian War (431–404) and they were reversed after four months in 411 and after a little more than a year on the later occasion. Thus the measures of Kleisthenes achieved stability, whether by satisfying all Athenians or by denying opportunities to dissidents.

In the course of the fifth century changes were made within the inherited framework of political organs. They were prompted by the growth in the power, prosperity, and population of the Athenians. In 483 a rich vein of silver was discovered in the mines at Laureion. The proceeds were used for building triremes. So the Athenians increased their fleet on a large scale. It numbered 200 triremes by 480 and contributed much to the victory over the Persians at Salamis. By launching the Delian League in 478 and maintaining it for more than seventy years they gained large opportunities of enrichment. Changes in the political organs can be reviewed by considering the assembly, the council, and the offices in turn.

Neither the measures of Kleisthenes nor fifth-century changes added to the formal competence of the assembly. It had always exercised ultimate authority in determining policy, ever since the Athenians became conscious of themselves as a community. In 632 (?), when Kylon occupied the Acropolis in an attempt to make himself tyrant, operations against him were entrusted to the nine archons by "the Athenians" (Thuc. 1.126.7–8). Later Solon wrote laws "for the Athenians at their bidding" (Hdt. 1.29.1). Later still, about 560, a bodyguard was granted to Peisistratos by "the community (demos) of the Athenians" (Hdt. 1.59.5). But before the fifth century meetings of the assembly may have been infrequent. In the time of Aristotle it had a regular schedule amounting to forty meetings each year (AP 43.3–6). No such schedule is attested for the fifth century. But the growth in the international power of Athens brought plentiful business and therefore frequent meetings.

The task of the council of 500 was to prepare business for the assembly. The rule was that no item could be brought before the assembly unless it had first been considered by the council.[5] Since undertakings of state policy required authorization by the assembly, the council acted as a central clearinghouse for public business of all kinds. By the middle of the fifth century the council had adopted a practice of dividing itself into ten sections or *prytaneiai*, each consisting of the councilors belonging to one phyle. The year was divided into ten parts, each of thirty-five or thirty-six days. Each *prytaneia* of fifty councilors was on duty for a tenth of the year. The men on duty took their meals in the office building. They called meetings of the council every day, except during festivals, and they drew up the agenda. They also called meetings of the assembly.[6]

Among annual offices the one called "the nine archons" had been inherited from archaic conditions. One of the nine, now often called "the eponymous archon" because his name served to designate the year, had only "archon" as his title. Two others had the titles of basileus and polemarch. The remaining six were called *thesmothetai*. In consequence of the reforms of Kleisthenes their number was raised to ten by adding an officer called "the secretary of the thesmothetai," although collectively they continued to be called "the nine archons." In 487 the Athenians decided to choose them henceforth not by election but by sortition (casting lots). Presumably competition had aroused bitterness and corruption; the reform brought these abuses to an end.[7] Until 457 the nine archons were chosen from the upper two of the four property classes into which Solon had divided the citizens. But in 457 a reform admitted men of the third class to eligibility. Later, although the requirement was not changed in name, men of even the lowest class were in fact admitted, no questions being asked (Arist. *AP* 26.2; cf. 7.4). In the sixth century the nine archons may have exercised some degree of political power. But in consequence of sortition there was no guarantee that they would be men of sufficient talent or ambition to assert themselves. Apart from tasks concerning festivals the significant function that remained to them was to preside in courts.

In the lifetime of Pericles the growing prosperity and international power of the Athenians brought an increase in public business, and many boards were created to take charge of it. With few exceptions each board was annual and consisted of ten men chosen by sortition. Aristotle said that in the middle of the fifth century there were as many as seven hundred such officers. The figure may have been an exaggeration, but at least it suggests an order of magnitude.[8] More information about such boards of ten is available for the fourth century. There were, for example, officers to lease public contracts (*poletai*), receivers to accept payments due to the state (*apodektai*), officers in charge of the dockyards, supervisors of the market, supervisors of weights and measures, and officers in charge of the grain supply. The Athenian habit was to reduce each task to small compass so that it could be handled by a board lacking expertise. The major exception among offices was the generalship. The commanders had to be men of military talent. So the ten generals were chosen each year by election and there was no restriction on re-election. Consequently, in the fifth century, the generalship was the chief prize for political ambition. Pericles was elected general each year for fifteen years (443/2–429/8).

Before turning from political to judicial organs, a puzzle should be noted. It concerns the Areopagos and the work of Ephialtes. Apart from the council of 500 there was another council, called the council of the Areopagos, because it met on that hill. It consisted of all who had held any of the nine archonships. It may have come into being at an early stage, when small meetings of leading men began to be differentiated from general gatherings of the citizens. Perhaps it had considerable influence on politics in the sixth century, although that is conjectural. Aristotle (*AP* 25.2) says that in 462/1 a reformer called Ephialtes took powers away from the council of the Areopagos and gave them to the council of 500, the assembly, and the courts. Aristotle does not say what the powers were. Moreover, he was writing more than twenty years after Isokrates had composed a treatise, in form an oration, called *Areopagitikos*. In this work Isokrates said that long ago the council of the Areopagos had exercised extensive supervision over the education and general behavior of the citizens. He did not give illustrative detail; he did not say how the Areopagos had lost the censorial power that he attributed to it; and he did not name Ephialtes. Isokrates does not elsewhere show himself to be well informed on Athenian history, and he composed the *Areopagitikos* at a time when some other Athenians were indulging in speculative and tendentious reconstruction of the past of their city.

Some historians, relying on Isokrates, hold that the council of the Areopagos had formerly been powerful and Ephialtes accordingly carried out a major reform. Others suppose that the reform was small in compass. A defensible, though somewhat conjectural, view is that it deprived the Areopagos of a role in the scrutiny (*dokimasia*) that men chosen to the nine archonships had to undergo before taking office. Certainly after 462/1 the only significant task performed regularly by the council of the Areopagos was to serve as a court for trying some kinds of homicide.[9]

JUDICIAL ORGANS

If a dispute between two fellow citizens over something considered valuable cannot be settled informally, and if the community has grown strong enough to inhibit self-help, the two parties go to court. In classical Athens nearly all lawsuits were judged by courts of the kind called *dikasteria* (singular *dikasterion*). In the fifth century each dikasterion had 501 members. These were called *dikastai* (singular *dikastes*) a word sometimes rendered as "judges" or "jurors," but these translations can suggest the modern distinction between question of law and question of fact, and so it is better to call the members of the court "dikastai." Each lawsuit had two stages. The first was a hearing before a public officer, such as one of the nine archons, to clarify the issue between the two parties. The other was a hearing before 501 dikastai, and these decided the dispute by vote. Each stage requires consideration.

Each of the nine archons was authorized to receive cases of a defined kind. For example, the eponymous archon received cases concerning the family; the polemarch received disputes between resident aliens (Arist. *AP* 56–9). As more offices were created, many of them were authorized to receive cases arising in connection with their tasks. Occasionally the first stage of proceedings was a hearing not before an

officer but before the council of 500 or the assembly; the citizen taking initiative believed that his allegation was a matter of public concern
and so he reported it to one of these bodies. Even so, the division of
procedure into two stages was observed, and so the function of the first
stage calls for note.

When a dispute begins, the parties often argue at cross purposes.
Before the issue between them can be presented to a court for judgment,
it must be formulated as a proposition to be put before the court, which
can then find for the plaintiff or for the defendant. In Athens the first
stage, where the issue was clarified, was called *anakrisis* and it concluded
with *antomosia*; that is, the one party asserted and the other denied the
same proposition on oath.[10] If the parties were stubborn, it might have
been difficult for the officer to induce them to accept his formulation.
But the archon, the basileus, and the polemarch each had the help of two
assessors (*paredroi*), whom he chose at his discretion.[11] The thesmothetai,
numbering six, could perhaps seek help from one another.

At the second stage the officer brought the two parties before a
dikasterion. In a private dispute (or *dike*) each was allowed the same
limited time for addressing the audience. After both had spoken, each
was allowed a shorter time for rebuttal. When the last speech had been
delivered, the dikastai decided the issue without deliberating; they voted
secretly by means of counters (Arist. *AP* 68.4). In a dike only a person
who believed that his interests were at issue could take action as plaintiff. There were also *graphai*, sometimes called "public actions," where
anyone who wished (*ho boulomenos*) could present himself as plaintiff.
The law provided graphai for each of two reasons. Some graphai were
directed against activities harming the community; for example, there
was a graphe against misconduct on embassies and one against embez-
zling public funds. In other cases the law provided a graphe because the
person whose interests were at issue could not take action at law. For
example, there was a graphe for harm to the material interests of an
orphan. The orphan, being under age, could not take action, and his
guardian, who ought to have acted for him, was the most likely defendant. The time allowed for hearing a graphe in a dikasterion was not
restricted, as for a dike. A whole day was allowed for a graphe, whereas
a single dikasterion could hear several dikai in one day.

To serve as dikastes one had to be a male citizen, one had to have
reached one's thirtieth year of life, and one had to swear an oath to judge
justly. A list of 6,000 men available for such service was kept and revised
each year.[12] Sortition was employed to draw as many panels of 501 as
were required on each court day from the total of 6,000. The procedure

of sortition was altered twice between the time of Aristophanes and that of Aristotle, presumably to diminish the risk of corruption.[13] Payment for service as dikastes was introduced on the motion of Pericles and was extended to the political offices. The rate of pay was modest. As judicial business grew in the fifth century, it would not have been possible to attract enough volunteers without offering compensation.[14]

The judicial procedure just described, with numerous panels of (typically) 501 drawn from a pool of 6,000, was in operation by 422, when Aristophanes composed the *Wasps*. One may wonder when and how it had arisen. It is reasonable to guess that, long before, when Athens had fewer people, less wealth, and less litigation, a single dikasterion of 501 male citizens aged at least thirty and bound by oath sufficed. Herodotos (6.104.2) says that in 493 Miltiades, fleeing from the Persians, arrived in Athens from the Thracian Chersonese and was tried and acquitted in a dikasterion. Some readers have dismissed this statement as anachronistic, but there is no specific reason to doubt it. The classical Athenians believed that the dikasteria had been created by Solon, when he compiled laws early in the sixth century.[15] Doubtless a single dikasterion, meeting when lawsuits arose, was enough in the time of Solon. The hypothesis that his laws provided for trial before a dikasterion gains in plausibility when one considers the anomaly in classical procedure, namely the cases which were tried by courts of a different kind. These were the courts for homicide.

The classical Athenians believed that their laws on homicide had been made by a legislator called Drakon and that he was active before the time of Solon. Not much can be asserted about Drakon with any confidence, but it is credible that at an early stage homicide was the first matter on which the embryonic polis provided a forensic procedure. The developed set of laws, providing for trial of various kinds of homicide, is reported by Demosthenes (23.22–99) and Aristotle (*AP* 57.2–4). As for other matters, procedure was in two stages. In the first the (presumed) killer and the relative(s) of the victim appeared before the basileus. The second and definitive stage was a hearing before the council of the Areopagos or before a body called the *ephetai*; the forum depended on the nature of the act of homicide. The Areopagos judged charges of intentional homicide and wounding, including poisoning and arson. The ephetai numbered fifty-one and met in different places to try different kinds of homicide.

Historians used to assume that the Areopagos was at first the sole court for homicide and judged all such cases indiscriminately, but later it deputed competence for some cases to the ephetai; on this view the latter would be a commission of the Areopagos. But in recent decades the view has been gaining favor that the ephetai were at first the sole court for homicide and limited competence was later transferred to the Areopagos.[16] The competence exercised by the ephetai when they sat in the temple of Athena Pallas provides a strong indication in favor of the newer view. There they judged charges of three kinds: involuntary homicide, planning (or instigating: *bouleusis*) homicide if one set an agent to carry out the deed, and killing a slave or an alien. If the ephetai at the Palladion exercised competence deputed to them by the Areopagos, it is impossible to say why three such disparate charges were assigned to the same court; they cannot be subsumed under a single principle. The better alternative is to suppose that the ephetai originally had competence for homicide of all kinds, but a later reform assigned to the Areopagos competence to judge the charge of killing an Athenian citizen intentionally with one's own hands. Then the competence still exercised by the ephetai after the reform was the residue. At the earlier stage the aim of procedure was neither to convict nor to punish the culprit but to bring the dispute between the killer and the relatives of the victim to an end. At this stage one relied on one's relatives for security. The later reform, assigning limited competence over murder of citizens to the council of the Areopagos, could only come about when the state had grown powerful enough to present itself as the primary guarantor of safety.[17]

All that is known about the identity of the ephetai is that they numbered fifty-one. That figure lends itself to comparison with the size of the dikasterion. Conjecturally one may suppose that, when a case arose, the fifty-one ephetai were chosen by casting lots among male citizens who had reached their thirtieth year and were bound by an oath. That is, the ephetai were the model after which the dikasterion was later created. There is then no need to doubt that the dikasterion (that is, the procedure for choosing by sortition 501 male citizens aged at least thirty and bound by an oath) was created by Solon or perhaps regularized by him from earlier practices.

Study of the oath sworn by classical dikastai accords with this hypothesis and leads to further conclusions. The oath began with the undertaking:

> I will vote in accordance with the laws and with the decrees
> of the people of Athens and of the council of five hundred,
> and on matters where there are no laws, I will vote in accordance with the most just opinion.[18]

Attention will be given here first to the notion of the most just opinion and then to the expression "the laws and the decrees."

When a dispute comes into court, the bearing of the law on the case is hardly ever crystal clear. If it were so clear, the parties would be likely to settle out of court. The dispute arises and is presented to a court for judgment because there is room for disagreement about the proper way of applying the law to the case. A modern judge has the task of interpreting or applying the law in the light of his superior understanding of the body of law. He reasons by analogy, often drawing on rulings reported from past cases where the law was applied. His ruling, or that of a higher court if the case is appealed, can in turn be cited in future cases to illustrate proper application of the law. In this manner stability in judging cases is achieved.

The matter can be approached from a different point of view. The English word "law" has two senses.[19] It can mean a particular measure, such as an act of a legislature. Alternatively it can mean a body of law, as when people speak of the law of inheritance, the law of sale, the law of landlord and tenant, or with even greater generality, Roman law or Californian law. Some languages have different words for the two senses. A particular measure appears in Latin as "lex" (and in other guises), in French as "loi," and in German as "Gesetz." A body of law is "ius" in Latin, "droit" in French, and "Recht" in German. The particular laws are understood to be specific manifestations of the underlying body of law. The task of a judge is to reason from the particular laws to the underlying body of law and bring that body of law to bear on the case before him.

The Athenians did not have the modern concept of law. By *nomoi* they meant particular measures. They did not recognize an underlying body of law, which could be brought to bear on a novel case.[20] They knew that parties, assisted by orators, could argue by analogy from acknowledged laws to buttress a claim, but they thought that both parties to a single case could do so with equal plausibility.[21] They did not recognize that legal argument can lead to a valid conclusion. It was left to the Romans to make that discovery.[22] So the Athenian dikastes swore to vote in accordance with the most just opinion. He would listen to the opinions presented by the two parties and he would vote for the one that seemed to him more just. Consequently there could be no appeal from the judgment of an Athenian court. In modern practice a litigant may appeal if he believes that the judge has made a mistake in applying the law to the case. An Athenian dikastes could not be mistaken about what he thought.

The dikastes also swore to vote in accordance with the laws and the decrees. Allusions to "the *nomoi* (laws) and the *psephismata* (decrees)" occur frequently in forensic speeches of the fourth century, and a passage of Aristophanes (*Thesm.* 361–2) shows that this stock phrase was already current in the fifth. Aristotle and the author of the Pseudo-Platonic *Definitions* tried to say what kind of content was proper for measures of the two kinds: a law should state a general rule, but decrees should regulate particular cases; a law should be permanent but a decree should have only temporary validity.[23] These utterances of the philosophers were perhaps an attempt to articulate Athenian beliefs.

The classical Athenians thought that Solon had written their laws. Decrees were made by vote of the council and the assembly. By the time of Pericles the code compiled in the first half of the sixth century can scarcely have been adequate. Writers of the late fifth century sometimes use the word *nomos* of decrees, that is, of measures passed by vote of the assembly.[24] Starting in 410 the Athenians set up commissions to revise the laws. The work was interrupted by defeat in the Peloponnesian War and the ensuing revolution, but it was resumed and brought to fruition in 403–399. Then or soon afterwards a procedure was created for amending the code. So in the fourth century the distinction between laws and decrees was clear. Nomoi were measures occurring in the code or the amendments to it, and psephismata were measures voted by (the council and) the assembly.

One of the measures adopted in 403/2 in connection with revision of the laws provided:

> No decree of the council or of the people shall have greater authority than a law.[25]

There was a court procedure to uphold this rule; it was called the *graphe paranomon* or action against a measure contravening the laws. If anyone thought that a decree contravened the laws, he could prosecute the proposer of the decree in a dikasterion. The challenger could have recourse to this procedure even if the decree had already been voted by the assembly. If the dikasterion found for the plaintiff, the decree ceased to be valid.

As already noted, in the fourth century one could tell readily which measures were nomoi and which were psephismata. But in the fifth century the difference was not so clear, for as also noted, writers sometimes used the word *nomos* of mere decrees. Yet the forensic procedure of the graphe paranomon already existed. It is attested in connection with events of 415, 411, and 406.[26] Thus even before the revision of the laws in 410–399 the Athenians believed that the assembly ought only to pass measures within the framework set by the laws. They had not thought out the consequences of that belief, and so there was an anomaly within their institutions. Clarification was achieved in consequence of the revision of the laws.

DEMOKRATIA AND INDEPENDENT COURTS: AN ASSESSMENT

Pericles, as portrayed by Thucydides, boasts thus of the Athenian constitution in the Funeral Speech (2.37.1):

> We enjoy a constitution which does not envy the laws of our neighbors. On the contrary we provide them more with a model than we imitate them. Admittedly, since our constitution is administered not for a few but for the majority, it is called *demokratia*. Nevertheless, as regards the laws everyone gets equal treatment in private disputes, and as regards public esteem, in so far as each has a claim to recognition, he is not honored for the most part because of his class-affiliation but because of his merits, and on the other hand in a case of poverty, if a man can do the state some service, he is not debarred by obscurity.

These remarks employ three key ideas: a name, equality before the law, and public esteem. Each of them calls for comment.

First the name. This passage of the speech is sufficient evidence for saying that the Athenian constitution had come to be called *demokratia* and this designation could not be rejected. But the manner in which Pericles accepts the designation requires attention. He seeks to excuse the name. Even though the constitution is called *demokratia*, he can proceed to insist on its merits.[27] Two further considerations confirm that the word required apology. One is the usage of Herodotos. He gives a supposed debate between three Persian grandees about forms of government (3.80–83). One of them, Otanes, advocates "the rule of the multitude (*plethos archon*)," but he does not utter the word *demokratia*. Instead he says: "The rule of the multitude has the most beautiful name of all, *isonomia*." Elsewhere (5.43) Herodotos could call the recommendation of Otanes a proposal for *demokratia*. But the advocate himself, as portrayed by Herodotos, avoided the word. It would have had to be excused.

The other consideration leading to the same conclusion springs from etymology. Generally etymology only provides a clue to meaning if it is transparent to the people employing the word. The etymology of *demokratia* was transparent, as was that of its stock contrast, *oligarchia*. In the latter word the root *arch-* indicated rule of a mild kind; the derived verb means "to lead, to begin." But in *demokratia* the element *krat-* implies severe rule. In the *Prometheus Bound* preserved among the works of Aischylos the executioners who tie Prometheus to a rock bear the names Kratos and Bia: "Force" and "Violence."

The second idea on which the speech of Pericles draws in relation to the constitution is "equal treatment in private disputes." Enough has been said above to show that the Athenian courts were designed to provide equal access to judicial remedies. Thucydides makes Pericles say that equal treatment is provided for everyone. Yet one may wonder whether wealth perhaps brought an advantage in litigation. If a rich man could hire an expensive rhetorician to compose a speech, was he more likely to win? No conclusive answer can be given. But at least the extant speeches in private cases (notably speeches of Isaios and in the Demosthenic corpus) show that humble people, as well as rich people, sought redress in court.

The third idea employed in the speech is public esteem. From the earliest times Greeks were addicted to the competitive pursuit of honor (prestige, status, reputation; English and Greek each has many words for the same idea). The attainment of personal distinction was the goal of a public career. Pericles asserts that in the public sphere each competitor was judged by his merits and none was excluded by poverty. That was true but it was not the whole truth. Public policy was limited by money, and to understand the ramified finances of the Athenian state required the leisure which private wealth brings.[28] But at least there was no institutional bar to exclude a poor man.

It will be well to linger over the pursuit of public honor and ask how ambitious men set about it. Thucydides provides guidance. Narrating the steps that led to revolution in 411, he mentions "sworn associations" (*xynomosiai*) which there were in the city "for law-suits and elections" (*epi dikais kai archais*, 8.54.4). That is, there were several such associations competing with one another. Each tried to help its own members in rivalry with members of the other associations. Hasty readers have sometimes called these associations "oligarchic clubs," but that is an error. The associations were designed for the established framework of the courts and the elections. In 411 they were persuaded to desist from competing and collaborate instead. The consequence was revolution. But that consequence arose from the circumstances of 411, not from the permanent aims of the associations.

Lawsuits and elections were the occasions for competition. As many extant speeches illustrate, the graphe and other types of public action gave rivals the opportunity to sue one another. The annual office filled by election, as distinct from sortition, was the generalship. Embassies sent when need arose were also elective. The prestigious activities for an Athenian were to speak effectively in the assembly and the courts (i.e., to act as a *rhetor*) and to lead armed operations (to act as a *strategos*) with success. In the fourth century *rhetores kai strategoi* became a stock phrase, approximating in meaning to the modern word "politicians." Competition for prestige in public life was essentially personal in character. Naturally differences of opinion could arise on immediate questions of policy. But a politician did not derive his raison d'être from proposing a distinctive policy. For the most part the question was not what goal to pursue, but who could be most effective toward achieving the agreed goal.[29]

The absence of parties determined by distinctive programs is a difference between Athenian demokratia and modern representative governments, that is, governments of the kind usually meant by "democracy." There were other differences. The modern citizen casts, or does not cast, his vote and expects his representative to work for him for a period of years until the next election. The Athenian could, if he wished, vote at numerous meetings of the assembly each year; he did not employ a representative to vote for him. Again, the distribution of mandates among constituencies in modern nations is intended to provide even representation. For contrast, some Athenian figures call for note. Demetrios of Phaleron, who governed Athens for the Macedonians from 317 until 307, conducted a survey of the population and found that there were 21,000 adult male citizens.[30] The greater prosperity of the Athenians in the time of Pericles doubtless maintained a larger population, as is indeed indicated by the figures which Thucydides (2.13.6–8) gives for the forces mobilized in 431. But the Pnyx, the place where the assembly met, had room only for about 6,000 people in the fifth century. In the fourth century it was enlarged so that it could accommodate between 6,500 and 8,000 people.[31] Thus in the assembly demokratia exemplified government of the people, for the people, by about a third of the people or fewer.

To assess the achievement of the Athenians in organizing society one must go back to the courts. As will be remembered, the dikasteria differed in composition from the assembly. Any male citizen who had reached his eighteenth year could attend the assembly and vote, but to serve as dikastes the age required was the thirtieth year, an oath had to be sworn, and one had to be included in the annual list of 6,000. The courts exercised authority independent of the assembly. That is, a judgment issued by a court could not be overruled by the assembly. Early in 323 a dikasterion found Demosthenes guilty of accepting a bribe from a Macedonian fugitive and sentenced him to a fine of fifty talents. Unable to pay, he withdrew into exile. In the ensuing summer the death of Alexander altered the balance of political forces and so the Athenians wished to recall Demosthenes. They could not declare the judgment of the court invalid. Instead the assembly gave Demosthenes fifty talents, so that he could pay the fine (Plut. *Dem.* 27.6). Indeed, not only was the assembly not superior in authority to the courts, but through the graphe paranomon a court could overrule a decree that had been voted by the assembly. The theory implied by the graphe paranomon was that the assembly could only pass decrees within the framework set by the laws, and the courts had power to uphold the laws.

The question of the relative authority of the laws and of measures voted by the assembly was not merely theoretical but was sometimes put to the test. The belief that the demos, the assembled community, should be free to do whatever it wished is mentioned on two occasions in extant information about Athenian deliberations. The first was in the fall of 406. The Athenians had defeated the Peloponnesians in a naval battle at Arginousai. But a storm sprang up and the victors did not collect the corpses or the wounded. In Athens the enemies of the generals who had exercised command aroused agitation against them. The council formulated a proposal for trying the generals collectively on a single vote and the trial was not to be in a dikasterion but in the assembly. When this proposal was put before the assembly, there was some opposition, but those in favor of the proposal shouted that the demos should be allowed to do whatever it wished (Xen. *Hell.* 1.7.12). The assembly passed the proposal and after hearing the two sides condemned the generals to death. The occurrence was a miscarriage of justice and the Athenians regretted it ever after, as is clear from Xenophon's account.

Again, in the spring of 348 Apollodoros, a member of the council of 500, proposed a motion for assigning some funds to a military purpose. The account of the matter is given in a speech composed about eight years later and says that one of the considerations swaying Apollodoros was the belief that the demos should be free to do whatever it wished with its own money. The motion was passed by the council and by the assembly. But a rival politician prosecuted Apollodoros by graphe paranomon. The dikasterion upheld the prosecutor and condemned Apollodoros to a fine of a talent ([Dem.] 59.3–8).

The conclusion should be that the Athenians did not entrust comprehensive power to a single organ. Authority was divided between the assembly and the courts. Admittedly there were defects in the institutions. Notably there was no provision for legal memory; that is, there was no assurance that like cases occurring at different times would be judged alike. But at least the judicial organs of the Athenians were independent of their political organs. That is why their constitutional structure deserves respect. For the independence of the judicial authority safeguards the liberty of the citizen.

SUGGESTIONS FOR FURTHER READING

W. R. Connor, *The New Politicians of Fifth-Century Athens* (Princeton: Princeton University Press, 1971); C. W. Fornara and L. J. Samons, *Athens from Cleisthenes to Pericles* (Berkeley: University of California Press, 1991); A. R. W. Harrison, *The Law of Athens*, 2 vols. (Oxford: Oxford University Press, 1968 and 1971); L. Kallet-Marx, *Money, Expense and Naval Power in Thucydides'* History *1–5.24* (Berkeley: University of California Press, 1993); D. M. Lewis et al., eds., *Cambridge Ancient History*, vol. 5, *The Fifth Century*, second edition (Cambridge: Cambridge University Press, 1992); J. H. Lipsius, *Das attische Recht und Rechtsverfahren*, 3 vols. (Leipzig: Teubner, 1905–1915; reprinted at Darmstadt: Wissenschaftliche Buchgesellschaft, 1966); R. Meiggs, *The Athenian Empire* (Oxford: Oxford University Press, 1972).

NOTES

1   R. Drews, *Basileus: The Evidence for Kingship in Geometric Greece* (New Haven: Yale University Press, 1983).

2   See M. Stahl, *Aristokraten und Tyrannen im archaischen Athen: Untersuchungen zur Überlieferung, zur Sozialstruktur und zur Entstehung des Staates* (Stuttgart: Steiner, 1987), pp. 137–232 (the basic inquiry). On conditions reflected in the *Odyssey* see A. G. Geddes, "Who's Who in Homeric Society?" *CQ* 34 (1984): 17–36. The development of the Athenian state was further complicated and delayed by the size of Attica, the territory that Athens eventually controlled. See Greg Anderson, "Alkmeonid Homelands, Political Exile and the Unification of Attica," *Historia*

49 (2000): 387–412. For Attica before Kleisthenes the importance of small groups based on locality or kinship has been emphasized by P. B. Manville, *The Origins of Citizenship in Ancient Athens* (Princeton: Princeton University Press, 1990).

3   There is much disagreement about the character of the reforms. The view followed here accords with that proposed by G. R. Stanton, "The Tribal Reform of Kleisthenes the Alkmeonid," *Chiron* 14 (1984): 1–41. The literary sources are Hdt. 5.66–9; Arist. *AP* 20–22.

4   Indeed F. J. Frost ("The Athenian Military before Cleisthenes," *Historia* 33 [1984]: 283–94) maintains, perhaps correctly, that previously there were no armed actions launched by the Athenian state; the few attested enterprises were carried out by men of private power.

5   This formulation is known from Plut. *Sol.* 19.1; there it has been retrojected on to a supposed Solonian council of 400.

6   Arist. *AP* 43.2–4. The standard study of the council is P. J. Rhodes, *The Athenian Boule* (Oxford: Oxford University Press, 1972; revised reprint, 1984).

7   Arist. *AP* 22.5. Aristotle (*Pol.* 5.1303a13–16) says that sortition was adopted at Heraia to put an end to corrupt practices. Disruptive competition is reported from Athens for the period 590–579 (Arist. *AP* 13.1–2).

8   Arist. *AP* 24.3: Aristotle says that there were 700 officers operating in Attica, apart from those sent abroad. For defense of Aristotle's estimate see M. H. Hansen, "Seven Hundred *archai* in Classical Athens," *GRBS* 21 (1980): 151–73.

9   G. L. Cawkwell ("*Nomophylakia* and the Areopagus," *JHS* 108 [1988]: 1–12) maintains that the Areopagos had had censorial power and Ephialtes put an end to this. P. J. Rhodes (n. 6, pp. 144–207) attributes extensive measures to Ephialtes. E. Ruschenbusch ("Ephialtes," *Historia* 15 [1966]: 369–76) shows how unreliable Isokrates and Aristotle are on Ephialtes; cf. E. Ruschenbusch, "*Patrios Politeia*. Theseus, Drakon, Solon und Kleisthenes in Publizistik und Geschichtsschreibung des 5. und 4. Jahrhunderts v. Chr.," *Historia* 7 (1958): 398–424.

10   The modern word is "joinder of the issue." In the fourth century a new procedure, called *paragraphe*, came to be widely used; this transferred much of the task from the officer to a preliminary session of the dikasterion. The officer's share was said to be reduced to *proanakrisis*. This new development is well attested and facilitates reconstruction of the officer's earlier function. See R. Sealey, *The Justice of the Greeks* (Ann Arbor: University of Michigan Press, 1994), pp. 134–7.

11   Arist. *AP* 56.1; cf. K. A. Kapparis, "Assessors of Magistrates (Paredroi) in Classical Athens," *Historia* 47 (1998): 383–93.

12   For the age limit: Arist. *AP* 63.3. For the total of 6,000: Aristoph. *Wasps* 655–63; cf. J. H. Kroll, *Athenian Bronze Allotment Plates* (Cambridge, MA: Harvard University Press, 1972), pp. 69–90.

13   The first procedure is known mainly from the *Wasps* of Aristophanes. The second, known from the *Ekklesiazousai* and the *Ploutos* of the same author, was introduced about 409 (see A. L. Boegehold, "Many Letters: Aristophanes *Plutus* 1166–7," in A. L. Boegehold et al., eds., *Studies Presented to Sterling Dow on His Eightieth Birthday*, Greek, Roman and Byzantine Monographs, no. 10 [Durham, NC: Duke University, 1984], pp. 23–30). The third is described by Aristotle *AP* 63–9. For a summary account see M. H. Hansen, *The Athenian Democracy in the Age of Demosthenes*, trans. J. A. Crook (Norman: University of Oklahoma Press, 1991), p. 183.

14 Introduction of pay for dikastai: Arist. *AP* 27.3; *Pol.* 2.1274a8–9. For discussion
of the rate and its economic significance see A. H. M. Jones, *Athenian Democracy*
(Oxford: Blackwell, 1957; paperback by Johns Hopkins University Press, 1986),
pp. 17–18, 49–50, 80–81.

15 Arist. *Pol.* 2.1273b41–1274a5; cf. *AP* 7.3, 9.1. Solon was archon in 594/3. He may
have carried his measures then or somewhat later, about 580–570.

16 This view has been espoused for different reasons by E. Ruschenbusch ("*Phonos*.
Zum Recht Drakons und seiner Bedeuting für das Werden des athenischen
Staates," *Historia* 9 [1960]: 129–54), M. Gagarin (*Drakon and Early Athenian Homi-
cide Law* [New Haven: Yale University Press, 1981], pp. 127–37), and R. Sealey
("The Athenian Courts for Homicide," *CP* 78 [1983]: 275–96).

17 Before the end of the fifth century ways were found to bring cases of homicide
before regular dikasteria; see E. M. Carawan, "*Ephetai* and Athenian Courts for
Homicide in the Age of the Orators," *CP* 86 (1991): 1–16. But the laws, revised in
the last years of the century, continued to provide for trials before the Areopagos
and the ephetai.

18 The oath was reconstructed from remarks of the orators by M. Fränkel, "Der
attische Heliasteneid," *Hermes* 13 (1878): 452–66. For the clause on voting in
accordance with the most just opinion see Dem. 20.118, 23.96, 39.40, 57.63;
Pollux 8.122.

19 "Law. 1.a. The body of rules, whether proceeding from formal enactment or
from custom, which a particular state or community recognizes as binding on its
members or subjects. (In this sense usually *the law*.) 2.a. One of the individual rules
which constitute the "law" (sense 1) of a state or polity. In early use only pl. The
plural has often a collective sense (after L. *jura, leges*) approaching sense 1." (*Oxford
English Dictionary*).

20 Cf. E. Ruschenbusch, "*Dikastérion pantón kyrion*," *Historia* 6 (1957): 257–65.

21 M. Hillgruber, *Die zehnte Rede des Lysias*, Untersuchungen zur antiken Literatur
und Geschichte, Band 29 (Berlin and New York: De Gruyter, 1988), pp. 105–20.

22 Cf. B. W. Frier, *The Rise of Roman Jurists. Studies in Cicero's pro Caecina* (Princeton:
Princeton University Press, 1985). The Roman discovery has been inherited by
modern states, although the judicial machinery is different. In Rome the rulings
preserved were answers given by jurisconsults to questions of law. In modern states
they are precedents embodied in judgments of courts. The same discovery was
made in Japan in the Tokugawa period (1603–1868). The courts of the shogunate
kept records of civil cases with the judgments and the grounds of the judgments as
precedents for future trials; see J. H. Wigmore, *Law and Justice in Tokugawa Japan,
Part I: Introduction* (Tokyo: Kokusai Bunka Shinkokai, 1969), pp. xxi–xxii; cf. J. H.
Wigmore, *A Panorama of the World's Legal Systems* (Washington, DC: Washington
Law Book Company, 1921), pp. 504–19.

23 Arist. *EN* 5.1137a31–38a2; [Plat.] *Def.* 415b; cf. Arist. *Pol.* 4.1292a4–7, 32–7.

24 Xen. *Hell.* 1.7.20 and 23; *Mem.* 1.2.42; Andok. 1.96.

25 Andok. 1.87; Dem. 23.87, cf. 24.30.

26 Andok. 1.17, 22 (for 415); Thuc. 8.67, cf. Arist. *AP* 29.4 (for 411); Xen. *Hell.*
1.7.12–13, 20–23 (for 406). Note also an occurrence of 414 or earlier: [Plut] *Ten
Orators* 833d; Harpok. s.v. *keleontes*; Antiph. frr. 8–14 (Blass).

27 The translation offered here tries to do justice to the tone of regret in the sentence.
In Greek that tone is indicated in the double employment of the particles *men* and

de. On interpretation of the sentence see R. Hirzel, *Themis, Dike und Verwandtes* (Leipzig: Teubner, 1907), p. 263 with n. 8; J. R. Grant, "Thucydides 2.37.1," *Phoenix* 25 (1971): 104–7.

28   L. Kallet-Marx, "Money Talks: Rhetor, Demos and the Resources of the Athenian Empire," in R. Osborne and S. Hornblower, eds., *Ritual, Finance, Politics: Athenian Democratic Accounts Presented to David Lewis* (Oxford: Oxford University Press, 1994), pp. 227–51.

29   See P. J. Rhodes, "Political Activity in Classical Athens," *JHS* 106 (1986): 132–44, and "Who Ran Democratic Athens?" in P. Flensted-Jensen et al., eds., *Polis and Politics. Studies in Ancient Greek History Presented to Mogens Herman Hansen on his Sixtieth Birthday* (Copenhagen: Museum Tusculanum Press, 2000), pp. 465–77.

30   Ktesikles, *FGrHist* 245 F 1 apud Athen. 6.272c; cf. Diod. 18.18.4–5 and Plut. *Phok.* 28.4. On an alternative interpretation 21,000 was the number of those able to bear arms and the total would be higher.

31   M. H. Hansen (n. 13), pp. 128–31.

11: ATHENS AND SPARTA AND THE COMING OF THE PELOPONNESIAN WAR

J. E. Lendon

INTRODUCTION

It was three days' walk from the borders of Attica to the crest of the vale of Laconia, from Athens, the city wreathed in violet, to Lacedaemon, clad in mountains and in bronze. The wayfarer from Athens left behind him the pandemonium of lucre, naval empire, and democracy, and entered the hushed streets of Sparta, where by an ancient law no coin might be found, where boys were schooled to silence and men to speak rarely and shortly, in the Laconic way. So close in miles but so contrary in manners, in the time of the Athenian statesman Pericles Athens and Sparta came to fight a great war together, the war we call the Peloponnesian War.

Two features of Sparta are especially important for understanding her relations with the Athens of Pericles. The first is the warlike quality of Spartan society. The toiling of Sparta's helots in the fields of Laconia and Messenia gave Spartans the leisure to devote themselves to hunting, athletics, and martial exercise. And the harsh Spartan upbringing, the whipping contests and starvation, and Spartan military training – no other state in fifth-century Greece trained all her citizen soldiers – left the Spartans supreme on the field of battle. This military dominance enabled the Spartans to forge an alliance of defeated, timid, or hopeful states, the Peloponnesian League (so we call it). Its members were wards against the rising of the helots, and allies against other enemies, especially against proud Argos, Sparta's old foe in the Peloponnese. But together Sparta's league was as strong as its mistress: Sparta could bully one town or a few, but not all and not the greatest, such as Corinth.

To lead her alliance to war Sparta needed in practice to gain her allies' consent.

The martial tone of Spartan society, moreover, manifested itself in an unusual degree of competitiveness between Spartan citizens. Ancient Greek society in general was extremely rivalrous, but nowhere was this competitiveness as publicly encouraged and institutionalized as at Lacedaemon. Boys competed relentlessly with one another in the course of their public education; young warriors competed for membership in the mess and in the *hippeis*, the "cavalry," an honor roll of 300 paradoxically arrayed on foot around the king in battle. So intense was this competition that fights were frequent (Xen. *Lac. Pol.* 4.6), and boys might be killed in struggles (Xen. *Anab.* 4.8.25; Plut. *Apop. Lac.* 233F–4A; *Lac. Apop.* 240E–F). Greybeards vied for membership in the Gerousia, the Spartan council of elders. The wider significance of this Spartan competitiveness is that it was not only displayed at home, but also projected into the international realm to govern relations between Lacedaemon and other states. "Slow to go to war, unless by necessity" (1.118.2)[1] the Spartans may have been, but young Spartans learned their definition of necessity in a Sparta where contests over rank and pride were decided by fighting. Looking back, Polybius thought the Spartans "the most rivalrous for honor, greedy for rulership, and overbearing toward the other Greeks" (6.48.8).

GREEK THINKING ABOUT THE CAUSES OF WARS

To investigate the origins of the Peloponnesian War is not only to trace the diplomatic history of the age of Pericles, but also to investigate the dynamics of Greek international politics, Greek thinking about why wars occur, and the ways in which that thinking was similar to and different from our own.

Thucydides, the historian of the war, is clear on why he thinks the war between Athens and Sparta broke out. "The truest cause of the war... was the growing greatness of the Athenians, and the fear this inspired, which compelled the Lacedaemonians to go to war" (1.23.6). Elsewhere he defines this "growing greatness" more exactly as the increase of Athenian power, *dynamis*, evident because "most of Greece was already subject to them" (1.88), and expands upon the nature of the threat Athenian *dynamis* posed: it was to Sparta's allies (1.118.2). This cause is sharply distinguished from the immediate events that led up to war, which Thucydides terms the "grounds for complaint" (*aitiai*) and "points of difference" (*diaphorai*) (1.23.5),[2] which are not the "truest cause" of the war, but which, however they did contribute, were in some way less important.

The majority of modern students of the fifth century B.C. have accepted Thucydides' explanation. They have done so because Thucydides argues for his explanation so skillfully, but also because the cause offered by Thucydides fits contemporary expectations so comfortably: their gut feeling is that fear of power *is* why wars break out. But this comfort is an artefact, an invisible result of the vast later influence of Thucydides on Western thought about relations between nations. Thucydides influenced Hobbes, his translator; and Thucydides and Hobbes together are the progenitors of the leading style in the contemporary study of international relations, called "Realism."[3] And unrigorous realism – analysis in terms of power and fear – is the vulgate of the age, the model of foreign relations unreflectively offered up in the newspapers: if looking out the window we approve of Thucydides' description of the landscape, we do so unaware that it was Thucydides who sited the window in the first place.

Thucydides' realism seems conventional and natural to us, yet his account of the causes of the war would have struck his contemporaries as surprising, or even perverse: hence his emphatic distinction between the "truest cause" and the mere "grounds for complaint" and "points of difference" (1.23.5–6), which others evidently thought were decisive; hence his emphatic reiteration of his cause (1.88; cf. 1.118.2); hence Thucydides' admission that *his* cause was not much discussed at the time (1.23.6). Thucydides' first book is shot through with subterranean arguments for his understanding of the causes of the war. Speeches that Thucydides puts in the mouths of historical figures keep mentioning the power of Athens (esp. 1.68–85.2), despite Thucydides' insistence that the Spartans' fear of Athens's power had not been much mentioned at the time. Had Thucydides' interpretation been natural to his audience he would hardly have had to prosecute so vigorous and ingenious a polemic.

The direction of Thucydides' argument suggests that many Greeks interpreted the origins of the war precisely in terms of the "grounds for complaint" and "points of difference" whose importance Thucydides worked to diminish. But modern historians have struggled to place these in a compelling narrative of the war's origins: to build a chain of causation to the outbreak of hostilities from the "grounds for complaint" and "points of difference." This is difficult because the "grounds for complaint" and "points of difference" are small things, taking place at the edge of the Greek mental world. They have nothing directly to do with Sparta, only with her allies, and arguably they touch upon her allies' pride more than their vital interests. Why on earth would the Spartans go to war with Athens over such things? But Greeks would have had far less trouble understanding this logic than we do: other Greek authors – and Thucydides in other passages – reveal the mechanics of causation that Thucydides rejected in this case. Looking back over the history of the Peloponnese from centuries later, Polybius ascribed its endless warfare to the fact that its inhabitants were "all both lordly and freedom-loving by nature, and inclined to be utterly unyielding about conceding first place" (5.106.5). The way he and other Greeks believed war arose from this struggle for first place – *proteion* – can be summarized thus:[4]

A. Greek states view themselves as ranked against each other (and barbarian states) by their relative *timē* or *axioma*, prestige or honor or worth.

- Rank is related to, and in part derivative of, the power of a state, but is conceptually distinct.[5] Myth and history contribute to rank, regardless of power.[6]
- Superior rank or supreme rank (*hegemonia*) conveys the right to honors and deferential compliance from other states.[7]
- A state believing that it is equal in rank to another must *not* defer to that other state, because that is an admission of inferiority.[8]

B. Wars result from perceived attempts to alter relative rank.

- Rank is upheld by deference, hurt by insult (*hybris*).
- War results when a state perceives that another has insulted it – practiced *hybris* upon it.[9]
- *Hybris* can be a military attack or any act of disrespect or failure of deference if deference is felt to be due, or the display of an arrogant attitude, "thinking big" (*mega phronein*).[10] In Thucydidean terms, acts of *hybris* are "grounds for complaint" and "points of difference."[11]
- Minor acts of disrespect and arrogant attitudes are constant, but war is not: states must be sensitized to view minor acts of disrespect as *hybris*.

C. The primary purpose of war over rank is revenge.

- The insulted state feels anger (*orgē*) and seeks revenge, which restores the previous relative ranking of the states.[12]

- Desire for vengeance is increased by the recollection and reinterpretation (or invention) of previous incidents as other acts of *hybris*.[13]
- If immediate revenge cannot be taken, the insulted state abides in enmity or hatred (*echthra* or *misos*) toward the insulting state.

D. Traditionally, revenge consists of victory in hoplite battle or ravaging the agricultural land of the enemy. "Do not practice *hybris*, lest your cicadas sing from the ground."[14]

Thucydides is hardly alone among Greek authors in ascribing the causes of wars to considerations of fear and power.[15] But this is a less common diagnosis than the theory of causation that traces war to conflict over rank. And this prevalent Greek conception of the origins of Greek wars – against which Thucydides was struggling to make room for his own – attracts our attention here for one very simple reason: Thucydides' fear-of-power explanation was wrong. As Donald Kagan showed in 1969, Athenian power was not growing.[16] And if Thucydides was wrong, our next resort for a cause should be the theory that Thucydides was fighting against, that the war broke out not over questions of power, but over questions of rank.[17]

In other words, rather than accept or try to repair Thucydides' power-and-fear explanation, it may be better to borrow the model of causation that underlies (for example) Diodorus of Sicily's description of the outbreak of a war between Argos and Mycenae in the 460s.

> At this time a war broke out between Argos and Mycenae for the following reasons. The Myceneans, because of the old worth (*axioma*) of their country, would not submit to the Argives, like the other cities of Argolis, but when they were given orders they alone paid them no heed. And they disputed with the Argives about the temple of Hera, and thought themselves worthy to conduct the Nemean games. . . . In sum, the Argives suspected them, fearing lest, if they grew more powerful, they would contend for the *hegemonia*, on account of the ancient pride of their city. The Argives, being estranged for these reasons (*aitiai*), having been eager of old to raise up their city, and thinking that this was a good opportunity . . . marched against the Myceneans.
>
> (11.65.1–3)[18]

The Argives and the Myceneans are rivals in rank: this rivalry is manifested especially in the religious sphere, with wrangling over temples and games. The Argives think they have the right to give orders to the Myceneans; the Myceneans, thinking themselves equal in rank – Mycenae was the ancient seat of Agamemnon – refuse to defer, refuse to obey, refuse even to notice. This failure of deference – an insult – is a *casus belli*. The Argives come to fear the power of the Myceneans, not because the latter's power is inherently terrifying, but because they diagnose a Mycenean thirst for rank: the Argives fear that the Myceneans will try to take from them the *hegemonia* – a term implying superiority especially in rank.[19] It is concern about rank that makes the Argives sensitive to the growth of Mycenean power. The conventional Greek thinking represented here – the refusal of a proud state to defer to another that considers itself superior in rank, and this being considered a cause of war – provides a handy tool with which to understand the origins of the Peloponnesian War.

THE FIFTY YEARS BEFORE THE PELOPONNESIAN WAR

Sparta was the leader of the Greek alliance formed to oppose Xerxes' invasion of Greece. The Spartans led the league by land and by sea, and their *hegemonia* was symbolized by their holding the honorable right of the line at the battle of Plataea (Hdt. 9.28; 479 B.C.).[20] But even while the war raged, the Athenians chafed at Spartan primacy, maneuvering (unsuccessfully) for command of the Greek fleet (Hdt. 7.161, 8.2–3).[21] And immediately after the war a controversy between Athens and Sparta displayed how nettling Athens found her inferior rank (?479/8 B.C.).[22] Hearing that the Athenians were rebuilding the walls of their ruined city, the Spartans sent to bid them desist.[23] This request from Sparta to Athens was the instruction of a superior in rank – a *hegemon* – to an inferior in rank, who could be expected to defer to her superior's desires. And this Athens was not prepared to do. Spartan interference was forestalled by guile and the walls were finished quickly: evidently a Spartan invasion was thought possible. And then the author of the deceit, Themistocles, told the Spartans forthrightly – Thucydides tells us – that Athens would defer to Sparta no longer. Hereafter Athens intended to be "of equal weight in the common councils" (1.89.3–92.1; quoted 1.91.7).

> Hearing these things, the Spartans manifested no open anger (*orgē*) towards the Athenians . . . because they were friendly

towards them because of their zeal in the Persian War, but nevertheless, not getting what they wanted they were secretly vexed.

(1.92.1)

The insolent Athenian failure to defer to Sparta, which considered herself supreme in rank, was a cause of *orgē*, anger, which was often sufficient to cause Greek states to go to war (so the Athenian fear of invasion was not ill-founded). But given the otherwise good relations between Athens and Sparta, Sparta was not sufficiently sensitized to Athenian insults for war to result.

Soon after the affair of the walls, events conspired to confirm Athenian pretensions to equality in rank by giving the Athenians the command at sea they had been denied during the war. There was still need for an allied fleet to protect Greece against the return of the Persians, to uproot Persia's remaining holdings in the Aegean (1.89.2, 1.94.2), and to take revenge upon the Persians for their invasion (1.96.1). But those allies supplying ships found the Spartan commander of the fleet – Pausanias, the victor of Plataea – harsh and strange; they intrigued to procure his recall to Lacedaemon, and refused to accept his successor. The allies appealed to the Athenians to take the lead (1.94–6; cf. 1.75.2).[24] This the Athenians did with alacrity, enrolling the cities around the Aegean in a new league that met on the sacred isle of Delos, and setting the contribution – in ships or treasure – of each of them (1.96–97.1, 99.3; ?477 B.C.). A story swims up from the murk – centuries later, perhaps an invention – that the Spartans debated whether this Athenian supremacy at sea could be endured, and many Spartans thought not, arguing that it should be wrested from the Athenians by war; but no action was taken. In the laconic croak of a Spartan elder: "it does not profit Sparta to dispute for the sea" (Diod. 11.50; ?475 B.C.). An Athenian speaker later in Thucydides draws out the rank implications of these events: "after the Persian wars we had a fleet, and so got rid of the rule (*archē*) and supremacy in rank (*hegemonia*) of the Lacedaemonians, it being no more fitting for us to obey them, than they us, except insofar as they were stronger at the time" (6.82.3). A restatement, in other words, of Themistocles' doctrine of the equality in rank between Athens and Sparta.

Subsequent Athenian actions against Persia are important because they tended to confirm Athens's sense that her rank was equal, at least, to that of Sparta. Why should the Athenians take second place to the Spartans, after they and their league defeated the Persians at Eurymedon, destroying 200 ships (1.100.1; ?467 B.C.)?[25] But in the years of Athens's eastern triumphs, relations between Sparta and Athens remained good because Athens's hammer of the Persians, Cimon, was a convinced admirer of Sparta (Plut. *Cimon* 16). Athenian politics immediately after the war was dominated by the rivalry of Cimon and Themistocles. Eventually Themistocles was exiled (?471/0 B.C.) and settled at Argos, Sparta's hereditary enemy in the Peloponnese. When the Spartans brought against him charges of conspiring with the Persians, his political enemies at Athens were delighted to connive, the Athenians were swayed to lay him under a sentence of death, and Themistocles was harried from Greece, fleeing ultimately to the court of the Great King of Persia (1.135.2–138).[26] On this occasion, unlike when Athens had rebuilt her walls, what the Spartan *hegemon* asked, Athens deferentially did.

Some years later (?464 B.C.) there was a great earthquake at Sparta followed by a revolt of the helots. The Spartans besieged the helots at Mt. Ithome in Messenia and called for the help of their allies and friends, including the Athenians, who came in force under Cimon (1.101.2–1.102.2). The controversy over the sending of this expedition – reported by Plutarch – reveals the range of Athenian attitudes toward their city's rank. The politician Ephialtes opposed the expedition, we are told, arguing that Athens "ought not help or raise up again a city that was a rival to Athens, but to let the pride of Sparta be overthrown and be trod underfoot." To Ephialtes the cities were rivals for rank, and the rebellion of the helots was an opportunity to surpass Sparta. His opponent Cimon, we are told, carried the Athenians with the argument that Athens "not allow Hellas to become lame, nor Athens to be deprived of her yokefellow" (Plut. *Cimon* 16.8). In Cimon's metaphors – of a man with two legs, and a yoke with two oxen – Athens and Sparta are equal in rank, and that is as it should be. But neither Athenian politician, not even the pro-Spartan Cimon, argued that Sparta was Athens's *hegemon*, and therefore had the right to deference and the compliance that flowed from deference. Both were heirs to Themistocles' declaration at Sparta that Athens would defer no longer.

"The first open point of difference (*diaphora*) between the Lacedaemonians and the Athenians was the result of this campaign" (1.102.3). The Spartans conceived a suspicion of the Athenians – thinking them "bold and revolutionary and of alien stock," Thucydides suggests (1.102.3) – and sent them away, alone of those who had come to help. The Spartans said nothing of their suspicions, claiming merely that the

Athenians were no longer needed. Seeing through the pretense, the Athenians

> took it ill and thought it unworthy of themselves to be treated so by the Lacedaemonians, and straight away after they got home, renounced the alliance against the Persians, and became allies of the Argives, the Spartans' enemies.
>
> (1.102.4; cf. Plut. *Cimon* 17.2; ?461/60 B.C.)[27]

Thucydides' description of this decisive break with Sparta – eventually to lead to war – fits very neatly into the Greek conception of war as arising from insult. But why the insult, when relations between Athens and Sparta had recently been so warm? The two cities had different senses of their relative rank. The Spartans were acting as supreme in rank, as *hegemon*. The alliance against the Persians that made their primacy manifest was still in force. Had not the Athenians sentenced Themistocles to death when the Spartans asked? Had not the Athenians come to Ithome when the Spartans called? These were the actions of a deferential inferior, an inferior one could order home when convenient, an inferior who would not be insulted by such treatment, or who, if insulted, would swallow its spleen. But neither anti- nor even pro-Spartan sentiment in Attica accepted that Athens was still Sparta's inferior. Athens came as an equal to Ithome – so even Cimon insisted. To dismiss an equal was to treat Athenians "unworthily" of their estimation of themselves: to insult them. The insult led to war; Cimon's association with the Spartans resulted in his exile when he returned to Athens (Plut. *Cimon* 17.2). Briefly his rival Ephialtes was supreme, but he was mysteriously murdered. Now Pericles began his ascent to predominance at Athens ([Arist.] *AP* 25–27.1).

The process of going to war over rank, as the Athenians were now doing, often involved both the reinterpretation of past dealings with the enemy as insults and the invention of grievances. In this light should be understood the odd tale that Thucydides tells of a secret Spartan agreement to invade Attica in support of the rebellion from the Athenian alliance of Thasos, an island in the northern Aegean (1.101.1–2; 465 B.C.).[28] It is alleged that the Spartans were conveniently prevented from keeping this engagement by the earthquake and the secession of the helots to Ithome. Thucydides no doubt thought the story true, but it has all the signs of a manufactured *casus belli*: at once secret and stillborn, it was quite impossible to prove or disprove. Perhaps there had been communication between Thasos and Sparta. In the hour of fury after the dismissal of Cimon from Ithome it is easy to imagine the angry invention or elaboration of such contacts.

The long war that now broke out – the so-called "First Peloponnesian War" (?461/60–446/5 B.C.) – went well for Athens at the start. Megara, the small state that controlled the northern approaches to the isthmus of Corinth, defected from the Spartan alliance to the Athenian because Corinth, another Spartan ally, was fighting her over their mutual border. "And the fierce hatred (*misos*) of the Corinthians for the Athenians arose first and especially from this" (1.103.4).[29] As long as the war was carried on primarily between Athens and Sparta's allies, Athens won more battles than she lost by land and sea (1.105–6). But when the Athenians and their allies met the Spartans and their allies at Tanagra in Boeotia, the Spartans won, and reemphasized their superiority in rank by ravaging the land of Megara when they passed through it on their way home (1.107–108.2; ?457 B.C.).[30] Two months later the Athenians were back in Boeotia, and by defeating the Boeotians at the battle of Oenophyta they made Boeotia their dependency. Aegina, an old enemy of Athens that had taken the Spartan side in this war, also surrendered to Athens (1.108.2–4; ?457 B.C.).[31] In neither case did the Spartans act. Nor had they invaded Attica in the years before Tanagra. Were they prevented by the Athenian possession of Megara (cf. 1.107.3)?[32] Or by the continued resistance of the helots on Ithome, or some dimly seen problems in the Peloponnese (cf. 1.118.2)?[33] But those considerations had not kept them mewed up in the Peloponnese earlier in the year, when they set out upon the campaign that ended at Tanagra.[34] And even then they had not marched out intending to fight the Athenians: the Athenians had brought them to battle when they were marching back from an adventure in Doris, their legendary homeland in the north (1.107.2–6).

Why were the Spartans so passive? Looked at in terms of rank, they had no reason to be otherwise. This was a war the Athenians had undertaken in quest of revenge for an insult: it was for the Athenians to march into Laconia. Athenian dread of doing so – of attacking the Spartans directly at all, on our evidence – before Tanagra upheld Sparta's claims to higher rank. At Tanagra Sparta vindicated that claim against an Athenian challenge, and with her supreme rank safe, felt no compelling reason to act subsequently. After Tanagra the Athenians raided around the coast of the Peloponnese and made a descent upon Laconia itself (1.108.5; ?456 B.C.). Diodorus's source interprets this raid correctly: it was undertaken "to humble the fame of the Spartans" (Diod. 11.84.3). It was revenge for the defeat at Tanagra, an attempt to re-assert the rank of the Athenians after their defeat.[35] The next set of Athenian raids of which we hear – upon the northern Peloponnese – were led by Pericles (1.111.2–3; ?454 B.C.).

A few years later, Cimon, who had returned from exile, arranged a truce for five years between the Athenians and Spartans (1.112.1; Plut. *Cimon* 18.1; 451 B.C.). But even if the two cities were no longer actively fighting each other, the truce did not put a stop to Athens's rivalry with Sparta for rank. One of Sparta's traditional claims to supremacy in standing was her guardianship of Delphi, the seat of the oracle of Apollo and the most hallowed spot in Greece. In the time of Cimon's truce the Spartans made an expedition – a so-called "Sacred War" – to free Delphi from the Phocians, an occupying power. No sooner had the Spartans departed than the Athenians marched out and placed Delphi back in the hands of the Phocians, their allies (1.112.5; ?449 B.C.). The Spartans had long enjoyed special privileges at Delphi, graven upon a bronze wolf: the Phocians granted the Athenians identical rights and carved them upon the same wolf (Plut. *Per.* 21.2).[36]

Around the same time, at Pericles' behest, the Athenians sent envoys out into Greece to invite all the Greeks to a great pan-Hellenic congress at Athens, to weigh what should be done about the temples that had been destroyed by the Persians, about the common sacrifices that were owed to the gods for the victory, and about freedom of the seas (?449 B.C.). The conference was never held: the Spartans opposed the meeting, and the envoys' invitation was refused in the Peloponnese. No wonder, because for the Athenians to call such a meeting in their city was to claim to be first in rank in Greece, and the summoning of ambassadors was an invitation to other Greeks to acknowledge that supremacy. Plutarch says that Pericles proposed this meeting to get the Athenian people to "think big" (*mega phronein*; Plut. *Per.* 17) – a usual term for a Greek state trying to advance itself in rank, often itself a cause of war: whatever the value of Plutarch's testimony, the Spartans and their allies probably interpreted Athenian intentions thus.

The Spartans had made good use of Cimon's truce to plot a victorious end to the First Peloponnesian War. As the last sands of the truce trickled out, much of Boeotia rebelled. The Athenians marched out all unready, were brought to battle, and were defeated at Coronea: to get her prisoners back Athens had to set Boeotia free (1.113; Plut. *Per.* 18.2–3). Then the nearby island of Euboea revolted, and Pericles had to lead the Athenian army over the water. Then came news that Megara had risen and rejoined the Spartan alliance and – lo! – a great Peloponnesian host was on the march for Attica. That army entered the territory of

Athens and ravaged the land, but the Athenians did not come out to fight them, and so the Spartans reaffirmed their superiority in rank. Having done so, they marched home, leaving the plucky Euboeans to their fate (1.114, 2.21.1; Plut. *Per.* 22.2; Diod. 12.6.1; 446 B.C.), much as they had the Boeotians after Tanagra.

The Thirty Years' Peace (446/5 B.C.) – the treaty between Athens and Sparta that concluded the First Peloponnesian War – had many wise provisions. Future disputes between Athens and Sparta were to be dealt with by arbitration (7.18.2; 1.140.2); states belonging to neither alliance could join either (1.35.2); but states listed in the treaty as allies of either could not change sides (1.40.2), as Megara had done at the outbreak of the First Peloponnesian War.[37] Yet peace could only be lasting if Sparta were willing to admit Athenian equality in rank, or Athens were willing to admit her inferiority. Neither was likely. To the contrary, Athens had been humiliated by the way the First Peloponnesian War had ended, and her humiliation was petrified in the treaty (4.21.3).[38] Not only had she to ratify her losses of Boeotia and Megara, but she had also to withdraw from bases she still held in the Peloponnese and the Megarid (1.115.1). The First Peloponnesian War, moreover, had made Sparta sensitive to Athens's pretensions. Before the war Sparta had been prepared to disregard slights such as the rebuilding of Athens's walls, but after the war she was to prove far more jealous of her honor and tender about challenges to her rank. Yet the treaty did satisfy Sparta's allies, without whom she could not in practice make war on Athens: in the short run, it was Sparta's allies who would keep the peace.

Any observer who hoped that the Athenians had been taught their place by the catastrophe that ended the First Peloponnesian War would have learned otherwise several years after the Peace when the Athenians led a colony to Thurii, in the south of Italy (?443 B.C.). This was a pan-Hellenic colony, whose members were drawn from the whole of Greece, including the Peloponnese (Diod. 12.9–11), but its leaders were Athenian. The foundation of Thurii was a claim to supreme rank in Greece parallel to Pericles' invitation to the pan-Hellenic congress to discuss the temples. It was a more modest gambit, but unlike the previous effort it was successful. When the new colony soon got in trouble (Diod. 12.23.2), Athens did nothing to help.[39] The colony was a matter of rank, not of strategic position, not of power: the most important point, that Athens could be accepted as leader of a pan-Hellenic enterprise, had been made.

With the Athenians still jousting for first place, and the Spartans feeling proud and touchy, any incident between them might easily lead to war. War almost broke out a few years after Thurii, when Athens's ally Samos revolted from the Athenian alliance (1.115.5–117; 440 B.C.). On this occasion the Spartans summoned their allies to deliberate about going to war with Athens, which means at least that powerful forces at Sparta were prepared to consider going to war themselves, if the essential aid of their allies could be secured. But the Corinthians – they were to claim – persuaded the allies to withhold their consent, and so nothing happened (1.40.5; cf. 1.41.2, 1.43.1). When Sparta's allies came shortly to change their minds, the major obstacle to war on Sparta's side would be removed.

The period after the Thirty Years' Peace was the era of the ascendancy of Pericles at Athens. After the exile of Pericles' last major rival a few years after the Peace (?443 B.C.), he was the predominant Athenian politician. Thucydides admired Pericles, but even so Thucydides emphasizes Pericles' consistent and stiff-necked resistance to the Spartans. "I have always held the same principle," Thucydides has him say, "not to yield to the Peloponnesians" (1.140.1). "He was the most powerful man of his time, and leading the state he opposed the Lacedaemonians in everything, and he did not suffer them to yield, but urged the Athenians on to war" (1.127.3). Yet there is to be detected in Athenian policy – as the future was to show – a remarkable scrupulosity in adhering to the terms of the treaty: a scrupulosity confirmed by the Spartans, who were to admit that when the war came it was they, not the Athenians, who had violated the Peace (7.18.2). The policy of Pericles – and Athens under Pericles' leadership – seems to have been to accept the territorial losses embodied in the Thirty Years' Peace, but resist utterly inferiority in rank. Pericles' Athens used the treaty as a shield to protect herself against Spartan revenge for her pretensions to standing.

The series of events that immediately preceded the outbreak of the war now present themselves. Although their relative chronology is not wholly clear, their importance was that they turned Sparta's allies against Athens. At some point after Samos Athens got into a dispute with Megara about the cultivation of sacred land on their mutual border and Megara's harboring of Athens's runaway slaves: a perfectly unexceptional boundary dispute between Greek cities of the kind that frequently led to war.[40] But instead of going to war with a Spartan ally – a breach of the treaty – Athens imposed a trade embargo upon the Megarians, forbidding them to trade in the markets and harbors of Athens and her confederacy (Thuc. 1.139.1–2; ?435 B.C.).[41] In an overwhelmingly agricultural world, this Megarian Decree hardly reduced the Megarians to beggary (as Aristophanes jokingly suggested [*Ach.* 535]): it was an insult, cunningly crafted because the Megarians could not themselves avenge it in blood without breaking the treaty.

Yet the key was Corinth – the city that boasted that she had prevented war over the rebellion of Samos. An old hatred existed between Corinth and her colony Corcyra, the island of Corfu in the northwest of Greece (1.25.3). A mother city expected deferential honor from a daughter, precedence at sacrifices and in the (acutely public) common assemblies of the Greeks. Instead the Corcyreans, wealthy in money and powerful in war, treated the Corinthians with contempt, being "raised up" by their nautical eminence, and associating themselves with the Phaeacians, the epic inhabitants of their island, who once had gloried in their ships (1.25.4; cf. 1.38.2–5). Between states locked in such hatred – with so much pent-up desire for revenge – war was likely to burst out over any difference, as it certainly had before (1.13.4; cf. Hdt. 3.49–53). The quarrel now was over Epidamnus, a colony of Corcyra's to the north on the mainland. Asked for help by Epidamnus, after the Corcyreans had refused her, the Corinthians jumped at the chance, driven by their grievances against Corcyra for the contempt in which Corcyra held them (1.26.1, 1.38.5). When the Corcyreans heard they flew into anger (1.26.3): now there was war between Corinth and Corcyra, as nice a case of a war depicted as arising from rivalry in rank as survives from antiquity.[42]

Initially Corcyra had the better of the war, and defeated the Corinthians in a sea battle (1.26.3–30; 435 B.C.). But the Corinthians kept up their anger – their desire for revenge – against the Corcyreans, and began to build a vast fleet (1.31.1). Report of this sent the Corcyreans to Athens to plead for an alliance, a plea that the Athenians granted (1.31.2–44.1), but with great care for their obligations under the Thirty Years' Peace. They agreed to a defensive alliance only, and only a small squadron would be sent to help, with Cimon's son Lacedaemonius, "the Spartan," as a commander, perhaps to emphasize Athens's lack of aggressive intent; and that small squadron was forbidden to fight unless Corcyra herself, or a possession of hers, was threatened (1.44.1–45.3, 1.53.2–4).

It is in understanding Athenian willingness to help Corcyra against Corinth that Thucydides' mechanics of fear and power come into their own. Thucydides is surely right that Athens's dependence on naval supremacy made it impossible for her to allow the possibility that the two other significant fleets in Greece – those of Corcyra and Corinth – would, with a Corinthian conquest of Corcyra, be combined under a single head, whether for the moment friendly or hostile (1.33.2, 1.35.5,

1.36.3, 1.44.2). Greek ethics backed Corinth's claim that Athens should not help Corcyra against her, and Thucydides portrays the Corinthians making ethical arguments to dissuade the Athenians: Athens owed Corinth neutrality, at least, in exchange for her intervention with Sparta's allies over Samos (1.37–43).[43] The claim that one good turn deserved another is the flip side of the Greek code of revenge – that one bad turn deserved another. But in this case fear of power – Athenian fear of the naval power of Corinth if Corinth reduced Corcyra to obedience – trumped ethical considerations.

Despite all Athens's safeguards, her ships ended up fighting against those of Corinth: worse, the arrival of a second Athenian squadron filched from Corinth the hope of making use of the victory she gained (1.46–55; 433 B.C.), and so interfered with Corinth's "avenging" herself on Corcyra (1.53.2). The contagion of Corinth's abiding anger now spread from her old enemy, Corcyra, to Athens.

> This was the first ground for complaint (*aitia*) that the Corinthians had for the war against the Athenians, that they had fought against them alongside the Corcyreans in time of treaty. Soon after this another point of difference (*diaphora*) tending towards war arose between the Athenians and the Peloponnesians: the Corinthians were devising to avenge themselves upon the Athenians, and the Athenians suspected their hatred (*echthra*).
>
> (1.55.2–56.2)

Corinth and Athens came to blows over another colony of Corinth's, Potidaea, on the Chalcidice in the northern Aegean, and a tribute-paying member of the Athenian confederacy. Athens suspected Corinth of encouraging Potidaea to revolt, and so demanded that she send home her magistrates (which Potidaea took from Corinth) and tear down her wall on the seaward side (1.56.2–57). The Potidaeans sent envoys to Athens to plead their case – but also to Sparta. And the Spartans gave Potidaea a conditional promise of support: they would invade Attica if Athens attacked Potidaea (1.58.1, 1.71.4). This fateful guarantee is a puzzle if viewed in terms of power politics: Potidaea had nothing to do with the security of Sparta, nor even with that of Corinth. Its significance lies instead in the world of rank. By asserting an interest in Potidaea, Sparta was demanding that Athens concede her inferiority by deferring to Spartan wishes. But the Athenians paid no attention, much as Mycenae had ignored the wishes of Argos in Diodorus's account of the outbreak of the war between them.

With Spartan assurances, Potidaea revolted from Athens. The Corinthians rushed volunteers and mercenaries from the Peloponnese to her aid, there was fighting around Potidaea, and the Athenians besieged the Potidaeans and their allies in the city (1.60.1–65; 432 B.C.). These were yet more grounds for complaint (*aitiai*): Athens's attack on Potidaea, and her siege of Corinthians and Peloponnesians inside Potidaea, on the one hand, and on the other the Peloponnesians' incitement of a tributary Athenian ally to revolt, and Peloponnesians' open – if unofficial – fighting alongside the Potidaeans against the Athenians (1.66).

When her anxiety about Potidaea and her men inside it made Corinth summon Sparta's allies to Sparta to urge the Spartans to go to war (1.67.1; 432 B.C.), the prerequisites of war were present. Feeling at Sparta was hostile to Athens: the Spartans had been prepared to go to war earlier when Samos revolted, and now Athens had refused to defer to Sparta in the matter of Potidaea. Of Sparta's allies, who as a body had prevented war over Samos, Megara – which had a long list of "grievances" (*diaphorai*), chief among them the Megarian Decree – was eager for revenge against Athens, as was Corinth. Corinth, indeed, had already tried to take that revenge through Potidaea, in a manner that did not directly violate the treaty: Corinth's subversion of Potidaea was parallel in intention to the Megarian Decree. Other cities too had causes for resentment: we are told especially of Aegina, an unwilling member of the Athenian confederacy since her surrender in the first Peloponnesian War (1.67.2–4, 2.27.1). But although the Spartans and then their allies voted for war (1.87–8, 1.118.3–119, 1.125.1), an actual attack upon Athens was still many months away.[44]

"During that time," Thucydides says, the Spartans "sent ambassadors to Athens alleging grievances, in order to have a better pretext for war, should the Athenians pay them no attention in any respect" (1.126.1). Thucydides is dismissive of the protracted diplomatic exchange that separated the formal Spartan and Peloponnesian votes for war from the outbreak of the war itself. To him the Spartans had voted to go to war from fear of Athenian power, more than because they were persuaded by their allies (1.88): once the decision was made on the basis of fear of power, everything else was a sideshow. But viewed from the standpoint of rank, this diplomatic activity takes on far greater importance. No recent event gave the Spartans reason to fear for their safety. And most recent developments did not directly affect even the honor of Sparta: Megara and Corinth had been humiliated, but those humiliations scarcely spotted the austere dignity of Lacedaemon. Sparta had threatened war with Athens over Potidaea not because she cared about Potidaea, but because she had chosen to test Athenian deference. Yet the Athenians had not – as far as we know – openly defied Sparta over Potidaea; they had merely ignored her. Best to repeat forthrightly, several times, the invitation to Athens to step down and to concede the supremacy of Sparta, in terms that could not be so easily ignored. Many Athenians might quail at an open challenge to the old commander of Hellas: the Spartans might well achieve the victory in standing they sought without war.

First the Spartans bade the Athenians to drive out the curse of the goddess, a hereditary taint attaching to Pericles through his mother's family (1.126–7). The very strangeness – to modern eyes – of the Spartans' citing an ancient bane as a grievance confirms to the modern reader Thucydides' suggestion that the Spartans were merely groping for pretexts. Yet the content of the Spartan demand is less important than the fact of a demand. The Spartans might have demanded nearly anything ("should the Athenians pay them no attention *in any respect*," Thucydides wrote of the ultimata): the question was whether the Athenians would climb down and grant it. The Athenians did not: they "retorted" (1.128.1, 1.135.1, 1.139.1) with a demand that the Spartans drive out not one but two curses. Not only did the Athenians refuse to defer and so admit their inferiority in rank, they insulted the Spartans.

Now the Spartans returned with more detailed ultimata: "they commanded the Athenians to withdraw from Potidaea, to leave Aegina autonomous, and especially, most plainly of all they said that there would not be war if they revoked the Megarian Decree" (1.139.1).[45] None of these had anything to do with the security of Sparta; none of them had anything to do with the pride of Sparta until Sparta chose to make them a test of Athenian deference, and demand that Athens yield to her on these points. But the position of Athens – of Pericles' Athens – was consistent. Athens would adhere to the treaty but not give in on any matter touching upon rank. Athens must refuse to do anything commanded by the Spartans, great or small, Thucydides has Pericles say in the speech he writes for him on this occasion, so that the Spartans "will learn to deal with you as equals" (1.140.5–41.1).[46] The Athenians replied that "they would do nothing at command" – an equal could not yield to commands – "but were ready to have their grievances settled in a fair and equitable manner by arbitration, according to the treaty" (1.145).[47] When the Athenians replied to these demands, they replied as well to a final Spartan mission, which bade them simply to let the Greeks be autonomous (1.139.3). This last was merely a slogan: the Athenians had not yielded to the primacy of the Spartans, and now there was to be war (431 B.C.).

The theory offered here, that the Peloponnesian War broke out over issues of rank, is confirmed by the history of how the Spartans carried on the war in its first seven years. Their strategy – except in the third year, when they turned aside to besiege Athens's small ally Plataea in Boeotia – was to invade Attica. When the Athenians did not come out to face them, they ravaged the fields and turned for home. The first time the Spartans invaded Attica they may well have expected the Athenians to face them in battle (2.20; cf. 2.11.6–8). But they continued their strategy of annual invasions long after it became clear that the Athenians would not emerge from their city and that their invasions alone were not compelling the Athenians to make peace. Why invade year after year? In fact, exactly because the Athenians would not come out to fight, these invasions served to confirm Sparta's superiority in rank, and the Peloponnesian ravaging of Attica brought revenge manifold upon the Athenians for their *hybris*; thus the repeated invasions fulfilled Sparta's war aims. The invasions were really about – in words Thucydides puts into the mouth of the commander of the first of them – the Peloponnesians "not revealing ourselves to be worse than our ancestors, or inferior to our own reputation" (2.11.2) and "the great reputation, good or ill, that is at stake from the outcome for us and our ancestors" (2.11.9). Perhaps Athens's annual raids around the Peloponnese are to be understood in part as revenge for Sparta's invasions, as Aristophanes believed (*Peace* 626);[48] perhaps also her annual invasions and ravagings of Megara can be understood in this way (2.31, 4.66.1) – the logic of revenge explaining why Athens invaded Megara not once every year, but twice.[49] Only eventually, as the war ground on, did its imperatives become more cruel: eventually the Peloponnesian War became not a duel over rank, but a savage struggle for survival.

CONCLUSION

The great majority of modern students have defended, and tried to justify, Thucydides' position that the Peloponnesian War broke out because of Spartan fear of the growth of Athenian power.[50] This paper begins from a position that is a minority position among modern scholars, but that I suspect would have commanded the assent of a majority of ancient Greeks: that Thucydides was wrong. It tries to explain the origins of the war by applying to Thucydides' narrative of events a way of thinking about the causes of wars with which Thucydides was well acquainted, and applied in other cases, but that he opposed applying in this case. Thucydides' error, if error it was, was the one into which historians – especially good historians – most commonly fall: he mistook a symptom for a fundamental cause. It is likely that the Spartans had always viewed Athenian power with a certain concern. It was a commonplace among Greeks that power and prosperity, especially if rapidly acquired, encouraged acts of *hybris* in their possessor (e.g., 3.39.4, 3.45.4, 4.18.2).[51] Athenian power, any Greek would understand, would predispose Athens to challenge Sparta's supremacy in rank. It is very likely, as well, that by the time war broke out between Athens and Sparta, Sparta did fear the power of Athens. But Spartan fear of Athens's power was not the ultimate cause of the war. That fear was a by-product of Sparta's realization that Athens would not concede Sparta's supremacy in rank, the old supremacy that Sparta cast in the sixth century, forged in the Persian War, and tempered in the First Peloponnesian War. Spartan fear was not of Athens's power in itself, but of Athens's using that power to dispute Sparta's rank – much as Argos had feared the growing power of Mycenae in Diodorus' story of the outbreak of war between them. The Athenian challenge to Spartan rank, rather than Spartan fear of Athenian power, was the truest cause of the war.

Who was responsible for the Peloponnesian War? The Spartans, for being willing to go to war rather than brook any challenge to their ancient primacy in standing? But there was no reason for Greece's hallowed *hegemon* to yield. The Athenians, as the dynamic party, for insisting on their equality – sometimes superiority – in rank to the Spartans, and being willing to go to war rather than yield the claim? But they could justify their pretension by their victories over the Persians and their dominion over Greeks.[52] The Corinthians, who began the chain of revenges and challenges to rank that were the proximate cause of the war? But few Greek states would have acted differently. The transcendent cause of the war was the culture of Greek foreign relations, embedded so deeply in Greek competitiveness and the ethics the Greeks inherited from their heroic past. The principle that created the Olympic games, that set potter against potter and playwright against playwright, the competitive principle that drove so much of what is remarkable about Greek civilization, that same principle drove Athens and Sparta to war.[53]

SUGGESTIONS FOR FURTHER READING

On Spartan ways and constitutional arrangements, the most important ancient sources are Xenophon's *Politeia of the Lacedaemonians* and Plutarch's *Life of Lycurgus*. For an introduction to the Spartans, J. T. Hooker, *The Ancient Spartans* (London: Dent, 1980), or, older, H. Michell, *Sparta* (Cambridge: Cambridge University Press, 1952). The essays in S. Hodkinson and A. Powell, eds., *Sparta: New Perspectives* (London: Duckworth, 1999), direct the reader to recent developments in the study of Sparta.

On Spartan military prowess, J. F. Lazenby, *The Spartan Army* (Warminster: Aris and Phillips, 1985); and on Sparta's relations with her allies, S. Bolmarcich, "Thucydides 1.19.1 and the Peloponnesian League," *GRBS* 45 (2005): 5–34. On the competitive culture of the Spartans, see J. E. Lendon, "Spartan Honor," in C. D. Hamilton and P. Krentz, eds., *Polis and Polemos* (Claremont, CA: Regina, 1997), pp. 105–26.

On Greek thinking about the origins and ethics of war, see H. van Wees, *Greek Warfare: Myths and Realities* (London: Duckworth, 2004), pp. 6–43. The argument offered in this paper expands upon J. E. Lendon, "Homeric Vengeance and the Outbreak of Greek Wars," in H. van Wees, ed., *War and Violence in Ancient Greece* (London: Duckworth, 2000), pp. 1–30. It is grounded in Greek conceptions of honor and revenge, which are the subject of controversy: see N. Fisher, "*Hybris*, Revenge, and *Stasis* in the Greek City-States," in H. van Wees, ed., *War and Violence in Ancient Greece* (London: Duckworth, 2000), pp. 83–123 (esp. 87–8 for the literature), with whom I am inclined to agree, but *contra* G. Herman, "Athenian Beliefs about Revenge: Problems and Methods," *Proceedings of the Cambridge Philological Society* 46 (2000): 7–27.

On the origins of the Peloponnesian War, the main source is Thucydides, book 1. Plutarch's lives of Themistocles, Cimon, and Pericles contribute details, as do the eleventh and twelfth books of Diodorus of Sicily. For a guide to reading Thucydides' account of the origins of the war, see C. Pelling, *Literary Texts and the Greek Historian* (London: Routledge, 2000), pp. 82–111. For the (very considerable) scholarship on the origins of the war, see the critical summary by E. A. Meyer, "*The Outbreak of the Peloponnesian War* after Twenty-Five Years," in C. D. Hamilton and P. Krentz, eds., *Polis and Polemos* (Claremont, CA: Regina, 1997), pp. 23–54. Most important are D. Kagan, *The Outbreak of the Peloponnesian War* (Ithaca, NY: Cornell University Press, 1969) and G. E. M. de Ste. Croix, *The Origins of the Peloponnesian War* (London: Duckworth, 1972).

NOTES

1   Unidentified references are to Thucydides.

2   So Crawley translates; my translations are often in debt to his.

3   A. M. Eckstein, "Thucydides, the Outbreak of the Peloponnesian War, and the Foundation of International Systems Theory," *International History Review* 25 (2003): 757–74.

4   Summarizing (and slightly expanding) J. E. Lendon, "Homeric Vengeance and the Outbreak of Greek Wars," in H. van Wees, ed., *War and Violence in Ancient Greece* (London: Duckworth, 2000), pp. 1–30 at 13–21. Illustrations there were mostly from Herodotus and Xenophon: here some corroborating references from Thucydides, Polybius, and Diodorus are given in the notes to illustrate how general this thinking was. See also H. van Wees, *Greek Warfare: Myths and Realities* (London: Duckworth, 2004), pp. 22–6.

5   Polyb. 20.4.1–4.

6   For a state with more rank than power, Tegea in Herodotus (9.26), which ranks higher than Corinth and Megara, although it brings fewer men to battle (Hdt. 9.28), and claims, on the basis of history and myth, to rank higher than Athens (Hdt. 9.26–7). Cf. Diod. 19.53–54.3.

7   Cf. 1.38.2–5, 1.120.1; Polyb. 33.16.3. On this theme, J. E. Lendon, "Xenophon and the Alternative to Realist Foreign Policy: *Cyropaedia* 3.1.14–31," *JHS* 126 (2006): 82–98.

8   5.111.4; cf. 1.140.5, 1.141.1.

9   Cf. 1.38.6; Polyb. 3.7.2.

10   For *mega phronein* and *hybris*, see D. L. Cairns, "*Hybris*, Dishonour, and Thinking Big," *JHS* 116 (1996): 1–32; Lendon (n. 7).

11   Cf. Diod. 11.52.2.

12   Cf. Polyb. 3.10.5, 3.13.1, 3.7.2.

13   Cf. Diod. 11.64.3; Polyb. 3.6.13.

14   Ravaging, quoted Arist. *Rh.* 1395a. See also Polyb. 23.15; cf. 9.33.10. Ravaging is an insult and produces anger in its turn, Thuc. 1.143.5, 2.11.7–8, 2.21.2, 2.22.1; Plut. *Per.* 33.3; Ar. *Ach.* 509–12. Being shut within walls is a humiliation in itself, Polyb. 21.10.6.

15   Cf. especially Polybius, e.g., 1.10.5–6, 1.83.3–4, 2.13.4.

16   D. Kagan, *The Outbreak of the Peloponnesian War* (Ithaca, NY: Cornell University Press, 1969), esp. pp. 345–6; a position vindicated against subsequent scholarly argument by E. A. Meyer, "*The Outbreak of the Peloponnesian War* after Twenty-Five Years," in C. D. Hamilton and P. Krentz, eds., *Polis and Polemos* (Claremont: Regina, 1997), pp. 23–54 at 27, 31–2.

17   As is implied by Aristophanes, *Ach.* 524–39, where a chain of revenges – partly absurd, this being comedy – causes the war: the mechanics of causation may be significant, even if the details are wrong. Cf. R. Sealey, "The Causes of the Peloponnesian War," *CP* 70 (1975): 89–109, who maintained that Thucydides

himself had originally conceived of the outbreak of the war in terms of a chain of vengeances – the "grounds for complaint" and "points of difference" – but had subsequently changed his mind and settled on Sparta's fear of Athenian power, yet never fully reconciled the two positions in his narrative. Evolution of Thucydides' thought in the other direction (from fear of power to *aitiai* and *diaphorai*) is no less possible (drawing out the implications of J. Ober, "Thucydides *Theoretikos*/Thucydides *Histor.* Realist Theory and the Challenge of History," in D. McCann and B. S. Strauss, eds., *War and Democracy* [Armonk: M. E. Sharpe, 2001], pp. 273–306).

18   It is generally accepted that in his account of classical Greek affairs the first-century B.C. Diodorus draws heavily upon the fourth-century B.C. historian Ephorus, and Ephorus in turn may have been drawing on the fifth-century B.C. Hellenicus, so his accounts can be defended (as, e.g., by J. H. Schreiner, *Hellanikos, Thukydides, and the Era of Kimon* [Aarhus: Aarhus University Press, 1997]). But the sources – indeed the veracity – of Diodorus's account are irrelevant here: we are interested in the intellectual mechanics that lie behind it, mechanics that appear to have changed little from the days of Herodotus to those of Diodorus.

19   For *hegemonia* in this sense, see J. Wickersham, *Hegemony and Greek Historians* (Lanham: Rowman and Littlefield, 1994).

20   Cf. 4.18.1, and C. W. Fornara and L. J. Samons, *Athens from Cleisthenes to Pericles* (Berkeley: University of California Press, 1991), p. 125, on Spartan moral authority in Greece.

21   Cf. Diod. 11.27.2–3: as a result of the Greek victory at Salamis, which was attributed to the Athenians, "the Athenians were puffed up, and it became clear to everybody that they intended to compete with the Lacedaemonians for hegemony on the sea, so the Lacedaemonians, seeing what was about to happen, acted in rivalry for honor to humble their pride" (cf. 11.55.6). The conventional-minded Diodorus (probably drawing on Ephorus) frequently interprets the events of the fifth century B.C. in terms of rank, as here.

22   It cannot be too much emphasized that the absolute dates of events between 479 and 431 B.C. are badly attested and extremely controversial, that even upon relative chronology (relied upon here, and sounder) there is disagreement, and that not all scholars even admit the existence of all the events that ancient authors describe: so, for example, Fornara and Samons (n. 20), hardly ranting radicals, doubt the ancient anecdotes that suggest friction between Athens and Sparta in the 470s (pp. 118–24), wonder (with many others) about Pericles' summoning of a pan-Hellenic congress in ?449 (p. 91), and juggle the chronology of the late 460s (pp. 127–9). The scope of this volume requires dogmatism and forbids attention to these tasty controversies.

23   Diodorus's interpretation (11.39.2): "seeing the great glory the Athenians had gained with their naval power, the Lacedaemonians suspected their increase, and decided to forbid the Athenians to rebuild their walls."

24   Diod. 11.59.1 interprets the Athenians' taking command at sea as "taking that glory from the Spartans."

25   Diodorus 12.2.1: "The Athenians were far the first in glory and courage, famous through almost the whole inhabited world. They caused their *hegemonia* to grow to such a degree that, by themselves, without the Lacedaemonians and Peloponnesians, they defeated great Persian forces by land and by sea, and humbled the

famous *hegemonia* of the Persians to such a degree, that they compelled them to set free all the cities of Asia" (cf. 11.71.5; Plut. *Cimon* 12.1).

26   Diod. 11.54.2–3 interprets: "The Lacedaemonians, seeing that Sparta was humbled by the treason of Pausanias the general, and that the Athenians were esteemed because no citizen of theirs had been convicted of treason, were eager to ensnare the Athenians in similar calumnies. So, since Themistocles was in high repute among the Athenians, and had a great reputation for excellence, they accused him of treason;" cf. 11.55.5: ". . . the Lacedaemonians were eager to slander and humble the city of the Athenians, and . . . the Athenians wanted to clear themselves of the charge brought against them. . . ."

27   Diod. 11.64.3 interprets: "The Athenians, thinking that they had been dishonored, then marched away. But afterward, being estranged from the Lacedaemonians, they fanned the fires of their hatred (*echthra*) more and more. Therefore they took this as the beginning of their estrangement, and afterward, when the cities wrangled [had *diaphorai*], they entered into great wars, and filled all of Greece with great woes."

28   I follow E. Badian's compelling impeachment of this story, "Thucydides and the Outbreak of the Peloponnesian War: A Historian's Brief," in E. Badian, *From Plataea to Potidaea: Studies in the History and Historiography of the Pentecontaetia* (Baltimore: Johns Hopkins University Press, 1993), pp. 125–62 at 134–6; cf. Fornara and Samons (n. 20), p. 127.

29   Diodorus describes the mutual raiding of Megara and Corinth as a *diaphora* (11.79.2).

30   Why did the Thebans call the Spartans in? Diodorus (11.81.1–2) guesses that "the Thebans, having been humbled by the alliance they made with Xerxes, sought a way to regain their ancestral strength and glory. Because all the other Boeotians held the Thebans in contempt and would not pay heed to them, the Thebans asked the Lacedaemonians to help them gain the *hegemonia* of all Boeotia."

31   Diod. 11.70.2 interprets: "This city, often successful in sea battles, was puffed up and abundantly supplied with money and triremes, and, in sum, always at odds with the Athenians;" cf. 11.78.3–4: "With their pride crushed by the magnitude of the disaster, they were compelled to join the tribute-paying league of the Athenians."

32   G. E. M. de Ste. Croix, *The Origins of the Peloponnesian War* (London: Duckworth, 1972), pp. 190–95.

33   Fornara and Samons (n. 20), pp. 133–7.

34   Nor had the Spartans come out when the Corinthians earlier seized the passes and fought the Athenians in the Megarid (1.105.3–6; ?458 B.C.).

35   Cf. Aristophanes *Peace* 626, where Athenian raids on Laconia during the Peloponnesian War are described as a form of revenge.

36   A dimly seen dispute in the 470s B.C. between Athens and Sparta over Delphi may reflect this rivalry as well (Plut. *Them.* 20.3–4).

37   De Ste. Croix (n. 32), pp. 293–4.

38   Cf. Diod. 12.7: the Athenians "humbled" by their defeat at Coronea.

39   Cf. Kagan (n. 16), p. 164.

40   Plutarch *Per.* 30.2–3 places it in a sequence of vengeances; also Aristophanes *Ach.* 524–39.

41   The Megarian decree is best placed before Athens's involvement with Corcyra (see below), because it then helps to explain the tension to which Thucydides alluded

in the speeches he composed about whether Athens should ally with Corcyra (1.33.3, 1.35.4, 1.36.1, 1.44.2, and esp. 1.42.2).

42 Cf. G. Crane, *Thucydides and the Ancient Simplicity* (Berkeley: University of California Press, 1998), pp. 93–105.

43 Cf. Crane (n. 42), pp. 105–24. For relations of reciprocity in Greek foreign relations, Lendon (n. 7).

44 It is dangerous to argue from the details of Thucydides' speeches, given that the historian admits that they contain an admixture of what Thucydides thought "appropriate under the circumstances" (1.22.1), and most contemporary students consider them very close to free compositions. But since Thucydides was opposed to interpreting the outbreak of the war in terms of rank, it is interesting how often rank and revenge arguments nevertheless creep into the debate Thucydides stages about whether the Spartans should go to war – the *hybris* of the Athenians (1.68.2), the need to avenge (1.86.2–3) and to act "worthily of Sparta" (1.86.5) – and the Corinthian speech urging the allies to war: again, revenge (1.121.5; cf. 1.141.7).

45 Aristophanes *Ach.* 536–9 confirms the special importance of the Megarian Decree to the Spartans; cf. Diod. 12.39.4; Plut. *Per.* 29.5.

46 Aristophanes confirms the Athenian hard line, by having a character note that if the Spartans had imposed an embargo – like the Megarian Decree – on the Athenians, the Athenians would have gone to war over it (*Ach.* 541–54); so, he says, they have no right to complain about the Spartans.

47 Thucydides has Pericles propose in a speech a set of aggressive tit-for-tat retorts to the Spartan demands: Athens will retract the Megarian Decree if Sparta abolishes her laws forbidding foreigners in Sparta; Athens will let her allies be autonomous if the Spartans do the same (1.144.2). We do not know if such retorts were included in the formal Athenian reply (or indeed how much they are to be credited, since they are presented in a speech [see above n. 44]). But if they were, or they were even suggested at Athens, they are parallel to Athens's reply to the Spartans' demand that she drive out the curse of the goddess: they suggest Athens's intractability over her rank.

48 Cf. Diod. 11.84.3.

49 Cf. 2.42.4 for Athenian actions in the first year of war being acts of revenge.

50 For a summary of such approaches see Meyer (n. 16), pp. 25–35.

51 Cf. Hdt. 5.91; Dem. 1.23; and see J. de Romilly, *The Rise and Fall of States According to Greek Authors* (Ann Arbor: University of Michigan Press, 1977), pp. 46–7.

52 As Thucydides has Pericles boast in speeches (2.41, 2.61.4, 2.63–4).

53 My thanks to E. A. Meyer, J. Dillery, S. Bolmarich, M. Lendon, and the editor of this volume.

CONCLUSION: PERICLES
AND ATHENS

L. J. Samons II

Pericles casts a long shadow. Undoubtedly the most important figure in the history of Athenian democracy, he nonetheless suffers from a kind of mythologization. Like George Washington or Abraham Lincoln, Pericles has become larger (and smaller) than life. To moderns, he often seems a kind of disembodied spokesman for democratic values, transmitted to us through less than careful readings, summaries, or decontextualized quotations from Thucydides' account of Pericles' Funeral Oration. Many people know that Pericles in that address called Athens the "school of Hellas," and that he praised Athenian government and society in contrast to the Spartans' regime. Yet few authorities have emphasized the primary thrust of the speech, which is thoroughly militaristic, collectivist, and unstintingly nationalistic.[1] Beside Pericles' image in the popular mind, and at times clouding the very picture of him, are the famous buildings on the Acropolis of Athens, built as part of the "Periclean" program of construction. In fact, the Parthenon and (a very small part of) Pericles' speech stand together as the most concrete modern images of ancient democracy and classical Athens.

This is a strange situation. For, like Pericles' career, the Parthenon is not a testament to Athenian democracy, humanism, or liberalism, although some scholars still hold versions of this view.[2] A temple to Athens's patron deity, Athena, the building was financed in part by money the Athenians had exacted from other Greek states.[3] Its frieze seemingly depicted (at least in part) the Athenian festival known as the Panathenaea (i.e., sacred rites that were "All Athena" or "All Athenian").[4] Inside the impressive structure, a colossal gold and ivory statue of Athena held the image of "Victory" (Nike) in her hand, while her sandals rested on images of the myth of Pandora, who had released troubles innumerable to man.[5] The Parthenon is first and foremost a monument to Athenian power, glory, and victory over both barbarians (such as the Persians) and, by implication if not direct representation, other Greeks. The building was a dedication to and housed a representation of the goddess that presided over and ensured Athenian superiority. The temple proclaims "Athena and Athens!" without so much as a hint of Panhellenism or "democratic" values. As David Lewis concluded, "To say that the Athenians built the Parthenon to worship themselves would be an exaggeration, but not a great one."[6]

A close examination of Pericles' Funeral Oration in Thucydides reveals a monument perhaps even more "nationalistic" – as opposed to "democratic" – than the Parthenon. After briefly dilating on Athens's open society and implicitly contrasting this with the control of individual lives putatively found in Sparta, Pericles passes quickly to the issue of Athens's power and the need for Athenian citizens, literally, to become "lovers" of the city (or its power: see below). Even Pericles' famous proclamation that Athens was a school, or "education," for Greece rests on a military foundation.

> In short, I say that as a city we are an education for Hellas, and I doubt if the world can produce a man, who where he has only himself to depend upon, is equal to so many emergencies, and graced by so happy a versatility as the Athenian. And that this is no mere boast thrown out for the occasion, but plain matter of fact, *the power of the state acquired by these habits proves.* For Athens alone of her contemporaries is found when tested to be greater than her reputation, and alone gives no occasion to her assailants to blush at the antagonist by whom they have been worsted, or to her subjects to question her title by merit to rule. *Rather, the admiration of the present and succeeding ages will be ours, because we have not left our power without witness, but have shown it by mighty proofs*; and because far from needing a Homer for our panegyrist, or other of his craft whose verses might charm for the moment only for the impression which they gave to melt at the touch of fact, *we have forced every sea and land to be the highway of our daring, and everywhere, whether for evil or for good, have left imperishable monuments behind us.* Such is the Athens for which these men, in the assertion of their determination

not to part with her, nobly fought and died; and well may every one of their survivors be ready to suffer in her cause.

(Thuc. 2.41, emphasis added) [7]

Such ideas are echoed later in the last speech of Pericles presented in Thucydides' work.

Remember, too, that if your country has the greatest name in all the world, it is because she never bent before disaster, and because *she has expended more life and effort in war than any other city, and has won for herself a power greater than any hitherto known,* the memory of which will descend to the latest posterity; even if now, in obedience to the general law of decay, we should ever be forced to yield, still *it will be remembered that we held rule over more Greeks than any other Greek state, that we sustained the greatest wars against their united or separate powers, and inhabited a city unrivaled by any other in resources and magnitude.* These glories may incur the censure of the slow and unambitious; but in the breast of energy they will awake emulation, and in those who must remain without them an envious regret. *Hatred and unpopularity at the moment have fallen to the lot of all who have aspired to rule others; but where odium must be incurred, true wisdom incurs it for the highest objects.*

(2.64, emphasis added)

Modern sensibilities recoil – or should recoil – from the naked nationalism of Pericles' orations, a nationalism that one cannot dismiss as merely empty rhetoric. Athens's consistent drive to Aegean hegemony after the 460s confirms this aggressive sense of national superiority as a guiding principle of Athenian interaction with other states and a fundament of the Athenians' self-image.[8] In contrast, one might speculate that in introducing "democratic values" into the Funeral Oration, Pericles was making a significant innovation, asking the Athenians to conceptualize themselves in a new or unusual way.[9] But even Pericles does not allow his image of Athens as a unique or superior state to rest primarily on its democratic form of government. For Pericles, Athens's superiority to other states stemmed from its power and from its citizens' character – a character that had facilitated the acquisition of that power.[10]

Of course, Athens *was* the cultural leader of fifth-century Hellas, but it is obvious from Thucydides and from other Athenian literature and iconography that the Athenian demos's image of itself rested more on Athens's military power and empire than on the city's cultural hegemony. Thus Pericles encourages the Athenians to "realize the power of Athens, and feed your eyes upon her every day, even becoming her lovers [*erastai*]; and then when all her greatness shall break upon you, you must reflect that it was by courage, sense of duty, and a keen feeling of honor in action that men were enabled to win all this" (2.43). Scholars question whether Pericles asks the Athenians to become the lovers "of *Athens*" or "of [Athens's] *power*."[11] The Greek is ambiguous, but the question is moot. Athens and its power were one and the same for Pericles: the city's power was its glory in the present and the assurance of its reputation in the future.

Pericles' speeches and career thus provide important evidence of the Athenians' martial self-image and of their early efforts to conceptualize their polis – but only in part – as a state with an unusual and superior government/society (*politeia*). Nevertheless, and despite his crucial role in the radicalization of Athenian democracy, Pericles himself has only recently begun to attract the scholarly attention he deserves.[12] These new studies represent a welcome development, for grappling with the problems of Pericles' biography, his political career, and his long-term influence must be central to any study of Athenian history in the fifth century.

PERICLES' BACKGROUND

Pericles' family background certainly made him unusual. His mother came from one of the most famous (and infamous) aristocratic families in Athens. This clan (the Alcmeonids) had produced the founder of Athenian *demokratia* (Cleisthenes). But it also suffered from the stigma of an apparently state-sanctioned curse incurred sometime in the late seventh century B.C., when an Alcmeonid official executed would-be revolutionaries after they had sought protection of the gods as suppliants at a sacred altar. These actions resulted in the family's expulsion from Athens and the subsequent purification of the city by a Cretan soothsayer.[13]

After this event the Athenian populace and the Alcmeonid family had a tumultuous relationship. Having secured their return from exile by the early sixth century, the family sought power by aligning themselves through marriage with the Athenian tyrant Peisistratus in the mid-500s. At the time, this must have been seen as a "popular" and antiaristocratic move, since the Peisistratid tyrants apparently sought power as champions of the people against some of the aristocrats that dominated Athens. This tactic clearly worked, because the tyrants' subsequent fall in 511/10 reportedly resulted from hostilities between the Peisistratids and certain aristocratic families (including the Alcmeonids), and from the Spartan policy of overthrowing tyrannies, and not from any hostility toward the tyrants within the Athenian demos at large. A few years later, it was the Alcmeonid Cleisthenes – Peisistratus's former brother-in-law and the grandson of another tyrant – who managed to pass the reforms in Athens that ultimately resulted in *demokratia* (ca. 507). Obviously a connection with tyrannical government or families in no way disqualified a leader from popular support in late sixth-century Athens.[14]

But Pericles' great-uncle Cleisthenes seems to have fallen from power shortly after the reform that created *demokratia*, perhaps because his government sought Persian protection in the face of continued Spartan interference in Athenian internal affairs. (The Spartans, having removed the Peisistratid tyrants, had returned to Athens and attempted to overthrow the regime instituted by the Peisistratids' relation Cleisthenes. The Athenian people successfully resisted their attempt, but then rejected an alliance with Persia apparently supported by Cleisthenes.)[15] Later, Pericles' relatives found themselves under suspicion of pro-Persian sympathies: Alcmeonids and those close to them were ostracized by vote of the Athenian demos.[16] Included in this banished group were Pericles' father, Xanthippus (who was married to an Alcmeonid), and his Alcmeonid uncle Megacles. Pericles thus spent important adolescent or early adult years during the mid- to late 480s as the son of an exile, probably returning to Athens with his father only after those ostracized were recalled in 481/0.

It has been reasonably suggested that all this left an indelible mark on Pericles' later political persona. Tainted by the religious curse on his mother's family, Pericles seemingly sought out the company of the growing number of rationalist philosophers present in Athens – men who were unlikely to treat such a stigma with anything but disdain.[17] The Spartans' role in the attack on Cleisthenes and Pericles' own sometimes troubled relations with philo-Spartan political forces in Athens (represented by Cimon and his allies) must have contributed to Pericles' virulently anti-Spartan foreign policy. His family's apparent inability to consolidate its power (or, rather, achieve supremacy) through typical aristocratic means (especially through land and cults) and their subsequent need to seek popular support – first through connections with the tyrants and then through *demokratia* – laid the groundwork for Pericles' own radicalization of the democratic regime and the demos's empowerment.[18]

PERICLES' POLITICAL CAREER

Our sources provide almost no information about Pericles' early political career. It appears likely that he entered politics somewhat late in life, perhaps fearing ostracism, given his father's experience, the curse on his mother's family, and the latter's connections with the Peisistratids.[19] He certainly served in Athens's military in the 470s, and we know he acted as the producer (*choregos*) of Aeschylus's *Persians* in 473/2. Beyond this, we know almost nothing else about his actions until he participated in the unsuccessful prosecution of the great Athenian general (and Athens's leading statesman) Cimon in 463. Even here he played a minor role, perhaps choosing not to antagonize Cimon or his then powerful pro-Spartan supporters. In any case, Pericles apparently presented a strictly *pro forma* prosecution.[20]

After his restrained prosecution of Cimon, Pericles most probably attached himself to the faction supporting Cimon's political enemy Ephialtes. When Ephialtes seized the opportunity presented by Cimon's expedition to the Peloponnese to put through his reforms (462/1), Pericles almost certainly supported him. After Ephialtes' subsequent murder, Pericles apparently emerged as the leader of the progressive faction.[21]

Unfortunately, we confront a virtual vacuum in the sources for Pericles' career between 463 and 451/0. Aeschylus's *Eumenides* may suggest that Pericles was seen as a major force among the reformers by 459/8, the year of the play's production,[22] but there is no direct evidence of his political activities in this period. We may infer from his later policies that Pericles favored the rejection of the Athenian alliance with Sparta against Persia (Thuc. 1.102) and supported the subsequent First Peloponnesian War, which pitted Athens against Sparta and its allies (especially Corinth) ca. 460–446. It is difficult to say the same about Athens's ultimately disastrous expedition to Egypt (459–454), apparently launched to assist Egypt's attempt to break free of Persian control and (surely) also in the hope of establishing Athenian influence in the rich lands of northeastern Africa.[23] Pericles' later actions and Plutarch's testimony suggest that the statesman probably would have preferred to focus Athens's attentions on projects closer to home, forgoing the war against

Persia in favor of extending Athens's Hellenic empire in the Aegean and on the Greek mainland.[24]

Pericles' desire to expand Athens's Greek holdings may also help explain the events surrounding the so-called Peace of Callias, an apparent agreement (formal or informal) between Athens and the Persian Great King Artaxerxes ca. 449 that ended Atheno-Persian hostilities in the Aegean. Pericles undoubtedly supported this agreement, which had been brought about by a renewal of active war with Persia (in Cyprus) after Cimon returned to Athens from ostracism ca. 451 (and arranged a truce with Sparta). Cimon's subsequent death allowed his political rivals like Pericles to take advantage of the situation.[25]

The campaign against the Persians suggests that Cimon briefly dominated Athenian foreign policy after his return in the late 450s; Pericles at that time apparently focused on domestic questions.[26] In 454/3, the treasury of the Delian League had been transferred to Athens, and increased expenditures on Athenian projects followed in short order.[27] Pericles' proposal to begin the payment of jurors from public funds probably occurred during this period, and the statesman's legislation to restrict Athenian citizenship to those with two Athenian parents in 451/0 suggests a reasonable historical context for the measure. When the benefits of Athenian citizenship were on the rise, it might seem both economically and politically expedient (from Pericles' standpoint) to limit this citizenship to those of strictly Athenian descent.[28] Since the law also effectively ended the Athenian aristocrats' practice of marrying into aristocratic non-Athenian families, it would tend to diminish any inter-polis aristocratic ties and/or feelings of "Panhellenism." We may assume that Pericles intended and welcomed both results.

The end of the war with Persia ca. 449 allowed Pericles and the Athenians to turn their attentions fully to Greece itself. Unfortunately for Athens, the peace also confirmed the allies' fears that tribute payment to Athens and Athenian domination of the Aegean were ultimately unrelated to any continuing war against the Persians. Apparently, some states demonstrated resistance or revolted, and the Athenians resorted to force to keep the "alliance" together.[29] Meanwhile, Athenian gains in central Greece were challenged by renewed hostilities with Sparta and a Boeotian coalition led by Thebes (448/7–447/6). When cities on the great island of Euboea also revolted, Pericles led a force there to reduce the poleis, only to learn that Megara had now revolted and murdered its Athenian garrison, opening the isthmus to a Peloponnesian invasion of Attica.[30] According to one tradition, Pericles solved the Spartan problem by bribing the advisors of the Spartan king Pleistoanax, who then failed to attack Athens and was forced to leave Sparta.[31] Nevertheless, the Athenians' loss to the Boeotians at Coronea in 447/6 signaled the end of Athens's land empire in central Greece, and, combined with the troubles in Euboea and elsewhere in the empire, led to a peace treaty with Sparta in 446/5 that was intended to last for thirty years.[32]

Despite the limited success of his presumed foreign policy initiatives in the early to mid-440s, Pericles enjoyed increasing influence in Athenian domestic affairs. Work on the Parthenon began in 447/6, and the Periclean building program as a whole poured large sums of money into Athenian pockets and Athens's economy.[33] Pericles' opponents apparently raised objections to the use of the funds paid by the members of the Delian League for such expenditures, but the program was obviously lucrative for the Athenian portion of the builders, artists, and workers involved, and thus popular. After the demos finally ostracized Pericles' chief political rival and the leading opponent of the program, Thucydides son of Melesias,[34] Pericles began his impressive run of fifteen consecutive years (443/2–429/8) as one of Athens's elected *strategoi*.[35]

Pericles supported, participated in, and probably proposed Athens's intervention in the conflict between its allies Samos and Miletus in 441. Having taken the Milesians' side, the Athenians ultimately voted to impose a democracy and a garrison on Samos and took Samian hostages. When the Samians balked, and some of their anti-Athenian exiles sought the assistance of a Persian satrap, the Athenians besieged the city for nine months before reducing it and then executing many Samian opponents of Athens's actions (440–439).[36]

A faction in Athens clearly resented the brutal treatment of an eminent and powerful ally such as Samos, and Pericles seems to have endured some criticism over his policy.[37] However, the statesman's enemies only succeeded in slandering Pericles' consort Aspasia and possibly indicting, exiling, or ostracizing one or more of his associates.[38] Meanwhile, contemporary jibes at Pericles and his associates may have been responsible for the decree the Athenians apparently passed in 440/39 prohibiting certain kinds of comic abuse.[39] This measure, repealed in 437/6, and (with more certainty) numerous fragments of lost comedies suggest that Pericles and his associates served as frequent butts of the comedians' jokes. (Favorite topics included Pericles' "tyrannical" control of Athens and the empire and the size and shape/baldness of the statesman's head, which one poet claimed was large enough to hold eleven couches.)[40] If comic poets' attacks on Pericles, his supporters, or his policies precipitated the measure, the decree nonetheless suggests that Pericles could still muster real support in the assembly. And the fact that the Samian War did not do any lasting harm to Pericles' overall popularity with the demos may be suggested by the fact that he was chosen to deliver a funeral oration for the Athenians who died in the war.[41]

Pericles' arguably greatest political success occurred in the late 430s, when he persuaded the Athenian populace to refuse all concessions to the Spartans (thus bringing on the Peloponnesian War in 431) and then persuaded the hoplite-farmers of Attica to move inside the city walls and allow their lands to be ravaged by Spartan invaders.[42]

Although scholars continue to debate the causes of the war, Thucydides points clearly to Pericles as the principal reason for the failure of Sparta's diplomatic efforts to secure peace. We may note that, according to Thucydides (1.140–44), Pericles opposed *all* concessions to Sparta on principle: that is, his policy rested on a commitment to absolute Athenian superiority rather than on a calculation of diplomatic or political advantage in particular circumstances.

> The Athenians, persuaded of the wisdom of [Pericles'] advice, voted as he desired, and answered the Lacedaemonians as he recommended, both on the separate points and in general: they would do nothing on dictation, but were ready to have the complaints settled in a fair and impartial manner by the legal method [i.e., arbitration], which the terms of the truce [of 446/5] prescribed. So the [Spartan] envoys departed home and did not return again.
>
> (1.145)

In this passage, as in few others in his history, Thucydides goes out of his way to attribute a policy to a single individual, who is able to persuade the members of the demos to follow him even against their own natural desires or judgment.

Later in his narrative the historian goes even further to establish Pericles' responsibility for the war's outbreak in 432/1. When the Spartans, upon actually marching toward Athenian territory, sent out a herald to test the waters for peace one last time, their spokesman found himself unable to address the Athenian people, "Pericles having already carried a motion against admitting either herald or embassy from the Lacedaemonians after they had marched out" (2.12). This passage is followed immediately by the report of a speech Pericles made to encourage the Athenian people as they faced the Spartan invasion (2.13). Putting all these passages together with Thucydides' praise of Pericles as one able "to lead the demos rather than to be led by them" (2.65), it becomes obvious that, for Thucydides, Pericles himself served as the *sine quo non* for the outbreak of the Peloponnesian War *in spring 431*. Larger forces and historical conditions admittedly created the environment within which Pericles' abilities and policies could bring about this war (at this time).[43] But when Aristophanes and others later joked that Pericles had started the war for personal motives (such as desiring to divert attention from certain legal problems), they were simply adding a comic twist to the obvious responsibility Pericles bore for the war that began in 431.[44]

Even after the war continued into its second year and the Athenians were suffering from a devastating plague, Pericles continued to support the conflict, touting the Athenian dominance and fame that he believed it would ensure, albeit in the face of great popular opposition. Although the demos fined Pericles and apparently removed him from office in this year (430/29), the Athenians subsequently reelected him. Pericles once more was serving as *strategos* when he died (probably from the plague) in 429/8.[45]

PERICLES' IDEAS

Pericles' political convictions and even the particular program he pursued as a result of those convictions – including peace (or at least détente) with Persia, imperial expansion into mainland Greece and tightened controls on the allies (all actions that risked hostilities with Sparta and its allies), and payments made to poorer Athenians in return for their participation in public service – seem comprehensible, if not predictable, given his family background and personal history. But it is less easy to explain the kind of abstraction that appears in Pericles' thoughts about Athens in the speeches Thucydides attributes to him. That Thucydides has colored these addresses with his own language and thought cannot be doubted, but the historian – who expresses his admiration of Pericles' political character in glowing terms – is unlikely to have invented the basic ideas contained in these orations.[46]

What these orations show, beyond a rhetorical brilliance that surely stems from Pericles at least as much as Thucydides,[47] is a fervent nationalism based on a belief in Athenian superiority – or rather, the belief that Athens *could* be superior given the right actions. These actions, in Pericles' view, included the adoption of the belief both in the superiority of the state over the individual and in the related moral value of public service and its ability literally to "act as a shield to cover up a man's other imperfections."[48] Pericles clearly approved of the fact that the Athenians "unlike any other nation," regarded the man who does not participate in the political life of the city through actions like serving on juries "not as unambitious but as useless" (2.40). Pericles returns to this theme in a later speech, opining that "national greatness is more for the advantage of private citizens, than any individual well-being coupled with public humiliation."[49]

Such ideas stand in stark contrast to the older Greek aristocratic ideal of individual *arete* – manly excellence or virtue exhibited to assert individual superiority and to gain the honor and rewards (*time*) such superiority produced. Achilles had famously cursed his fellow Achaeans and withdrawn from the war with Troy after Agamemnon had insulted his honor or *time* (*Iliad* book 1). By placing his own status above his duties to the group, Achilles thereby demonstrated a conception of human excellence based not on morality or responsibility to others, but rather on an individual's performance of great deeds (Achilles was "the best of the Achaeans" because of his military prowess). This conception carried little or no ethical content beyond the duty to one's own honor, a duty over which the group exercised virtually no claim.[50] Pericles, on the other hand, asserted the city's absolute claim on an individual's services and the ability of state service to compensate for personal failings. Somewhat ironically, in their apparent distance from ideas of individual morality, Pericles' views recall Homeric values, although Pericles replaces the individual's duty to his own honor with the individual's duty to provide for the state's reputation.

Pericles' collectivist ideal also fell afoul of other conceptions of excellence and duty current in mid-fifth-century Athens. Sophocles' *Antigone* demonstrates that by ca. 441 some Athenians were already grappling with conflicts between man's duty to the state and his responsibility to obey divine and "unwritten" laws. Although the playwright and the statesman served as generals together and are sometimes depicted as friends, their world-views exhibit a stark contrast – a contrast one might characterize (roughly) as that between the "humanistic" (Pericles) and the "religious" (Sophocles) orientations.[51] Where Sophocles asked his audience to respect and fear man's qualities while evaluating him against a higher (and divine) standard, Pericles' values suggest that there is no higher standard than the admiration of future generations *of men*.

Adding to the contemporary conflict over Athenian values exhibited in Sophocles' *Antigone* may have been the views of Socrates, who by the 430s probably had begun to propound an even more radical concept of personal excellence – a concept that emphasized individual ethics. Socrates apparently placed an individual's duty to divine law and to his own soul above that to the state. Thus, Socrates reminds the Athenians in Plato's *Apology*, he remained aloof from politics. Pericles clearly would have had little sympathy with such notions, as they had the potential of robbing the state of the kind of service and devotion the statesman believed so important.

Of course, the ideal of civic responsibility and public service was hardly unknown to fifth-century Athenians. But Pericles seemingly had taken this concept – ultimately based on utility, community of religious and other sentiments, and natural patriotism – and developed it into a fervent nationalism designed to underpin Athenian power and superiority and ensure Athens's place in history. That is, Pericles' abstract ideal looks toward Athens's future reputation even more than to its present situation or its inherited past. It is, therefore, explicitly *not* a utilitarian or moral view of duty and service. As Pericles states in Thucydides, "even if now, in obedience to the general law of decay, we should ever be forced to yield, still it will be remembered that we held rule over more Greeks than any other Greek state" (2.64). These views, perhaps less than remarkable in modern societies, which are focused on the future and thus obsessed with "progress" and creating a better world "for our children," made Pericles a very unusual thinker for fifth-century Greece.[52]

It was Athens's power, and not her cultural or political superiority, on which Pericles relied for Athens's future reputation: Pericles did not tell the Athenian people that they would be remembered for their democracy or for Sophoclean tragedy or for the Parthenon, but rather for their rule over other Greeks. This equation – "Athenian power = reputation in the future" – seems to have been a central idea for Pericles, who pursued the goal of Athenian supremacy in Hellas throughout his career. This theme also pervades the Age of Pericles, pulling together the policies of hostility toward Sparta and the radicalization of the democracy through empowering the demos, the members of which would – in turn – provide Athens with the votes and manpower necessary to ensure her dominant position in Hellas.

To understand how important this idea of Athens's reputation was to Pericles, one need only note that the statesman apparently believed that individual Athenians' contemplation of their state's future reputation (as opposed to their own personal safety or honor) actually should comfort the citizens suffering from the loss of their children and bolster them in the face of a war now aggravated by the outbreak of a deadly plague. In the event, the statesman somewhat overestimated the Athenians' willingness to sacrifice themselves on the altar of their city's future reputation. Nevertheless, Pericles' overall career clearly demonstrates his ability to sell his conception of Athens and state service to the demos at large. As Thucydides put it, Pericles was able to lead the people, and thus to persuade them to take unpopular actions.

> Pericles indeed, by his rank, ability, and known integrity, was enabled to exercise an independent control over the multitude – in short, to lead them instead of being led by them; for as he never sought power by improper means, he was never compelled to flatter them, but, on the contrary, enjoyed so high an estimation that he could afford to anger them by contradiction. Whenever he saw them unseasonably and insolently elated, he would with a word reduce them to alarm; on the other hand, if they fell victims to a panic, he could at once restore them to confidence. In short, what was nominally a democracy became in his hands government by the first citizen. With his successors it was different. More on a level with one another, and each grasping at supremacy, they ended by committing even the conduct of state affairs to the whims of the multitude. This, as might have been expected in a great and sovereign state, produced a host of blunders . . .
> (2.65)[53]

In Thucydides' opinion, Pericles' accomplishments, skill, and integrity separated the statesman from later demagogues, who simply pandered to the demos by inciting their baser passions or by simply telling them what they wished to hear. Pericles, on the other hand, turned the populace toward policies *he* deemed appropriate, policies he honestly believed were best for Athens and, especially, for her future reputation.

The events of Pericles' career demonstrate that a voting populace can be led into difficult, treacherous, or simply unpopular political territory by an individual with sufficient persuasive powers and impressive personal character – an individual who is willing to risk removal from office or the loss of power by contradicting majority opinion. But it is also clear that many of Pericles' political and military actions resulted in real economic gains for the Athenian electorate. Payments for public service and the massive building program helped earn him the basic support of the poorer members of the demos, whose service in the Athenian navy (in turn) took some military pressure off the middle-class hoplite-farmers who made up the infantry. This last group, like the sailors and even many aristocrats, also enjoyed the benefits Athens's empire brought to the city, including the markets it opened for their surplus produce and the lands it provided for their occupation.[54] Pericles' support of imperial policies like the planting of Athenian colonies and cleruchies around the Aegean and the collection and use of tribute from "allied" Greek states never seems to have wavered.[55] The idea that the Athenians thereby were ensuring a place in history for their city as well as material advantages for themselves undoubtedly encouraged the natural view that their polis was special, and perhaps helped allay any fears that their empire was unjust. It is surely no coincidence that Pericles' more "popular" acts – including the building program and the creation of jury pay – came in his early or middle career. By the late 430s, Pericles' long-established political influence and public reputation enabled him to push the citizenry into a deadly and far from universally popular war with Sparta.

Pericles asked the Athenians to align their interests with those of the state and the Athenian leader apparently practiced what he preached. For Pericles risked his own life numerous times in service to his country, both proposing military actions in the assembly and then leading them on the battlefield. Pericles' individual courage and real commitment to his policies cannot be questioned.[56]

Moreover, however skeptical his personal religious beliefs may have been, we have every reason to believe that Pericles performed all the religious duties of his political office as general and the religious actions that were expected of him as an Athenian citizen and father without demur. Had he not done so, we certainly would expect to hear about this in the historical record, which contains numerous unflattering details about Pericles' personal and public life and associates him closely with men of heterodox views like the philosopher Anaxagoras.[57] Pericles may have been thought by some to share Anaxagoras' strange opinions, but that apparently did not lead even to any rumor (much less an accusation) that he failed to perform his religious duties. We may also note that Pericles sponsored and served as a commissioner for the Athenian building program, which resulted in the rejuvenation of the sacral center of Athens and served religious as much as political or economic purposes. Again, Pericles' actions, not his personal views about the gods, established his essential piety in most Athenian eyes.[58]

Economically, Pericles seems to have subordinated personal gain to his own ideas about justice and public service. Despite his wealth, he reportedly lived on such a strict budget that it led to poor relations with his sons.[59] In short, his actions seem to reflect an Athenian ideal that money was not a thing to be pursued for its own sake. In this way, Pericles' life demonstrates the fact that Athenian society at large placed a value on allowing other concerns to influence one's economic decisions.[60]

According to Thucydides, Pericles' Funeral Oration ended with a firm reminder of Pericles' conception of the individual Athenian's duty to the state.

> Comfort, therefore, not condolence, is what I have to offer to the parents of the dead who may be here. Numberless are the chances to which, as they know, the life of man is subject; but fortunate indeed are they who draw for their lot a death so glorious as that which has caused your mourning, and to whom life has been so exactly measured as to terminate in the happiness in which it has been passed. Still I know that this is a hard saying, especially when those are in question of whom you will constantly be reminded by seeing in the homes of others blessings of which once you also boasted: for grief is felt not so much for the want of what we have never known, as for the loss of that to which we have long been accustomed. Yet you who are still of an age to beget children must bear up in the hope of having others in their stead; not only will they help you to forget those whom you have lost, but will be to the state at once a reinforcement and a security; for never can a fair or just policy be expected of the citizen who does not, like his fellows, bring to the decision the interests and apprehensions of a father. And those of you who have passed your prime must congratulate yourselves with the thought that the best part of your life was fortunate, and that the brief span that remains will be cheered by the fame of the departed. For it is only the love of honor that never grows old; and honor it is, not gain, as some would have it, that rejoices the heart of age and helplessness.
>
> Turning to the sons and brothers of the dead, I see an arduous struggle before you. When a man is gone, all are wont to praise him, and should your merit be ever so transcendent, you will still find it difficult not merely to overtake, but even to approach their renown. The living have envy to contend with, while those who are no longer

in our path are honored with a goodwill into which rivalry does not enter. On the other hand, if I must say anything on the subject of female excellence to those of you who will now be in widowhood, it will be all comprised in this brief exhortation. Great will be your glory in not falling short of your natural character; and greatest will be hers who is least talked about among men whether for good or bad.

My task is now finished. I have performed it to the best of my ability, and in words, at least, the requirements of the law [demanding a funeral oration] are now satisfied. If deeds be in question, those who are here interred have received part of their honors already, and for the rest, their children will be brought up till manhood at the public expense: the state thus offers a valuable prize as the garland of victory in this race of valor, for the reward both of those who have fallen and their survivors. And where the rewards for merit are greatest, there are found the best citizens.

And now that you have brought to a close your lamentations for your relatives, you may depart.

(Thuc. 2.44–6)

This long passage is quoted and discussed far less frequently than Pericles' brief discussion of democracy and his argument for the superiority of Athenian liberality to the Spartans' strict way of life in the same speech. Perhaps this is so because these words hardly seem consistent with the popular view of Athenian democracy and humanism. Indeed, no part of this passage (apart from the complex sentences and the demeaning remarks about women[61]) would be in any way out of character in a Spartan oration over the dead. The abstract notion that honor (and not children or grandchildren) makes old age pleasant and that such honor may be gained from the death of one's children surely would have been applauded in Sparta, where the ideal mother told her son to return from battle with his shield "or on it."

One should also note that Pericles' encouragement to produce more children is aimed at the middle-aged and older men present: most middle-aged mothers of sons old enough to die in combat could not be expected to produce "replacements" for their dead sons. Indeed, it is only the widows among the women in the audience that receive any kind of special attention, and probably few of these women will have become the new wives of those Athenian men still young enough to produce reinforcements for the state. Among other things, Pericles' oration should remind us that Athenian *demokratia* in its Periclean form was not an ancient version of modern liberalism or social democracy, and that Pericles and his fellow Athenians were far more like their contemporary Spartan adversaries than like twenty-first-century democrats.

If one extrapolates from the reports about Pericles' lack of sociability and his apparent unwillingness to express much basic human sympathy for the parents of Athens's dead soldiers in the Funeral Oration, at least one potential motivation for Pericles' political actions in favor of the demos disappears.[62] No evidence suggests that Pericles loved the common members of the demos (any more than he loved his fellow aristocrats) or that he sought to improve their conditions out of humanitarian concerns. Rather, in the landless mass of citizens Pericles saw an untapped source of Athenian power and the crucial support for Athenian dominance. In short, Pericles seems to have believed that it was necessary to raise the demos (even at the expense of the aristocrats) so that his policies might succeed and so that Athens might thus triumph (both then and in history).

This essentially nonpolitical goal of ensuring Athens's place in history and Pericles' own personal integrity separate him from the demagogues who came after him. Where they looked for success in the assembly or on the battlefield in order to gain power in the present, Pericles sought to make Athens powerful in order to ensure the city's future reputation. And Pericles' ideals, his integrity, and his personal charisma, combined with his ability to abstract himself and other individual Athenians from their real political environment in order to focus on Athens's position in history, made Pericles both the greatest and the most dangerous leader Athens ever produced.

If unmitigated praise for Pericles is therefore unjustified, we may pause to focus on one of his admirable qualities that stands out most starkly in the modern democratic world. Even if Pericles' proposals sometimes stemmed in part from a plan to ingratiate him with the demos at large (as a means to achieve his greater goal), the evidence we have demonstrates clearly that he occasionally spoke harshly and critically to the Athenian people. Confident in his own powers of persuasion and loyal to his own ideals, Pericles felt no compunction about telling the Athenian demos that they were wrong. "If you are angry with me," he states early in his last speech in Thucydides, when the Athenians were enduring a plague that increased the suffering caused by the Peloponnesian War, "you are angry with a man who is, as I think, second to no man either in knowledge of the proper policy or in the ability to expound it, and who is moreover not only a patriot but an honest one" (2.60). In the same speech, Pericles reminds his audience that *they* had voted for the very war for which they now wished to blame him. One is hard pressed to imagine a modern elected leader in the midst of an unpopular war or economic recession (much less a plague!) proclaiming to the electorate (in essence), "I am smart and honest; if you are angry with me, it is because you are neither smart nor honest with yourselves, since you have become fickle, while I have remained the same." Let us remember that by speaking in this way and by proposing and then supervising politically dangerous policies (such as war with Sparta), Pericles risked immediate removal from office, fines, ostracism, and even execution by the populace he addressed.

RECONSIDERING THE "AGE OF PERICLES"

Pericles led the Athenians in the military campaigns and tribute collection that undergirded their empire, supported and supervised the public construction that made Athens the most impressive polis in Hellas, and proposed the public expenditures that empowered and enriched the Athenian demos. Within this superheated environment and surely in part in response to it, Sophocles composed his greatest tragedies while Euripides polished and Aristophanes learned their craft. At the same time, Pericles prepared and then encouraged Athens to fight a war with Sparta that would ultimately debilitate the Hellenic city-state system and end the lives of tens of thousands of Greeks. Thucydides' speeches suggest that Pericles himself clearly understood the risks he (and Athens) ran by undertaking such actions. But the statesman considered these risks acceptable in view of the potential gain for Athens's position in history.

For many, Pericles has come to represent things like the empowerment of the poorer citizens and the ideals of humanism and democracy (especially "liberty and equality"), while the term "Periclean Athens" usually brings to the mind sublime literature and architecture (rather than war, nationalism, and imperialism). But we have seen that neither egalitarianism nor humanism, nor the rich theological world-view of Sophocles, nor the moral philosophy of Socrates can be identified as the defining ideals of Periclean Athens or of Pericles himself. And while fifth-century Athenian literature does occasionally seem to praise or encourage the Athenian practice of democracy, this theme appears in only a very small part of Athenian drama.[63] More frequently, dramatists such as Sophocles and Euripides seem to be questioning the values or practice of *demokratia* or humanistic ideals as much as reaffirming them.[64] In general, the themes that flow through this literature are far more universal than praising or condemning the particular form Hellenic polis government could take.[65] Certainly one may justifiably associate great literature and drama with Periclean Athens. But we should hesitate to credit Pericles himself or democratic politics with their particular form or superlative quality, unless we admit that artists such as Sophocles and Thucydides (and perhaps even the great sculptor Pheidias) may be seen as critics of the Age of Pericles as much as products of it.[66]

Moreover, Pericles got it wrong. Athens is *not* remembered today because she "spent more lives" or "ruled more Greeks than any other Greek state." Most people without a detailed knowledge of Greek history – and some with it – would (wrongly) associate those dubious accomplishments with Sparta. Instead of the long passages on Athens's power and military successes in Pericles' speeches, it is the relatively few words about democracy that are quoted repeatedly by those wishing to characterize the Athenian regime or Pericles himself.

But the few words praising an open society or election based on merit in Pericles' speeches should not be allowed to overshadow the pervading theme of his orations and of the years he led Athens. That theme was *Athenian power*. And even if one believed that Pericles felt compassion for the lowest Athenian citizens (despite sending thousands of them to their deaths), this would say nothing about the thousands of allied Greeks, metics, and slaves exploited systematically by the Athenian people.[67] Pericles, after all, was not some kind of twentieth-century leader defending "democracy" or "the poor and underprivileged" against the attacks of those opposed to "freedom." Pericles used *demokratia* as a force to build Athenian power, and that meant "spending more life" than any other Greek state as much as it necessitated allowing those without property to vote in the assembly or serve (with payment) on Athenian courts. Under Pericles, the Athenian demos was offered a very plain exchange. If the common citizens would serve repeatedly in the military and vote for Pericles, his supporters, and their policies, they would receive in return payments for their public service, an increase in their political power, and the glory and wealth that attended their empire. When combined with Pericles' insistence that Athenians owed their first duties to the state, that these duties would compensate for their private failings, and that Athens ran a terrible risk if it gave up its empire, it is understandable why this message ultimately succeeded.

Pericles' contributions to the age associated with his name occurred because he acted as a genuine leader in his society, proving himself willing to run great risks, including losing his life, in order to continue to express his sincerely held opinions. As we have seen, Pericles was removed from office and fined on at least one occasion, and his friends and associates endured popular criticism and perhaps even political and legal attacks because of their association with the statesman. Despite this, Pericles "led the people instead of being led by them," in the words of Thucydides (2.65), demonstrating his willingness to oppose the will of the people and directly contradict the demos. His determination to upbraid the people, to tell them when they were wrong, to assert his own wisdom and the wisdom of his policies in the face of public fines, exile, or execution, stands in stark contrast to the timid modern democratic politician's fear of merely failing in a reelection bid. And Pericles' success in creating particular policies and then convincing the Athenians to follow him (even when his views were unpopular) during a tumultuous period of Greek history demonstrates just how much – for good or ill – one man can accomplish within a democratic regime.

Pericles remains today one of the few individuals in Western history whose name can stand for an entire historical epoch by calling to mind political, social, artistic, literary, and intellectual aspects of the period. As the leader of Athens's most progressive and militaristic faction, panegyrist of Athenian natural superiority and collectivism, proponent of Athens's greatest public construction project, and associate or friend of some of the city's (and era's) greatest minds, Pericles defined his age even as he radically altered it. It is therefore in no way inappropriate to think of the mid-fifth century in Athens as the "Age of Pericles," as long as we understand that the term represents much more than democracy, drama, and the Parthenon, and as long as we remember that for other Greeks and even for some Athenians, Periclean Athens evoked not only admiration and respect, but also resentment and fear.[68]

SUGGESTIONS FOR FURTHER READING

A. J. Podlecki, *Perikles and his Circle* (London: Routledge, 1998), provides a detailed treatment of Pericles' career and his relations with his associates and contemporaries. For the statesman's background and politics, see especially C. W. Fornara and L. J. Samons, *Athens from Cleisthenes to Pericles* (Berkeley: University of California Press, 1991). Donald

Kagan, *Pericles of Athens and the Birth of Democracy* (New York: Simon and Schuster, 1991), presents a very useful (and generally favorable) over-view of Pericles' career and historical significance. Victor Ehrenberg, *Sophocles and Pericles* (Oxford: Blackwell, 1954), is still valuable on the intellectual and social milieu of mid-fifth-century Athens, its subjects' worldviews, and much else. W. R. Connor's *The New Politicians of Fifth-Century Athens* (Princeton: Princeton University Press, 1971) empha-sizes Pericles' role as a precursor to leaders such as Cleon who followed him and has an excellent treatment of the emerging political vocabulary of the fifth century. Readers interested in Plutarch's biography of Pericles should be aware of P. Stadter's helpful work, *A Commentary on Plutarch's Pericles* (Chapel Hill: University of North Carolina Press, 1989).

NOTES

1   For a notable exception, see P. Rahe, *Republics Ancient and Modern* (Chapel Hill: University of North Carolina Press, 1992), pp. 198 ff.

2   See, e.g., J. J. Pollitt, *Art and Experience in Classical Greece* (Cambridge: Cambridge University Press, 1972), pp. 71–97, and Brook Manville and Josiah Ober, *A Company of Citizens* (Boston: Harvard Business School Press, 2003), pp. 1–5. For the Parthenon itself, see also Lapatin in this volume, pp. 135–42.

3   This has been denied; but see L. J. Samons, *Empire of the Owl: Athenian Imperial Finance* (Stuttgart: Steiner, 2000), pp. 41–50.

4   On the Panathenaea and the celebratory procession the frieze may depict, see R. Parker, *Athenian Religion: A History* (Oxford: Oxford University Press, 1996), pp. 91–2, and J. Neils, ed., *Worshipping Athena: Panathenaia and Parthenon* (Madison: University of Wisconsin Press, 1996); on the name, cf. N. Robertson, "Athena's Shrines and Festivals," in Neils, p. 56: "Panathenaia presumably means 'Rites of all Athenians.'"

5   On Pandora's presence here, cf. J. Pollitt (n. 2), pp. 98–9, and Lapatin in this volume, p. 136.

6   D. M. Lewis, *CAH* V².139. On the subject in general, cf. David Castriota, *Myth, Ethos and Actuality: Official Art in Fifth-Century B.C. Athens* (Madison: University of Wisconsin Press, 1992). For a more optimistic interpretation of the Parthenon and its sculpture, see Pollitt (n. 2), pp. 64–110.

7   Translations of Thucydides in this chapter are those of R. Crawley, often adapted, sometimes based on the revisions of T. E. Wick, Thucydides, *The Peloponnesian War* (New York: Modern Library, 1982).

8   On the Athenians' self-image, see L. J. Samons, "Democracy, Empire and the Search for the Athenian Character," *Arion* 8.3 (2001): 128–57. On the role of honor and rank in inter-polis relations in fifth-century Greece, see Lendon in this volume (as will be clear, we differ somewhat on the causes of the Peloponnesian War).

9   On the Athenian funeral orations (*epitaphioi*) in general, see Nicole Loraux, *The Invention of Athens: The Funeral Oration in the Classical City,* trans. Alan Sheridan (Cambridge, MA: Harvard University Press, 1986), who overemphasizes the

importance of democracy in these speeches (p. 64), especially relative to Athens's military virtues and history.

10   Long after Pericles' death, Athenians continued to identify the special qualities of Athens primarily in military rather than political terms: see, e.g., Isocrates *Panegyricus,* Plato *Menexenus,* Lysias 2.

11   See, e.g., Hornblower, *CT* 1.311.

12   For recent attempts to treat Pericles, see Donald Kagan, *Pericles of Athens and the Birth of Democracy* (New York: Simon and Schuster, 1991); C. W. Fornara and L. J. Samons, *Athens from Cleisthenes to Pericles* (Berkeley: University of California Press, 1991), esp. pp. 23–36; Charlotte Schubert, *Perikles* (Darmstadt: Wissenschaftliche Buchgesellschaft, 1994); and A. J. Podlecki, *Perikles and His Circle* (London: Routledge, 1998).

13   See *AP* 1, Plut. *Solon* 12, and Diog. Laert. 1.110, with Fornara and Samons (n. 12), pp. 6–7.

14   See L. J. Samons, "Mass, Elite and Hoplite-Farmer in Greek History," *Arion* 5.3 (1998): 110–15, with the additional material in "Revolution or Compromise?" in E. W. Robinson, ed., *Ancient Greek Democracy: Readings and Sources* (Oxford: Blackwell 2004), pp. 113–22, and Fornara and Samons (n. 12), pp. 13–23, 37–58. On the origins of the name *demokratia,* see Sealey in this volume, pp. 238, 250–51.

15   Hdt. 5.70–73, with Fornara and Samons (n. 12), pp. 19–23, and Samons (n. 14, 1998): 110–15.

16   See Hdt. 6.115, 121–4; *AP* 22.

17   See Fornara and Samons (n. 12), pp. 24–36; Plut. *Per.* 4–6. Podlecki (n. 12), pp. 30–31, also considers Pericles a "rationalist," but does not associate this with his family background. On the intellectual climate of Athens in this period, see Wallace in this volume.

18   Fornara and Samons (n. 12), pp. 1–36; cf. Podlecki (n. 12), pp. 1–10, 156.

19   Fornara and Samons (n. 12), pp. 23–9. On Pericles' early career, cf. Podlecki (n. 12), pp. 11–16, 35–54, and Kagan (n. 12), pp. 26–45. For popular associations of Pericles with Peisistratus, see Plut. *Per.* 7, 16.

20   *AP* 27, Plut. *Per.* 7, 10. It is also possible that Pericles acted as a collusive prosecutor in Cimon's case. For although Pericles' father Xanthippus had prosecuted Cimon's father Miltiades a generation earlier (in somewhat murky circumstances: Hdt. 6.136), Cimon's family and the Alcmeonid clan had a long-running relationship stretching back into (at least) the mid-sixth century: see Samons (n. 8): 145–7 and *What's Wrong with Democracy? From Athenian Practice to American Worship* (Berkeley: University of California Press, 2004), pp. 101–4, 239–40 n. 13, and on the prosecution, cf. also R. Sealey, "The Entry of Pericles into History," *Hermes* 84 (1956): 237–8. (In fact, Cimon's wife Isodice was an Alcmeonid and one of Pericles' sons married a member of Cimon's family. Both marriages suggest that, whatever the families' political persuasions, no inveterate enmity existed between them.) Pericles eventually took a clearly anti-Cimonian line in politics, but his actual break with Cimon (and/or his policies) may have come some time after the trial of 463. Pericles' later actions would then have suggested an interpretation of the trial that made his policy seem consistently anti-Cimonian throughout his career.

21   See *AP* 25–7, Plut. *Per.* 7–10. For Ephialtes' reforms see also the Introduction and Sealey in this volume, pp. 243–4; for the view that Pericles' role in the reforms

has been exaggerated in (some) ancient and modern treatments, see Fornara and Samons (n. 12), pp. 24–8, and L. J. Samons, "Aeschylus, the Alkmeonids, and the Reform of the Areopagos," *CJ* 94 (1998/99): 221–33. Podlecki (n. 12), pp. 46–7, supports the conventional view, but concedes that Ephialtes may have been recorded "as the principal mover" (p. 46) in documents recording the legislation. The arguably best and least tendentious reference to the reforms in our sources (*AP* 35.2) attributes the measures to Ephialtes and a certain Archestratos and makes no mention of Pericles. At the very least, this reference makes it virtually certain that Pericles himself did not make the formal motion(s) that led to the reforms.

22 Samons (n. 21).

23 Thuc. 1.104, 109–10. Plut. *Per.* 20 explicitly reports that Pericles opposed an expedition to Egypt, but the temporal context is unclear and the report could simply reflect a logical inference by Plutarch or his source based on Pericles' later policy of avoiding conflict with Persia.

24 Plut. *Per.* 20–23 describes Pericles' interest in a mainland Greek empire, although the biographer cites this as an example of Periclean moderation, since he attempted to restrain the demos from foreign adventures beyond Greece.

25 For the "peace" and its possible results, see also Introduction, p. 15 with n. 62, and Rhodes in this volume, p. 27.

26 Plut. *Per.* 10 (cf. *Cim.* 17) reports a secret agreement between Pericles and Cimon by which Pericles would propose Cimon's recall from ostracism and the two would then divide their power into domestic (Pericles) and foreign (Cimon) spheres. Again, this may be no more than an inference from later events.

27 Pericles was a member of the board of generals in 454/3, and his later use of the allied money justifies the inference that he supported the transfer: see Samons (n. 3), pp. 92–106.

28 For the citizenship law, see *AP* 26.4, with Podlecki (n. 12), pp. 159–61 (containing a useful summary of recent scholarship on possible motives for the measure) and Rhodes, p. 28 and Patterson, pp. 163, 168–9 in this volume.

29 For the resistance and revolts in the late 450s – mid-440s, see R. Meiggs, *The Athenian Empire* (Oxford: Oxford University Press, 1972), pp. 109–28, 152–74, with P. J. Rhodes, *CAH* V².54–61, and D. Lewis, *CAH* V².127–38. On the relationship between Athenian democracy and imperialism in general, see Rhodes in this volume.

30 Thuc. 1.112–15; Plut. *Per.* 22–3.

31 Plut. *Per.* 22–3; Ar. *Clouds* 858–9, with *schol.* (= Fornara 104).

32 Thuc. 1. 113, 115; Plut. *Per.* 24; Lewis, *CAH* V².133–8.

33 Parthenon work: *IG* i³ 436; Pericles' responsibility for the building program and public payments from the work: Plut *Per.* 12–14, 31. Podlecki (n. 12), pp. 69–70, 78–9, 86–7, 101–9, 157–8, discusses Pericles' direct involvement (perhaps exaggerated by our sources) with Pheidias and the building program as a whole, concluding that he exercised "general oversight of [the construction of the Odeion] along with other building projects" (p. 79). On this work see also Lapatin in this volume.

34 Plut. *Per.* 12, 14; for the building program debate, analysis of Plutarch's report, and references to other literature, see Samons (n. 3), pp. 41–50, 154–7; for Pericles and Thucydides son of Melesias, see Podlecki (n. 12), pp. 83–8.

35 Plut. *Per.* 15–16.

36　Thuc. 1.115–17, Plut. Per. 24–8, with C. W. Fornara, "On the Chronology of the Samian War," JHS 99 (1979): 9–17, and D. Lewis, CAH V².143–5.

37　Plut. Per. 24, 28.

38　Plut. Per. 24, 31–32, with Fornara and Samons (n. 12), pp. 34–5. The dates and specific nature of any formal or informal attacks on Pericles' associates (such as Anaxagoras, Pheidias, Damon, and Aspasia) are problematic. For the ostracism of Damon (recently doubted), see R. W. Wallace "Damon of Oa: A Music Theorist, Ostracized?" in P. Murray and P. Wilson, eds., Music and the Muses: The Culture of Mousike in the Classical Athenian City (Oxford: Oxford University Press, 2004), pp. 249–67; for the others, see, e.g., Podlecki (n. 12), pp. 31–4, 101–17.

39　Schol. Ar. Ach. 67 = Fornara 111. Other explanations of the measure are, of course, possible.

40　For fragments of the lost comedians ridiculing Pericles, see Plut. Per. 3–4, 13, 16, 24, 33, with Podlecki (n. 12), pp. 169–76.

41　Plut. Per. 28, with Arist. Rhet. 1365a, I.7.31–3; on the procedure for selecting the orator for the funeral ceremony, see Pl. Menex. 234a–6a.

42　Thuc. book 1, esp. 1.140–46; Plut. Per. 32–4.

43　For another view of the war's outbreak, see Lendon in this volume, pp. 270–75, and cf. Raaflaub, pp. 96–102. The view propounded here is admittedly heterodox (see Samons [n. 20], pp. 124–31, for a more thorough justification). The Spartans are sometimes blamed for the outbreak of the Peloponnesian War because they opened direct hostilities by invading Attica, because they refused arbitration, which they apparently should have accepted under the terms of the treaty of 446/5 (Thuc. 1.78.4, 140: see esp. G. E. M. de Ste. Croix, The Origins of the Peloponnesian War [London: Duckworth, 1972], e.g., pp. 55–6, 65, 290; cf. also Hornblower, CT 1.227–8, and E. Badian, From Plataea to Potidaea: Studies in the History and Historiography of the Pentecontaetia [Baltimore: Johns Hopkins University Press, 1993], pp. 142–4), and because the Spartans later even condemned themselves for their refusal (see Thuc. 7.18, with de Ste. Croix, locc. cit.). But this condemnation, fair enough if we (like the religiously scrupulous Spartans) wish to judge the ultimate morality of a foreign policy based on the letter of a treaty, ignores the realities of the situation in 432/1. Simply put, the Spartans had nothing with which to bargain in any arbitration. Every matter in contention stemmed from Athenian actions against Spartan allies, and thus the only possible result of any "arbitration" would have been Spartan acceptance (and thus legitimation) of some part of the Athenians' aggressive policies. Sparta's decision to refuse arbitration is thus more than comprehensible, while its willingness to concede most of Athens's gains informally and without arbitration shows the Spartans' real desire to avoid this war. The Spartans clearly were willing, in fact, to ignore their allies the Corinthians' complaints against Athens if the Athenians would only give up the decree limiting the trade of Megara (another of Sparta's allies), but the Spartans could not be forced into any formal recognition of Athens's claims against Peloponnesian interests. In other words, the Spartans needed some concession from Athens to take back to their Peloponnesian allies, both as a demonstration that Sparta had not completely abandoned them to Athenian dominance and as an excuse to avoid war (cf. Lendon in this volume, pp. 273–5). It was Pericles' policy of refusing any concession that brought on the conflict in spring 432/1.

44 For Aristophanes' lampoons of the war's causes, see *Acharn.* 513–39 with schol. on 532, *Peace* 605–6 with schol.

45 See Thuc. 2.60–65, with Hornblower, *CT* 1.341; Plut. *Per.* 35. On Pericles' career, see also Rhodes in this volume, pp. 32–3.

46 Thuc. 2.65 with 1.22. On speeches in Thucydides cf. also Rhodes, p. 36 and Lendon, p. 281 n. 44 in this volume.

47 Many sources beyond Thucydides testify to Pericles' skills as an orator: see Plut. *Per.* 7, 8, 15, Plato *Menex.* 235e, *Phaedrus* 269e–70a, schol. Ar. *Acharn.* 530; for a collection of relevant texts in translation, see Fornara 74.

48 Thuc. 2.42; see also p. 300.

49 Compare Nicias's view expressed before the Athenian assembly (Thuc. 6.9), a speech where Nicias echoes Thucydides' description of Sicily (6.2–6), and which thus may be thought to express other opinions shared by the historian: "not that I think a man need be any the worse citizen for taking some thought for his person and estate; on the contrary, such a man would for his own sake desire the prosperity of his country more than others...."

50 But compare Hector's part in the *Iliad*: his concerns for the city and its reaction to his actions may reflect the influence of early polis values.

51 For a somewhat similar view, see V. Ehrenberg, *Sophocles and Pericles* (Oxford: Blackwell, 1958). For Sophocles and Pericles as "probably friends," cf. Podlecki (n. 12), pp. 121–4 (p. 124), and Kagan (n. 12), p. 133, who writes, "Sophocles appears to have been part of Cimon's circle of friends, who joined in the general union with the Pericleans after Cimon's return from exile and remained friendly with Pericles thereafter."

52 For the more typical Greek emphasis on not falling short of one's ancestors, see Thuc. 1.144, Dem. 14.41.

53 Plutarch *Per.* 15 expands on Thucydides' opinion, but draws a line between an early demagogic portion of Pericles' career (before the ostracism of Thucydides son of Melesias) and the later, statesmanlike period: cf. Gomme, *HCT* 1.65–70, Ehrenberg (n. 51), p. 87, and Fornara and Samons (n. 12), pp. 29–34.

54 Obviously only the sons of poorer hoplite-farmers (who would not inherit sufficient property to maintain their position) and those below this status would be likely to participate in Athenian colonies and cleruchies established in the empire. But we must conclude that this offered a major safety valve for forces that, in other *poleis*, would have been likely to cause unrest.

55 For Pericles' support of colonies and cleruchies (Athenian settlements on lands seized within other states), see esp. Plut. *Per.* 11, 19–20; cf. Podlecki (n. 12), pp. 62–4, and Meiggs (n. 29), pp. 260–62.

56 For Pericles' military exploits, see esp. Plut. *Per.* 18–28, with Podlecki (n. 12), pp. 55–76, who also discusses his foreign policy.

57 These details mainly appear in Plutarch's life of Pericles, and some are undoubtedly later inventions. However, we happen to know that in the fifth century a certain Stesimbrotus of Thasos wrote a work on Pericles, Thucydides (son of Melesias, not the historian), and Themistocles. This work contained, at least, contemporary gossip, which was therefore available to Plutarch. The comic poets also provided Plutarch with ample contemporary material on Pericles. For Pericles and Anaxagoras, see Podlecki (n. 12), pp. 23–31.

58 Although a modern might conclude (as does Wallace in this volume, p. 219) that Pericles was probably an atheist, his actions apparently did not lead to this conclusion by (at least the majority of) his contemporaries; cf. Ehrenberg (n. 51), pp. 41–46, 92. For contemporary Athenian religious attitudes and practices, see Boedeker in this volume.

59 See Plut. *Per.* 16, 36, and cf. Kallet in this volume, pp. 73–4.

60 For the complex nature of the Athenian economy, see Kallet in this volume.

61 For the view that these remarks do not demean women, see Patterson in this volume, pp. 171–2; cf. Raaflaub, p. 115.

62 Pericles' lack of sociability: Plut. *Per.* 5, 7. See Plato *Menex.* 247c–8d, for a "funeral oration" that is significantly more personal in its words for the parents of the dead, and Arist. *Rhet.* 1365a, I.7.34, which attributes a compassionate phrase lamenting the loss of Athens's young men to a (perhaps different) funeral oration of Pericles.

63 E.g., Euripides *Suppliants* 399–494; cf. Aeschylus *Eumenides*, esp. 681ff. (on the establishment of the Areopagus council), and see also Henderson in this volume. For an attempt to use the scattered literary references to construct a fifth-century defense of democracy, see K. Raaflaub, "Contemporary Perception of Democracy in Fifth-Century Athens," *C&M* 40 (1989): 33–70.

64 See, for example, Sophocles *Ant.* 368–411 (end of the "Ode to Man"), and Eur. *Ion* 590ff.

65 For the minimal role democracy played in the fifth-century Athenians' self-image, see Samons (n. 8). Democracy's relative prevalence in Aristophanic comedy is as telling as its virtual absence from other fifth-century literary and artistic forms.

66 Recent work, especially by Simon Goldhill – "The Great Dionysia and Civic Ideology," *JHS* 107 (1987): 58–76 (also published in Winkler and Zeitlin, eds., *Nothing to Do with Dionysos?* [Princeton: Princeton University Press, 1990], pp. 97–129) and "Civic Ideology and the Problem of Difference: The Politics of Aeschylean Tragedy, Once Again," *JHS* 120 (2000): 34–56 – has usefully emphasized the particular social and historical context of Athenian tragedy. Yet the association (and indeed identification) of this context with democracy per se seems to me much exaggerated. For a corrective, see P. J. Rhodes, "Nothing to Do with Democracy: Athenian Drama and the *Polis*," *JHS* 123 (2003): 104–19, and cf. Henderson in this volume and J. Griffin, "The Social Function of Attic Tragedy," *CQ* 48 (1998): 39–61.

67 For the metics and slaves, see Patterson in this volume.

68 I thank the University of California Press for permission to reprint and adapt portions of Loren J. Samons II, *What's Wrong with Democracy? From Athenian Practice to American Worship* (Berkeley: University of California Press, 2004).

BIBLIOGRAPHY

Abramson, H., "A Hero Shrine for Phrontis at Sounion?" *CSCA* 12 (1979): 1–19.

Adcock, F. E., *Thucydides and His History* (Cambridge: Cambridge University Press, 1963).

Adkins, A. W. H., *Moral Values and Political Behaviour in Ancient Greece from Homer to the End of the Fifth Century* (New York: Norton, 1972).

Aleshire, Sara B., "The Demos and the Priests: The Selection of Sacred Officials at Athens from Cleisthenes to Augustus," in R. Osborne and S. Hornblower, eds., *Ritual, Finance, Politics: Athenian Democratic Accounts Presented to David Lewis* (Oxford: Oxford University Press, 1994), pp. 325–37.

Anderson, Greg, "Alkmeonid Homelands, Political Exile and the Unification of Attica," *Historia* 49 (2000): 387–412.

Anderson, Greg, *The Athenian Experiment: Building an Imagined Political Community in Ancient Attica, 508-490 B.C.* (Ann Arbor: University of Michigan Press, 2003).

Andrewes, A., *The Greek Tyrants* (London: Hutchinson, 1956).

Andrewes, A., "Phratries in Homer," *Hermes* 89 (1961): 129–40.

Andrewes, A., "The Theramenes Papyrus," *ZPE* 6 (1970): 35–8.

Andrewes, A., "The Opposition to Pericles," *JHS* 98 (1978): 1–8.

Arias, P. E., M. Hirmer, and B. B. Shefton, *A History of Greek Vase-Painting* (London: Thames & Hudson, 1962).

Badian, E., *From Plataea to Potidaea: Studies in the History and Historiography of the Pentecontaetia* (Baltimore: Johns Hopkins University Press, 1993).

Balcer, J. M., *The Athenian Regulations for Chalkis* (Wiesbaden: Steiner, 1978).

Barner, W., et al., eds., *Literatur in der Demokratie. Für Walter Jens zum 60. Geburtstag* (Munich: Kindler, 1983).

Beard, Mary, *The Parthenon* (Cambridge, MA: Harvard University Press, 2003).

Bérard, C., et al., *A City of Images: Iconography and Society in Ancient Greece*, trans. D. Lyons (Princeton: Princeton University Press, 1989).

Best, J. G. P., *Thracian Peltasts and Their Influence on Greek Warfare* (Groningen: Wolters-Noordhoff, 1969).

Bickerman, E. J., "Autonomia: Sur un passage de Thucydide (I. 144. 2)," *RIDA* 5 (1958): 313–44.

Blank, D., "Socratics vs. Sophists on Payment for Teaching," *CA* 4 (1985): 1–49.

Blok, J., "Virtual Voices: Toward a Choreography of Women's Speech in Classical Athens," in A. Lardinois and L. McClure, eds., *Making Silence Speak* (Princeton: Princeton University Press, 2001), pp. 95–116.

Blundell, Sue, *Women in Ancient Greece* (Cambridge, MA: Harvard University Press, 1995).

Boardman, J., *Greek Gems and Finger Rings* (London: Thames & Hudson, 1970).

Boardman, J., *Greek Sculpture: The Classical Period* (London: Thames & Hudson, 1985).

Boardman, J., "Trade in Greek Pottery," *OJA* 7 (1988): 27–33.

Boardman, J., *Athenian Red Figure Vases: The Classical Period* (London: Thames & Hudson, 1989).

Boardman, J., ed., *The Oxford History of Classical Art* (Oxford: Oxford University Press, 1997).

Boedeker, Deborah, *Descent from Heaven. Images of Dew in Greek Poetry and Religion* (Chico, CA: Scholars Press, 1984).

Boedeker, Deborah, "Paths to Heroization," in Deborah Boedeker and David Sider, eds., *The New Simonides* (Oxford: Oxford University Press, 2001), pp. 148–63.

Boedeker, D., and K. A. Raaflaub, eds., *Democracy, Empire, and the Arts in Fifth-Century Athens* (Cambridge, MA: Harvard University Press, 1998).

Boegehold, A., "Many Letters: Aristophanes *Plutus* 1166–67," in A. L. Boegehold et al., eds., *Studies Presented to Sterling Dow on His Eightieth Birthday*, Greek, Roman and Byzantine Monographs, no. 10 (Durham, NC: Duke University, 1984), pp. 23–30.

Boegehold, A., "Perikles' Citizenship Law of 451/0" in A. Boegehold and A. Scafuro, eds., *Athenian Identity and Civic Ideology* (Baltimore: Johns Hopkins University Press, 1994), pp. 57–66.

Boegehold, A., *The Athenian Agora*, vol. 28, *The Lawcourts at Athens* (Princeton: American School of Classical Studies at Athens, 1995).

Boegehold, A., and A. Scafuro, eds., *Athenian Identity and Civic Ideology* (Baltimore: Johns Hopkins University Press, 1994).

Boersma, J. S., *Athenian Building Policy from 561/0 to 405/4 B.C.* (Groningen: Wolters-Neordhoff, 1970).

Bolmarcich, S., "Thucydides 1.19.1 and the Peloponnesian League," *GRBS* 45 (2005): 5–34.

Bourriot, F., *Recherches sur la nature du génos*, 2 vols. (Lille: Université de Lille, 1976).

Bradeen, D. W., "The Popularity of the Athenian Empire," *Historia* 9 (1960): 257–69.

Bremmer, Jan, "The Birth of the Term 'Magic,'" *ZPE* 126 (1999): 1–12.

Bruit Zaidman, L. and P. Schmitt Pantel, *Religion in the Greek City*, trans. P. Cartledge (Cambridge: Cambridge University Press, 1992).

Brumfield, Allaire C., *The Attic Festivals of Demeter and Their Relation to the Agricultural Year* (Salem, NH: Arno, 1981).

Bugh, G. R., *The Horsemen of Athens* (Princeton: Princeton University Press, 1988).

Bundrick, S., *Expressions of Harmony: Representations of Female Musicians in Fifth-Century Athenian Vase Painting* (Ph.D. dissertation: Emory University, 1998).

Bundrick, S., *Music and Image in Classical Athens* (New York: Cambridge University Press, 2005).

Burke, E. M., "The Economy of Athens in the Classical Era: Some Adjustments to the Primitivist Model," *TAPA* 122 (1992): 199–226.

Burkert, W., *Greek Religion*, trans. J. Raffan (Cambridge, MA: Harvard University Press, 1985).

Cahill, N., *Household and City Organization at Olynthus* (New Haven: Yale University Press, 2002).

Cairns, D. L., "*Hybris*, Dishonour, and Thinking Big," *JHS* 116 (1996): 1–32.

Calhoun, G. M., "Oral and Written Pleading in Athenian Courts," *TAPA* 50 (1919): 177–93.

Camp, J. M., *The Athenian Agora: Excavations in the Heart of Classical Athens* (London: Thames & Hudson, 1986).

Camp, J. M., *The Archaeology of Athens* (New Haven: Yale University Press, 2001).

Carawan, E. M., "*Ephetai* and Athenian Courts for Homicide in the Age of the Orators," *CP* 86 (1991): 1–16.

Carey, C. "Old Comedy and the Sophists," in D. Harvey and J. Wilkins, eds., *The Rivals of Aristophanes. Studies in Athenian Old Comedy* (London: Duckworth and the Classical Press of Wales, 2000), pp. 419–36.

Cargill, J., *The Second Athenian League: Empire or Free Alliance?* (Berkeley: University of California Press, 1981).

Carter, L. B., *The Quiet Athenian* (Oxford: Oxford University Press, 1986).

Cartledge, P., "The Silent Women of Thucydides: 2.45.2 Re-viewed," in R. Rosen and J. Farrell, eds., *Nomodeiktes. Greek Studies in Honor of Martin Ostwald* (Ann Arbor: University of Michigan Press, 1993), pp. 125–32.

Cartledge, P., "The Effects of the Peloponnesian (Athenian) War on Athenian and Spartan Societies," in D. R. McCann and B. S. Strauss, eds., *War and Democracy* (Armonk: M. E. Sharpe, 2001), pp. 104–23.

Cartledge, P., "The Political Economy of Greek Slavery," in P. Cartlege, E. Cohen, and L. Foxhall, eds., *Money, Labour and Land: Approaches to the Economies of Ancient Greece* (London: Routledge, 2002), pp. 156–66.

Cartledge, P., E. E. Cohen, and L. Foxhall, *Money, Labour and Land: Approaches to the Economies of Ancient Greece* (London: Routledge, 2002).

Castriota, David, *Myth, Ethos, and Actuality. Official Art in Fifth-Century B.C. Athens* (Madison: University of Wisconsin Press, 1992).

Catling, H. W., "Archaeology in Greece, 1988–89," *Archaeological Reports* 35 (1989): 3–116.

Cavaignac, E., "Les dékarchies de Lysandre," *REH* 90 (1924): 285–316.

Cawkwell, G. L., "*Nomophylakia* and the Areopagus," *JHS* 108 (1988): 1–12.

Ceccarelli, P., *La pirrica nell'antichità greco romana* (Pisa: Istituti Editoriali e Poligrafici Internazionali, 1998).

Chambers, M., "Four Hundred Sixty Talents," *CP* 53 (1958): 26–32.

Christ, M., "Ostracism, Sycophancy, and the Deception of the Demos: [Arist.] *Ath Pol.* 43.5," *CQ* 42 (1992): 336–46.

Christ, M., "Conscription of Hoplites in Classical Athens" *CQ* 51 (2001): 398–409.

Clairmont, C., "The Lekythos of Myrrhine," in G. Kopcke and M. Moore, eds., *Studies in Classical Art and Archaeology: A Tribute to Peter Heinrich von Blanckenhagen* (Locust Valley: J. J. Augustin, 1979), pp. 103–10.

Clairmont, C., *Patrios Nomos: Public Burial in Athens during the Fifth and Fourth Centuries B.C.*, 2 vols. (Oxford: B.A.R., 1983).

Clairmont, C., *Classical Attic Tombstones*, 9 vols. (Kilchberg: Akanthus, 1993).

Cohen, E., *The Athenian Nation* (Princeton: Princeton University Press, 2000).

Cole, T., *The Origins of Rhetoric in Ancient Greece* (Baltimore: Johns Hopkins University Press, 1991).

Connor, W. R., *The New Politicians of Fifth-Century Athens* (Princeton: Princeton University Press, 1971).

Connor, W. R., "Early Greek Land Warfare as Symbolic Expression," *PP* 119 (1988): 3–29.

Connor, W. R., "'Sacred' and 'Secular': ἱερά καὶ ὅσια and the Classical Athenian Concept of the State," *Ancient Society* 19 (1988): 161–88.

Connor, W. R., "City Dionysia and Athenian Democracy," *Classica et Mediaevalia* 40 (1989): 7–32 = W. R. Connor et al., eds., *Aspects of Athenian Democracy* (Copenhagen: Museum Tusculanum Press, 1990), pp. 7–32.

Connor, W. R., M. H. Hansen, K. A. Raaflaub, B. S. Strauss, eds., *Aspects of Athenian Democracy* (Copenhagen: Museum Tusculanum Press, 1990).

Coulson, W. D. E., O. Palagia, T. L. Shear, Jr., H. A. Shapiro, and F. J. Frost, eds., *The Archaeology of Athens and Attica under the Democracy*, Oxbow Monograph 37 (Oxford: Oxbow, 1994).

Coulton, J. J., *Ancient Greek Architects at Work* (Ithaca, NY: Cornell University Press, 1977).

Cox, C., *Household Interests: Property, Marriage Strategies, and Family Dynamics in Ancient Athens* (Princeton: Princeton University Press, 1998).

Crane, G., *Thucydides and the Ancient Simplicity* (Berkeley: University of California Press, 1998).

Croally, N. T., *Euripidean Polemic: The Trojan Women and the Function of Tragedy* (Cambridge: Cambridge University Press, 1994).

Csapo, E., and W. J. Slater, *The Context of Ancient Drama* (Ann Arbor: University of Michigan Press, 1995).

Davies, J. K., "Society and Economy," in D. M. Lewis, J. Boardman, J. K. Davies, and M. Ostwald, eds., *The Cambridge Ancient History*, vol. 5, *The Fifth Century B.C.*, second edition (Cambridge: Cambridge University Press, 1992), pp. 287–305.

Davies, J. K., "Accounts and Accountability in Classical Athens," in S. Hornblower and R. Osborne, eds., *Ritual, Finance, Politics. Athenian Democratic Accounts Presented to David Lewis* (Oxford: Oxford University Press, 1994), pp. 201–12.

Davies, J. K., "Ancient Economies: Models and Muddles," in H. Parkinson and C. Smith, eds., *Trade, Traders and the Ancient City* (London and New York: Routledge, 1998), pp. 225–56.

Detienne, Marcel, "The Violence of Wellborn Ladies," in Marcel Detienne and Jean-Pierre Vernant, eds., *The Cuisine of Sacrifice among the Greeks* (Chicago: University of Chicago Press, 1989): 129–47.

Dillon, M., and L. Garland, eds., *Ancient Greece: Social and Historical Documents from Archaic Times to the Death of Socrates* (New York: Routledge, 2000).

Donohue, A. A., and M. D. Fullerton, eds., *Ancient Art and Its Historiography* (Cambridge: Cambridge University Press, 2003).

Dover, K. J., *Aristophanes Clouds* (Oxford: Oxford University Press, 1968).

Dover, K. J., *Thucydides*, Greece & Rome New Surveys in the Classics, no. 7 (Oxford: Oxford University Press, 1973).

Dover, K. J., *Greek Popular Morality in the Time of Plato and Aristotle* (Berkeley: University of California Press, 1974).

Dover, K. J., "The Freedom of the Intellectual in Greek Society," *Talanta* 7 (1976):24–54.

Drews, R., *Basileus: The Evidence for Kingship in Geometric Greece* (New Haven: Yale University Press, 1983).

Ducrey, P., *Le traitement des prisonniers de guerre dans la Grèce antique* (Paris: De Boccard, 1968).

Eckstein, A. M., "Thucydides, the Outbreak of the Peloponnesian War, and the Foundation of International Systems Theory," *International History Review* 25 (2003): 757–74.

Eder, W., ed., *Die athenische Demokratie im 4. Jahrhundert v. Chr.: Vollendung oder Verfall einer Verfassungsform?* (Stuttgart: Steiner, 1995).

Ehrenberg, V., *Sophocles and Pericles* (Oxford: Blackwell, 1954).

Engen, D., *Athenian Trade Policy, 415–307 B.C.: Honors and Privileges for Trade-Related Services* (Ph.D. dissertation: University of California, Los Angeles, 1996).

Erickson, B. L., *Late Archaic and Classical Crete. Island Pottery Styles in an Age of Historical Transition, ca. 600–400 B.C.* (Ph.D. dissertation: University of Texas, Austin, 2000).

Euben, J. P., J. Wallach, and J. Ober, eds., *Athenian Political Thought and the Reconstruction of American Democracy* (Ithaca, NY: Cornell University Press, 1994).

Fantham, Elaine, et al., *Women in the Classical World* (New York: Oxford University Press, 1994).

Faraone, Christopher A., "The Agonistic Context of Early Greek Binding Spells," in Christopher A. Faraone and Dirk Obbink, *Magika Hiera: Ancient Greek Magic and Religion* (New York: Oxford University Press, 1991), pp. 2–32.

Ferrari, G., "The Ancient Temple of the Acropolis at Athens," *AJA* 106 (2002): 11–135.

Figueira, T. J., *The Power of Money: Coinage and Politics in the Athenian Empire* (Philadelphia: University of Pennsylvania Press, 1998).

Finley, M. I., "Was Greek Civilization Based on Slave Labour?" in M. I. Finley, ed., *Slavery in Classical Antiquity* (Cambridge: Heffer & Sons, 1960), pp. 53–72.

Finley, M. I., *Democracy, Ancient and Modern*, second edition (London: Hogarth/New Brunswick: Rutgers University Press, 1985; orig. edition, 1973).

Finley, M. I., "The Fifth-Century Athenian Empire: A Balance Sheet," in P. D. A. Garnsey and C. R. Whittaker, eds., *Imperialism in the Ancient World* (Cambridge: Cambridge University Press, 1978), pp. 103–26.

Finley, M. I., *Ancient Slavery and Modern Ideology* (New York: Viking Press, 1980).

Finley, M. I., *Economy and Society in Ancient Greece*, B. Shaw and R. Saller, eds. (New York: Viking, 1982).

Finley, M. I., *The Ancient Economy*, new edition (Berkeley: University of California Press, 1999).

Fisher, N., "*Hybris*, Revenge, and *Stasis* in the Greek City-States," in H. van Wees, ed., *War and Violence in Ancient Greece* (London: Duckworth, 2000), pp. 83–123.

Flashar, Martin, "Die Sieger von Marathon: Zwischen Mythos und Vorbildlichkeit," in Martin Flasher, Hans-Joachim Gehrke, and Ernst Heinrich, eds., *Retrospektive: Konzepte von Vergangenheit in der griechisch-römischen Antike* (Munich: Biering & Brinkmann, 1996), pp. 63–85.

Fontenrose, Joseph, "The Hero as Athlete," *CSCA* 1 (1968): 73–104.

Ford, A., "Sophists without Rhetoric: The Arts of Speech in Fifth-Century Athens," in Yun Lee Too, ed., *Education in Greek and Roman Antiquity* (Leiden: Brill, 2001), pp. 85–109.

Fornara, C. W., "The Date of the Callias Decrees," *GRBS* 11 (1970): 185–96.

Fornara, C. W., "On the Chronology of the Samian War," *JHS* 99 (1979): 7–18.

Fornara, C. W., ed. and trans., *From Archaic Times to the End of the Peloponnesian War* (Cambridge: Cambridge University Press, 1983).

Fornara, C. W., "Thucydides' Birth Date," in R. M. Rosen and J. Farrell, eds., *Nomodeiktes: Greek Studies in Honor of Martin Ostwald* (Ann Arbor: University of Michigan Press, 1993), pp. 71–80.

Fornara, C. W., and L. J. Samons II, *Athens from Cleisthenes to Pericles* (Berkeley: University of California Press, 1991).

Forrest, W. G., "An Athenian Generation Gap," *YCS* 24 (1975): 37–52.

Fowler, Robert L., "Greek Magic, Greek Religion," in R. Buxton, ed., *Oxford Readings in Greek Religion* (Oxford: Oxford University Press, 2000), pp. 317–43.

Foxhall, L., "Household, Gender and Property in Classical Athens," *CQ* 39 (1989): 22–44.

Foxhall, L., "Farming and Fighting in Ancient Greece," in J. Rich and G. Shipley, eds., *War and Society in the Greek World* (London: Routledge, 1993), pp. 134–45.

Foxhall, L., "Women's Ritual and Men's Work in Ancient Athens," in R. Hawley and B. Levick, eds., *Women in Antiquity: New Assessments* (London: Routledge, 1995): 96–110.

Foxhall, L., and H. A. Forbes, "Sitometreia: The Role of Grain as a Staple in the Ancient Greek World," *Chiron* 12 (1982): 41–90.

Fränkel, M., "Der attische Heliasteneid," *Hermes* 13 (1878): 452–66.

French, A., *The Growth of the Athenian Economy* (New York: Barnes & Noble, 1964).

Frier, B. W., *The Rise of Roman Jurists. Studies in Cicero's pro Caecina* (Princeton: Princeton University Press, 1985).

Frost, F. J., "The Athenian Military before Cleisthenes," *Historia* 33 (1984): 283–94.

Fullerton, M. D., *Greek Art* (Cambridge: Cambridge University Press, 2000).

Gabrielsen, V., *Remuneration of State Officials in Fourth Century B.C. Athens*, Odense University Classical Studies xi (Odense: Odense University Press, 1981).

Gabrielsen, V., *Financing the Athenian Fleet* (Baltimore: Johns Hopkins University Press, 1994).

Gaebel, R. A., *Cavalry Operations in the Ancient Greek World* (Norman: University of Oklahoma Press, 2002).

Gagarin, M., *Drakon and Early Athenian Homicide Law* (New Haven: Yale University Press, 1981).

Gagarin, M., *Antiphon the Athenian. Oratory, Law, and Justice in the Age of the Sophists* (Austin: University of Texas Press, 2002).

Gager, John G., *Curse Tablets and Binding Spells from the Ancient World* (New York: Oxford University Press, 1992).

Garlan, Y., *War in the Ancient World: A Social History* (London: Chatto and Windus, 1975).

Garland, R., "Religious Authority in Archaic and Classical Athens," *ABSA* 79 (1984): 75–123.

Garland, R., *The Piraeus from the Fifth to the First Century B.C.* (Ithaca, NY: Cornell University Press, 1987).

Garland, R., *Introducing New Gods: The Politics of Athenian Religion* (Ithaca, NY: Cornell University Press, 1992).

Garnsey, P. D., "Grain for Athens," in P. Cartledge and F. D. Harvey, eds., *Crux: Essays in Greek History Presented to G. E. M. de Ste. Croix* (London: Duckworth 1985), pp. 62–75.

Garnsey, P. D., *Famine and Food Supply in the Graeco-Roman World* (Cambridge: Cambridge University Press, 1988).

Geddes, A. G., "Who's Who in Homeric Society?" *CQ* 34 (1984): 17–36.

Gill, D., and M. Vickers, "Reflected Glory: Pottery and Precious Metal in Classical Greece," *JdI* 105 (1990): 1–30.

Giovannini, A., "Le Parthénon, le tresor d' Athéna et le tribut des alliés," *Historia* 39 (1990): 129–48.

Giovannini, A., "La participation des alliés au financement du Parthénon: *aparchè* ou tribut?" *Historia* 46 (1997): 145–57.

Goldhill, S., *Reading Greek Tragedy* (Cambridge: Cambridge University Press, 1986).

Goldhill, S., "The Great Dionysia and Civic Ideology," *JHS* 107 (1987): 58–76, also published as "The Great Dionysia and Civic Ideology," in J. J. Winkler and F. I. Zeitlin, eds., *Nothing to Do with Dionysos?* (Princeton: Princeton University Press, 1990), pp. 97–129.

Goldhill, S., "Representing Democracy: Women at the Great Dionysia," in R. Osborne and S. Hornblower, eds., *Ritual, Finance, Politics: Athenian Democratic Accounts Presented to David Lewis* (Oxford: Oxford University Press, 1994), pp. 347–69.

Goldhill, S., "Civic Ideology and the Problem of Difference: The Politics of Aeschylean Tragedy, Once Again," *JHS* 120 (2000): 34–56.

Gomme, A. W., *The Population of Athens in the Fifth and Fourth Centuries, B.C.* (Oxford: Blackwell, 1933).

Gomme, A. W., A. Andrewes, and J. K. Dover, *A Historical Commentary on Thucydides*, 5 vols. (Oxford: Oxford University Press, 1945–81).

Graf, F., *Magic in the Ancient World* (Cambridge, MA: Harvard University Press, 1997).

Grant, J. R., "Thucydides 2.37.1," *Phoenix* 25 (1971): 104–7.

Gregory, J., *Euripides and the Instruction of the Athenians* (Ann Arbor: University of Michigan Press, 1991).

Griffin, J., "The Social Function of Attic Tragedy," *CQ* 48 (1998): 39–61.

Griffith, J. G., "A Note on the First *Eisphora* at Athens," *AJAH* 2 (1977): 3–7.

Griffith, M., "Brilliant Dynasts. Power and Politics in the *Oresteia*," *CA* 14 (1995): 62–129.

Grote, G., *A History of Greece*, 12 vols. (London: J. Murray, 1846–1856; London: reprint edition, 1869–1884; 10-volume edition, 1888).

Guthrie, W. K. C., *A History of Greek Philosophy*, vol. 3, *The Fifth-Century Enlightenment* (Cambridge: Cambridge University Press, 1969).

Guthrie, W. K. C., *A History of Greek Philosophy,* vol. 4, *Plato: the Man and His Dialogues. Earlier Period* (Cambridge: Cambridge University Press, 1975).

Hahnemann, C., *Incarnating Democracy* (Ph.D. dissertation: Brown University, 1997).

Hall, J., *Ethnic Identity in Greek Antiquity* (Cambridge: Cambridge University Press, 1997).

Halliwell, S., "The Uses of Laughter in Greek Culture," *CQ* 41 (1991): 279–96.

Hamel, D., *Athenian Generals. Military Authority in the Classical Period* (Leiden: Brill, 1998).

Hansen, M. H., "How Often Did the Athenian Dikasteria Meet?" *GRBS* 20 (1979): 243–6.

Hansen, M. H., "Misthos for Magistrates in Classical Athens," *SO* 54 (1979): 5–22.

Hansen, M. H., "Seven Hundred *archai* in Classical Athens," *GRBS* 21 (1980): 151–73.

Hansen, M. H., *Demography and Democracy: The Number of Athenian Citizens in the Fourth Century B.C.* (Herning: Systime, 1985).

Hansen, M. H., *Three Studies in Athenian Demography* (Copenhagen: The Royal Danish Academy, 1988).

Hansen, M. H., *The Athenian Democracy in the Age of Demosthenes*, trans. J. A. Crook (Oxford: Blackwell, 1991).

Hansen, M. H., ed., *The Ancient Greek City-State* (Copenhagen: Royal Danish Academy of Sciences and Letters, 1993).

Hansen, M. H., "The 'Autonomous City-State': Ancient Fact or Modern Fiction?" in M. H. Hansen and K. Raaflaub, *Studies in the Ancient Greek Polis*, Historia Einzelschriften 95 (Stuttgart: Steiner, 1995), pp. 21–43.

Hansen, M. H., "The Trial of Sokrates – From the Athenian Point of View" (Copenhagen: Royal Danish Academy of Sciences and Letters, 1995), *Hist.-fil.-Medd.* 71: 1–31.

Hansen, M. H., and K. A. Raaflaub, eds., *Studies in the Ancient Greek Polis*, Historia Einzelschriften 95 (Stuttgart: Steiner, 1995).

Hanson, V. D., *Warfare and Agriculture in Classical Greece* (Pisa: Giardini, 1983; second edition, Berkeley: University of California Press, 1998).

Hanson, V. D., *The Western Way of War: Infantry Battle in Classical Greece* (New York: Knopf, 1989).

Hanson, V. D., ed., *Hoplites: The Classical Greek Battle Experience* (London: Routledge, 1991).

Hanson, V. D., *The Other Greeks: The Family Farm and the Agrarian Roots of Western Civilization* (New York: Free Press, 1995).

Hanson, V. D., "Hoplites into Democrats," in J. Ober and C. Hedrick, eds., *Démokratia* (Princeton: Princeton University Press, 1996), pp. 289–312.

Hanson, V. D., "Democratic Warfare, Ancient and Modern," in D. R. McCann and B. S. Strauss, eds., *War and Democracy* (Armonk: M.E. Sharpe, 2001), pp. 3–33.

Harris, Diane, "Freedom of Information and Accountability," in R. Osborne and S. Hornblower, eds., *Ritual, Finance, Politics. Athenian Democratic Accounts Presented to David Lewis* (Oxford: Oxford University Press, 1994), pp. 213–25.

Harris, Diane, *The Treasures of the Parthenon and Erechtheion* (Oxford: Oxford University Press, 1995).

Harris, E., "Workshop, Marketplace and Household: The Nature of Technical Specialization in Classical Athens and Its Influence on Economy and Society," in P. Cartledge, E. E. Cohen, and L. Foxhall, eds., *Money, Labour and Land: Approaches to the Economies of Ancient Greece* (London and New York: Routledge, 2002), pp. 67–99.

Harris, W. V., *Ancient Literacy* (Cambridge, MA: Harvard University Press, 1989).

Harrison, A. R. W., *The Law of Athens*, 2 vols. (Oxford: Oxford University Press, 1968–1971).

Harvey, D., and J. Wilkins, eds., *The Rivals of Aristophanes. Studies in Athenian Old Comedy* (London: Duckworth and the Classical Press of Wales, 2000).

Hasebroek, J., *Trade and Politics in Ancient Greece* (London: G. Bell, 1933).

Haselberger, L., ed., *Appearance and Essence: Refinements of Classical Architecture* (Philadelphia: University Museum Press, 1999).

Hedrick, C., "Reading, Writing, and Democracy," in R. Osborne and S. Hornblower, eds., *Ritual, Finance, Politics: Athenian Democratic Accounts Presented to David Lewis* (Oxford: Oxford University Press, 1994), pp. 157–74.

Hedrick, C., "Democracy and the Athenian Epigraphical Habit," *Hesperia* 68 (1999): 387–439.

Henderson, Jeffrey, "*Lysistrate*: The Play and Its Themes," *YCS* 26 (1980): 153–218.

Henderson, Jeffrey, "The *dêmos* and the Comic Competition," in J. J. Winkler and F. Zeitlin, eds., *Nothing to Do with Dionysos? Athenian Drama in its Social Context* (Princeton: Princeton University Press, 1990), pp. 271–313.

Henderson, Jeffrey, "Women and the Athenian Dramatic Festivals," *TAPA* 121 (1991): 133–47.

Henderson, Jeffrey, "Comic Hero versus Political Elite," in A. H. Sommerstein et al., eds., *Tragedy, Comedy and the Polis* (Bari: Levante Editori, 1993), pp. 307–19.

Henderson, Jeffrey, "Attic Comedy, Frank Speech, and Democracy," in D. Boedeker and K. Raaflaub, eds., *Democracy, Empire, and the Arts in Fifth-Century Athens* (Cambridge, MA: Harvard University Press, 1998), pp. 255–73, 405–10.

Henderson, Jeffrey, ed. and trans., *Aristophanes*, 4 vols., (Cambridge, MA: Loeb Classical Library, 1998–2002).

Henderson, Jeffrey, "Demos, Demagogue, Tyrant in Attic Old Comedy," in K. A. Morgan, ed., *Popular Tyranny: Sovereignty and Its Discontents in Ancient Greece* (Austin: University of Texas Press, 2003), pp. 155–79.

Henry, M., *Prisoner of History: Aspasia of Miletus and Her Biographical Tradition* (New York: Oxford University Press, 1995).

Herman, G., "Athenian Beliefs about Revenge: Problems and Methods," *Proceedings of the Cambridge Philological Society* 46 (2000): 7–27.

Herrmann, P., "Zu den Beziehungen zwischen Athen und Milet im 5. Jahrhundert," *Klio* 52 (1970): 163–73.

Hignett, C., *Xerxes' Invasion of Greece* (Oxford: Oxford University Press, 1963).

Hillgruber, M., *Die zehnte Rede des Lysias*, Untersuchungen zur antiken Literatur und Geschichte, Band 29 (Berlin and New York: De Gruyter, 1988).

Hirzel, R., *Themis, Dike und Verwandtes* (Leipzig: Teubner, 1907).

Hodkinson, S., and A. Powell, eds., *Sparta: New Perspectives* (London: Duckworth, 1999).

Hölkeskamp, K.-J., *Schiedsrichter, Gesetzgeber und Gesetzgebung im archaischen Griechenland* (Stuttgart: Steiner: 1999).

Hölkeskamp, K.-J., "(In-)Schrift und Monument. Zum Begriff des Gesetzes im archaischen und klassischen Griechenland," *ZPE* 132 (2000): 73–96.

Holladay, A. J., "The Détente of Kallias?" *Historia* 35 (1986): 503–7.

Hölscher, T. "Images and Political Identity: The Case of Athens," in D. Boedeker and K. A. Raaflaub, eds., *Democracy, Empire, and the Arts in Fifth-Century Athens* (Cambridge, MA: Harvard University Press, 1998), pp. 153–83.

Hooker, J. T., *The Ancient Spartans* (London: Dent, 1980).

Hornblower, S., *A Commentary on Thucydides*, 2 vols. (Oxford: Oxford University Press, 1991–1996).

Hornblower, S., "The Religious Dimension to the Peloponnesian War," *HSCP* 94 (1992): 169–97.

Hornblower, S., *Thucydides*, second edition (London: Duckworth, 1994).

Hunt, P., *Slaves, Warfare, and Ideology in the Greek Historians* (Cambridge: Cambridge University Press, 1998).

Hunt, P., "The Slaves and the Generals of Arginusae," *AJP* 122 (2001): 359–80.

Hunter, Virginia, *Policing Athens* (Princeton: Princeton University Press, 1984).

Hunter, Virginia, "Status Distinctions in Athenian Law," in V. Hunter and J. Edmonson, eds., *Law and Social Status in Classical Athens* (Oxford: Oxford University Press, 2000), pp. 1–29.

Hunter, V. and J. Edmonson, eds., *Law and Social Status in Classical Athens* (Oxford: Oxford University Press, 2000).

Hurwit, J., *The Athenian Acropolis* (Cambridge: Cambridge University Press, 1999).

Hurwit, J., *The Acropolis in the Age of Pericles* (Cambridge: Cambridge University Press, 2004).

Immerwahr, H., *Attic Script* (Oxford: Oxford University Press, 1990).

Isager, S., and M. H. Hansen, *Aspects of Athenian Society in the Fourth Century B.C.* (Odense: Odense University Press, 1975).

Isager, S., and J. E. Skydsgaard, *Ancient Greek Agriculture* (London and New York: Routledge, 1992).

Jacoby, Felix, "*Patrios Nomos.* State Burial in Athens and the Public Cemetery in the Kerameikos," *JHS* 64 (1944): 37–66.

Jameson, M. H., "Agriculture and Slavery in Classical Athens," *CJ* 73 (1977/78): 122–45.

Jameson, M. H., "Agricultural Labor in Ancient Greece," in B. Wells, ed., *Agriculture in Ancient Greece* (Stockholm: Swedish Institute of Athens, 1992), pp. 135–46.

Jameson, M. H., "Religion in the Athenian Democracy," in Ian Morris and Kurt Raaflaub, eds., *Democracy 2500? Questions and Challenges* (Dubuque: Kendall/Hunt for the American Institute of Archaeology, 1998): 171–95.

Jameson, M. H., "On Paul Cartledge, 'The political economy of Greek slavery'," in P. Cartledge, E. Cohen, L. Foxhall, eds., *Money, Labour and Land: Approaches to the Economies of Ancient Greece* (London: Routledge, 2002), pp. 167–74.

Jenkins, I., *The Parthenon Frieze* (Austin: University of Texas Press, 1994).

Jenkyns, R., *The Victorians and Ancient Greece* (Cambridge, MA: Harvard University Press, 1980).

Jones, A. H. M., *Athenian Democracy* (Oxford: Blackwell, 1957; paperback edition: Johns Hopkins University Press, 1986).

Jones, N. F., *Public Organization in Ancient Greece: A Documentary Study* (Philadelphia: American Philosophical Society, 1987).

Jones, N. F., *The Associations of Classical Athens: The Response to Democracy* (Oxford: Oxford University Press, 1999).

Joss, Kelly, *Re-constructing the Slave: An Examination of Slave Representation in the Greek Polis* (Ph.D. dissertation: University of St. Andrews, 2006).

Kagan, D., *The Outbreak of the Peloponnesian War* (Ithaca, NY: Cornell University Press, 1969).

Kagan, D., *The Peace of Nicias and the Sicilian Expedition* (Ithaca, NY: Cornell University Press, 1981).

Kagan, D., *The Fall of the Athenian Empire* (Ithaca, NY: Cornell University Press, 1987).

Kagan, D., *Pericles of Athens and the Birth of Democracy* (New York: Simon and Schuster, 1991).

Kagan, D., *The Peloponnesian War* (New York: Viking, 2003).

Kallet-Marx, L., "Did Tribute Fund the Parthenon?" *CSCA* 20 (1989): 252–66.

Kallet-Marx, L., "The Kallias Decree, Thucydides, and the Outbreak of the Peloponnesian War," *CQ* 39 (1989): 94–113.

Kallet-Marx, L., *Money, Expense and Naval Power in Thucydides' History 1–5.24* (Berkeley: University of California Press, 1993).

Kallet-Marx, L., "Thucydides 2.45.2 and the Status of War Widows in Periclean Athens," in R. Rosen and J. Farrell, eds., *Nomodeiktes. Greek Studies in Honor of Martin Ostwald* (Ann Arbor: University of Michigan Press, 1993), pp. 133–44.

Kallet-Marx, L., "Money Talks: Rhetor, Demos and the Resources of the Athenian Empire," in R. Osborne and S. Hornblower, eds., *Ritual, Finance, Politics. Athenian Democratic Accounts Presented to David Lewis* (Oxford: Oxford University Press, 1994), pp. 227–51.

Kallet, L., "Accounting for Culture in Fifth-Century Athens," in D. Boedeker and K. A. Raaflaub, eds., *Democracy, Empire, and the Arts in Fifth-Century Athens* (Cambridge, MA: Harvard University Press, 1998), pp. 43–58.

Kallet, L., *Money and the Corrosion of Power in Thucydides: The Sicilian Expedition and Its Aftermath* (Berkeley: University of California Press, 2001).

Kallet, L., "*Demos Tyrannos*: Wealth, Power and Economic Patronage," in K. Morgan, ed., *Popular Tyranny: Sovereignty and Its Discontents in Classical Athens* (Austin: University of Texas Press, 2003), pp. 117–53.

Kannicht, R., "Dikaiopolis. Von der Schwierigkeit, ein rechter Bürger zu sein," in W. Barner et al., eds., *Literatur in der Demokratie. Für Walter Jens zum 60. Geburtstag* (Munich: Kindler, 1983), pp. 246–57.

Kapparis, K. A., "Assessors of Magistrates (Paredroi) in Classical Athens," *Historia* 47 (1998): 383–93.

Karavites, P., *Capitulations and Greek Interstate Relations* (Göttingen: Vandenhoeck and Ruprecht, 1982).

Karavites, P., "ἐλευθερία and αὐτονομία in Fifth Century Interstate Relations," *RIDA* 29 (1982): 145–62.

Keen, A., "'Grain for Athens': Notes on the Importance of the Hellespontine Route in Athenian Foreign Policy before the Peloponnesian War," *Electronic Antiquity* 1 (1993).

Kerferd, G. B., "The First Greek Sophists," *CR* 1 (1950): 8–10.

Kerferd, G. B., *The Sophistic Movement* (Cambridge: Cambridge University Press, 1981).

Kerferd, G. B., ed., *The Sophists and Their Legacy* (Wiesbaden: Steiner, 1981).

Keuls, Eva, *The Reign of the Phallus* (New York: Harper and Row, 1985).

Kerkhof, R., *Dorische Posse, Epicharm und attische Komödie* (Munich and Leipzig: Saur, 2001).

Knox, B. M. W., *Oedipus at Thebes: Sophocles' Tragic Hero and His Time* (New Haven: Yale University Press, 1957).

Knox, B. M. W., *Word and Action. Essays on the Ancient Theater* (Baltimore: Johns Hopkins University Press, 1979).

Knox, B. M. W., "Athenian Religion and Literature," in D. M. Lewis et al., eds., *The Cambridge Ancient History,* vol. 5, *The Fifth Century B.C.,* second edition (Cambridge: Cambridge University Press, 1992), pp. 268–86.

Kraut, R. ed., *The Cambridge Companion to Plato* (Cambridge: Cambridge University Press, 1992).

Krentz, P., "Casualties in Hoplite Battles," *GRBS* 26 (1985): 13–20.

Krentz, P., "Fighting by the Rules: The Invention of the Hoplite Agôn," *Hesperia* 71 (2002): 23–39.

Kroll, J. A., *Athenian Bronze Allotment Plates* (Cambridge, MA: Harvard University Press, 1972).

Kyle, D. G., "The Panatheniac Games: Sacred and Civic Athletics," in J. Neils, ed., *Goddess and Polis: The Panathenaic Festival in Ancient Athens* (Princeton: Princeton University Press, 1992), pp. 77–101, 203–8.

Lambert, S. D., *The Phratries of Attica* (Ann Arbor: University of Michigan Press, 1993).

Lapatin, K. D. S., "Pheidias elephantourgos," *AJA* 101 (1997): 663–82.

Lapatin, K. D. S., *Chryselephantine Statuary in the Ancient Mediterranean World* (Oxford: Oxford University Press, 2001).

Lapatin, K. D. S., "The Fate of Plate and Other Precious Materials: Towards a Historiography of Ancient Greek Minor (?) Arts," in A. A. Donohue and M. D. Fullerton, eds., *Ancient Art and Its Historiography* (Cambridge: Cambridge University Press, 2003), pp. 69–91.

Lardinois, A., and L. McClure, eds., *Making Silence Speak: Women's Voices in Greek Literature and Society* (Princeton: Princeton University Press, 2001).

Larson, Jennifer, *Greek Heroine Cults* (Madison: University of Wisconsin Press, 1995).

Lazenby, J. F., *The Spartan Army* (Warminster: Aris & Phillips, 1985).

Lazenby, J. F., "The Killing Zone," in V. D. Hanson, ed., *Hoplites: The Classical Greek Battle Experience* (London: Routledge, 1991), pp. 87–109.

Leader, R., "In Death Not Divided: Gender, Family, and State on Classical Athenian Grave Stelae," *AJA* 101 (1997): 683–99.

Lendon, J. E., "Spartan Honor," in C. D. Hamilton and P. Krentz, eds., *Polis and Polemos* (Claremont, CA: Regina, 1997), pp. 105–126.

Lendon, J. E., "Homeric Vengeance and the Outbreak of Greek Wars," in H. van Wees, ed., *War and Violence in Ancient Greece* (London: Duckworth, 2000), pp. 1–30.

Lendon, J. E., *Soldiers and Ghosts: A History of Battle in Classical Antiquity* (New Haven: Yale University Press, 2005).

Lendon, J. E., "Xenophon and the Alternative to Realist Foreign Policy: *Cyropaedia* 3.1.14–31," *JHS* 126 (2006): 82–98.

Lewis, D., "Who Was Lysistrata?" *ABSA* 50 (1955): 1–12.

Lewis, D. "The Thirty Years' Peace," in D. M. Lewis et al., eds., *The Cambridge Ancient History*, vol. 5, *The Fifth Century B.C.*, second edition (Cambridge: Cambridge University Press, 1992), pp. 121–46.

Lewis, S., *News and Society in the Greek Polis* (Chapel Hill: University of North Carolina Press, 1996).

Linders, Tullia, *The Treasurers of the Other Gods in Athens and Their Functions* (Meisenheim am Glan: Hain, 1975).

Lissarrague, F., *The Aesthetics of the Greek Banquet: Images of Wine and Ritual*, trans. A. Szegedy-Maszak (Princeton: Princeton University Press, 1990).

Lloyd, G. E. R., *Magic, Reason and Experience* (Cambridge: Cambridge University Press, 1979).

Lloyd, G. E. R., *The Revolutions of Wisdom. Studies in the Claims and Practice of Ancient Greek Science* (Berkeley: University of California Press, 1987).

Lloyd-Jones, H., trans., *The Libation Bearers* (Englewood Cliffs, NJ: Prentice-Hall, 1985).

Loomis, W. T., *Wages, Welfare Costs and Inflation in Classical Athens* (Ann Arbor: University of Michigan Press, 1998).

Loraux, N., *The Invention of Athens. The Funeral Oration in the Classical City*, trans. A. Sheridan (Cambridge, MA: Harvard University Press, 1986).

Loraux, N., *Children of Athena*, trans. C. Levine (Princeton: Princeton University Press, 1993).

Luce, J. V., *An Introduction to Greek Philosophy* (London: Thames and Hudson, 1992).

Lyons, Deborah, *Gender and Immortality: Heroines in Ancient Greek Myth and Cult* (Princeton: Princeton University Press, 1997).

MacDowell, D. M., *The Law in Classical Athens* (Ithaca, NY: Cornell University Press, 1978).

MacDowell, D. M., *Aristophanes and Athens* (Oxford: Oxford University Press, 1995).

Malkin, Irad, *Religion and Colonization in Ancient Greece* (Leiden: Brill, 1987).

Manfredini, M., and L. Piccirilli, *Plutarco, La vita di Solone* (Milan: Mondadori, 1977).

Manville, P. B., *The Origins of Citizenship in Ancient Athens* (Princeton: Princeton University Press, 1990).

Manville, Brook, and Josiah Ober, *A Company of Citizens* (Boston: Harvard Business School Press, 2003).

Mark, I. S., *The Sanctuary of Athena Nike in Athens*, Hesperia Supplement 26 (Princeton: American School of Classical Studies at Athens, 1993).

Matthaiou, A. P., "περὶ τῆς IG I³ 11," in A. P. Matthaiou, ed., *ΑΤΤΙΚΑΙ ΕΠΙΓΡΑΦΑΙ. ΠΡΑΚΤΙΚΑ ΣΥΜΠΟΣΙΟΥ ΕΙΣ ΜΝΗΜΗΝ Adolf Wilhelm (1864–1950)* (Athens: ΕΛΛΗΝΙΚΗ ΕΠΙΓΡΑΦΙΚΗ ΕΤΑΙΡΕΙΑ, 2004), pp. 99–122.

Mattingly, H. B., "Periclean Imperialism," in *Ancient Society and Institutions: Studies Presented to Victor Ehrenberg on His Seventy-Fifth Birthday* (Oxford: Blackwell, 1966): 193–223; also published (with revisions) in G. Wirth, ed., *Perikles und seine Zeit*, Wege der Forschung 412 (Darmstadt: Wissenschaftliche Buchgesellschaft, 1979), pp. 312–49, also published in H. B. Mattingly, *The Athenian Empire Restored* (Ann Arbor: University of Michigan Press, 1996), pp. 147–79.

Mattingly, H. B., *The Athenian Empire Restored* (Ann Arbor: University of Michigan Press, 1996).

Mattusch, C., *Greek Bronze Statuary* (Ithaca, NY: Cornell University Press, 1988).

Mattusch, C., "The Eponymous Heroes: The Idea of Sculptural Groups," in W. D. E. Coulson et al., eds., *The Archaeology of Athens and Attica under the Democracy* (Oxford: Oxbow Books, 1994), pp. 73–82.

Mattusch, C., *Classical Bronzes* (Ithaca, NY: Cornell University Press, 1996).

McCann, D. R., and B. S. Strauss, eds., *War and Democracy* (Armonk: M.E. Sharpe, 2001).

McInerney, Jeremy, *The Folds of Parnassos: Land and Ethnicity in Ancient Phokis* (Austin: University of Texas Press, 1999).

Meier, C., *The Greek Discovery of Politics*, trans. D. McLintock (Cambridge, MA: Harvard University Press, 1990).

Meier, C., *The Political Art of Greek Tragedy* (Baltimore: Johns Hopkins University Press, 1993).

Meiggs, R., "The Political Implications of the Parthenon," in G. T. W. Hooker, ed., *Parthenon and Parthenos*, Greece & Rome suppl. vol. 10 (Oxford: Oxford University Press, 1963), pp. 36–45.

Meiggs, R., *The Athenian Empire* (Oxford: Oxford University Press, 1972).

Meiggs, R., *Trees and Timber in the Ancient Mediterranean World* (Oxford: Oxford University Press, 1982).

Meiggs, R., and D. Lewis, *A Selection of Greek Historical Inscriptions to the End of the Fifth Century B.C.*, revised edition (Oxford: Oxford University Press, 1988).

Meijer, P. A., "Philosophers, Intellectuals and Religion in Hellas," in H. S. Versnel, ed., *Faith, Hope and Worship: Aspects of Religious Mentality in the Ancient World* (Leiden: Brill, 1981), pp. 216–63.

Meritt, B. D., H. T. Wade-Gery, and M. F. McGregor, eds., *The Athenian Tribute Lists*, 4 vols. (Cambridge, MA and Princeton: The American School of Classical Studies at Athens, 1939–1953).

Meyer, E. A., "Epitaphs and Citizenship in Classical Athens," *JHS* 113 (1993): 99–121.

Meyer, E. A., "*The Outbreak of the Peloponnesian War* after Twenty-Five Years," in C. D. Hamilton and P. Krentz, eds., *Polis and Polemos* (Claremont, CA: Regina, 1997), pp. 23–54.

Meyer, H. D., "Vorgeschichte und Gründung des delisch-attischen Seebundes," *Historia* 12 (1963): 405–46.

Michell, H., *Sparta* (Cambridge: Cambridge University Press, 1952).

Mikalson, J. D., *The Sacred and Civil Calendar of the Athenian Year* (Princeton: Princeton University Press, 1975).

Mikalson, J. D., *Athenian Popular Religion* (Chapel Hill: University of North Carolina Press, 1983).

Miller, M., *Athens and Persia in the Fifth Century B.C.* (Cambridge: Cambridge University Press, 1997).

Mirhady, D. C., "The Athenian Rationale for Torture," in V. Hunter and J. Edmondson, eds., *Law and Social Status in Classical Athens* (Oxford: Oxford University Press, 2000), pp. 53–74.

Mitchell, Lynette G., and P. J. Rhodes, eds., *The Development of the Polis in Archaic Greece* (London: Routledge, 1997).

Mitchell, S., "Hoplite Warfare in Ancient Greece," in A. B. Lloyd, ed., *Battle in Antiquity* (London: Duckworth, 1996), pp. 87–105.

Moles, J., "Herodotus Warns the Athenians," *Papers of the Leeds International Latin Seminar* 9 (1996): 259–84.

Molho, A., K. Raaflaub, and J. Emlen, eds., *Athens and Rome, Florence and Venice: City-States in Classical Antiquity and Medieval Italy* (Stuttgart: Steiner, 1991).

Moore, J. M., ed. and trans., *Aristotle and Xenophon on Democracy and Oligarchy* (Berkeley: University of California Press, 1975).

Morgan, K. A., ed., *Popular Tyranny: Sovereignty and its Discontents in Ancient Greece* (Austin: University of Texas Press, 2003).

Morris, I., and K. A. Raaflaub, eds., *Democracy 2500? Questions and Challenges*, Archaeological Institute of America Colloquium series (Dubuque, IA: Kendall/Hunt, 1998).

Morrison, J. S., J. Coates, and N. B. Rankov, *The Athenian Trireme*, second edition (Cambridge: Cambridge University Press, 2000).

Mueller, R., "Sophistique et démocratie," in B. Cassin, ed., *Positions de la sophistique*, Colloque de Cerisy (Paris: J. Vrin, 1986), pp. 179–93.

Munn, M., *The School of History. Athens in the Age of Socrates* (Berkeley: University of California Press, 2000).

Natali, C., "*Adoleschia, Leptologia*, and the Philosophers in Athens," *Phronesis* 32 (1987): 232–41.

Nehamas, A., "Eristic, Antilogic, Sophistic, Dialectic: Plato's Demarcation of Philosophy from Sophistry," *History of Philosophy Quarterly* 7 (1990): 3–16.

Nehamas, A., *Virtues of Authenticity. Essays on Plato and Socrates* (Princeton: Princeton University Press, 1999).

Neils, J., ed., *Worshipping Athena: Panathenaia and Parthenon* (Madison: University of Wisconsin Press, 1996).

Neils, J., *The Parthenon Frieze* (Cambridge: Cambridge University Press, 2001).

Neils, J., et al., *Goddess and Polis: The Panathenaic Festival in Classical Athens*, exhib. cat. (Princeton: Princeton University Press for Hood Museum of Art, Dartmouth College, Hanover, NH, 1992).

Newiger, H.-J., "War and Peace in the Comedy of Aristophanes," *YCS* 26 (1980): 219–37.

Nielsen, I., *Cultic Theatres and Ritual Drama: A Study in Regional Development and Religious Interchange between East and West in Antiquity* (Aarhus: Aarhus University Press, 2002).

Nightingale, A., "Sages, Sophists, and Philosophers: Greek Wisdom Literature," in O. Taplin, ed., *Literature in the Greek and Roman Worlds* (Oxford: Oxford University Press, 2000), pp. 156–91.

Nixon, L., and S. Price, "The Size and Resources of Greek Cities," in O. Murray, ed., *The Greek City: From Homer to Alexander* (Oxford: Oxford University Press, 1990), pp. 137–70.

Nock, Arthur Darby, *Essays on Religion and the Ancient World*, Zeph Stewart, ed., (Cambridge, MA: Harvard University Press, 1972).

Ober, J., "Thucydides, Pericles, and the Strategy of Defense," in *The Craft of the Ancient Historian: Essays in Honor of Chester G. Starr* (Lanham, MD: University Press of America, 1985), pp. 171–88 = *The Athenian Revolution* (Princeton: Princeton University Press, 1996), pp. (53–)55–71 and (72–)73–85.

Ober, J., "The Rules of War in Classical Greece," in M. Howard et al., eds., *The Laws of War* (New Haven: Yale University Press, 1994), pp. 12–26 with 227–30.

Ober, J., "Civic Ideology and Counterhegemonic Discourse: Thucydides on the Sicilian Debate," in A. L. Boegehold and A. C. Scafuro, eds, *Athenian Identity and Civic Ideology* (Baltimore: Johns Hopkins University Press, 1994), pp. 102–26.

Ober, J., "Thucydides *Theoretikos*/Thucydides *Histor*: Realist Theory and the Challenge of History," in D. McCann and B. S. Strauss, eds., *War and Democracy* (Armonk: M. E. Sharpe, 2001), pp. 273–306.

Ober, J., "Tyrant-Killing as Therapeutic Stasis: A Political Debate in Images and Texts," in K. A. Morgan, ed., *Popular Tyranny: Sovereignty and Its Discontents* (Austin: University of Texas Press, 2003), pp. 215–50.

Ober, J., and C. Hedrick, eds., *Démokratia* (Princeton: Princeton University Press, 1996).

Ober, J. and B. Strauss, "Drama, Rhetoric, and the Discourse of Athenian Democracy," in J. Winkler and F. Zeitlin, *Nothing to Do with Dionysos?* (Princeton: Princeton University Press, 1990), pp. 237–70.

Osborne, R., *Demos: The Discovery of Classical Attika* (Cambridge: Cambridge University Press, 1985).

Osborne, R., *Classical Landscape with Figures* (Dobbs Ferry: Sheridan House, 1987).

Osborne, R., "Women and Sacrifice in Classical Greece," *CQ* 43 (1993): 392–405.

Osborne, R., "The Economics and Politics of Slavery at Athens," in A. Powell, ed., *The Greek World* (London: Routledge, 1995), pp. 27–43.

Osborne, R., "Religion, Imperial Politics, and the Offering of Freedom to Slaves" in V. Hunter and J. Edmondson, eds., *Law and Social Status in Classical Athens* (Oxford: Oxford University Press, 2000), pp. 75–92.

Osborne, R., and S. Hornblower, eds., *Ritual, Finance, Politics: Athenian Democratic Accounts Presented to David Lewis* (Oxford: Oxford University Press, 1994).

Ostwald, M., *Autonomia* (Atlanta: Scholars Press, 1982).

Ostwald, M., *From Popular Sovereignty to the Sovereignty of Law. Law, Society, and Politics in Fifth-Century Athens* (Berkeley: University of California Press, 1986).

Ostwald, M., "Philosophy, Rhetoric and Science," in D. M. Lewis et al., eds., *The Cambridge Ancient History*, vol. 5, *The Fifth Century*, second edition (Cambridge: Cambridge University Press, 1992), pp. 338–51.

Ostwald, M., "Public Expense: Whose Obligation? Athens 600–454 B.C.E.," *PAPhS* 139 (1995): 368–79.

Parke, H. W., *Festivals of the Athenians* (Ithaca, NY: Cornell University Press, 1977).

Parke, H. W., *Greek Mercenary Soldiers*, reprint edition (Chicago: Ares, 1981).

Parker, R., *Athenian Religion: A History* (Oxford: Oxford University Press, 1996).

Parkinson, H., and C. Smith, eds., *Trade, Traders and the Ancient City* (London and New York: Routledge, 1998).

Patterson, C., *Pericles' Citizenship Law of 451/0 B.C.* (New York: Arno, 1981).

Patterson, C., "The Case Against Neaira and the Public Ideology of the Athenian Family," in A. Boegehold and A. Scafuro, eds., *Athenian Identity and Civic Ideology* (Baltimore: Johns Hopkins University Press, 1994), pp. 199–216.

Patterson, C., *The Family in Greek History* (Cambridge, MA: Harvard University Press, 1998).

Patterson, C., "The Hospitality of Athenian Justice: The Metic in Court," in V. Hunter and J. Edmonson, eds., *Law and Social Status in Classical Athens* (Oxford: Oxford University Press, 2000), pp. 93–112.

Patterson, C., "Athenian Citizenship Law," in D. Cohen and M. Gagarin, eds., *The Cambridge Companion to Greek Law* (New York: Cambridge University Press, 2005), pp. 267–89.

Patterson, Orlando, *Freedom: Freedom in the Making of Western Culture* (New York: Basic Books, 1991).

Pavan, M., *L'avventura del Partenone* (Florence: Sansoni, 1983).

Pelling, C., *Literary Texts and the Greek Historian* (London: Routledge, 2000).

Pickard-Cambridge, A., *The Dramatic Festivals of Athens*, rev. J. Gould and D. M. Lewis, second edition (Oxford: Oxford University Press, 1988).

Podlecki, A., *Perikles and his Circle* (London: Routledge, 1998).

Pollitt, J. J., *Art and Experience in Classical Greece* (Cambridge: Cambridge University Press, 1972).

Pollitt, J. J., *The Art of Ancient Greece: Sources and Documents*, second edition (Cambridge: Cambridge University Press, 1990).

Popper, Karl, *The Open Society and Its Enemies*, vol. 1, *The Spell of Plato* (London, 1945; fifth edition, Princeton: Princeton University Press, 1966).

Powell, A., ed., *The Greek World* (London: Routledge, 1995).

Powell, B., *Writing and the Origin of Greek Literature* (Cambridge: Cambridge University Press, 2002).

Price, J., *Thucydides and Internal War* (Cambridge: Cambridge University Press, 2001).

Pritchett, W. K., "Marathon," *University of California Publications in Classical Archaeology* 4, no. 2 (1960): 137–89.

Pritchett, W. K., *The Greek State at War*, 5 vols. (Berkeley: University of California Press, 1971–1990).

Quass, F., Review of W. R. Connor et al., eds., *Aspects of Athenian Democracy* (Copenhagen: Museum Tusculanum Press, 1990), *Gnomon* 67 (1995): 28–9.

Raaflaub, K. A., "Contemporary Perceptions of Democracy in Fifth-Century Athens," *C&M* 40 (1989): 33–70.

Raaflaub, K. A., "City-State, Territory, and Empire in Classical Antiquity," in A. Molho et al., eds., *City-States in Classical Antiquity and Medieval Italy* (Stuttgart: Steiner, 1991), pp. 565–88.

Raaflaub, K. A., "Homer to Solon: The Rise of the Polis. The Written Sources," in M. H. Hansen, ed., *The Ancient Greek City-State* (Copenhagen: Royal Danish Academy of Sciences and Letters, 1993), pp. 41–105.

Raaflaub, K. A., "Democracy, Power, and Imperialism in Fifth-Century Athens," in J. P. Euben et al., eds., *Athenian Political Thought and the Reconstruction of American Democracy* (Ithaca, NY: Cornell University Press, 1994), pp. 103–46.

Raaflaub, K. A., "Father of All, Destroyer of All: War in Late Fifth-Century Athenian Discourse and Ideology," in D. R. McCann and B. S. Strauss, eds., *War and Democracy* (Armonk: M. E. Sharpe, 2001), pp. 307–56.

Raaflaub, K. A., "Philosophy, Science, Politics: Herodotus and the Intellectual Trends of His Time," in E. J. Bakker et al., eds., *Brill's Companion to Herodotus* (Leiden: Brill, 2002), pp. 164–83.

Raaflaub, K. A., *The Discovery of Freedom in Ancient Greece* (Chicago: University of Chicago Press, 2004).

Raaflaub, K. A., et al., *Origins of Democracy in Ancient Greece* (Berkeley: University of California Press, forthcoming).

Raaflaub, K., and N. Rosenstein, eds., *War and Society in the Ancient and Medieval Worlds* (Washington, DC: Center for Hellenic Studies, 1999).

Rahe, P., "The Primacy of Politics in Classical Greece," *AHR* 89 (1984): 265–93.

Rahe, P., *Republics Ancient and Modern* (Chapel Hill: University of North Carolina Press, 1992).

Rahe, P., "Justice and Necessity: The Conduct of the Spartans and the Athenians in the Peloponnesian War," in M. Grimsley and C. J. Rogers, eds., *Civilians in the Path of War* (Lincoln: University of Nebraska Press, 2002), pp. 1–32.

Randall, R. H., Jr., "The Erechtheum Workmen," *AJA* 57 (1953): 199–210.

Rasmussen, T., and N. Spivey, eds., *Looking at Greek Vases* (Cambridge: Cambridge University Press, 1991).

Reeder, E. D., et al., *Pandora: Women in Classical Greece* (Baltimore: The Walters Art Gallery, 1995).

Rehm, R., *The Play of Space* (Princeton: Princeton University Press, 2002).

Rengakos, A. and A. Tsakmakis, eds., *Brill's Companion to Thucydides* (Leiden: Brill, forthcoming).

Rhodes, P. J., *The Athenian Boule* (Oxford: Oxford University Press, 1972; revised reprint, 1984).

Rhodes, P. J., "On Labelling Fourth-Century <Athenian> Politicians," *LCM* 3 (1978): 207–11.

Rhodes, P. J., "Athenian Democracy after 403 B.C.," *CJ* 75 (1979/80): 305–23.

Rhodes, P. J., *A Commentary on the Aristotelian Athenaion Politeia* (Oxford: Oxford University Press, 1981; revised reprint, 1993).

Rhodes, P. J., *The Athenian Empire*, Greece & Rome New Surveys in the Classics 17 (Oxford: Oxford University Press, 1985).

Rhodes, P. J., "Political Activity in Classical Athens," *JHS* 106 (1986): 132–44.

Rhodes, P. J., "The Ostracism of Hyperbolus," in R. Osborne and S. Hornblower, eds., *Ritual, Finance, Politics: Athenian Democratic Accounts Presented to David Lewis* (Oxford: Oxford University Press, 1994), pp. 85–98.

Rhodes, P. J., "Who Ran Democratic Athens?" in P. Flensted-Jensen et al., eds., *Polis and Politics. Studies in Ancient Greek History Presented to Mogens Herman Hansen on his Sixtieth Birthday* (Copenhagen: Museum Tusculanum Press, 2000), pp. 465–77.

Rhodes, P. J., "Public Documents in the Greek States: Archives and Inscriptions. Part I," *G&R* 48.1 (2001): 33–44.

Rhodes, P. J., "Public Documents in the Greek States: Archives and Inscriptions. Part II," *G&R* 48.2 (2001): 136–53.

Rhodes, P. J., "Nothing to Do with Democracy: Athenian Drama and the Polis," *JHS* 123 (2003): 104–19.

Rhodes, P. J., with D. M. Lewis, *The Decrees of the Greek States* (Oxford: Oxford University Press, 1997).

Rhodes, Robin Francis, *Architecture and Meaning on the Athenian Acropolis* (Cambridge: Cambridge University Press, 1995).

Rich, J., and G. Shipley, eds., *War and Society in the Greek World* (London: Routledge, 1993).

Ridgway, B. S., *Fourth-Century Styles in Greek Sculpture* (Madison: University of Wisconsin Press, 1997).

Ridley, R. T., "The Hoplite as Citizen," *AC* 48 (1979): 508–48.

Roberts, J. W., *City of Socrates* (London: Routledge, 1984).

Robertson, M., *A History of Greek Art*, 2 vols. (Cambridge: Cambridge University Press, 1975).

Robertson, M., *The Art of Vase-Painting in Classical Athens* (Cambridge: Cambridge University Press, 1992).

Robertson, N. D., "The True Nature of the 'Delian League,' 478–461 B.C.," *AJAH* 5 (1980): 64–96, 110–33.

Roisman, J., *The General Demosthenes and His Use of Military Surprise* (Stuttgart: Steiner, 1993).

Romilly, J. de, "Thucydides and the Cities of the Athenian Empire," *BICS* 13 (1966): 1–12.

Romilly, J. de, *The Rise and Fall of States According to Greek Authors* (Ann Arbor: University of Michigan Press, 1977).

Romilly, J. de, *The Great Sophists in Periclean Athens* (Oxford: Oxford University Press, 1992).

Roochnik, D., *Of Art and Wisdom: Plato's Understanding of Techne* (University Park: Pennsylvania State University Press, 1996).

Rosen, R. M., and J. Farrell, eds., *Nomodeiktes: Greek Studies in Honor of Martin Ostwald* (Ann Arbor: University of Michigan Press, 1993).

Rosenbloom, D., "Myth, History, and Hegemony in Aeschylus," in B. Goff, ed., *History, Tragedy, Theory* (Austin: University of Texas Press, 1996), pp. 91–130.

Rosivach, V., "Manning the Athenian Fleet," *AJAH* 10 (1985 [1993]): 41–66.

Roussel, D., *Tribu et cité* (Paris: Les Belles Lettres, 1976).

Ruschenbusch, E., "*Dikastérion pantón kyrion*," *Historia* 6 (1957): 257–65.

Ruschenbusch, E., "*Patrios Politeia*. Theseus, Drakon, Solon und Kleisthenes in Publizistik und Geschichtsschreibung des 5. und 4. Jahrhunderts v. Chr.," *Historia* 7 (1958): 398–424.

Ruschenbusch, E., "*Phonos*. Zum Recht Drakons und seiner Bedeuting für das Werden des athenischen Staates," *Historia* 9 (1960): 129–54.

Ruschenbusch, E., "Ephialtes," *Historia* 15 (1966): 369–76.

Ste. Croix, G. E. M. de, "The Character of the Athenian Empire," *Historia* 3 (1954–1955): 1–41.

Ste. Croix, G. E. M. de, *The Origins of the Peloponnesian War* (London: Duckworth, 1972).

Ste. Croix, G. E. M. de, *The Class Struggle in the Ancient Greek World* (London: Duckworth, 1981).

Samons, L. J., II, "Athenian Finance and the Treasury of Athena," *Historia* 42 (1993): 129–38.

Samons, L. J., II, "Kimon, Kallias and Peace with Persia," *Historia* 47 (1998): 129–40.

Samons, L. J., II, "Mass, Elite and Hoplite-Farmer in Greek History," *Arion* 5.3 (1998): 99–123.

Samons, L. J., II, "Aeschylus, the Alkmeonids, and the Reform of the Areopagos," *CJ* 94 (1998/99): 221–33.

Samons, L. J., II, *Empire of the Owl: Athenian Imperial Finance*, Historia Einzelschriften 142 (Stuttgart: Steiner, 2000).

Samons, L. J., II, "Democracy, Empire, and the Search for the Athenian Character," *Arion* 8.3 (2001), 128–57.

Samons, L. J., II, "Revolution or Compromise?" in E. W. Robinson, ed., *Ancient Greek Democracy: Readings and Sources* (Oxford: Blackwell, 2004), pp. 113–22.

Samons, L. J., II, *What's Wrong with Democracy? From Athenian Practice to American Worship* (Berkeley: University of California Press, 2004).

Schaps, D., "The Women of Greece in Wartime," *CP* 77 (1982): 193–213.

Schmitz, W., *Wirtschaftliche Prosperität, soziale Integration und die Seebundpolitik Athens* (Munich: tuduv, 1988).

Schreiner, J. H., *Hellanikos, Thukydides, and the Era of Kimon* (Aarhus: Aarhus University Press, 1997).

Schubert, Charlotte, *Perikles* (Darmstadt: Wissenschaftliche Buchgesellschaft, 1994).

Schuller, W., *Die Herrschaft der Athener im ersten attischen Seebund* (Berlin: de Gruyter, 1974).

Scott-Kilvert, I., trans., *The Rise and Fall of Athens: Nine Greek Lives* (London: Penguin, 1960).

Scullion, S., "Tragic Dates," *CQ* 52 (2002): 81–101.

Scullion, S., "Nothing to Do with Dionysus: Tragedy Misconceived as Ritual," *CQ* 52 (2002): 102–37.

Seaford, R., "The Social Function of Attic Tragedy: A Response to Jasper Griffin," *CQ* 50 (2000): 30–44.

Sealey, R., "The Entry of Pericles into History," *Hermes* 84 (1956): 234–47.

Sealey, R., "The Causes of the Peloponnesian War," *CP* 70 (1975): 89–109.

Sealey, R., *A History of the Greek City States* (Berkeley: University of California Press, 1976).

Sealey, R., "The Athenian Courts for Homicide," *CP* 78 (1983): 275–96.

Sealey, R., "The Tetralogies Ascribed to Antiphon," *TAPA* 114 (1984): 71–85.

Sealey, R., *The Athenian Republic* (University Park: Pennsylvania State University Press, 1987).

Sealey, R., *The Justice of the Greeks* (Ann Arbor: University of Michigan Press, 1994).

Shapiro, H. Alan, *Myth into Art. Poet and Painter in Classical Greece* (London: Routledge, 1994).

Shay, J., *Achilles in Vietnam* (New York: Simon & Schuster, 1994).

Shay, J., *Odysseus in America: Combat Trauma and the Trials of Homecoming* (New York: Scribner, 2002).

Shefton, B., "Reflections on the Presence of Attic Pottery at the Eastern End of the Mediterranean during the Persian Period," *Transeuphratène* 19 (2000): 75–81.

Seibert, J., *Die politischen Flüchtlinge und Verbannten in der griechischen Geschichte* (Darmstadt: Wissenschaftliche Buchgesellschaft, 1979).

Sickinger, J. P., *Public Records and Archives in Classical Athens* (Chapel Hill: University of North Carolina Press, 1999).

Sickinger, J. P., "Literacy, Documents, and Archives in the Ancient Athenian Democracy," *American Archivist* 62 (1999): 229–46.

Siewert, P., *Der Eid von Plataia* (Munich: Beck, 1972).

Siewert, P., *Die Trittyen Attikas und die Heeresreform des Kleisthenes* (Munich: Beck, 1982).

Silk, M. S., ed., *Tragedy and the Tragic. Greek Theatre and Beyond* (Oxford: Oxford University Press, 1996).

Sinclair, R. K., *Democracy and Participation in Classical Athens* (Cambridge: Cambridge University Press, 1988).

Sluiter, I., and R. M. Rosen, eds., *Free Speech in Classical Antiquity* (Leiden: Brill, 2004).

Smarczyk, Bernhard, *Untersuchungen zur Religionspolitik und politischen Propaganda Athens im Delisch-Attischen Seebund* (Munich: tuduv, 1990).

Snodgrass, A. M., *Archaic Greece* (Berkeley: University of California Press, 1980).

Snodgrass, A. M., "The Rise of the Polis: The Archaeological Evidence," in M. H. Hansen, ed., *The Ancient Greek City-State* (Copenhagen: Royal Danish Academy of Sciences and Letters, 1993), pp. 30–40.

Sommerstein, A. H., "How to Avoid being a Komodoumenos," *CQ* 46 (1996): 327–56.

Sommerstein, A. H., "Platon, Eupolis and the 'Demagogue-Comedy'," in D. Harvey and J. Wilkins, eds., *The Rivals of Aristophanes. Studies in Athenian Old Comedy* (London: Duckworth and the Classical Press of Wales, 2000), pp. 437–51.

Sommerstein, A. H., "Harassing the Satirist: The Alleged Attempts to Prosecute Aristophanes," in I. Sluiter and R. M. Rosen, eds., *Free Speech in Classical Antiquity* (Leiden: Brill, 2004), pp. 145–74.

Sommerstein, A. H., S. Halliwell, J. Henderson, and B. Zimmermann, eds., *Tragedy, Comedy and the Polis* (Bari: Levante Editori, 1993).

Sourvinou-Inwood, C., *Studies in Girls' Transitions: Aspects of the Arkteia and Age Representation in Attic Iconography* (Athens: Kardamitsa, 1988).

Sourvinou-Inwood, C., "Something To Do with Athens: Tragedy and Ritual," in R. Osborne and S. Hornblower, eds., *Ritual, Finance, Politics: Athenian Democratic Accounts Presented to David Lewis* (Oxford: Oxford University Press, 1994), pp. 269–90.

Sourvinou-Inwood, C., "What Is Polis Religion?" in Richard Buxton, ed., *Oxford Readings in Greek Religion* (Oxford: Oxford University Press, 2000): 13–37.

Spence, I., "Perikles and the Defence of Attika during the Peloponnesian War," *JHS* 110 (1990): 91–109.

Spence, I., *The Cavalry of Classical Greece* (Oxford: Oxford University Press, 1993).

Stadter, P., *A Commentary on Plutarch's Pericles* (Chapel Hill: University of North Carolina Press, 1989).

Stadter, P., "Pericles among the Intellectuals," *Illinois Classical Studies* 16 (1991): 111–24.

Stafford, Emma, *Worshipping Virtues* (London: Duckworth, 2000).

Stahl, M., *Aristokraten und Tyrannen im archaischen Athen: Untersuchungen zur Überlieferung, zur Sozialstruktur und zur Entstehung des Staates* (Stuttgart: Steiner, 1987).

Stanier, R. S., "The Cost of the Parthenon," *JHS* 73 (1953): 68–76.

Stansbury-O'Donnell, M. D., "Polygnotos's Iliupersis: A New Reconstruction," *AJA* 93 (1989): 203–215.

Stansbury-O'Donnell, M. D., "Polygnotos's Nekyia: A Reconstruction and Analysis" *AJA* 94 (1990): 213–35.

Stanton, G. R., "The Tribal Reform of Kleisthenes the Alkmeonid," *Chiron* 14 (1984): 1–41.

Stears, K., "Dead Women's Society: Constructing Female Gender in Classical Athenian Funerary Sculpture," in N. Spencer, ed., *Time, Tradition and Society in Greek Archaeology* (London: Routledge 1995), pp. 109–31.

Steiner, D., *The Tyrant's Writ* (Princeton: Princeton University Press, 1994).

Stewart, A., "History, Myth, and Allegory in the Program of the Temple of Athena Nike at Athens," in Herbert L. Kessler and Marianna Shreve Simpson, eds., *Pictorial Narrative in Antiquity and the Middle Ages. Studies in the History of Art*, vol. 16 (Washington, DC: National Gallery of Art, Washington, 1985), pp. 53–74.

Stewart, A., *Greek Sculpture: An Exploration* (New Haven: Yale University Press, 1990).

Stockton, D., "The Peace of Callias," *Historia* 8 (1959): 61–79.

Stockton, D., *The Classical Athenian Democracy* (Oxford: Oxford University Press, 1990).

Straten, F. T. van, "Gifts for the Gods," in H. S. Versnel, ed., *Faith, Hope and Worship: Aspects of Religious Mentality in the Ancient World* (Leiden: Brill, 1981), pp. 65–151 and Plates 1–64.

Strauss, B. S., *Athens after the Peloponnesian War* (Ithaca, NY: Cornell University Press, 1986).

Striker, G., "Methods of Sophistry," in *Essays on Hellenistic Epistemology and Ethics* (Cambridge: Cambridge University Press, 1996), pp. 3–21.

Stroud, R. S., *The Axones and Kyrbeis of Drakon and Solon*, California Studies in Classical Philology 19 (Berkeley: University of California Press, 1979).

Taplin, O., "Fifth-Century Tragedy and Comedy: A *Synkrisis*," *JHS* 106 (1986): 163–74.

Taplin, O., "Comedy and the Tragic," in M. S. Silk, ed., *Tragedy and the Tragic. Greek Theatre and Beyond* (Oxford: Oxford University Press, 1996), pp. 188–202.

Taylor, M. W., *The Tyrant Slayers: The Heroic Image in Fifth Century B.C. Athenian Art and Politics*, second edition (Salem, NH: Ayer, 1991).

Thomas, R., *Oral Tradition and Written Record in Classical Athens* (Cambridge: Cambridge University Press, 1989).

Thomas, R., *Literacy and Orality in Ancient Greece* (Cambridge: Cambridge University Press, 1992).

Thomsen, R., *Eisphora* (Copenhagen: Gyldendal Boghandel, 1964).

Thorne, J. A., "Warfare and Agriculture," *GRBS* 42 (2001): 225–53.

Thucydides, *The Peloponnesian War*, trans. R. Warner (London: Penguin, 1972).

Thucydides, *The Peloponnesian War*, trans. R. Crawley, rev. T. E. Wick (New York: Modern Library, 1982).

Thür, G., ed., *Symposion 1993. Vorträge zur griechischen und hellenistischen Rechtsgeschichte* (Cologne: Böhlau, 1994).

Todd, S. C., *The Shape of Athenian Law* (Oxford: Oxford University Press, 1993).

Tournikiotis, P., ed., *The Parthenon and Its Impact in Modern Times* (Athens: Melissa, 1994).

Traill, John S., *The Political Organization of Attica: A Study of the Demes, Trittyes, and Phylai, and Their Representation in the Athenian Council* (Princeton: American School of Classical Studies at Athens, 1975).

Trianti, I., "Παρατηρήσεις σε δύο ομάδες γλυπτών του τέλους το 6ου αιώνα από την Ακρόπολη," in W. D. E. Coulson et al., eds., *The Archaeology of Athens and Attica under the Democracy* (Oxford: Oxbow, 1994), pp. 83–91.

Tritle, L., "Hector's Body: Mutilation of the Dead in Ancient Greece and Vietnam," *AHB* 11 (1997): 123–36.

Tritle, L., *From Melos to My Lai* (London: Routledge, 2000).

Tyrrell, William Blake, and Frieda S. Brown, *Athenian Myths and Institutions* (New York: Oxford University Press, 1991).

Vanderpool, Eugene, "An Inscribed Stele from Marathon," *Hesperia* 11 (1942): 329–37.

Vasunia, P., *The Gift of the Nile: Hellenizing Egypt from Aeschylus to Alexander* (Berkeley: University of California Press, 2001).

Vernant, J.-P., *Les origines de la pensée grecque* (Paris: Presses Universitaires de France, 1962), also published as *The Origins of Greek Thought* (Ithaca, NY: Cornell University Press, 1982).

Versnel, Henk S., ed., *Faith, Hope and Worship: Aspects of Religious Mentality in the Ancient World* (Leiden: Brill, 1981).

Versnel, Henk S., "Religion and Democracy," in Walter Eder, ed., *Die athenische Demokratie im 4. Jahrhundert v. Chr.* (Stuttgart: Steiner, 1995), pp. 367–87.

Vickers, M., and D. Gill, *Artful Crafts: Ancient Greek Silverware and Pottery* (Oxford: Oxford University Press, 1994).

Vlastos, G., *Socrates, Ironist and Moral Philosopher* (Ithaca, NY: Cornell University Press, 1991).

Walbank, M. B., "Criteria for the Dating of Fifth-Century Attic Inscriptions," in D. W. Bradeen and M. F. McGregor, eds., ΦΟΡΟΣ: *Tribute to Benjamin Dean Meritt* (Locust Valley, NY: Augustin, 1974), pp. 161–9, also published (with revisions) as "Criteria for Dating" in M. B. Walbank, *Athenian Proxenies of the Fifth Century B.C.* (Toronto and Sarasota: Stevens, 1978), pp. 31–51.

Wallace, R. W., *The Areopagos Council* (Baltimore: Johns Hopkins University Press, 1989).

Wallace, R. W., "The Athenian Laws against Slander," in G. Thür, ed., *Symposion 1993* (Cologne: Böhlau, 1994), pp. 109–24.

Wallace, R. W., "Private Lives and Public Enemies: Freedom of Thought in Classical Athens," in A. Boegehold and A. Scafuro, eds. *Athenian Identity and Civic Ideology* (Baltimore: Johns Hopkins University Press, 1994), pp. 127–55.

Wallace, R. W., "Speech, Song and Text, Public and Private. Evolutions in Communications Media and Fora in Fourth-Century Athens," in W. Eder, ed., *Die athenische Demokratie im 4. Jahrhundert v. Chr.* (Stuttgart: Steiner, 1995), pp. 199–217.

Wallace, R. W., "Solonian Democracy," in I. Morris and K. A. Raaflaub, eds., *Democracy 2500? Questions and Challenges* (Dubuque, IA: Kendall/Hunt, 1998), pp. 11–29.

Wallace, R. W., "The Sophists in Athens," in K. Raaflaub and D. Boedeker, eds., *Democracy, Empire, and the Arts in Fifth-Century Athens* (Cambridge, MA: Harvard University Press, 1998), pp. 203–22.

Wallace, R. W., "Damon of Oa: A Music Theorist, Ostracized?" in P. Murray and P. Wilson, eds., *Music and the Muses: The Culture of Mousike in the Classical Athenian City* (Oxford: Oxford University Press, 2004), pp. 249–67.

Wallinga, H. T., *Ships and Sea-Power before the Great Persian War* (Leiden: Brill, 1993).

Wees, H. van, "Politics and the Battlefield: Ideology in Greek Warfare," in A. Powell, ed., *The Greek World* (London: Routledge, 1995), pp. 153–78.

Wees, H. van, "The Development of the Hoplite Phalanx," in H. van. Wees, ed., *War and Violence in Ancient Greece* (London: Duckworth, 2000), pp. 125–66.

Wees, H. van, ed., *War and Violence in Ancient Greece* (London: Duckworth, 2000).

Wees, H. van, *Greek Warfare: Myths and Realities* (London: Duckworth, 2004).

Westlake, H. D., "Ionians in the Ionian War," *CQ* 29 (1979): 9–44, republished in *Studies in Thucydides and Greek History* (Bristol: Bristol Classical Press, 1989), pp. 113–53.

Whitby, M., "The Athenian Grain Trade in the Fourth Century B.C.," in H. Parkinson and C. Smith, eds., *Trade, Traders and the Ancient City* (London: Routledge, 1998), pp. 102–28.

Whitehead, D., *The Ideology of the Athenian Metic* (Cambridge: Cambridge University Press, 1977).

Wickersham, J., *Hegemony and Greek Historians* (Lanham, MD: Rowman and Littlefield, 1994).

Wigmore, J. H., *A Panorama of the World's Legal Systems* (Washington, DC: Washington Law Book Company, 1921).

Wigmore, J. H., *Law and Justice in Tokugawa Japan, Part I: Introduction* (Tokyo: Kokusai Bunka Shinkokai, 1969).

Williams, D., and J. Ogden, *Greek Gold: Jewelry of the Classical World* (New York: Abrams/Metropolitan Museum of Art, 1994).

Wilson, P., *The Athenian Institution of the Khoregia* (Cambridge: Cambridge University Press, 2000).

Wood, E. M., *Peasant-Citizen and Slave* (London and New York: Verso 1988).

Woodruff, P., "Rhetoric and Relativism: Protagoras and Gorgias," in A. A. Long, ed., *The Cambridge Companion to Early Greek Philosophy* (Cambridge: Cambridge University Press, 1999), pp. 290–310.

Wycherley, R. E., *The Stones of Athens* (Princeton: Princeton University Press, 1978).

Yalouri, E., *The Acropolis: Global Fame, Local Claim* (Oxford: Berg, 2001).

INDEX

Contributors have used latinized (Pericles, Laurium) or transliterated (Perikles, Laureion) forms in accordance with their preferences. The index usually lists the form appearing most frequently in the volume.